NELSON
The Immortal Memory

CONWAY CLASSICS

The Conway Classics series presents exceptional works of maritime literature and naval reference beautifully produced at affordable prices for the library of any sea-faring enthusiast and collector.

RELATED NAVAL TITLES FROM THE CONWAY CLASSICS SERIES

The British Battle-Fleet
Its Inception and Growth throughout the centuries
Fred T Jane
Introduction by Antony Preston

The British Battle-Fleet, first published in 1912 when the naval arms race with Germany was nearing its climax, is rightly seen as a classic, read as much for its views on the future of naval warfare as its detailed statistics. Fred T Jane covers the sweep of British naval history from Alfred the Great to the Dreadnought era. This new edition is complete with colour illustrations by W L Wyllie RA and an incisive new introduction.

Hardback, 230 x 150 mm, 440 pages, 24 colour plates, 48 black and white illustrations
ISBN 0 85177 723 6

All the World's Battleships
1906 to the present
edited by Ian Sturton

All the World's Battleships provides the technical data, gives the design background and outlines the careers of the world's battleships and battlecruisers. Organised by nation, type and class, each vessel is described in detail and every page is illustrated with plans and historic photographs. The ship histories include references to important technical and political developments in the various navies of the world.

Hardback, 280 x 216 mm, 192 pages, Over 500 photographs and diagrams
ISBN 0 85177 691 4

North American orders: Brassey's Inc., PO Box 960, Herndon, VA 22070, USA

For a free catalogue of all titles in the Conway Classics series and additional publications from Conway Maritime Press, please contact:

The Sales Department
Conway Maritime Press
33 John Street
London WCIN 2AT
Telephone: 0171-753 7777
Fax: 0171-753 7795
E-mail: brasseys@dial.pipex.com
Web: http://www.brasseys.com

NELSON
The Immortal Memory

David Howarth

&

Stephen Howarth

CONWAY CLASSICS

© David Howarth and Stephen Howarth, 1988

First published in the United Kingdom in 1988 by J.M. Dent & Sons Ltd.

This edition published in 1997 in the Conway Classics series by Conway Maritime Press,
an imprint of Brassey's (UK) Ltd, 33 John Street, London WC1N 2AT
Telephone: 0171-753 7777
Fax: 0171-753 7795
E-mail: brasseys@dial.pipex.com
Web: http://www.brasseys.com

North American orders: Brassey's Inc., PO Box 960, Herndon, VA 22070, USA

British Library Cataloguing in Publication Data is available on request.
Library of Congress Cataloguing-in-Publication Data: A catalog record for this book is
available on request.

ISBN 0 85177 720 1

Printed in Great Britain by Redwood Books, Trowbridge

'There is but one Nelson.' *Admiral Lord St Vincent*

'To any other Nation the loss of Nelson would have been irreparable; but in the British Fleet off Cadiz, every Captain was a Nelson.' *Admiral Villeneuve*

Contents

CONTENTS

List of Illustrations

Trafalgar Day

EACH YEAR, AT eight o'clock in the morning on 21 October, the Royal Navy observes a private ritual. The flags of the most memorable signal ever flown by a British warship are hoisted again to the mastheads and yards of HMS *Victory*, now lying in her permanent dry dock in Portsmouth: England expects that every man will do his duty.

This is Trafalgar Day, the anniversary of a victory so devastating and so complete that it put an end to war at sea for a century. The quarterdeck of the ship is crowded with senior officers and a guard of ratings; there are trumpeters from the Royal Marines; a few privileged guests stand under the break of the poop. It is a strictly organized crowd; it has not assembled merely to celebrate a victory long ago, but also to express its affection for a single man of the hundreds who died that day in battle: Horatio Nelson, the Admiral who flew that signal on this ship ('to amuse the fleet', he said) as she very slowly approached her enemies off Cadiz in 1805. To an observer, the privacy and intimacy of the annual ceremony are especially noticeable: the participants are formed in a hollow square – the honour guard at its forward end, trumpeters at its after end, officers on either side – surrounding a small plaque mounted on the deck, and all are facing inboard. Outside the ship, the normal morning life of the town and port carries on. Prayers are read, including the Naval Prayer and Nelson's own prayer, written in his cabin two decks below, on that same day in 1805; and the Commander-in-Chief Naval Home Command lays a wreath on the plaque, marking the spot where Nelson fell when he was shot by a musketeer from the rigging of a French ship grappled alongside.

Nelson was the most brilliant and most honoured naval leader Britain has produced. But brilliance and honour are not the whole reason why he is still remembered with the unique affection this ceremony shows. He is remembered not mainly because he was a great admiral, a great tactician, or even a great hero in the military sense – but because he was an exceptionally kind and lovable man. Not that he was a saint, far from it: he was vain, sometimes irritable, often self-pitying, and unfaithful to his wife in one tremendous love affair. Yet somehow his human faults seem to have made the people who knew him love him all the more. No admiral ever won such personal devotion. When he died at Trafalgar, his fleet forgot its victory in an astonishing spontaneous outburst of grief: the commander they lost seemed more important to them than the triumph they had won. Many of them expressed their feelings then and there. The despatch sent to the Admiralty by Admiral Collingwood as second-in-command might well have glorified the victory; but he wrote, 'My heart is rent with the most poignant grief.' Captain Blackwood, the senior frigate captain, wrote home to his wife: 'On such terms it was a victory I never wished to have witnessed.' And Thomas Hardy, captain of HMS *Victory* and tough as leather: 'His death I shall forever mourn.' A sailor down in the gloom of a gundeck found a stub of pencil and a piece of paper, and wrote home: 'Our dear Admiral Nelson is killed ... Chaps that fought like the devil sit down and cry like a wench.' And Dr Scott, who was the Admiral's chaplain: 'When I think, setting aside his heroism, what an affectionate, fascinating little fellow he was, I become stupid with grief.'

These are not terms in which the navy often remembers admirals. But even now, nearly two centuries after his death, it still looks on Nelson with respect and unique affection. Any account of his life should ask the question why, and try to find the answer.

1

'Poor Horatio'

HE WAS A fierce and skilful fighter, but a gentle, kindly man; so one can write of his deeds without the sin of exalting violence. His life ended in a classic heroic climax at the height of battle, but it had started in rural simplicity and peace, in the hamlet of Burnham Thorpe, within distant sound of the sea on the northern coast of Norfolk.

'I was born September 29th, 1758, in the Parsonage House, was sent to the high school at Norwich, and afterwards removed to North Walsham; from whence, on the disturbance with Spain relative to the Falkland Islands, I went to Sea with my uncle Captain Maurice Suckling, in the Raisonable of sixty-four guns.'

Nelson was a prolific writer – seven large volumes of his letters, despatches and memoranda were published in the 1840s, followed over a century later by an eighth; and they were only the ones that happened to have survived. Sometimes he made a particular effort to ensure the preservation of a document: for example, there are two copies – one in the National Maritime Museum at Greenwich, the other in the Public Records Office at Kew – of his last diary and his prayer before Trafalgar, and he wrote both copies himself. More often, his letters were kept by correspondents – even before he became famous – for the simplest and best of reasons: he was far away from those who loved him, and the letters brought him closer. They were and are a pleasure to read, for his voice comes through clearly – chatty, warm-hearted and considerate, with an elegance of style derived from his own wide reading, and the rhythms of the King James Bible – and no doubt the letters were reread many times. In that sense, he wrote a continuing, informal autobiography from the age of fifteen to his dying day. But, in his only attempt at formal autobiography, the terse paragraph above was all he ever wrote about his childhood; and even

3

there he left out the fact that between schools at Norwich and North Walsham, he went to a third, at Downham Market. It was not unhappy memories of childhood which made him write so briefly of it; he just did not think it would interest anyone. Historians have had to use scraps of information, and even of imagination, to fill the gap.

What he called the Parsonage House has gone: it was a mile away from the church, and was pulled down in his lifetime. Apart from that, Burnham Thorpe has not changed very much. It is still a remote and peaceful little place, with a large church nearly six hundred years old, a few farm houses, a big village green (now a playing field) with a stream running through it, a pub, a windmill or two, and a population recorded in the 1950s as two hundred and forty-seven. Of course there are not many corners of England which are so quiet now as they were when Nelson was a boy. On the most tranquil summer's day, even at Burnham, you can hear the rumble of distant traffic; but closer at hand there are still the sounds of the place as it used to be: the horses and carts, the cattle and the bells of churches far and near, and the birds – especially the curlews, piping on the sea marshes which border the parish to the north.

The Parsonage House was quite large; it had to be, because the Reverend Edmund Nelson, who was Rector of the parish, and his wife Catherine had eleven children. It was not an unusual number then, nor was it unusual that three of them died in infancy.

One may most easily imagine this homely middle-class family at its Sunday dinner, the spartan but plentiful food, mutton and beef from farms in the parish, vegetables from the parsonage garden, sometimes perhaps a present of rabbits or geese or even pheasants from the neighbouring grand estate of Holkham: at the head of the table, the father, a gentle and loving man, but strict too and always respected; at the foot, the mother, about whom little is known except that (in Nelson's later words) she 'hated the French'; and seated along the sides, a grandmother who often lived with them, a nurse named Blackett, and the cheerful gang of children – five boys and three girls. Maurice, the eldest, was fourteen in 1767; he became a clerk in the Navy Office. William was ten, less than eighteen months older than Horatio; he took Holy Orders like his father and, by no other virtue than that of outliving both Maurice and Horatio, became an earl. The oldest girl, Susannah, was twelve, and the youngest, another Catherine – usually known as Kitty – was only a few months old. They were all fond of each other. The remaining sister and two brothers –

4

Anne, Edmund and Suckling, whose unusual Christian name was his mother's maiden name – were all younger than Horatio, and died in their twenties or thirties; but the survivors, while always closely united, were very ordinary people. It is a total mystery what chance of heredity produced one genius in this simple family.

At Christmas in 1767, the family was shattered by tragedy. In the space of a week, in the depths of winter, the children's mother and grandmother died. It was a loss that could never really be made good, but as they came to terms with it, some of the children did their best to express their sympathy for their father. Susannah, the twelve-year-old daughter, took over running the household, but then apprenticed herself to a milliner and later got a job in a shop. The two oldest boys were at boarding school and stayed there, but the third of them, Horatio, decided he wanted to leave school and go to sea to 'provide for himself'.

That decision has left an impression that the Reverend Edmund was desperately hard up, but he cannot in fact have been more impoverished than any country parson with a large family. He himself had a habit of taking long holidays in Bath, the west country spa, to escape from the winter wind of Burnham, and he went on doing so after his wife died, presumably leaving the younger children in the care of Blackett. And the family had influential friends, who would certainly not have let it go hungry. Catherine Nelson's father was Dr Maurice Suckling, prebendary of Westminster, her brother Maurice was a senior captain in the Royal Navy and the Sucklings had landed property in Norfolk. Further back, she was also related to the wealthy neighbouring family of Walpole. Horatio, the rather pompous name she gave to her third son, was a Walpole family name. He did not like it. At home, the family called him Horace, which at least had an English air, and to most other people in his later life he was simply Nelson – or, of course, My Lord.

The Reverend Edmund came of humbler but learned stock. He liked to remind people that his father was another Norfolk parson, yet had been to Eton and Cambridge. But his mother was the daughter of a Cambridge baker – perhaps an undergraduate indiscretion. It is possible Catherine's family regretted she had not made a grander marriage.

When Horatio made up his mind, he asked his older brother William to write to his father, who was at the time in Bath, to tell him what he wanted to do. It is not recorded why he asked William to write, or why he chose the sea; but he may have thought William was a more persuasive letter-writer, and as for the sea, there are two likely reasons. The first was Burnham itself.

It is only three miles from the church to the open sea. But the sea, all along that coast, seems strangely remote: it is hidden behind at least a mile of salt marshes and dunes, crossed by ancient dykes and ditches and divided by tidal creeks. The nearest creek, only a mile from home, reaches in to another Burnham, Burnham Overy – there are ten Burnhams in the district, each with a different second name – and Burnham Overy has a quay, or staithe, and good shelter for fishing boats which lie at anchor or, at low water, angled in the mud, even in winter when the north-east wind whistles in across the marshes. Burnham Overy is a natural magnet for a small boy, the place where Nelson would have learnt the feel of a boat, as soon as he was big enough to walk there and clamber aboard; would have learnt also to work an oar and hoist a sail as soon as his arms could do it, and perhaps even to set a course along the winding creek and out through the sandbanks to the open sea.

The other reason was his uncle, Captain Suckling. Horatio had certainly met him, and certainly heard his sea-faring stories: he remembered one when he was sailing into battle at Trafalgar on the day he died. The children would look out for his name in the newspaper, and one day they read of the Falklands 'disturbance', and that he had been given a new command. Their father was not altogether surprised when William's letter reached him in Bath; indeed, he may have been grateful to have a son who knew exactly what he wanted to do. He saw no difficulties, and wrote to his brother-in-law, who replied with oft-quoted and heavy-handed humour: 'What has poor Horatio done, who is so weak, that he should be sent to rough it out at sea? But let him come, and the first time we go into action a cannon ball may knock off his head and provide for him at once.'

HMS *Raisonnable* (strictly, the name has two *ns*, though Nelson spelt it with one) was lying at Chatham on the Medway. To get there from Burnham was quite a formidable expedition. So far as one knows, the little boy had never before been outside Norfolk, and had only travelled about twenty miles within it, when he went to school. Peter, his father's odd-job-man, put him on the coach to King's Lynn. The Rector met him there and accompanied him to London. They arrived in winter, early in 1771; and from the capital his father sent him on by coach, for the final stage of the journey, alone.

The boy was a little over twelve, and very small for his age – as a man he was under five foot six – and Chatham was a busy bewildering place with thousands of sailors and 'dockyard mateys', hundreds of officers and scores of ships. Something must have gone wrong: either the Rector and Captain Suckling had not arranged a rendezvous, or else Suckling could not be there, or else Horatio arrived at an unexpected hour. Whatever the reason, he could not find his ship, or anyone who could spare the time to tell him what to do or where to go. Finally he was shown the way, but once on board he found no waiting uncle, nor anyone who would pay the least attention to him. His entire first night on a warship was spent waiting on deck. He grew up to be famously fearless, but his introduction to the navy, that first day and night in Chatham, may have been the most daunting experience of his life.

By coincidence, the naval dockyard at that time contained his last ship as well as his first. In his loneliness, he can scarcely have imagined that one day he would also walk her decks, as a commander-in-chief; but he must have seen her, for she was lying close to the two-decked, 64-gun *Raisonnable*, and she was markedly larger – a first-rate, three-decked ship of the line, her sides pierced for one hundred guns. As yet her stern was unadorned, for her name, in yellow letters twelve inches high, would not be painted on until later that summer. But first-rates were rare, and merited curiosity; so perhaps, when he finally met his uncle, he may have learned a few other things about the impressive ship – that she had been launched six years before, was still untried in battle, and would be called *Victory*. However, if he had time for that, it would have been very brief; for 'poor Horatio' was in the navy now, signed on as a captain's servant, and pitched in to do the best he could in a harsh, rigorous and completely unfamiliar way of life.

Servant was the technical word for such boys: in fact, they were apprentice officers. It was an extremely tough existence for children – living crowded in the cockpit, below the waterline of a ship, dark and damp and comfortless and cold; instantly doing whatever they were told; always able and willing to race to the masthead 170 feet above the deck; long hours of school, and the same food the sailors had. As another twelve-year-old wrote at that time, 'We live on beef which quite makes your throat cold in eating it, owing to the maggots which are very cold when you eat them, like calves' foot jelly or blomonge, being very fat indeed.' The writer must have been a tough little boy, for he added emphatically, 'I do like this life very much.'

Like it or not, this was the usual way – practically the only way – to start a career as a naval officer. One of the perquisites of a captain was the right to carry thirty or forty servants on his ship's books. Some captains, besides their stewards, cooks and valets, carried superfluous men like barbers and musicians; but most made up the numbers by taking the sons of their friends to sea, and good ones took a great interest in the education of their crowd of little boys. One consequence of this was that almost all naval officers came from a narrow social class. On the whole, they were not aristocrats – those went into the army. They were certainly not what were called the lower classes; in fact most crews disliked the few men, known as tarpaulin captains, who had worked their way up from a humble beginning. Most of them were the minor landed gentry, the squires of England. It was an unfair system, with no pretence of democracy. But it did at least produce officers who had lived under naval tradition from their childhood, and were intensely proud of the service.

In the end, HMS *Raisonnable* never had to go to the Falkland Islands; on the contrary, she remained in the rather ignominious job of guardship in the Medway. The disturbance with Spain which Nelson had mentioned was one of the early outbreaks of an international squabble which has still not been settled to universal agreement. The Falkland Islands, far in the South Atlantic, were not much use to anybody except as a shelter for ships rounding Cape Horn. They were first visited by the Elizabethan sailor Captain Davis. In 1764 the French explorer de Bougainville made a settlement there, and claimed the islands for France. In the next year Captain Byron arrived, formed another settlement, and made a claim for Britain. The French and English settlers stayed there for some time before either group discovered the other existed. A few years later, the Spaniards made a claim, but very soon withdrew it, and it was left to the then non-existent republic of Argentina to pursue the Latin line over a century later. The naval expedition for which Captain Suckling fitted out his ship in the year Nelson joined her, 1771, did not take place until 1982.

When he said he 'went to sea' in the *Raisonnable*, Nelson meant, in the contemporary sense, that that was his first naval billet. In the modern sense of the phrase, he did not really go to sea at all in her – the furthest she went while he was on board was twelve miles downriver to Sheerness, at the mouth of the Medway; and soon after he joined her, the quarrel over the Falklands blew over, and the ship was paid off. Suckling was appointed to the larger *Triumph*, 74 guns, which was lucky for the young servants because he could take them with him. But the *Triumph* also was lying at Chatham as guardship, and had no immediate prospect of moving. Suckling knew his nephew needed sea-time to start him on his climb up the ladder of promotion; but he could not find any naval ship that was starting a suitable voyage with a suitable captain, so he transferred the boy to a merchant ship belonging to the trading house of Hibbert, Purrier and Horton, and named *Mary Ann*. On 25 July 1771, she sailed from London for the West Indies. Her route took her past Kent's North Foreland, through the Straits of Dover – giving Nelson his first glimpse of a country he would come to detest obsessively – and on down the Channel. Thus, somewhere between the Scillies and Ushant, he first saw an empty horizon ahead, first felt the motion of a ship in the open ocean, first looked down at a bow-wave, up at taut rigging and drawing sails, first worked aloft in a rolling ship – and also, very probably, first felt seasick: for he was sick in bad weather all his life.

Little is known of that first voyage. It lasted about a year, in which time *Mary Ann* called at Jamaica and Tobago, and presumably many of the islands in between. Beyond that, the only certain records are that the captain was named John Rathbone, that he had served under Suckling as master's mate in the naval ship *Dreadnought*, and that the voyage had a deep effect on Nelson. 'If I did not improve my education,' he wrote long afterwards, 'I returned a practical seaman.' He was thirteen, quite old enough in those days to think of himself as a practical seaman, but young enough to feel a little too conceited about it. He also returned 'with a horror of the Royal Navy', for he had thoroughly absorbed the prevailing attitude of merchant seamen towards the king's ships. Pay there was always lower than in merchant ships, and notoriously late in coming; discipline was severe; leave was minimal; and – particularly in time of war, when the chronic shortage of volunteers was worst – the infamous press gangs would make up the shortfall by force. Nelson characterized the whole 'with a saying ·then constant with the seamen: "Aft the most honour, forward the better man"' – because officers were quartered aft and crews forward. 'It was many weeks before I got in the least reconciled to a man-of-war, so deep was the prejudice rooted; and what pains were taken to instil this erroneous principle in a young mind!' Yet the experience served him well in later life, for it taught him two things which he never forgot: an outsider's view of the Royal Navy, and a sailor's view of his officers.

Clearly, he was rather a handful when he returned to Suckling in the *Triumph*. But Suckling welcomed him back with courtesy and kindness, with the last year's news of the family – his father was in good health, and still the Rector, and Maurice, the oldest brother, had asked for Suckling's influence to get a job in the Navy Office – and also with a sensible and effective way of directing his energy. He promoted the bumptious boy to midshipman, and 'as my ambition was to be a seaman, it was always held out as a reward, that if I attended well to my navigation I should go in the cutter and decked long-boat' – not as a passenger, but as a working member of the crew, and later, in command.

Thus, in the first months back under Captain Suckling's eye, Nelson learned to sail a boat in the estuaries of the Medway and the Thames. Francis Drake was another boy who had had his first lessons there, and naval youngsters still do, still using the same rather clumsy boats that Nelson would have known. It is just as good a place to learn now as it was then: strong tides, and miles of mudbanks and shifting sandbanks covered at high water – these are the best of teachers. And the satisfaction of growing competence and confidence is just the same too – 'By degrees,' Nelson said, 'I became a good pilot, and confident of myself among rocks and sands, which has many times since been of the very greatest comfort to me.'

Exciting as his new skills were, Nelson evidently viewed them only as a means to an end, a way of getting on in the service to which he was (at least for the time being) entirely 'reconciled'. To swing round a buoy in the Medway was not his idea of naval life, so he set about finding a voyage for himself; and in 1773 he decided what it should be. The great news of the day was that two naval ships were to make a scientific expedition to the Arctic. Without a war to provide satisfactory employment and assist promotion, such rare expeditions were the only real way for a junior officer to improve his status. Competition to take part was correspondingly keen, and at first there seemed little chance that the young midshipman would be accepted: until his fifteenth birthday – still some months away – he would officially be a boy, and he was told no boys were going, 'as being of no use'. However, as still happens to a certain extent, age limits were not an absolute bar to a competent person, but a useful means of rejecting the incompetent. Nelson was plainly becoming as competent as many older men, and on his own admission, 'nothing could prevent my using every interest to go.' He had met the captain of one of the ships, who had the unusual name of Skeffington Lutwidge, and shrewdly persuaded him that he was not applying as a boy, but as a practical seaman, to do a grown man's job. No doubt Captain Suckling put in a good word for him, while Nelson himself 'begged I might be coxswain; which, finding my ardent desire for going with him, Captain L. complied with, and has continued the strictest friendship to this moment.' He had not yet met the senior of the two captains, Constantine Phipps, who later became Lord Mulgrave, but 'he also', he wrote, 'continued his kindest friendship and regard to the last moment of his life.' This was the first time Nelson is seen to exercise his persuasive charm. Until then, he probably did not know he had it, and nobody now can quite define its quality. But looking back, one can see the results. Every captain he served under, even the earliest, was aware of it, and all – except one, perhaps – remained his firm friends for the rest of their lives, or his.

The Arctic expedition had two objectives – to sail as close as possible to the North Pole, and to renew the search which the English had been pursuing since Elizabethan times for a north-east passage by way of Siberia to the Pacific Ocean. In terms of science and exploration, it was not a success. The two ships – Phipps' *Racehorse* and Lutwidge's ominously named *Carcass* – set out on 4 June 1773, reached Spitzbergen on 28 June, and two days later were stuck in the ice. Sending Lutwidge out with the master of *Racehorse* to see if there was any way through, Phipps learned that 'they had ascended a high mountain, whence they commanded a prospect extending to the east, and north-east, ten or twelve leagues, over one continued plain of smooth unbroken ice, bounded only by the horizon' – and there, drifting somewhat with the floes, they remained. With 'the weather exceedingly fine and mild, and unusually clear, the scene', Phipps recorded, 'was beautiful and picturesque', and the ships' companies were allowed to play on the ice all day – probably many of them were not much further from boyhood than Nelson. But as the ice gradually piled up and threatened to crush the ships' hulls, plans had to be made to abandon them and escape in the boats – just the kind of thing which, as the navy was learning, would bring Nelson to the fore. 'I exerted myself', he remembered later, 'to have the command of a four-oared cutter, which was given me, with twelve men; and I prided myself in fancying I could navigate her better than any other boat in the ship.'

It is quite likely that he could. Certainly, by then, he would have fared little worse than anyone else; and one may guess that his twelve men agreed, for he already had some of the key characteristics which would make him the navy's best-loved commander: an infectious enthusiasm, a pleasure in seamanship and a buoyant self-confidence, matched by confidence in his sailors, and a sympathetic understanding for them as well. No doubt there was a good deal of adolescent cockiness too; but it seems that even from the beginning, all the elements were present, and most people tolerated his cockiness as later they tolerated his vanity.

At length, however, the ships were got out safely, returning to England to be paid off on 15 October – just over a fortnight after Nelson's fifteenth birthday – and the only well known result of the expedition was a story which he would probably have liked to forget. With one seaman, he left his ship by walking across the ice in a fog. When it cleared, they were seen, a long way off, trying to attack a polar bear with one musket between them which did not work. Captain Lutwidge had to fire a gun to frighten the bear away. During the reprimand that followed, Nelson explained (according to Lutwidge) that he wanted to take the bearskin home as a present for his father. It was Lutwidge who told the story, never Nelson, and Nelson's Victorian biographers, eager hero-worshippers, quoted it to prove his courage when he was a boy. A rather ridiculous painting, done many years later to prove the same point, shows the youth about to club an astonished and frightened-looking bear with the butt of his musket. In fact, there was a crevasse between him and his prey, and as Lutwidge must have told him very clearly, the episode was much more foolish than brave. But it is worth remembering all the same, for it is one of the first records of some other characteristics he never lost: a degree of recklessness when faced with a goal he wanted very much; a readiness to disobey orders, at the risk of his career and even his life; and perhaps even then, the unforced affectionate charm which so often let others overlook his faults.

2

'Well then ... I will be a hero!'

HIS NEXT VOYAGE, the third before he was sixteen, was again his own choice, though his uncle again arranged it. After the Arctic, he chose to go to the tropics, and he joined a squadron of four ships sailing from Spithead to the East Indies – 'Nothing less than such a distant voyage could in the least satisfy my desire for maritime knowledge.' The squadron's flagship, *Salisbury*, was a fourth-rate – the term for a middle-sized warship mounting between 50 and 70 guns. With 50, *Salisbury* was one of the smallest of her rate, and her squadron sisters, all classed as sixth-rates, were very much smaller still: *Swallow*, the littlest, mounted only 16 guns; *Coventry* had 28. Midshipman Nelson was in the 20-gun frigate *Seahorse*.

Again, he served under an admiral (this time Sir Edward Hughes) who showed him 'the greatest kindness'. The master of the *Seahorse*, Captain George Farmer, had once served under Captain Suckling – hence his swift acceptance of Suckling's nephew into his frigate. But he was the only one of Nelson's early commanders who may not have remembered him afterwards with affection – that was not something he valued. He was a strict disciplinarian: his first lieutenant was court-martialled and 'relieved of his duties', and in the course of the voyage he recorded three hundred times in his meticulous log that men had been lashed at the gratings. It must have been a miserable experience, for a youth who had always been treated with kindness, to have to witness all those barbaric punishments. But it may have confirmed in Nelson the belief he often taught to others when he himself rose to command: that severity was not the best way to create a happy or efficient crew. All he recorded of this commander was that he was 'a very clever man', and that 'we constantly took the lunar observations.' 'Lunars' were a celestial method of fixing longitude, used between the inventions of, first, the sextant in about 1731, and then the chronometer in about 1773. But they involved a rather difficult observation and a very laborious calculation, and only the most expert navigators learnt to use them. For Nelson, that was certainly a useful lesson from the fierce Captain Farmer.

This was a voyage of adventures new to Nelson. At first his station in the ship was keeping watch from the fore-top; later he was placed on the quarterdeck, directly assisting the more senior officers. They called at Funchal, no doubt to re-stock the wardroom with Madeira wine, then they rounded the Cape and stood along the northern edge of the 'roaring forties', as far as the desolate island of St Paul, before they turned north for India: it was a very long way round, but the usual route under sail. Then came Madras, Calcutta, round to Bombay and up the Persian Gulf to Basrah, and back to Trincomalee in Ceylon, which Nelson thought the best harbour for its size in the world. (He said the same, years later, of Portoferraio in the Italian island of Elba, and of Milford Haven in Wales.) Altogether, as he noted, he 'visited almost every part of the East Indies', and at least once indulged in an evening's gambling. He was enormously successful, and won £300; but whether it was beginner's luck or the skill of experience, he realized shortly afterwards that if he had lost such a sum, he would have been ruined. He promptly decided never to take such risks again, and he scarcely ever did – at least, not at the card-table.

This exotic voyage around the treasury of the empire came to an abrupt end in December 1775. Returning to Bombay after more than a year at sea, he fell seriously ill with some kind of tropical fever, and the surgeon said a voyage back to England was his only chance of recovery. The first available ship was not due to leave for home until March 1776, but he was transferred to her straight away. She was the frigate *Dolphin*, famous as the first vessel to have sailed twice round the world, and the first English ship to have landed in Tahiti. Yet that probably meant little to him, ill as he was – he seems to have caught malaria, and suffered recurring bouts of fever throughout the rest of his life.

What he needed now was rest, a cooler climate, and a chance to get rid of his infection. He received all three on the journey to England, which took six months. Always generous with his gratitude, he put his recovery down to his captain, James Pigot, 'whose kindness at that time saved my life.' But that voyage as a passenger was most remarkable for a strange experience which marks the real end of

Nelson's youth, and the beginning of his rise to fame.

What happened was a bad attack of depression, the sort of thing that teenagers often suffer from: he was still only seventeen. What was remarkable, however, was the way he came out of it, and, typically, never forgot it. Talking about it very much later, he recalled how he 'felt impressed with the feeling that I should never rise in my profession.' Very ill, without a patron to act in his interest, he felt defeated by the difficulties he had to surmount, and 'could discover no means of reaching the object of my ambition'. He had 'a long and gloomy reverie in which I almost wished myself overboard.' He did not record how long the gloom lasted; given his illness and inactivity, it was probably some weeks. But then came the deliverance, a kind of sudden vision: 'a glow of patriotism was kindled within me, and presented my King and country as my patron. My mind exulted in the idea. Well then, I exclaimed, I will be a hero! And confiding in Providence, I will brave every danger.'

To those grandly spoken words he added one of the few enigmatic things he ever wrote: 'From that time, a brilliant orb was suspended before my mind's eye.' Friends and colleagues recorded that he spoke of this 'orb' in later life almost as if it were a physically visible object; and, even if he half-knew that the depression was caused by his fever, he seems to have half-believed that the orb was a light from heaven which beckoned him to glory.

Senior connections – people who would exert 'interest' on one's behalf – were invaluable to any young man in the navy, or wishing to join it. But when Nelson, in his self-pitying depression, reflected on 'the little interest I possessed', he had forgotten how much his Uncle Maurice's interest had already helped him. Perhaps he thought that Captain Suckling's influence had gone as far as it could; the uncharacteristic ingratitude shows just how ill and low he must have felt. But what he did not know was that while he had been exploring the East Indies, Suckling had been made Comptroller of the Navy and head of the Navy Board. He was more influential than ever, and as eager as ever to help. Many midshipmen would have been glad of an uncle with half the interest; and to be fair to Nelson, this was the only time he forgot what he owed to the captain.

Either Suckling, or the navy in its collective wisdom, knew that the cure for depression was action. *Dolphin* had only been two days at home when, late in September 1776, Nelson was ordered to serve as acting fourth lieutenant in the 64-gun ship of the line *Worcester*,

Captain Mark Robinson, on convoy duty from the Channel ports to Gibraltar. If he had a weak constitution, it was trying it pretty hard, after two years in the tropics, to act as an officer of the watch in the Channel and the north Atlantic in mid-winter. But he survived, and proved to himself and his captain that although he was only just eighteen (he joined the ship three days before his birthday), he could be relied upon to stand a watch – 'Captain Robinson used to say, "he felt as easy when I was on deck, as any officer in the ship."'

His next test was the formal examination for the confirmed rank of lieutenant. On 9 April 1777, he was summoned to face the examining board of three senior captains. He was confused to find that one of the three facing him across the table was his Uncle Maurice, and that evidently the other two had not been told of the relationship. Perhaps Maurice had hoped that a friendly face would give him confidence, but it had an opposite effect. What was an examinee supposed to do? Go along with what seemed a deception, or confess that he knew the examiner very well? Address him as Sir, or as Uncle? Nelson guessed that he ought to behave as if he had never seen him before, and when he had got over his confusion he answered the questions they gave him promptly and well. At the end, Suckling stood up and introduced his nephew. The others naturally asked why he had not told them before. 'I did not wish the younker to be favoured,' he is said to have replied. 'I felt convinced he would pass a good examination; and you see, gentlemen, I have not been disappointed.'

This exam was one of the novelties Samuel Pepys had introduced about a century before, when he was Comptroller of the Navy, as Suckling had become. A similar exam is still used today. Pepys himself would probably have approved Captain Suckling's light-hearted behaviour. He had introduced the exam because he had been extremely annoyed that any young man of good birth should have been able simply to buy an active commission (as they still could in the army) and take a responsible position without any knowledge of the service at all. But, where a candidate had the knowledge and ability, Pepys was content that the exam should be a mere formality; and Nelson's examiners quickly recognized his experience. 'He produceth Journals kept by himself in the *Carcass*, *Seahorse*, *Dolphin*, and *Worcester*,' said their report, 'and Certificates from Captains Suckling, Lutwidge, Farmer' – despite his beastliness, Farmer could be fair – 'Pigott, and Robinson, of his diligence, &c.: he can splice, knot, reef a sail, &c., and is qualified to do the duty of an Able seaman and Midshipman.'

Everyone knew Nelson would pass, and Suckling was so sure of it that he even arranged a posting for him beforehand.

Strictly speaking, Nelson was too young to be a lieutenant – he was still well under nineteen, and the lower age limit was twenty – but this was another naval regulation which, as everyone knew, was made to be stretched judiciously, and Suckling stretched it. Within a week, Nelson was able to send a jubilant and jocular letter to his brother William, who was then at Christ's College, Cambridge. 'I passed my Degree as Master of Arts on the 9th instant,' he wrote, 'and received my Commission on the following day, for a fine Frigate of 32 guns. So now I am left in the world to shift for myself, which I hope I shall do, so as to bring credit to myself and my friends.' Twenty-two years later, when he wrote his one and only formal autobiographical sketch, he got the date of his 'Degree' wrong – surprisingly, in view of its import-ance to him, and of the other details he remembered. But he only placed it one day earlier, and by then, nobody would have begrudged him an extra day's seniority.

The 'fine Frigate' was *Lowestoffe*, Captain William Locker, and Nelson was to be her second lieutenant. Suckling had probably chosen her because he had the highest opinion of Locker, and because she was under orders for active duty in Jamaica. Nelson had been seven years in the navy without being anywhere near the cannon ball which Suckling had said might take off his head. But the American War of Independence had broken out in 1775, which was why *Worcester* had been on convoy duty, and the West Indies were the likeliest place for action – not so much against naval ships, for the Americans had very few, but against their privateers. If Lieutenant Nelson was not killed in battle or by disease (and disease was much more probable), the Caribbean was the best spot for combat experience, prizes and possible promotion.

As a captain for the youthful Nelson, Locker was another fortunate choice, yet another officer who remained a life-long friend, a man to whom Nelson wrote regular grateful letters whenever he was bewil-dered by events. Before *Lowestoffe* sailed from her berth at Sheerness they had a short shore leave, and Locker told Nelson, when he had known him for only a few days, that he ought to have his portrait painted. This was not a suggestion Locker made to every junior officer: he seems to have sensed, with unusual foresight, that his very young lieutenant was going to make history. He took him to the London studio of a member of the Royal Academy – a Swiss-French artist named Rigaud – and the result was the first of the many portraits of Nelson, and perhaps the most revealing. Rigaud began it when his subject was eighteen years old. When Nelson came home nearly four years later, the artist added a West Indian background and the insignia of a captain; for Nelson had been promoted Captain when he was twenty.

That teenage portrait has a special interest, because Nelson remained in many ways like a teenager most of his life – enthusiastic, impulsive, rather naive, cheerful and sociable but with moods of introspective gloom. This early portrait may show more of the real person than some of the later ones, when his face was lined with worry and pain, and his uniform was loaded with decorations.

Certainly Rigaud reflects some of the charm that everyone saw in the boy; Nelson was already showing the genius for friendship which was his finest characteristic and the foundation of his success. It was not at all unusual then for a man to love another and to say so openly: there was thought nothing shameful or effeminate in it. But the web of friendship Nelson spread through the navy was without equal. He never forgot a friend and never lost the art of making new ones. It was not only his seniors who became his friends; so did hundreds of men of his own age, many of whom became famous in later years under his command. And not only officers: when the second ship he commanded was paid off after years in the Indies – he was twenty-two at the time – it was naturally a moment when most men longed to go home; but the entire crew volunteered to serve with him again, a naval tribute which may still be unique.

Rigaud's portrait makes Nelson look slender, which he was, but also reasonably tall, which he was not. In fact, he was small all over, so that the sword in the portrait looks too clumsy a weapon for the hands that rest on the hilt of it. But the most striking thing in the portrait, as it undoubtedly was in life, is the face – not remarkably handsome, not in the least belligerent, but rather gentle, calm and sensitive, and after two hundred years of history, still instantly recognizable.

Indeed, the whole ambience of that portrait is of gentle calm. Its pose is unselfconscious and relaxed. It suggests humility. Humility was not a quality that Nelson was famous for, but some men could bring it out in him, and Locker was one of them.

To become a national hero needs not only skill and courage, but also luck, and Nelson was certainly lucky in joining the navy at an auspicious moment. It had already won the supremacy at sea on which he was to put the final seal. That supremacy was achieved in 1759, the year after he was born, when the navy won three resounding victories over the French, at Quebec, Lagos and Quiberon Bay. After that, the navy was totally confident and always seeking battle, while its ancient enemies, the French and the Spaniards, were always seeking to avoid it. The only thing that shook its self-esteem was the American War of Independence, when it had to fight on the far side of the Atlantic while its enemy fought close to its home bases. English admirals in the West Atlantic, from Halifax to Jamaica, fought under many disadvantages. They were months away from the source of their orders, and aware also of political dissension at home. They were not sure of getting the support they relied on from the Admiralty. Many officers did not like fighting against the Americans, who did not seem like foreigners, and some even resigned, feeling that the only real enemies at sea were, as they had always been, the French and Spaniards.

Jamaica, therefore, where *Lowestoffe* was bound, was an uncomfortable station, where the navy was less sure of itself than it was accustomed to be. Three other factors added to its discomfort. First, it was unhealthy, full of fevers which nobody understood; the navy out there lost ten times more men through fever than it lost in battle. Secondly, the navy's Caribbean allies were a slave society, and many English people were beginning to feel uneasy about the morals of slavery. Finally, it was hot. Of course it still is, and its heat attracts holiday visitors, wearing appropriate lightweight clothes or bathing suits. But in those days, naval officers seem to have worn the same thick cumbersome uniform, layers and layers of it, whatever the climate, and not to have thought of swimming for exercise or to keep cool.

Nevertheless, a return even to that sultry climate, which he had first visited in the merchant vessel *Mary Ann*, must have been welcome to Nelson; for while *Lowestoffe* was being made ready for sea, a particularly unpleasant duty came his way: the command of a press-gang.

Impressment, or pressing, as a means of manning the navy, had already existed under parliamentary approval for more than two hundred years. As a royal prerogative it began very much earlier, but in 1556 an Act passed under Mary Tudor established that Thames watermen were not exempt from the press. This was the first of many Acts of Parliament regulating the practice, and the need did not finally fade until 1853, when the introduction of continuous service in the navy meant that seamen could actually make a career of naval service, earning a pension after a given number of years. Naturally the press was extremely unpopular among its victims, and the navy did not favour it much more, for jail-birds and vagrants forced unwillingly into ships did not easily make an efficient crew – hence the frequent need for stern discipline on board. During Nelson's lifetime, as opposition to the slave trade grew, opposition to the press grew too among citizens of conscience. In 1791, one such, identifying himself only as 'a freeholder', wrote in a vigorous essay of objection: 'It is a reflection upon the British Empire, whose laws, in the general, are so well calculated to defend every subject, that so cruel a method should be adopted to man our fleets; and argues a disgrace upon the naval service, that our ships of war cannot be manned without violence ... Britons hurry Britons into captivity!'

Unfortunately no one could think of a better alternative – or none, at least, that looked plausible on paper. The critical freeholder could offer only two solutions. The first was that every freeholder like himself and every shipowner should provide, respectively, 20 per cent of his income and one sailor per ship to man the national fleet. There was little chance of that. His second solution could almost have been written by Nelson. Certainly, implausible as it sounded then, Nelson would have agreed with every word: the navy should see itself, and should be seen, not as 'a punishment or a penance for every vagrant or vagabond, but rather as an honourable station, a scene of glory, in which they may distinguish their courage and capacity'. Nelson did not enjoy commanding a press-gang. In April 1777 – whether because of the chilly vapours from the river or from a psychological cause linked to his distaste for the duty – he fell suddenly and seriously ill with an apparent recurrence of his malaria, and had to be carried back to the rendezvous by his midshipman assistant. In those night-time searches on the banks of the Thames, the navy did not seem 'an honourable station' at all. But less than thirty years later, when he died at Trafalgar, his victories had made it exactly that; and they had also brought a practical end to impressment. It remained a legal way of manning the fleet until the mid-nineteenth century, but its only use had been in time of war, as a last resort; so, when the Napoleonic Wars were finally won, the press-gangs were never actually needed again.

3

'The merest boy of a captain'

FRIGATES SUCH AS *Lowestoffe* were small. They were fully rigged three-masted vessels, of 700 tons or thereabouts (one-third the tonnage of HMS *Victory*) and in the Royal Navy were usually about 130 feet long with a beam of 36 feet or so – foreign navies built them slightly larger. As a rule, they had only a single covered gundeck, and a single open flush deck above it, and since to operate efficiently they needed a crew of around 260, there was very little room on board for the strict formalities of naval life; their officers lived at close quarters with the men. But they were invaluable: their ratio of length to beam – nearly four to one – meant that they could sail closer to the wind than larger ships, and they were the fastest vessels in the navy. Their job was not to join the line of battle, but normally to sail alone, to scout ahead of the fleets and report the movements of the enemy: to be 'the eyes of the fleet', as Nelson called them in later years, when he was a fleet commander, and urgently needed the information only frigates could provide. Frigate captains therefore needed exceptional skill in navigation, and every member of their crews had to be expert in ship-handling and working aloft in any weather. They were the ancestors of the crews of destroyers.

Most young officers find the smallest ships are the best for independent adventure, and with a daring captain, a British frigate in the West Indies in 1777 had good prospects. Convoying eighteen merchantmen, *Lowestoffe* crossed the Atlantic in the summer, and reached Jamaica in July – the hottest and driest part of the year – with Nelson recovered from his bout of illness. He was already in an optimistic mood once more; and when he met another lieutenant on the station, he realized he really was lucky.

'There is not a man or officer in the Ship that would not consider a removal as a kind of promotion', wrote Cuthbert Collingwood. However, if it was almost impossible for a seaman to choose his ship, it was not much easier for an officer; and a frigate officer stuck with a laggardly captain had to endure immense frustration. 'What a country this is at present to make a fortune in', he lamented. 'All kinds of people are wallowing in their wealth acquired by prizes, and so extraordinary an exception are we that to be "as unfortunate as the *Hornet*" is become a proverbial saying, and the Black girls sing our poverty in their ludicrous songs.'

Collingwood and Nelson had met once before, in 1773, when Collingwood was twenty-five years old and Nelson fifteen. In 1777, despite the age difference of ten years and three days, Collingwood was less than two years Nelson's senior as a lieutenant. The difference was not so much one of ability as of 'interest', and if he had never realized it before, Nelson must have realized then how fortunate he was with his Uncle Maurice. Collingwood, born in Newcastle upon Tyne, came like Nelson from a large family – he had seven sisters and two brothers, five of whom died in childhood or young adulthood. Like Nelson, he sought the help of a naval relative, Richard Brathwaite or Braithwaite, to get him into the navy; yet though Braithwaite eventually became an admiral, he had nothing like the influence of Captain Suckling.

Added to that was the matter of timing. Collingwood had joined the navy in 1761, and was rated midshipman in 1766; but during the period following the 'year of victories', 1759, a teenager without influence had had little opportunity for distinction or promotion. It was not until the American War of Independence that his chance came: he was commissioned a lieutenant by Admiral Graves 'on the day the battle was fought at Bunker's Hill, where I was with a party of seamen, supplying the army with what was necessary to them.' By then he was twenty-seven years old, and he may have thought his luck had changed at last; but his new captain, Robert Haswell, soon put paid to that hope. Collingwood described Haswell's character as 'a strange compound of extravagant pride and abject meanness', and he was right.

Haswell was referred to as captain because he was *Hornet*'s commanding officer; yet she was only a sloop-of-war – even smaller than a frigate, with a tonnage of about 400, and a complement of around 120 men. Haswell had been a lieutenant for eighteen years, and in command for fourteen; but he had never progressed to a larger vessel. Had Collingwood become as embittered as his commanding officer, there would have been little chance of harmony between him and the newly arrived, somewhat upstart young Nelson. But as it was a firm and enduring friendship sprang quickly; and it was not just because of Nelson's beguiling charm. In spite of the difference in their ages, the two lieutenants – one still a teenager, the other nearly thirty years old – shared a deep devotion to their service. Describing Haswell's lack of such devotion, Collingwood remarked that when possible prizes were sighted, he 'left off even the ceremony of chasing them, and allowed them to pass unmolested sometimes within half a gunshot'; and he added with pointed sarcasm, 'There's a man to support the honour and interests of his country; would to heaven I was clear of him.'

Rather than jealousy towards Nelson, he felt only relief that a kindred spirit had arrived. From then on, their careers touched often, until, at Trafalgar, Collingwood was Nelson's second-in-command of the fleet. In the West Indies, as obscure junior officers, they drew well known but not very skilful portraits of each other; twenty-eight years later, distinguished and powerful, they still wrote to each other in the warmest terms – Nelson would begin his letters 'My dear Coll', or sometimes 'My dearest friend', and, with only the touch of respect that Nelson's quicker promotion had come to demand, Collingwood would reply: 'I am, my dear friend, affectionately yours.'

A frigate might be small and adventurous, but *Lowestoffe* was neither small enough nor adventurous enough to please Nelson. However, she had a tender, a diminutive armed schooner captured from the Americans, which Captain Locker had named *Little Lucy* after his daughter. Locker, the most sensitive of captains, observed that Nelson was longing to take *Little Lucy* to sea. He allowed him to choose a crew, and let him go.

Thus it was in *Little Lucy* that Nelson first went to sea in a ship he could call his own. Since she was only a tender, he was under Locker's command, but Locker had given him a free hand, and he made the most of it. No one is quite sure where the word 'schooner' comes from; some say it was a word invented in Massachusetts, where this type of vessel probably originated, while others maintain it derives from a Scottish word meaning to skip over the water. The latter is apt for Nelson's time: two-masted, with a fore-and-aft rig and a square topsail on the foremast, schooners were popular with fishermen and the navy alike for their speed, manoeuvrability and small crew numbers. As fishing boats, they could be first to the fish and first home; as naval patrol craft, they could be armed with carronades – stubby guns which threw a heavy charge over a short range – or long nine-pounders. In *Little Lucy*, Nelson skipped over the water north-eastwards from Jamaica, up through the Windward Passage between Cuba and Haiti, and then explored the southern Bahamas and the shallow seas between them, too shallow even for a frigate. 'In this vessel', he wrote much later in his *Memoir*, 'I made myself a complete pilot for all the passages through the Keys, islands situated on the north side of Hispaniola.' No doubt he did. Anyone who had piloted boats in the muddy tides of the Medway could do the same in the crystal waters of the Bahamas, where a pilot could see the bottom long before he hit it. Nevertheless, feeling a way for *Little Lucy* must have been the greatest fun, the sort of thing that most sea-minded young men would have loved: watching the shoals of many-coloured fish in shallow waters, taking shelter at night in the creeks of an enemy shore, always ready to fight a way out of a tight corner or to escape, if the odds were too great, by the tricks of good seamanship – and always sure, after each adventure, of a sympathetic welcome from Captain Locker. Nelson knew how lucky he was – 'I am most exceedingly obliged for the good opinion you entertain of me', he wrote to Locker, addressing him as 'my most worthy friend'. Few junior officers could have had such a good relationship with their commanders; if poor Collingwood knew of it, Nelson's position must have seemed like heaven to him.

It was delightful, but it could not last. Like any ambitious junior officer, Nelson had to think constantly of promotion, and the process of promotion began again in 1778, when two things happened about the same time. The first was that Locker fell ill – as most English people did in Jamaica – and the second was that a new commander-in-chief was appointed to the Indies. This was Admiral Peter Parker, who, four years later, would be made a baronet, and who already had a wife with the formidable reputation of a figurehead. Parker and Captain Suckling had been comrades-in-arms, and with the aid of that connection and a recommendation from the ailing Locker, Nelson was accepted into Parker's flagship, *Bristol*, as third lieutenant.

The move took place in July, and turned out to be one of the most fortunate events in young Nelson's life; for in the same month his Uncle Maurice died. By the time the sad news arrived – perhaps made slightly less sad by a bequest of £500 – the Parkers had established themselves firmly as Nelson's new friends and protectors. Both of the

Parkers (they were comparatively old – the admiral was fifty-six) came to look on Nelson as if he had been their son. Very quickly, Admiral Parker moved him up to first lieutenant, and for all her daunting stateliness, Nelson evidently delighted Mrs Parker as well. She nursed him in her house ashore at a time when he had a bad attack of fever; and whenever he distinguished himself in later life, after every great battle he fought, she wrote him affectionate letters of congratulation, saying how proud his own mother would have been. He always wrote back gratefully. 'I am as sensible as ever', his letter said after the Battle of Copenhagen in 1801, 'that I owe my present position in life to your and good Sir Peter's partiality for me.' Outspoken gratitude was always one of Nelson's attractive qualities; and Sir Peter had indeed been 'partial' to him, for in December 1778, he had promoted him again, to the rank of master and commander, and appointed him to a brig called *Badger*.

A brig was another type of small vessel, between the average schooner and a frigate in size; it was usually a two-masted square-rigged ship which was often used as a training vessel for boys. *Badger*, however, was on active service, presumably because the Royal Navy was short of ships in the Indies. The war with the American colonies was dragging on – already longer than anyone in Britain had expected – while during 1778, the French had also declared war against Britain. As ships were held at home to meet the cross-Channel threat, Nelson, in *Badger*, was sent to fend off American privateers from a huge stretch of Central America. Generally called the Mosquito Coast, it covered nearly a thousand miles of the mainland, from Mexico almost down to Panama.

This was a much more serious task than the expeditions in *Little Lucy*, and Parker must have had exceptional faith in Nelson's powers of single-handed command, and especially in his navigation. The officer in charge of a brig had the formal rank of master and commander. This was usually an interim rank between lieutenant and captain, and was reserved for ships – usually of less than 20 guns – too small to merit both a captain and a sailing master of their own. The rank did not make an officer a captain, it only implied that he was being considered for the next and most important promotion of all; but it did bring with it the courtesy title of captain, and therefore, from December 1778, just over a year after passing his exam as a lieutenant, Horatio could call himself Captain Nelson.

He did well. The settlers of that aptly named unhealthy shore were mostly British, but living in a country the Spaniards claimed as their own, and in fear that Spain might join in the war against Britain. To Nelson they entrusted the task of presenting their situation to the British authorities in Jamaica. One can only imagine the conversations, and the encouragement that even a single small naval ship provided, because the sole direct record of the episode is Nelson's own brief one, written twenty-one years later. By then he was a viscount in Britain and a duke in Naples, and had been showered with regal gifts and the freedom of great cities. Yet he still remembered with pleasure how the Mosquito Coast settlers 'unanimously voted me their thanks, and expressed their regret on my leaving them'. Thanks were all they could give to the boyish commander of the solitary brig; but it was the first time he had received a public expression of gratitude, and it must have meant a great deal to him.

During that period, the first half of 1779, Nelson also captured a French ship off the north-east coast of Jamaica – the first of his own as captain. It took two days' search to find its identifying papers. They turned up at last, hidden in an old shoe, and Nelson wrote to Locker: 'I sincerely wish it was in my power to show some small return for the very many favours I have received, but I am sure you do not think me ungrateful ... I know you will be pleased with this little earnest of success.'

It was in Oliver Cromwell's time that naval officers and crews were first given a formal right to the value of the ships and cargoes they captured – a right which, of course, only took effect in wartime. The shares were varied from time to time by Act of Parliament, and the seaman's share was always a minute proportion of the captain's or the admiral's. Many captains made fortunes in a single happy fight, while their seamen only got enough to get drunk on; but once in a while a prize was so rich that even the seaman's share was worth more than years of his pay. There were many memorable jackpots. In 1762, when Nelson was a very small boy, two British frigates captured a Spanish treasure ship; vessel and cargo were valued then at more than half a million pounds. In 1799, three frigates brought two more Spanish ships into Plymouth, laden with 2,811,526 dollars and a cargo of cocoa. At the time, an ordinary sailor's wage was about £14 a year, and from each of those prizes every seaman and marine involved got £182. 4s. 9½d – rather more than thirteen years' pay. But each midshipman got £791, warrant officers £2,468, lieutenants

£5,091; and each captain was awarded £40,730.

Ordinary seamen were very well aware of the disparity. A cartoon of the period shows a sailor kneeling in prayer by a cannon, just before a fight. An officer approaching says, 'Why, Starboard! How is this – at prayers when the enemy is bearing down upon us – are you afraid of them?' 'Afraid!', replies the sailor. 'No! I was only praying that the enemy's shot may be distributed in the same proportion as the prize money, the greatest part among the Officers.' And a second sailor whispers to a third, 'Why don't you say Amen to that, Tom?'

Nevertheless, it was a practical arrangement. Fighting men of whatever rank at sea received small wages, but on top of that they had, as it were, tickets in a tremendous lottery. It was always hard to man the naval fleet; without the lure of this gamble it would have been impossible. Without it, the boredom and discomfort of life in wartime would have been much harder to bear. And without it, the navy would certainly not have fought so eagerly as it did against such heavy odds. Even their tactics and gunnery training were designed for the winning of prize money. The navy did not fight or shoot to sink the enemy's ships, it fought to capture them and bring them home intact. No doubt British seamen were as patriotic as anyone else, but what they talked about when they sighted an enemy fleet was not the victory they might win for Britain, it was the prize money they could hope to win for themselves; they counted it and spent it in anticipation. Soldiers fought from a sense of military glory that was drilled into them, but in naval annals the thought of a glorious victory is far less often found than the thought of a profitable prize. And on the whole it was perhaps a healthier frame of mind; certainly naval wars were fought with less hatred and bitterness, and with more courtesy and compassion, than wars on land.

So no captain could have refused a chance for a prize. It would have been unfair for everyone else in his ship: they all expected a share of it – his officers and seamen of every rating, not to mention his commander-in-chief. Yet on a later occasion, when he was stationed again off the American coast, Nelson captured a vessel from Boston and then gave it back, signing a certificate of immunity from further capture for its owner. His crew do not seem to have disapproved of that: the vessel was a fishing boat, the owner a fisherman who piloted them safely through shoal water, and probably many of Nelson's men were fishermen too. Nevertheless, the event was so unusual that, at least once, the fisherman returned voluntarily with provisions for his merciful captors, and kept his certificate even when the War of Independence was over – a curiosity which became a proud memento when Nelson's name was famous in every ocean.

Nelson never mentioned the incident himself: he did not speak much of his own acts of kindness or generosity, for they came naturally to him. He was much more proud of his acts of bravery or seamanship – perhaps because, physically, he was such a slight man – and he would speak of those in terms which now seem unusually vain. The French ship taken off Jamaica was his first capture when nominally a captain, but he already had experience of prizes, and one involved an action 'which', as he put it, 'presaged my character; and as it conveys no dishonour to the officer alluded to, I shall relate it.'

While he was commander of *Little Lucy*, *Lowestoffe* made several captures, including one when he happened to be on board. It was an American privateer which *Lowestoffe* overhauled in heavy weather. The prize was carrying so much sail that she almost foundered before she hove to. It was normally the first lieutenant's duty to board a prize, and Nelson was only second. The boat was made ready and launched, and the first lieutenant went below for his hanger – a short sword, more convenient than the standard long sword when boarding. He could not find it. Captain Locker was also below, looking at his charts. When he came on deck and saw his boat still alongside he shouted: 'Have I no officers in this ship who can board the prize?' The master ran to the gangway, but Nelson got there first, saying, 'It's my turn now, and if I come back it's yours.' He very nearly did not come back. A great wave carried the boat in right over the deck of the privateer and out again. Choosing the right moment Nelson jumped, held on while the privateer surrendered, and as the gale separated them from *Lowestoffe*, took command. Decades later he still thought of 'this little incident' with satisfaction, and as he told the story, remarked: 'I know it is my disposition that difficulties and dangers do but increase my desire of attempting them.'

Many of the things Nelson wrote about himself were boastful and seem distasteful to a modern reader, but in justice one has to read them in their context. Almost all of them come from a memoir he wrote in 1799, and sent to two men called Clarke and McArthur, who were jointly occupied in writing the earliest of his many biographies. Nelson was at sea in the Mediterranean at the time, and Clarke and McArthur seem not to have asked for his permission to write a biography, or even told him they were doing so. Nevertheless, when he heard of it, he wrote to McArthur:

'My dear Sir, I send you a sketch of my life, which I am sensible wants your pruning-knife, before it is fit to meet the public eye; therefore, I trust you and your friend will do that, and turn it into much better language. I have been, and am very unwell, therefore you must excuse my short letter. I did not even know that such a book as yours was contemplated, therefore I beg you will send me the two volumes, and consider me as a sincere friend to the undertaking. That every success may attend you, is the sincere wish of your obliged friend, Horatio Nelson.'

Printing that graceful note at its beginning gave an air of authorization to the work, which turned out to be three volumes; but it was misleading. McArthur was a clergyman and Clarke was an admiral's secretary, and they could not be expected to know the whole of Nelson's history or of his motives. A basic reason for his writing the account as he did was to make sure, so far as he could, that they got things right, and especially that they put the cause of his actions before the Admiralty, which he believed had often misjudged him. However, they did not do what he asked. They did not use a pruning-knife at all, but published the whole thing. What he had written was a guide to them and a self-justification to the Admiralty; but it all appeared as part of his biography, and since it was the only account of his life that was written in the first person, it has been eagerly used by biographers ever since. It makes him seem very conceited, which few people thought him at the time. It is quite different from the contents of his letters, which are kind and affectionate, careful to express his admiration for his friends and colleagues. In short, this document, written for the private guidance of Clarke and McArthur, should never have been regarded as a basis for the truth about Nelson's character. Sometimes he accused himself of vanity, and sometimes it was true: he liked praise as much as the next person, and the adulation poured upon him in later life would have turned anyone's head. But somehow it always turned back again, in a way which would not have happened if vanity had been a fundamental part of his character. Perhaps it is a matter of interpretation, but it seems fairer to say that if he had a permanent weakness of character, it was not vanity, but the inability to be anything other than frank. In an ideal world, that would not be a failing.

Vain or not, Nelson's patrol of the Mosquito Coast proved him to Admiral Parker, and on his return to Jamaica, Parker rewarded him with the highest appointment he could give: on 11 June 1779, he promoted Nelson to the rank of post-captain.

The rank signified that an officer was capable of commanding a ship of twenty guns or more; Nelson was given command of the 28-gun frigate *Hinchinbrook*, with a complement of about two hundred men. To be 'made post', as the phrase went, was the most critical step in an officer's career. The new captain's name was 'posted' in the Navy List, and it was an appointment for life. Subsequent promotion was strictly by seniority; nobody could be promoted over his head. When Nelson became a captain, he was still only twenty years old. Thereafter, he only had to live long enough, without disgrace, and he was sure to become an admiral.

As commander-in-chief in the Indies, Parker made many captains, because he had many vacancies to fill. Captains were being lost not through battle so much as through fever: the old wardroom toast, 'A bloody war and a sickly season' (which brought quick promotion), was often proposed. Locker's health had lasted only a year before he was invalided home; but he reached England and retired in safety to London. The space for Nelson's promotion came because the captain of the *Hinchinbrook* was killed by accident. 'We all rise by *deaths*', he wrote a few years later to his brother William, who had become a vicar. 'I got my rank by a shot killing a Post-Captain, and I most sincerely hope I shall, when I go, go out of [the] world the same way; then we all go in the line of our Profession – a *Parson* praying, a Captain fighting.'

In the long run, this way of promotion had disadvantages. A young post-captain had to wait a very long time before he could hope for a further step up the ladder: Nelson himself waited eighteen years, and many of his contemporaries even longer. Lord St Vincent, who was another commander-in-chief, was quoted as saying that he would promote a hundred captains to open the way for one who was needed as an admiral. But the one who was needed did not necessarily become a flag officer, for the other ninety-nine could clog the higher ranks. The system meant that the navy came to have far too many senior captains and admirals, and most of them, with no hope of ever getting a ship to command, found themselves year after year ashore on half-pay. The worst congestion came when the size of the navy was being cut down after the end of the Napoleonic Wars. Next time naval war was declared, in the Crimea in the 1850s, there were unemployed lieutenants in their sixties, admirals who had not set foot on a ship for most of a lifetime, and commanders-in-chief who were over eighty and did not quite understand the changes that had happened since they had been boys. In making Nelson post at twenty, Parker was looking a very long way ahead, hoping at least that in twenty-five years' time Nelson would be fit for higher command. Presumably Parker thought he would, and presumably – which may have been just as important – the redoutable Lady Parker thought the same.

Nelson was then unassailably a captain, but he still did not look like one. A little later, by chance, on board the *Barfleur* – the flagship of Lord Hood, at anchor in the narrows off Staten Island – he was to meet no less a person than Prince William Henry, the son of King George III. The prince was then a midshipman, and 'had the watch on deck,' as he wrote later, 'when Captain Nelson ... came in his barge alongside, who appeared to be the merest boy of a captain I ever beheld; and his dress was worthy of attention. He had on a full-laced uniform; his lank unpowdered hair was tied in a stiff Hessian tail, of an extraordinary length; the old-fashioned flaps of his waistcoat added to the general quaintness of his figure, and produced an appearance which particularly attracted my notice; for I had never seen anything like it before, nor could I imagine who he was, nor what he came about. My doubts were, however, removed when Lord Hood introduced me to him. There was something irresistibly pleasing in his address and conversation; and an enthusiasm, when speaking on professional subjects, that showed he was no common being.'

No common being: Admiral Parker, Lord Hood, the prince, everyone recognized in spite of his meagre dress that Nelson had the uncommon qualities of a captain. These had two aspects, not easily combined. First there was the intellectual, almost bookish, understanding of naval strategy and tactics, and the social grace to talk of these things with his seniors; and secondly the ability to control a difficult, diverse and potentially dangerous crew of several hundred men and weld them into an efficient, contented company.

Nelson was an exceptionally kindly man all his life, but he could be extremely tough if he thought the good of the service demanded it. Everyone knows the fearsome punishments the navy used in those days, especially the flogging with the cat-o'-nine-tails. Nelson's instinct undoubtedly was to avoid such barbarities, but he was perfectly capable of ordering a man to be flogged: he could never have been a captain otherwise. It may be difficult to see these things through modern eyes, but ships then in wartime were manned partly by volunteers, partly by men rounded up by the press-gang, and partly by vagrants and layabouts and minor criminals who were sentenced to the ships instead of prison. So in every naval crew there were extremely lawless elements.

However, nobody wanted to be shipmates with a man who got drunk, stole, murdered or endangered them all by sleeping on watch; and a good sailor knew as well as anyone that there had to be drastic punishments. Crews did not like captains who were too easy-going. What they looked for in a captain was first and foremost professional competence, which would get them out of tight corners and win them prize money, and after that, strict justice in accordance with the naval law and custom which everyone understood.

That was precisely what Nelson was able to give them: supreme confidence, firm naval justice and also a certain touch of his own; a touch of human sympathy and understanding and humour, and always generous praise and thanks for jobs well done. Perhaps nobody now can put it exactly into words, but the fact is that all through his life his crews responded to his personality with total loyalty and devotion.

4

'This confounded voyage'

TO BE MADE post at twenty was unusual, but there was something even more unusual about Nelson's appointment: he was promoted to command before he had ever been present at a battle, and experience of combat was generally held to be essential before a man was given control of a warship. And there was yet another oddity in his promotion: the vessel he was appointed to command, the frigate *Hinchinbrook*, was out on a cruise – presumably under her first lieutenant, since her captain was dead. Nobody knew where she was, and she had been gone so long that the rumour had spread that she was lost.

It was disappointing to have been made post and have no ship, but it was especially disappointing because a major sea battle was expected any day. A large French fleet had been sighted passing Hispaniola (modern-day Haiti) and steering west. Jamaica lay in its path and the island was in turmoil, expecting invasion: 'Jamaica is turned upside down since you left it', wrote Nelson to the convalescent Locker. Without a vessel to call his own, he was given command of the battery of Fort Charles – an incongruous job for a naval officer. It was fortunate that he and Collingwood were not jealous of each other. Had they been so, it would have been Nelson's turn to feel a pang of envy. Each time he had been promoted, Admiral Parker had made Collingwood his successor – first, in a blessed release from the unlucky *Hornet* and her detestable captain, Collingwood had gone to *Lowestoffe*, then on to take charge of *Badger* – so now, though not yet a post-captain, he was contentedly sailing the sea and catching prizes while Nelson was on shore, gazing across the ocean and hoping that *Hinchinbrook* might arrive before the French.

Nelson took comfort in telling himself that the Fort Charles battery was the most important post on the island: it commanded the approaches to the main fleet anchorage, Port Royal, and to the principal towns, Kingston and Spanish Town. Manned largely by soldiers and by slaves who were loaned by plantation owners, it could not compare with a naval command; yet it was valuable, for it gave him an insight into the army's way of working, and the principles of defence from a landsman's point of view. Before long, this chance addition to his service experience began to pay off.

Working on shore for three months, Nelson was exposed to the raffish bachelor society of the island, who risked the ravages of the cheapest rum and the temptations of black mistresses. However, the only thing that seems to have worried him was the prospect of becoming a prisoner of war: 'I think you must not be surprised', he told Locker, 'to hear of my learning to speak French.' As usual, he made some good and lasting friends ashore: notably Captain the Hon. William Cornwallis, a naval officer known to the fleet as 'Billy Blue', who was conspicuous later in the blockade of France before Trafalgar, and Mr Hercules Ross, a leading planter and businessman, who 'behaved in a very public-spirited manner', volunteering his own vessels for naval use.

Yet the French armada – 125 ships, including twenty ships of the line, with transports carrying an army reported as 25,000 strong – passed Jamaica by, and sailed on westwards to Spanish-held Cuba. The fear of the Mosquito Coast settlers had finally come true: Spain had joined the war against Britain. But, at any rate for the time being, the threat of invasion subsided; *Hinchinbrook* turned up safe and sound; and, on his own quarterdeck at last, Nelson thankfully faced his new crew and the minor ordeal of 'reading himself in' – reading the terms of his commission aloud to the ship's company, so that his authority was certain. As soon as she could possibly be ready, he took the frigate happily to sea. In company with two other warships, *Hinchinbrook* left Port Royal in the middle of September 1779, shortly before Nelson's twenty-first birthday, and by the end of the year 'we took four sail, for which I shall share about eight hundred pounds sterling'. With adventure, excitement and hard cash coming out of it, those months were the best kind of life the navy could offer a young man, and Nelson made the most of it.

It was just as well that he did. In January 1880, while Admiral Parker made ready to take out a fleet in search of the French, Nelson was ordered on a cruise that was landlocked. The army had hatched a grandiose plan to land a force at the mouth of the Rio San Juan, a river that maps showed as rising in Lake Nicaragua and flowing to the Caribbean. So, perhaps because he was one of the very few naval officers who knew it, Nelson was sent back to the Mosquito Coast.

From the time of Drake, the San Juan had attracted adventurers, but apart from the local Indians and a few Spaniards, nobody was thought to have been up it since the days of the buccaneers a century before. Though the river ran into the Caribbean, its source was only twenty miles from the Pacific, the 'South Sea', so it seemed to suggest a feasible route for ships to cross between the oceans. Yet from the lake to the north or eastern sea, the San Juan ran a hundred miles, and in Nelson's time nobody knew anything about it, except that it was all in territory the Spaniards claimed as their own. Nelson's task with *Hinchinbrook* was to escort a convoy of troopships to the river mouth, and wait there on guard until the troops came back.

It was a thoroughly badly organized expedition, and Nelson said as much. ('How it will turn out, God knows!' he wrote to Locker.) To begin with, the troops were delayed, and proved to be a mixture of regular soldiers with volunteers and irregulars, unemployed sailors, prisoners-of-war let out of prison to enlist, deserters, freebooters and drunks. With this 'riotous, troublesome set of people' (as Nelson saw them), the general who made the plan intended 'to possess the lake of Nicaragua, which may be looked upon as the inland Gibraltar of Spanish America ... and by our possession of it, Spanish America is severed in two.' The idea was that they would be joined spontaneously by large numbers of local Indians, who, encouraged by 'plenty of presents', could be guides and pilots – but on sighting the white men, most of the Indians ran away, thinking (quite reasonably) that they would be abducted as slaves for Jamaica.

It took time to persuade them otherwise, and before the expedition upriver was ready to depart, the dry season was two months old. By then the river was so low that boats, even the Indians' dug-outs, had often to be unloaded and hauled by men wading in the shallows. It was obvious the journey would be much more difficult than it had looked, and Nelson did not believe soldiers would ever successfully manage it. Collingwood was his second-in-command, so – never a man to let a job go half done, and in spite of his orders – Nelson offered to leave *Hinchinbrook* off the mouth of the river and lead the army with two of her boats and fifty men of her crew. Major Polson, the soldiers' commanding officer, accepted gratefully, and remembered later how 'a light-haired boy came to me in a little frigate. In two or three days he displayed himself, and afterwards he directed all the operations.'

It was a nightmare journey. The British, hitherto confined to the islands, knew almost nothing about the hazards of a tropical rainforest: the risk of snake-bite, the vampire bats, the sunstroke by day and chilly damp by night, the poisonous plants and insects, the frightening night-time noises, the occasional attacks by alligators or jaguars, and above all the diseases – malaria, dysentery, flux and yellow fever, which the navy graphically called black vomit. 'The climate was deadly', wrote Collingwood. 'No constitution could resist its effects.'

Nor did they know about the Spanish defences: they assumed there would be some, but did not know where they were. There were no forts at the river mouth, and they guessed that if the Spaniards had built any, they had come down from the head of the river in Lake Nicaragua to do so. The first, a battery on an island in midstream, turned out to be fifty-four miles upriver – fifteen days' harrowing journey. By then, the expedition's doctor had noticed that 'the soldiery ... were frequently of very little use', and it was left to the sailors to 'board' ('if I may be allowed the expression') the enemy outpost, Nelson leading them barefoot – his shoes got stuck in the mud.

Two days and sixteen miles later, not far below the lake, they came on a powerful fortress: the Spaniards called it a castle. Nelson favoured a quick attack, but, overruling him, the shore commander decided on a formal siege. It took eleven days. Before the fortress surrendered, the besieging men were dying by dozens. Their ammunition ran out, and so did their food, until they were forced to subsist on a broth of boiled monkeys (which, after seeing what they looked like in the copper, Nelson refused to eat). When the survivors finally entered the fortress, it turned out the Spaniards were no better off. As worthy of his profession as he could be, the expedition's doctor (who was named Dancer) recorded and published his observations, for the benefit of others. The fortress, he wrote, was 'worse than any prison', a collection of 'wretched houses or sheds, consisting chiefly of semi-putrid skins'; its defenders were 'provided with nothing which could lend either them, or us, the least comfort'; and the rainy season had started, raising the river to a torrent.

Nelson was not present when the pathetic, disgusting place opened its gates to the British: he had been recalled. He had his full share of the diseases – the malaria from his early Eastern voyage came back; with some of his men, he contracted manchineel poisoning after drinking from an infected pool; and from the hordes of mosquitoes, he caught yellow fever, which was nearly always fatal. He probably had dysentery as well. But at the very last moment when any boat, even a canoe, could have struggled up against the flood, a message came from Admiral Parker. This informed him that his friend Collingwood had been made post too, and given command of *Hinchinbrook*. Nelson was to make his way down to the sea again, hand *Hinchinbrook* over to his friend, return to Jamaica and take over command of a bigger and better frigate, the 44-gun *Janus*.

It was a promotion which almost certainly saved his life, though in fact he was never able to assume his new command; he was far too ill. Nelson was often close to death in his career, but never closer to a lingering end than in the sordid, steaming camps of the Rio San Juan. He was sent down river in a canoe which took only three days with the flood behind it, where it had taken three weeks on the journey up. The remaining crew of *Hinchinbrook* were shocked to see him when he was carried on board, shivering with fever, emaciated, sallow, speechless and apparently paralysed. But he was among friends. They took him in a corvette to Jamaica, where he had to be carried ashore in his cot. The hospital was generally thought to be only a gateway to the cemetery, so it was decided the best place for him was a lodging house run by Cuba Cornwallis, 'a well-known and respectable negress who saved the life of many naval officers'. There he remained for a while, until Mrs Parker (who would not be 'her ladyship' for another two years) took him under her wing, nursing him at her home. There is a story that Nelson refused any medicine, until the Parkers hit on the device of getting their smallest daughter to give it to him. It sounds quite likely: he was usually a pretty bad patient, but he was fond of children – a characteristic which can hardly be called a weakness, yet which helped, later on, to bring about some of the saddest times of his life.

Although he was so weak, he managed to write a letter to General Dalling, the governor of the island, congratulating him on the capture of Fort San Juan. Dalling was the man who had conceived the plan, and who had written, with supreme confidence: 'I do not see how we can fail to bring about that grand object, a communication between sea and sea . . . I cannot, I say, perceive how the enemy, with the force they can bring against us, could be able, but after a considerable time indeed, and after infinite loss of time, treasure and men, to drive us out of the country.'

He was not the first to fall prey to the dream of linking the oceans, and far from the last: a hundred years later, when de Lesseps began trying to dig a canal across the isthmus, the jungle had not changed; the same diseases were still there; and it was said that a labourer died for every foot of canal dug out. Dalling fared just as badly – of *Hinchinbrook*'s complement of two hundred, 145 died in Nelson's and Collingwood's periods of command, 'and', wrote Nelson, 'I believe very few, not more than ten, survived of that ship's crew.' Collingwood confirmed it, adding that 'all the ships that were as long there suffered in the same degree: the transports' men all died, and some of the ships having none to take care of them, sunk in the harbour; but transport ships were not wanted, for the troops they brought were no more; they had fallen, not by the hand of an enemy, but sunk under the contagion of the climate.' The jungle confounded General Dalling's calculations; the Spaniards simply let it do their work for them, and retook the fort as soon as the rains ended.

All considered, Nelson's letter to Dalling was much more generous than it need have been. Dalling's polite reply attributed the success (such as it was) 'in a great measure' to Nelson, and later that summer, when Nelson was still an invalid, the general wrote a letter about him to the Admiralty. It appears to have sprung from motives of genuine sympathy and admiration – 'Such minds, my lord, are most devoutly to be wished, for government's sake' – but it makes one wonder just how obtuse the general could be. He suggested that if a squadron was going to the 'southern ocean', Nelson should be employed there – the reason being that 'Captain Nelson's constitution is rather too delicate for the service under my direction on this northern one.'

One thing quickly became clear: Nelson was not going to recover properly in Jamaica. Indeed, Jamaica's surgeon-general, Dr Moseley, said firmly that he would die if he stayed in the Indies. It was certain he could never effectively take command of *Janus*, so at the end of August 1780 – four full months after his return from the San Juan expedition – he reluctantly wrote to Admiral Parker: 'Sir, Having been in a very bad state of health ... I am therefore to request you will be pleased to permit me to go to England.' Parker sent his permission the same day, 'with his very sincere wishes for your speedy recovery.' But as he told the Admiralty, he was not at all sure Nelson would survive: 'Captain Nelson is so emaciated and in so bad a state of health that I doubt whether he will live to get home. I wish much for his recovery.

His abilities in his profession would be a loss to the service. A board of three naval surgeons confirms that he has multiple infections of malaria, together with "bilious vomitings, nervous headaches, visceral obstructions and many other bodily infirmities," and that to remain in the tropics would be attended with fatal consequences.'

However, Nelson still had a spark of life in him. Two things helped: firstly, the fact that in all the recriminations over the expedition, nobody had put any blame on him, and that retrospectively the army command agreed the quick assault he advised would have been better than a siege. Secondly, there was the promise of returning to England. With this, Nelson managed to write to several of his friends: 'Hope revives within me'; and on 4 September, on board the ship of the line *Lion*, he began the long journey home.

Her captain was the Honourable William Cornwallis, whom Nelson had befriended during his spell in command of the Fort Charles battery and who, twenty years later, as an admiral, had charge of the Channel fleet. Like Captain Pigot in the *Dolphin*, when Nelson had had his first bout of malaria, Cornwallis looked after the patient with such 'care and attention' that Nelson regarded him as a second life-saver. He was certainly humanitarian: Cuba Cornwallis, the Jamaican nurse, had taken his name after being freed from slavery by him. He was also one of the most important men Nelson had come to know well – a post captain of fifteen years' seniority; veteran of the Seven Years' War, the conquest of Canada and the battle of Quiberon Bay; friend of many experienced and influential officers, and younger brother of General Charles Cornwallis, the first marquis.

General Cornwallis has the misfortune to be remembered now mainly as the man who, on 19 October 1781, had to surrender his army at Yorktown, Virginia, to joint French-American forces – a defeat which effectively ensured America's independence. That defeat was the direct result of a four-day naval battle, the Battle of the Chesapeake, and the lessons learned from it affected British naval thinking profoundly.

The battle was fought in a desultory way between a French fleet, under Admiral de Grasse, and a British fleet under Admiral Graves. Both were bearing supplies to their respective armies in and around Yorktown. De Grasse arrived first and had the larger fleet. He was, moreover, a very able commander, but he should not have won the battle. The advantages of weather, so necessary to a sailing fleet, were all with the British. On the day of battle, the two sides identified each other at about 11 a.m. – to their equal astonishment, for neither knew the other was in the area at all. The wind was north-north-west, comfortably astern of Graves' fleet approaching from New York, and very uncomfortably on the port beam when de Grasse began beating out to sea from Chesapeake Bay. The flood tide, entering the bay, also opposed de Grasse and hindered his ships' movements; Graves should have been able to wait and pick off the French ships one by one as they emerged. But he did not. Instead, sticking rigidly to his navy's *Fighting Instructions*, he formed his fleet into line of battle: a line ahead, his ships following each other, parallel with those French who had come out. The line ran east to west, and became nearly as unmanoeuvrable as the one de Grasse was trying to form.

A few hours of firing ensued, only to break off at nightfall; and the following day Graves' second-in-command, Rear Admiral Sir Samuel Hood, wrote unhappily that 'yesterday the British fleet had a rich and most plentiful harvest of glory in view, but the means to gather it were omitted'. Both he and Graves recognized the errors: 'The enemy's van was not very closely attacked', said Hood. 'There was a full hour and a half to have engaged it before any of the rear could have come up.' And Graves, who had flown the signal for line ahead virtually all day, now said that when that signal was out 'at the same time with the signal for battle, it is not to be understood that the latter signal shall be rendered ineffectual by a too strict adherence to the former.'

By then it was too late, and anyway he was wrong: the *Fighting Instructions* were not made to be broken, and in them the line ahead was paramount. Graves could not expect his captains to second-guess him. The *Instructions* were already over a hundred years old – the first printed edition came out in 1672 – and had come to be regarded as something close to Holy Writ, disobeyed at one's peril. Yet by sticking rigidly to them off Minorca in 1756, the Royal Navy had lost its useful Mediterranean base, Port Mahon; and in 1781, after reading of the Battle of the Chesapeake, Nelson predicted a greater disaster: 'What sad news from America!' he wrote to Captain Locker. 'I much fear for Lord Cornwallis: if something be not immediately done, America is lost.'

Of course it was, but the lesson of the Chesapeake was quickly learned: seven months afterwards, in April 1782, with William Cornwallis as one of his captains, Hood was again second-in-command in a battle against de Grasse – the last sea battle of the war. This time, though, off the group of islets known as The Saints, between Guadeloupe and Dominica, Admiral Sir George Rodney was in command. Throwing the *Fighting Instructions* out, he led his ships through the French line. Five of the thirty enemy vessels were captured, including the flagship. Hood was convinced that if Rodney had continued the battle after dark, many more prizes would have been taken, and in some ways it was an inconsequential victory; there was the satisfaction of taking de Grasse prisoner, but it had no effect on the outcome of America's War of Independence. In other ways, however, it was of the greatest consequence: for the first time, the tactic of breaking an enemy line was introduced. Nelson, by then, was (very ungraciously) convoying merchant ships from England to Canada; it was in Newfoundland that he first heard about the Battle of the Saints, and compared its successful new tactic with the defeat of the old line of battle off the Chesapeake. It was a vivid guide, and one which he followed – even against actual orders – whenever he could, literally until the day he died.

For a man still inclined to be seasick, especially when he had nothing to do, crossing the Atlantic as a passenger in the late part of the year must have been an ordeal rather than a convalescence. *Lion* met such gales that the crossing lasted eighty days (Nelson's twenty-second birthday took place during the voyage), and although she was a big ship she was reported lost. They finally anchored off Spithead on 24 November, and, back in England at last, Nelson stayed for a while in Admiral Parker's London house. There, he saw his old friend Captain Locker, and Rigaud, the artist, who made ready to add the West Indian background and captain's insignia to his four-year-old portrait of Nelson. Locker was going to hang the bright and gentle picture in his room with two others, and ill as he was, Nelson was able to joke about the idea: 'I must be in the middle, for God knows, without good supporters, I shall fall to the ground ... it will not be the least like what I am now, that is certain; but you may tell Mr Rigaud to add beauty to it, and it will be much mended.'

But even with friends and fires to warm him, he was not recovering his health; so at the turn of the year he followed his father's example and went to Bath, which through its supposed medicinal springs had won a reputation for curing anything. The milder climate too would benefit an invalid accustomed to the tropics. When he arrived, his father was so horrified by his sickly appearance that he engaged an eminent and expensive surgeon, who prescribed rest, drinking the rather disgusting waters three times daily, and bathing in the hot springs every other day. One cannot tell which of these treatments was effective – for several weeks he still had to be carried to and from bed, and seems to have been partly paralysed, perhaps because of the manchineel poisoning, which affects the nervous system – but by the end of January 1781, he wrote to Locker: 'Thank God, I am now upon the mending hand.'

Still, the cure was slow, and as the weeks of treatment went by, he grew concerned at their expense, wondering how he would meet the doctor's bill. When it was presented, however, he exclaimed with surprise that it was too little. 'Pray, Captain Nelson,' the honest doctor is said to have replied, 'Allow me to follow what I consider to be my professional duty. Your illness, sir, was brought on by serving your King and Country, and believe me, I love both too well to be able to receive any more.'

Quite apart from his generosity, the physician's words impressed Nelson: years later, he told the story to his wife. Grateful, but as ever an unwilling patient ('I do not sit very easy under the hands of a doctor') he began to lobby for a new command. In April, with the coming of spring, he returned to London, announcing his complete recovery – 'I never was so well in health since you knew me, or that I can remember', he told Locker. Yet in his eagerness for employment, and with the chance of service in America, he overstated his well-being. He continued to suffer from sporadic paralysis, followed by painful swelling, in his left arm and leg. He was told he really must recover fully; and now, with the weather fine, he knew the best place to go. Burnham Thorpe was still home to him, and his family were still his closest friends.

Captain Suckling had, during his lifetime, done all for the Nelsons that any uncle could; and on his death he bequeathed five hundred pounds to each of his nephews, and a thousand to each of his nieces. When Horatio arrived to visit the family in Norfolk, he found the legacies had changed the lives of every one of them, and especially of his sisters, who – with the exception of Kate, who was only fifteen and had not yet started – had all been enabled to buy their way out of their apprenticeships to 'female trades'. Susannah had married Thomas Bolton, a prosperous merchant of corn and coal in the seaside town of Wells-next-the-Sea, not far from Burnham, and was starting a large, cheerful and noisy family. Anne and Kate were at home looking after their father, the Rector. Of the boys – now, of course, young men – Maurice still had his office job in the Admiralty; Edmund had gone to Ostend as assistant in the counting-house of his brother-in-law Bolton; Suckling – at sixteen, the youngest – was apprenticed to a linen-draper, and was already inclined to drink too much with the local farmers. As for William, he was determined to follow his father and become a curate. But he was a large, humourless and rustic man who appeared all his life to be more mercenary than Christian, and always strained the patience of the rest. Worse, his latest whim was to be a naval chaplain, which he thought was romantic, and he expected Horace to find him a good appointment.

That visit to Norfolk, and Nelson's convalescence, were brought to an end by the news he was hoping for: shortly before his twenty-third birthday, he was appointed commander of a ship. His first task would be to commission her into the navy, for she was a captured French merchantman. However, it was a further two months before she arrived at the Nore for fitting out; and even then, in spite of the long wait, when the time came he was 'so ill as hardly to be kept out of bed'. Maybe it was only a bout of flu; he did not say what exactly ailed him.

Nelson soon declared himself 'perfectly satisfied' with his officers and men; and though *Albemarle* was only another frigate (and at 28 guns, not much of a frigate), at first he refused to admit there was anything wrong with her. But she was never a good sailer: unless the wind was directly behind her, she was so slow that even he came to say the French had only taught her to run away.

He was badly disappointed, too, with the task the Admiralty gave him. Whether through sheer thoughtlessness, or because he had not seen active service for a year and a half, his orders were to convoy 260 merchantmen from Denmark to England. To be given such a job after eighteen months of severe and almost continuous illness disgusted him. Eighteen years later, he still remembered indignantly how he was kept that whole winter in the North Sea – 'it would almost be supposed to try my constitution'.

On his return from Denmark, he was ordered to Portsmouth to take in eight months' provisions. That pleased him: it suggested a long cruise, perhaps to India or the Far East. But, anchored with other vessels in the Downs during a wild, stormy night, a large and heavy storeship broke loose and drove down on his lightly built frigate.

Albemarle's bowsprit and foremast were ripped away. 'Alas,' Nelson wrote, as the chance of an eastern cruise vanished, 'how short-sighted are the best of us. All done in a few minutes! We ought to be thankful we did not founder. Such are the blessings of a sea life!' He got the ship to Portsmouth, but it was three months before he could get her out again, and in the course of the repairs the dockyard shortened her masts, which no doubt made her safer, but also even slower and more difficult to handle.

Instead of an eastern cruise, he was ordered to escort a convoy to the west, across the Atlantic by way of Cork in Ireland, to Newfoundland and thence to Quebec in the St Lawrence – and this at the very time that Admiral Rodney was making naval history in the Battle of the Saints. 'I want much to get off from this confounded voyage', Nelson wrote. 'Mr Adair [his admiral's doctor] has informed me that if I were sent to a cold damp climate, it would make me worse than ever.' As if unable to find anything else good about it, he added: 'We are all alive.' But to his own surprise, he found that crossing the Atlantic in summer agreed 'better with me than I expected'; and back in American waters, life took on a new aspect. For the first time, Nelson fell in love.

5

'What a prize!'

HER NAME WAS Mary Simpson, and she was sixteen years old. Her family, originally Scots, had settled in Quebec, where Nelson met them shortly before his twenty-fourth birthday.

He had arrived there on 1 July 1782. If he first saw Mary then, it would have been a fleeting encounter, for three days later *Albemarle* was sent on an independent cruise – a welcome change, which at least indicates that by the end of his convoy duty, his admiral recognized his ability. The voyage lasted almost eleven weeks, and brought a good deal of adventure but little profit: 'We have indeed taken, seen and destroyed more enemies than is usually done in the same space of time; but not one has arrived in port' – which meant, of course, that no prize money could be paid. One of the vessels was the fishing schooner which he captured and later released. 'However, I do not repine at our loss; in other things we have been very fortunate.' In mid-August *Albemarle* had run into a French squadron of one frigate and four ships of the line, which 'gave us a pretty dance for between nine and ten hours ... Upon the clearing up of a fog, they were within shot of us, and chased us the whole time about one point from the wind.' It was one of the occasions when the pilotage he had learnt as a boy in the Medway was of 'great comfort', for they only managed to escape by sailing deliberately into shoal waters studded with sand banks. Without its larger companions, the enemy frigate was challenged, took fright, and made off; and Nelson added candidly, 'Our escape we think wonderful.'

However, they must have been very badly provisioned at the start of the voyage, for after little more than a fortnight they ran out of fresh food. For eight weeks Nelson and his officers lived on salt beef, and he noted that the men had not had a fresh meal since the day

45

they sailed from Portsmouth, five and a half months before. Not surprisingly, when they returned to Quebec on 17 September, they were all thoroughly 'knocked up with the scurvy' – gums soft and swollen, livid spots on the skin, physically weakened and easily exhausted. One hopes the first meeting with Mary did not take place at once: Nelson cannot have been a pretty sight.

Mary, however, was. No portrait of her exists, but the local paper, reporting on a ball she had attended, described her as having 'heavenly charm', and a 'noble and majestic air'. Such words sound a little unlikely as a description of a sixteen-year-old, but presumably there must have been something of the truth in them, and, in the exaggerated way of a young lover, Nelson accorded her every virtue.

There is no way of knowing how Mary responded to him, for very little has been recorded about this first romance. The little that does remain shows that, at least briefly, Nelson was head over heels: after a month in port, he was ordered to convoy troops to New York, and before he left he came ashore to announce that he would not budge without seeing Mary and 'laying myself and my fortune at her feet.' It was ingenuous, and rather pathetic; his fortune was nonexistent, and he himself was only an undistinguished junior captain. Nor did he see Mary again. Alexander Davison, a businessman and a friend of Mary's father, noticed him as he was being rowed unexpectedly ashore and met him to find out the reason. The two men got into a vigorous argument, with Davison predicting that soon Nelson would have nothing at all to offer Mary, for if he left the navy for no better reason than being in love, the 'utter ruin' of his career must inevitably follow. '"Then let it follow," exclaimed Nelson, "for I am resolved to do it." "And I also", replied his friend, "positively declare that you shall not."'

It was one of the rare occasions when Nelson's resolve did not carry him through: Davison more or less forced him to return to his ship and make ready for the convoy. 'A very pretty job at this late season of the year,' said Nelson crossly, 'for our sails are at this moment frozen to the yards.' But he went all the same, and in the end evidently bore no ill-will – Davison became another of his lifelong friends, and when Nelson had more than fishing boats to dispose of, he asked Davison to be his prize-agent.

From Quebec to New York overland is only four hundred miles or so. By water – down the St Lawrence, across its Gulf, through Cabot Sound, around Nova Scotia and on past Boston (which was then held by the French) – it is at least four times as far. With only a single other warship in company and winter biting them all, *Albemarle* had to shepherd and chivvy twenty-three merchantmen to their destination. It is no wonder that Nelson was reluctant; but after a voyage of three weeks, when he reached Sandy Hook at the mouth of New York's Lower Bay, he was extremely pleased that Davison had made him go. For anchored there was a British squadron of thirteen ships of the line, led by *Barfleur*, the flagship of Admiral Hood – another country parson's son, and now, after his part in the Battle of the Saints, no longer Sir Samuel, but Lord Hood. As was customary for a captain arriving in port, Nelson went to pay his respects to its commander-in-chief, a certain Admiral Digby. He found Lord Hood there as well. Digby commended the young captain on the safe delivery of his merchant flock, and remarked that he had come to a fine station for prize money. Nelson agreed politely, then added: 'But the West Indies is the station for honour.'

The flattering observation was followed by a direct request, and the pleasant discovery that Lord Hood had known Nelson's Uncle Maurice well – Captain Suckling's 'interest' in his nephew extended beyond the grave. Less than a week after their first meeting, Nelson wrote delightedly to Locker: 'I am a candidate, with Lord Hood, for a line-of-battle ship. He has honoured me highly by a letter, for wishing to go off this station to a station of service, and has promised me his friendship.'

The county of Dorset, in southern England, was well known for its seafaring traditions. Admiral Digby was a Dorset man, from Minterne, in the centre of the county; Admiral Hood, thirty-five years older than Nelson, was from Dorset as well, born in the small town of Beaminster, on the edge of the North Dorset Downs, only eight miles from the sea.

Twelve miles south-east of Beaminster, and also eight miles from the sea – for the coast there runs south-eastwards – there is a moderately grand residence known as Kingston Russell House. In Nelson's day it belonged to the Duke of Bedford, but, in the year Horatio was born, it was rented and lived in by an elderly widower called Thomas Masterman. He had two daughters, and in 1762 – presumably being too infirm, or lonely, to live by himself – he asked his elder daughter, her husband and their four daughters to move in. They did so, and when he died the following year, took over the tenancy. They remained in residence a further fourteen years, producing two more daughters and three sons.

Like many parents faced with the pleasant problem of naming children, the tenants of Kingston Russell House looked for inspiration back into their joint family history. Three of the daughters were given names from their father's side; the other three probably came from their mother's side. The first and third of the sons were christened Joseph and John respectively, both being names of long standing on their father's side; and with the second son, born on 5 April 1769, the parents found a happy combination, a name shared by both sides. The infant was called after his maternal grandfather, whose first name, Thomas, happened to have been shared by one of his father's more distinguished relatives. That gentleman, who had died in 1732, had been a local Member of Parliament, a knight, and an admiral. On 7 April 1769, when the baby boy was two days old, he was christened Thomas Masterman Hardy.

The family's naval connections had not stopped in 1732. Another Hardy knight, Sir Charles the elder, was a Lord Commissioner of the Admiralty when he died in 1744, and after being Governor of New York, his son Sir Charles the younger (who earned his knighthood – it was not a baronetcy) was second-in-command of the memorable chase and victory in Quiberon Bay in 1759. So there was every chance that in time, at least one of the new generation – Joe, Jack or Tom, as they were known – would join the navy; and in the autumn of 1781, Tom did so.

He was twelve and a half years old then, the same age as Nelson had been when he first found his way into HMS *Raisonnable*; and he joined in exactly the same way, being taken into the brig *Helena* as a 'Captain's servant' by her commanding officer, Francis Roberts, who was a friend of the family. Roberts was a decent sort – he actually allowed young Hardy to bring his dog Bounce with him. The animal did not care for its master's new life and uniform: 'I was very angry with Bounce,' says Hardy's first surviving letter, written to his brother Joe in 1782 – 'he would not know me until I had put on my old coat. Captain Roberts likes him very much.' Roberts added a postscript to the letter, confirming this: 'We were glad to find the dog safe; I think him a very fine one.' Thomas, he said, was 'a very good boy, and I think will make a complete seaman one day or other.' Of course Roberts was right, and Tom remained a dog-lover all his life too; fifty-five years later, when he was the venerable Governor of Greenwich Hospital, his favourite pet was another dog named Bounce.

At the end of April 1782, Roberts was promoted to command the guardship *Seaford*, and took the boy (and presumably Bounce) with him. They remained on that duty for exactly twelve months; and so, as Hardy embarked on his own naval career, Nelson in New York was writing cheerfully to Locker in London about the welcome possibility of a line-of-battle ship. Far apart geographically, in age and in rank, he and Hardy had never heard of each other; but their names would become inextricably linked.

The year that Hardy was born also saw the birth – in very different circumstances – of two other boys whose names were one day to become famous. The father of one was an English aristocrat called Wesley. His son, born on 1 May, was christened Arthur. Arthur's elder brother Richard became Lord Mornington, and changed the family name back to its older form, Wellesley; and much later, Arthur himself earned in battle the title by which he is known: the Duke of Wellington.

The other boy, born on 15 August, was the son of a Corsican lawyer with an Italianate name, Buonaparte. To the rising generation of Britons, the family name would become the most fearful word they knew. In time, it took a more French form, Bonaparte, and one day the infant would crown himself emperor of France; but for most people today, even among the French, he is simply Napoleon. The baptismal name has itself become something like a title.

Meanwhile, in 1782, there were as well two women – as yet unknown to each other – who, while in most ways they had nothing in common, nevertheless shared two basic circumstances, and would share a third. Each had a child; neither had a husband; and so, in the way of the time, each had to seek a protector.

The first woman, Frances Herbert Woolward, born a few months before Nelson, was a daughter of colonial society: her father, William Woolward, had been senior judge in the balmy island of Nevis in the Lesser Antilles; her uncle, John Richardson Herbert, was president of the island's council. She was twenty when her father died; when she was twenty-one, she married his surgeon, Dr Nisbet. Soon after their wedding, the doctor fell ill with sunstroke and the couple came 'home' to England, where their son, Josiah, was born. But seventeen months later, in a house in the Cathedral Close in Salisbury, the doctor died. His widow – Fanny, as she was known – did the only thing she could, and begged her uncle for a safe haven back in the Caribbean. He agreed happily. He was a widower, without any intention of remarrying, but he was fond of Fanny; if she wished, she could run his household and act as hostess in his frequent social gatherings. She accepted with gratitude, and returned to the sun.

The second woman, Emily Hart, had no such security. Seven years younger than the widow Fanny Nisbet, she was the daughter of an illiterate blacksmith named Henry Lyon, who called her Emy. She was born near Liverpool, and before she was a teenager went to work as an under-nursemaid for a local family. At thirteen she was a maid-servant in London, and for the next three years held various menial posts: gossip subsequently said that apart from assisting a fruiterer in St James's Market, she had worked in a brothel and posed nude for artists. Some of it was true, some not, for she became the subject of much malicious talk. But at the age of sixteen, she was taken by a wealthy young baronet, Sir Harry Fetherstonhaugh, to be his mistress; by him she conceived her first child; and by him she was cast out, whereupon she invented for herself the fictional surname of Hart. In the custom of the age, she already had a second 'official' lover, the art-collecting Honourable Charles Greville, second son of the Earl of Warwick. Though he knew she was pregnant with a child probably not his own, he took her in. At some point she began to be known as Emma; and after the child was born – a little girl, also named Emma, and swiftly sent to live with her grandmother – Greville introduced his mistress to the artist Romney. He was entranced, for she was outstandingly beautiful, and in 1782 he began painting the first of many pictures of her.

As Nelson, filled with pleasant anticipation, sailed towards the West Indies, 'the station for honour', and as little Thomas Hardy played off duty with his dog on the English Channel, the Honourable Arthur Wesley was a privileged schoolboy at Eton, twenty miles west of London, and Cadet Buonaparte was at the Royal Military School in Brienne, a hundred miles east of Paris. There he had just been assessed as possessing the necessary firmness of character to join the French navy. The following year, the visiting inspector changed his recommendation: the cadet – 'a scowling shabby boy who spoke French very badly' – was to be given a career in the Artillery.

It is intriguing to think of the three boys and the young man at this moment: Nelson, the oldest, still only twenty-four, still a rather obscure naval captain; Hardy, Wellington and Napoleon, all born within a few months of each other, and still barely teenagers – each of the four pursuing his own dreams and ambitions, and each destined to affect the others' lives deeply, either as distant but professional colleagues (Nelson and Wellington met only once), as intimate friends, or as implacable enemies. It is also strange, and sad, to think of the two women at the same moment – single mothers, the one respectable and demure, the other with beauty as her sole asset – and to contemplate how Nelson would come to love them both, in such different ways that in Emma he found his greatest joy, and in Fanny his most guilty grief.

In the winter of 1782–3, however, all this was part of an unknown – even unlikely – future, for on 20 January 1783 a preliminary treaty of peace was signed at Versailles between Great Britain, France, Spain and the new nation America, bringing to an end America's long war for independence. Ratification of the treaty would come much later, and even news of the preliminary peace could be passed only slowly around the world. By chance, Nelson unintentionally came close himself to delaying its arrival. Leaving New York's icy November, *Albemarle* accompanied Lord Hood's squadron south and reached Port Royal in February, the most benevolent time of year there – rainfall low, sunshine plentiful, and the thermometer comfortably in the 70s Fahrenheit. In company with the brig *Drake*, Nelson was sent on a cruise of reconnaissance, and during the night of 16 February chased but lost a French ship. It was the vessel bringing tidings of peace to America.

As far as the Caribbean was concerned, the struggle went on until definite news arrived to stop it. On 25 February, Nelson wrote: 'We are all in the dark in this part of the world, whether it is peace or war.' He for one was happy that the war should carry on, because he was making a notable mark at last. Jamaica was chronically short of naval stores, including topmasts for line-of-battle ships – 'there was not one in the island' – when 'providentially a French mast-ship came alongside the *Albemarle*, who captured her: she had nearly a hundred topmasts for large ships, with a number of lower masts and yards; and will clear upwards of 20,000 pounds. What a prize, if the fleet had not been in sight! They do not deserve to share for her: we had chased to leeward, and she had passed every ship in the fleet without being noticed.'

He could not have been more pleased with his situation in Lord Hood's fleet, and wrote to Locker that it 'must be in the highest degree flattering to any young man: he treats me as if I were his son, and will, I am convinced, give me anything I can ask of him.' It was also shortly before this that Nelson had had his first encounter with royalty, when midshipman Prince William Henry gained his memorable impression of the unkempt young captain.

William, the third son, and third of fifteen children, of King George III, was then aged eighteen. He had been a midshipman for five years, and knew very well the difficulties of being made post, as well as the importance that even a junior post-captain had in his officers' lives. Nelson was only six years older than the prince, and with his shabby clothes and youthful appearance scarcely looked like a made man; William's impression of 'the merest boy of a captain' was fair. Lord Hood, however, now specifically told the prince that if he wanted to learn about naval tactics, he should ask Nelson, who 'could give him as much information as any officer in the fleet.' Nelson was thrilled at the thoughtful recommendation. Considering that William was not an ordinary midshipman but a prince of the blood, it offered Nelson, a parson's son, almost unlimited potential benefits – 'I cannot make use of expressions strong enough to describe what I felt', he wrote. Hood certainly would not have paid such a compliment lightly, but with the similarity of their backgrounds, he may also have felt sympathy for Nelson, perhaps seeing in his ambitious, energetic and struggling new captain an image of what he himself had once been.

The idea of a royal sailor starting a career at the bottom, junior to many commoners, was still somewhat startling. Frederick the Great, King of Prussia, commented that 'as our young nobility in general never learn anything, they of course are exceedingly ignorant. In England one of the King's sons, wishing to interest himself, has not scrupled to set out as a common sailor.' Nelson, for his part, was pleased to find Prince William really was 'a seaman, which you could hardly suppose' and credited him 'with the best temper, and great good sense'; but he also predicted that the prince would be 'a disciplinarian, and a strong one.' The prediction was correct, and William became a renowned libertine as well – a combination which made his friendship something of a mixed blessing later on.

As for the prince, his view of Nelson was interesting, quite apart from the vivid physical description he left. He found Nelson 'warmly attached' to the king, which cannot have surprised him much, for few aspiring commoners would neglect to flatter a royal connection. But there was evidently something rather more to Nelson's remarks than simple flattery, because what the prince recalled in later years was how he 'had the honour of the King's service, and the independence of the British navy, particularly at heart.' Nelson had not yet met, or even seen, King George; before meeting Prince William, probably the only idea he had of the monarch's appearance was from looking at the coins in his pocket. And remembering his adolescent vision ('a glow of patriotism ... presented my King and country as my patron') it seems clear he had an especially 'warm attachment' to the king as an idea, a symbol of all that was good about his country, rather than as a real person like himself. If the prince saw that, he may also have seen that it was an unfeigned loyalty.

William was by no means always right in his judgments. 'Throughout the whole of the American war', he said 'the height of Nelson's ambition was to command a line-of-battle ship'. This was true; but then he added: 'As for prize-money, it never entered his thoughts.' The episode with the mast-ship showed how wrong that was. Yet the briefest of his observations was also one of the most telling: Nelson, he said, was 'singularly humane'. The prince himself was not. 'In my own ship I go on pretty well', he wrote to Nelson later. 'I have had two Courts Marshal, one on the Master at Arms who was broke [deprived of his rank] and received 100 lashes.'

By then he was a post-captain too, using both his naval and royal authority to the utmost, often in a manner which Nelson found unnecessary, unpleasant and difficult to cope with. But in the spring of 1783, Nelson felt privileged and happy to escort the midshipman around the Caribbean. Before the half-unwelcome news of peace filtered through in April, *Albemarle* made a couple of quick captures – a French brig, which Nelson kept, and a launch belonging to the king of Spain, filled with Frenchmen and Germans claiming to be scientists, whom he let go. Knowing that peace was around the corner, perhaps he did not want to cause complications for an impending diplomatic event. One of the attractive aspects of the eighteenth century is the speed at which erstwhile enemies began visiting each other quite amicably as soon as they stopped fighting. In early May Prince William was on hand to make the appropriate gesture: a royal visit to Spanish-held Havana, accompanied by Captain Nelson; and whatever effect this had politically, it laid the basis of their lifelong friendship.

No more war. There was nothing for it but to go home, and find what employment, if any, a naval officer could obtain in peace. On 25 June

1783 *Albemarle* anchored at Spithead, and the following day Nelson wrote to Locker: 'After all my tossing about, my dear friend, here at last I am arrived safe and sound. I found orders for the Albemarle to be paid off at this place. On Monday next I hope to be rid of her.' On 3 July she was indeed paid off, and it was then that 'the whole ship's company offered, if I could get a ship, to enter for her immediately.' The 'common sailors' (in King Frederick's disdainful phrase) could not have made a clearer demonstration of their feeling for Nelson. It is the first record of the personal loyalty that he inspired in his crews, and it touched him: as he said, it was something which 'must flatter any officer'. Yet the reason was quite simple. 'The disgust of the seamen to the navy', he wrote, 'is all owing to the infernal plan of turning them over from ship to ship; so that men cannot be attached to their officers, nor their officers care the least about the men.' No one told him to care about his men – indeed, the system worked against it – but naturally and instinctively, he did, and they cared about him in return.

However, though he spent a lot of time and effort making certain that his 'good fellows' received all the wages owed them, he himself did not feel inclined to go back to sea at once, because exciting things were happening on shore. For the first time, he actually met the king. Such things did not occur by chance; to be presented at court you required a connection with someone who was not only very promi-nent, but who also had confidence in you. Lord Hood was one of the heroes of the year, and by arranging Nelson's presentation he demonstrated, as clearly as the 'common sailors', the confidence he felt in the youthful captain.

Everything appears to have gone off entirely satisfactorily, and King George was 'exceedingly attentive', as Nelson wrote rather smugly. Better still, there was a royal invitation to go down from London to Windsor, there to bid farewell to Prince William before he embarked on a grand tour of the Continent. Best of all, there was a friend to relax with and to hear the sensational news – Alexander Davison, who had put such a brusque end to Nelson's wooing in Canada, and who was now staying at Lincoln's Inn in London. Meeting there on the evening after his presentation at court, Nelson flung off his uniform – his 'iron-bound coat', as he called it – borrowed a dressing gown, and settled down to tell all. He did not say, afterwards, if they spoke of Mary. No doubt he asked about her, but he had clearly got over her by then; and he must have felt strongly that without Davison's intervention on

the beach at Quebec, nothing of the rest would have come to pass –
no meeting with Lord Hood, none with the prince, none with the king.
He still regretted that he had not made a fortune in the American war,
but reckoned from the attention paid to him that there was not a speck
on his character. Altogether, he was in a daze of happiness – 'I cannot
afford to live on board, in such a way as is going at present' – and
who could blame him: there was so much happening on shore. Indeed,
it was one of those periods in a growing career when everything goes
right, and all seems set for a future free of pitfalls.

In the autumn of 1783 – he had just turned twenty-five years old –
he decided to take the opportunity of peace to pay a visit to France.
Speaking the language could be a useful professional asset, but since
there had been no French invasion of Jamaica, he had never had to
learn it; so he arranged to travel with a French-speaking friend from
the *Lowestoffe* days, James Macnamara, now a captain too. Late in
October, with six months' leave of absence from the Admiralty, they
set off for Calais.

As always, he wrote some long and vivid letters to Locker, putting
down his impressions of it all – descriptions which show as much of
their author as of the things and people around him. To begin with,
'Our travels, since we left you, have been extended to much greater
length than I apprehended; but I must do Captain Mac the justice to
say, it was all my doings, and in a great measure against his advice.'
Mac had been to France before, and 'as he had experienced the difficulty
of attempting to fix in any place where there are no English', said they
should go straight from Calais to stay in St Omer, twenty-five miles
inland; but Nelson was determined to tour. In five days they covered
135 miles, on a circular route from Calais to Marquise and on south
to Boulogne, thence to Montreuil and down to Abbeville, and back
northwards to St Omer. There he stopped, as Mac had said he should
from the start, and wrote to Locker: 'Experience bought is the best,
and I have paid for mine pretty dearly.'

They had travelled in post-chaises, which were meant to be the
fastest and most comfortable carriages; 'but I am sure we did not get
on more than four miles an hour. I was highly diverted on seeing what
a curious figure the postillions, in their jack-boots, and such rats of
horses, made together. Their chaises have no springs, and the road is
generally paved like London streets [with cobbles] ... We were pretty
well shaken together.' For their first night in France they stopped at

'an inn, they called it; I should have called it a pig-sty. We were put into a room with two straw beds, and with great difficulty they mustered up clean sheets, and gave us two pigeons for supper, and laid wooden-handled knives. O what a transition from happy England! But we laughed at the repast, and went to bed with a determination that nothing should ruffle our tempers.'

In fact they slept very well, and breakfasted next day in Boulogne – 'full of English, I suppose because wine is so very cheap.' Things change little. Thereafter, they passed through 'the finest corn country that I ever beheld, diversified with fine woods, and sometimes, for two miles together, through noble forests' until they came to Montreuil. Laurence Sterne had written about it in *Sentimental Journey*, and, staying in the same place as he had, they found his recommendation good: a jolly landlord, 'partridges twopence halfpenny a couple, pheasants and woodcocks in proportion.' They would have liked to have stayed longer, but there was nowhere to rent, for 'there is no middling class of people. Sixty noblemen's families live in the town, who own the vast plain around it; the rest are very poor indeed.' So onward, with regret, to Abbeville, which was passed without comment; and there 'I determined, with Mac's advice, to steer for St Omer.'

Nelson had had enough of touring. Arriving in St Omer, he promptly dropped anchor and did not budge until his return to England in January 1784. He was surprised to find that 'instead of a dirty, nasty town, which I had always heard it represented,' it was actually 'a large city, well paved, good streets, and well lighted.' They lodged with a French family with two daughters, 'very agreeable young ladies... One always makes our breakfast, the other our tea, and we play a game at cards in the evening; therefore I must learn to speak French, if it is only for the pleasure of talking to them, for they do not speak a word of English.' He restricted his contact with the large number of other English visitors, ostensibly on the conscientious basis that he would learn no French otherwise. But his choice of people to visit and people to avoid is significant. In spite of his glittering new connections, Nelson was still very much a provincial Englishman. There were two fellow naval officers there, 'two noble captains ... They wear fine epaulettes, for which I think them great coxcombs; they have not visited me, and I shall not, be assured, court their acquaintance.' Certainly they were showing off, for epaulettes were not yet part of the British naval uniform; but there speaks the provincial with little money, jealous of show and willing to make a snap judgment. It is pleasant to note that in later years, when he met the two dandies through the course of duty, he liked them both, and came to count one of them, Alexander Ball, among the closest of his many friends.

There were only two English contacts whose company he sought out, and they were both of his own kind. One was the brother of another ex-*Lowestoffe* officer, and the other was the family of a clergyman named Andrews, whose offspring included a naval officer, and two 'most agreeable daughters, about twenty years of age, who play and sing to us whenever we go.' After a month in St Omer, Nelson admitted to Locker: 'The French goes on but slowly ... I must take care of my heart, I assure you.'

He was beginning to show a definite susceptibility to a pretty face, particularly when he was in uncomfortable circumstances – one has to be really Francophile to enjoy northern France in the winter. Indeed, once again, he was completely bowled over. Miss Andrews, he declared, was 'the most accomplished young woman my eyes ever beheld ... Had I a million of money, I am sure I should at this moment make her an offer of them.' But he had not; all that he had was his half-pay of £130 a year. He went so far as to write to his uncle William Suckling, asking for an allowance of a hundred a year until he could support a family, and his uncle would have given it to him – he later did so, when Nelson finally took the plunge. But before Uncle William's reply could reach him, Nelson unexpectedly returned to England, and would not tell anyone exactly why.

One of his sisters, Anne, had died suddenly, but although her death upset him greatly, this does not appear to have been his reason. To Locker, he wrote, with circumspection, that 'some little matters in my accounts' forced his return. It may have been that he was simply running out of money, and realized he could not really afford marriage; or perhaps he had proposed to Miss Andrews and had been turned down. Equally, he might just have fallen out of love with her as swiftly as he had fallen in, and had the sense to realize it. Whatever the cause, the relationship must have ended in an amicable way: Miss Andrews' naval brother remained on the best of terms with Nelson, which would not have been the case otherwise.

He did make one gratifying discovery in France: one of the 'scientists' he had captured and released in the Caribbean turned out to be a prince, a general in the French army, the second-in-command at the Battle of Yorktown, and brother of the heir-apparent to the electorate of Bavaria. Nelson only found this out when his erstwhile captive sent him 'a most polite invitation' to come and visit. He did not have time to accept before his return to England, but the implication pleased him: 'The present elector is eighty years of age, and this nobleman's brother is upon his death-bed; so most probably I shall have had the honour of taking prisoner a man who will be a sovereign prince of Europe, and bring into the field nearly a hundred thousand men.'

It was the kind of idea he liked, and he must have regretted whatever circumstances they were which forced him so precipitately back to England. On the whole, however, he had not liked France very much, apart from the food, the countryside, and his landlord's daughters. His travels had been very limited, but he had remarked on some of the country's social conditions – the pitiable general poverty, the lack of a 'middling class', the desperately unequal ownership of land – which, only five years later, would pitch the unhappy nation into its long and bloody revolution. (If he thought what those conditions might bring, he did not record it; certainly, had he been able to accept the Bavarian prince's invitation and so got inside the walls of the great châteaux, he would have seen the glitteringly ostentatious lives of the French nobility at first hand, and the full and painful contrast between court and country would have been inescapable.)

In general, though, he had found French people rather comical, and some of his own colleagues objectionable; the weather was no doubt cold and wet; the travel was uncomfortable. Altogether, his memories of the time cannot have been good. In later years, he always said that his obsessive hatred of France and the French sprang from his loathing for their revolutionary politics, which was a perfectly good reason. But he might have hated them a little less if, as a peaceful visitor, he had gone to the south, or at least gone in the summer. Certainly, things might have been rather different if he had fallen in love with one of his landlord's two daughters, but they had little chance in competition with the comforting familiarity, in a foreign land, of a Church of England home; and when Nelson left France in January 1784, he left it for ever. In all the years he spent later blockading its coast, he never again set foot on its shores.

6

'Many disagreeable adventures'

THERE WAS ANOTHER reason for Nelson's sudden return to England, whatever the truth about his apparent lack of funds and, possibly, his unsuccessful attempts at courtship. A turn of events nearer home seems also to have been strongly influential in his decision.

The nearest the English had come to revolution had been during their civil war, over a century before. Since the restoration of Charles II in 1660 the idea of parliamentary democracy had, in a haphazard way, been taking shape, and members of parliament were chosen by election – even if corruption was rife. The monarch, however, was still entitled to appoint his ministers and, if a ministry was to survive, parliamentary support and royal support were equally vital. With the ending of the American War of Independence, government in Britain had been through two years of turmoil: the resignation of one prime minister, the death of another, and a coalition led by two men who loathed each other and whom the king deeply disliked. In December 1783, King George III dismissed them both, and astonished everybody with his new appointee – as a verse of the time said, it was 'A sight to make surrounding nations stare, A kingdom trusted to a schoolboy's care.' For the new First Lord of the Treasury and Chancellor of the Exchequer, William Pitt the Younger, was only twenty-four years old – exactly the same age as Nelson.

While he was in St Omer, Nelson must have read about the new appointment, and its implications for politics at home. Scarcely anyone in the existing parliament supported Pitt; the ministry could not survive long on royal favour alone, and soon there would be no alternative but to call a general election. Clearly Nelson was intensely excited by the whole business: because on his return to London in January 1784 he set about trying to be adopted as a candidate for the new parliament.

No doubt he said to himself, Why not? The country was at peace; there was no prospect of immediate naval employment; he had gained as much promotion as he could; why not a second career? It could only enhance his future prospects, if he did well. Pitt and he were exact contemporaries; if one could be prime minister, there was no reason why the other should not be a member of his parliament. Other naval officers were thinking of standing – Lord Hood was one, and had said (as Nelson wrote after dining with him) that 'his house was always open to me, and that the oftener I came the happier it would make him.' At first the young hopeful was coy in his letters – perhaps he wanted to surprise his friends and family by being able to announce himelf suddenly as Captain Horatio Nelson, RN, MP. 'London has so many charms', he wrote to his brother William, 'that a man's time is wholly taken up.' He said he had been 'running at the ring of pleasure', which made it sound as though he was leading a hectic social life. He had indeed attended a levée at St James's, and had 'danced attendance' on people of influence; but, impoverished as he was, the impression of being a man about town was probably misleading. It is more likely that the 'ring of pleasure' was the company of the other young would-be politicians he met at Lord Hood's.

Gradually, though, he let it out – 'tonight the ministry will try their strength. I shall not conclude my letter till late, as perhaps I may hear how matters are likely to go' – and expressed his own views: the dismissed coalition, led by Charles James Fox, were 'a turbulent faction that are striving to ruin their Country', and Nelson and his friends hoped to 'unkennel Fox from Westminster.'

'Mr Pitt, depend upon it, will stand against all opposition', he declared in another letter. 'An honest man must always in time get the better of a *villain*.' Of course Pitt did prevail, and with the minimum of delay. Calling the election in March 1784, he won convincingly, and with the support of the people and the king began twenty-one years of almost uninterrupted governance. Nelson, however, had no part in it at all.

He had hoped to capitalize on his family's political connections, the Walpoles – as, similarly, had his brother William, now ordained and looking for a rectory of his own. But in a disillusioned letter to William, Nelson wrote that they had turned out to be 'the merest set of Cyphers – in public affairs, I mean ... As to your having enlisted under the banner of the Walpoles, you might as well have enlisted under those of my grandmother.' Nelson had not been taken on anywhere as a candidate; and finally, on 31 January, he wrote: 'I have done with politics; let who will get in, I shall be left out.'

While it lasted, though, the brief flirtation with another way of life was as ardent and optimistic as his passions for Mary Simpson and Miss Andrews, and when it was over, he was correspondingly cast down – 'pulled down most astonishingly', he wrote. He even thought of going back to France, but since 'no charming woman will go with me', he made do with Norfolk. To members of his family, his immediate future seemed unpromising. Yet whether through habit or as a fall-back, he had taken the opportunity, while in London, of calling on Lord Howe, First Lord of the Admiralty; and on 18 March he was appointed to a new command, the 28-gun frigate *Boreas*. Brother William was evidently surprised, for Nelson wrote heavily to him: 'You ask, by what interest did I get a Ship? I answer, having served with credit was my recommendation to Lord Howe ... Anything in reason that I can ask, I am sure of getting from his justice.'

William's surprise was actually quite understandable: there were many captains ashore on half-pay, and no obvious reason why Nelson should have been a lucky one, especially since he had exerted himself towards politics. Lord Hood probably had something to do with the appointment; it is even possible that he purposefully did something unknown to Nelson to keep him out of politics and reserve him for the navy. Whatever the background reality, though, the command seemed to William a splendid opportunity – for himself. Here, he decided, was the perfect chance to become a naval chaplain, and nothing Nelson could say would make him change his mind. Neither their father's advanced age and uncertain health; nor the recent death of their sister; nor the fact that *Boreas* was too small to have an official chaplain; nor even the further fact that William had just been offered a rectory – none of it made any difference, and Nelson gave in. 'Come when you please, I shall be ready to receive you', he wrote at last. 'Bring your canonicals and sermons. Do not bring any Burnham servants.'

Bound for the West Indies to take part in the constant naval patrols, HMS *Boreas* sailed from Long Reach at daylight on Monday 12 April, just after high water; and as Locker read in a letter from Nelson, until they reached the open ocean, the voyage was not a happy one. 'Since I parted from you,' he wrote, 'I have encountered many disagreeable adventures.' They had scarcely weighed anchor when 'the damned pilot – it makes me swear to think of it – ran the Ship aground, where she lay with so little water that the people could walk round her till next high water. That night, and part of the next day, we lay below the Nore with a hard gale of wind and snow; Tuesday I got into the Downs; on Wednesday I got into a quarrel with a Dutch Indiaman who had Englishmen on board, which we settled, after some difficulty. The Dutchman has made a complaint against me; but the Admiralty fortunately has approved my conduct – a thing they are not very guilty of when there is a likelihood of a scrape.'

It took six days to arrive at Spithead, and there Nelson had to take on board some less than welcome passengers: Lady Hughes, chatterbox wife of the commander-in-chief of the Leeward Islands, and Rosy, their unmarried, exceedingly unattractive daughter. The only thing as plain as poor Rosy was her mother's determination to find her a husband. Observing bluntly that 'the mother will be the handsomer in a few years', Nelson was horrified to realize that whatever the gorgeous Miss Andrews might have thought, Lady Hughes's opinion was that a young post-captain would be a very suitable match. Instant action was required to make it clear he was unavailable. Putting himself ashore, he hired two horses and 'a young girl' as a riding partner, and set off for a pleasant trot, no doubt being as obvious as possible about the whole business.

It was nearly a disaster. He could not control his mount, and as he clung on desperately, the 'blackguard horse' bolted, 'carried me all around the works into Portsmouth by the London gates, through the town, out at the gate that leads to [the] Common, where there was a waggon in the road, which is so very narrow that a horse could scarcely pass. To save my legs, and perhaps my life, I was obliged to throw myself from the horse, which I did with great agility; but, unluckily, upon hard stones, which has hurt my back and my leg ... It was a thousand to one that I had been killed.' And 'to crown all,' the girl's horse bolted too, and was stopped by a complete stranger.

One may readily imagine Nelson hobbling and cursing back to *Boreas*, and the girl, perhaps disdainful of him, going gratefully away on the arm of the 'gallant young man' who 'saved her from the destruction which she could not have avoided.' However, the bruises and embarrassment were worth while: though Lady Hughes was still 'an eternal clack', she took the point, and did not press Rosy further on the unwilling captain. After all, there were plenty of other young men around.

Lady Hughes was evidently a realistic and good-natured woman. As she talked *Boreas* – '*dear* Boreas' – across the Atlantic, she took a great liking to Nelson, and understood his rebuff of Rosy too well to hold it against him. Very much later, she wrote about the voyage; and although she was self-deprecating – 'As a woman, I can only speak of those parts of his professional conduct which I could comprehend' – she left a vivid and oft-quoted picture of Nelson's views of captaincy. He had taken about thirty midshipmen with him, mostly (in the usual way) the sons of friends and relatives. Among such a number, said Lady Hughes, 'it may reasonably be supposed there must have been timid spirits, as well as bold. The timid he never rebuked, but always wished to show them he desired nothing that he would not instantly do himself: and I have known him say, *Well, sir, I am going a race to the mast-head, and beg I may meet you there.* No denial could be given to such a request; and the poor little fellow instantly began to climb the shrouds. Captain Nelson never took the least notice in what manner it was done, but when they met in the top, spoke in the most cheerful terms to the midshipman, and observed how much any person was to be pitied who could fancy there was any danger, or even anything disagreeable in the attempt.'

Of course there could be a great deal of danger going aloft – one slip could be fatal – and first time off, it can be most disagreeable to climb perhaps 140 feet up the swaying, windy rigging. However large the vessel, its deck looks unnervingly small from such a height, and at the mast-head, you seem to be on an inverted pendulum, swinging out over the water from side to side in a most disconcerting way. But as Lady Hughes noticed, 'After this excellent example, I have seen the same youth who before was so timid, lead another in like manner, and repeat his commander's words.'

She also noticed how much attention Nelson paid to the midshipmen's schooling – not only in navigation and seamanship, but also in the social graces. When they eventually reached Barbados and went to dine with the governor, Nelson asked Lady Hughes's permission to take one of the midshipmen along, explaining to her and the governor: 'I make it a rule to introduce them to all the good company I can, as they have few to look up to, besides myself, during the time they are at sea.'

Such consideration was admirable, but Nelson's consciousness of his rank had another side, which earned him enemies and hindered his career. He showed it first in Madeira. On arrival there at the beginning of June, he and Lady Hughes paid the customary visits to the governor and the consul. The consul did not return the compliment as he should have done, saying the goverment had not provided him with a boat for such purposes. Nelson thought this a paltry excuse, and promptly banned any further contact with him. Apart from anything else, this meant that he was not invited to a party in *Boreas* to celebrate the king's birthday on Friday 4 June. It may have been just as well for him, in one way. A word which often crops up in Nelson's letters is 'bumper', meaning a glass of wine full to the brim. When 'drinking a toast in a bumper', the idea was to down it all in one go without spilling a drop – and at the party, 'after dinner, the healths of the king, queen, and their thirteen children [they still had two more to come] were drunk in as many bumpers.'

The Nelson brothers both took advantage of such opportunities as the island afforded: two days after the party, William conducted divine service on board, and received 'thanks for his excellent discourse'; the captain, meanwhile, ordered four and a quarter casks of Madeira for friends at home and abroad. When they set sail again after a week in port, Nelson's good humour was much restored, even though (as he disparagingly said of the ladies) his ship was still 'pretty well filled with *lumber*.' He lectured the ship's company on the diet and hygiene necessary to survive a four-year tour of the tropics; when crossing the equator, they had the usual jollifications, with 'King Neptune' coming on board and ducking all those who had not been through the ceremony before; and soon he had relaxed sufficiently to describe Rosy and Lady Hughes as 'very pleasant good people'. Unfortunately he found he could do little with Rosy's brother, who was one of the midshipmen; and when they arrived in the Leeward Islands, towards the end of June 1784, Admiral Sir Richard Hughes turned out to be the same as the rest of the family – bearable, but quite ineffectual.

'Tolerable,' was Nelson's opinion, 'but I do not like him, he bows and scrapes too much for me.' There seemed little to recommend him as a commander-in-chief: he lived in an ordinary boarding house ('not much in the style of a British Admiral', said Nelson sniffily); he had only one eye – not the result of some glamorous action, but of trying unsuccessfully to spear a cockroach with a table fork; now, all he wanted in Barbados was a quiet life. It did not take long for Nelson to reach a firm conclusion: 'The Admiral and all about him are great ninnies.' And with that began one of the most infuriating periods of Nelson's career.

It was not only the difference in personalities which raised his hackles, and which made the next nine months on the station wretched and frustrating for him. In his *Memoir*, he gave a succinct description of the real problem he faced in the West Indies: 'The Americans, when Colonists, possessed almost all the trade from America to our West India Islands; and on the return to Peace [after the War of Independence], they forgot, on this occasion, they became foreigners, and of course had no right to trade in the British Colonies.' But of course they were trading, and no one was trying to stop them: 'Our Governors and Custom-house Officers pretended that by the Navigation Act they had a right to trade; and all the West Indians wished what was so much in their interest.'

Nelson had found he was senior captain on the station, and he took his responsibility seriously: he knew the trade was illegal and foretold strategic problems if it was not stopped. But Admiral Hughes was extremely weak-willed. 'He is led', Nelson wrote to Locker, 'by the advice of the Islanders to admit the Yankees to a Trade; at least to wink at it. He does not give himself the weight I think an English Admiral ought to do. I, for one, am determined not to suffer the Yankees to come where my ship is; for I am sure, if once the Americans are admitted to any kind of intercourse with these Islands ... they will become first the Carriers, and next have possession of our Islands, are we ever again embroiled in a French war.'

This makes Nelson sound very anti-American, which he was not – in later years, in the Mediterranean, he was glad to offer free protection to American merchant ships there. He had no orders to do so, and knew he was making a gesture of international consequence by giving the shelter of the British flag to Americans; but as he said at that time, 'I am sure of fulfilling the wishes of my sovereign, and I hope of strengthening the harmony which so happily subsists between the two nations.'

Similarly, in the Caribbean in 1784, fulfilling the wishes of the sovereign was all he wanted to do, and he was certain what those wishes must be. The Navigation Act spelled them out clearly. Hughes claimed to have no specific orders from Britain – 'Very odd,' said Nelson, 'as every captain of a man-of-war was furnished with the statutes of the Admiralty, in which was the Navigation Act.' Hughes then asserted that 'he had never seen the book.' Of course Nelson promptly showed it to him; he 'seemed convinced', said he had not noticed the Act before, and issued orders for its enforcement. 'Having given Governors, Custom-house Officers and Americans notice of what I would do,' the *Memoir* continues, 'I seized many of their Vessels, which brought all parties upon me ...'

It was impossible to argue against the strict legality and correctness of Nelson's actions, yet only four people in the whole of the British Caribbean supported him. Hughes, as commander-in-chief, should have been one of them, but he was not: in December 1784, after pressure from traders, governors and corrupt customs officers through- out the region, he rescinded his order of enforcement. His new instruc- tion was that foreign merchantmen should be stopped and their approach reported to the local governor, who would then decide whether they should be allowed into port or not. If they were, Nelson was 'on no account to hinder or prevent such foreign vessel from going in accordingly, or to interfere any further in her subsequent proceedings.'

This was the most serious dilemma Nelson had ever faced. 'I must either disobey my orders,' he told Locker, 'or disobey Acts of Parlia- ment, which the admiral was disobeying.' He decided on the former. 'I wrote to the Admiral that I should decline obeying his orders, till I had an opportunity of seeing and talking to him, at the same time making him an apology.' Sir Thomas Shirley, a general in the army and Governor-General of the Leewards, was outraged, and told Nelson plainly that 'old respectable officers of high rank, long service and a certain life are very jealous of being dictated to in their duty by young gentlemen.' That is certainly true, and Shirley must have been considerably taken aback by Nelson's vigorous reply: 'I have the honour, Sir, of being as old as the Prime Minister of England, and think myself as capable of commanding one of His Majesty's ships as that Minister is of governing the State.'

It is a revealing remark. Most people thought he was being excess- ively officious – and rashly so, from the career point of view: Hughes warned him that if he carried on, he would be bound to 'get into a scrape'. But, 'trusting to the uprightness of my intentions', Nelson did carry on; and the example of Pitt may have given him strength. Perhaps he remembered his own words of a year before, and saw himself in them: 'Mr Pitt, depend upon it, will stand against all oppo- sition. An honest man must always in time get the better of a *villain*.'

He needed all his strength of conviction to maintain his stance. In January 1785 he wrote to Locker, 'The longer I am on this Station the worse I like it'; and a few weeks later, in a long letter to the Admiralty, described another breach. On 5 February he had sailed into English Harbour, the dockyard in Antigua, and there found HMS *Latona* flying a broad pendant, the emblem of a commodore.

'As her captain was junior to me, I sent to know the reason for her wearing it. Her Captain came on board, who I asked the following questions: Have you any order from Sir Richard Hughes to wear a broad pendant? *Answer*: No. *Question*: For what reason do you then wear it in the presence of a Senior Officer? *Answer*: I hoisted it by order of Commissioner Moutray. *Question*: Have you seen by what authority Commissioner Moutray was empowered to give you orders? *Answer*: No. *Question*: Sir, you have acted wrong, to obey any man who you do not know is authorized to command you. *Answer*: I feel I have acted wrong; but being a young captain, did not think proper to interfere in this matter, as there were you and other older Officers upon this Station.'

For his part, Nelson thought it perfectly proper to interfere whenever he saw something happening contrary to English or naval law, but his junior colleague's caution is understandable, for John Moutray was a very senior naval captain: he had been made post in the year Nelson was born. However, his present job, as commissioner for the naval dockyard, was a civil post. Hughes had authorized him to act as commander-in-chief on the station in the absence of a senior officer, yet as Nelson told him, with extraordinary bluntness: 'Until you are in commission I cannot obey any order I receive from you. I know of no superior officers besides the lords commissioned of the Admiralty, and my seniors on the post list.'

Altogether, Nelson's actions during this period – his only peacetime commission – came near to professional suicide. Though technically right, he was creating immense ructions with influential men, and causing the far-off Admiralty no end of trouble. He also put himself at severe financial risk. Just after the collision with Moutray, the islanders of Nevis banded together to sue him for the trade he had lost them, claiming £40,000 from a man whose full pay was £260 a year.

'I was so persecuted from one island to another', he wrote, 'that I could not leave my Ship.' For eight weeks he remained in *Boreas* to avoid arrest, writing to his uncle William Suckling (who had worked all his life for the Customs), to Hughes, the Admiralty, the secretary of state and – trusting on his slight connection – even to the king. Hughes by then was thinking of getting some senior captains out from England, so that Nelson could be court-martialled, but the civil trial in Nevis intervened; and to Nelson's immense relief the judge shared his attitude to the law. In spite of the islanders' plaintive description of a marine sentry as 'a man with a drawn sword' who they were sure was there to cut their throats, the seizures of American ships were upheld. Nelson was acquitted; and three months later, a reply came from England, saying that his costs would be met by the Treasury. The Admiralty acknowledged he was right, but simultaneously they used an unusually subtle device to indicate their displeasure with the captain who stuck so punctiliously to the rules. The rules, or naval tradition at least, said that after any action, praise or blame went to the most senior officer involved; and as Sir Richard was commander-in-chief, he and Governor Shirley received official commendation for their hard work and efforts in protecting British trade.

The only four people in the British Caribbean to give Nelson their support throughout this troubled time were two naval officers and two civilians. As it gradually became clear that, come what may, he was going to stick up for what he believed to be right, other junior officers rallied; but only the Collingwoods were with him from the start. Cuthbert, his old friend from the days when they were both made post by Admiral Parker, sailed in mid-September 1784 from Spithead in the newly built frigate *Mediator*. In mid-December it was actually he who made the first move against illegal West Indian trade, by stopping an American merchantman from entering Antigua. His brother Wilfred, commander of the sloop-of-war *Rattler*, was a year younger (thirty-four years old at the time) but looked older: 'Wilfred is always call'd old Collingwood', Cuthbert remarked with amusement, 'and has been taken for fifty.' To Admiral Hughes, they presented a strong-minded trio – as Cuthbert said with some understatement, 'Because our diligence reflects on his neglect, he dislikes us.'

They gave a united front to General Shirley as well. 'I shall take this opportunity of informing Your Excellency', wrote Cuthbert Colling-wood, 'I have reason to believe Foreigners (that is, Americans) do find means to impose on the Customs House, proofs which will not stand the test of inquiry, to procure papers authorizing them to trade hither … Is it amazing that I should, in obedience to my orders, endeavour to restrain this to the limits prescribed to it by law?' It was not; but what was a little surprising, at the least, was the identity of the two supportive civilians. One was John Herbert, president of the council of Nevis, who said in court that Nelson had only done his duty, and – though he knew he would lose a lot of money if the illegal trading was suppressed – offered to stand bail for ten thousand pounds. The other was Mrs Moutray, wife of the commissioner whose right to a broad pendant Nelson had challenged; and her support was all the more surprising, because both she and her husband knew that Nelson was deeply in love with her.

Any close friend could have predicted it. His brother William, finding the climate more than he could take, had sailed back to England after three months in the Caribbean, and until the Collingwoods arrived, he had no one to confide in, and many problems to solve. He first met the Moutrays when they offered him accommodation while *Boreas* was being repainted in English Harbour. Before long he confessed to Locker: 'Was it not for Mrs Moutray, who is *very very* good to me, I should hang myself in this infernal hole ... Her equal I never saw in any country or in any situation.'

So much for Mary Simpson and Miss Andrews. Of course, a married woman has a distinct attraction for many a young man: the husband is a convenient barrier to full responsibility, and the wife, being un-attainable, is all the more appealing. Mrs Moutray was much younger than her husband, and they had one child – an eleven-year-old boy who intended to join the navy, and who brought out Nelson's fatherly streak. But her main charms were simply that she was a sympathetic and civilized woman. The role of comforter came naturally to her: Cuthbert Collingwood was included under her soothing wing, and in her house he and Nelson drew the portraits of each other which have become famous – they gave the pictures to her, and fortunately she kept them. Both men remained in friendly contact with her for many years; she and Collingwood were still corresponding after Nelson was dead. Collingwood, however, never wore his heart on his sleeve. Later, a junior officer who did not know him closely said that 'in body and mind he was iron, and very cold iron – in heart I believe the same, except one small soft corner, accessible only to his family.' Nelson's heart was easily accessible, particularly when he faced problems, and for a brief time Mrs Moutray had the whole of it.

'I never passed English Harbour without a call, but alas! I am not to have much comfort', he told William. 'My dear, sweet friend is going home. I really am an April day; happy on her account, but truly grieved were I only to consider myself.' The family were obliged to return to England, Moutray's health being poor. Mrs Moutray kindly promised Nelson that, if his father took his youngest, favourite sister to Bath, she would get in touch. 'What an acquisition for any female to be acquainted with,' he said adoringly, 'what an example to take pattern from!' After they had gone, the infatuation lingered, and he could not resist the painful pleasure of visiting their empty house. He had known all along that this romance was hopeless: but his attachment was utterly sincere and he felt the loss deeply. Without Mrs Moutray, English Harbour could only be forlorn. 'E'en the trees drooped their heads' – one, indeed, had tactfully died – and 'all was melancholy; the road is covered with thistles; let them grow. I shall never pull one of them up. By this time I hope she is safe in old England. Heaven's choicest blessings go with her.'

Nelson in love was so obvious about it that onlookers could only be embarrassed or amused. It appears Commissioner Moutray was amused; at any rate, he was sufficiently old and experienced to tolerate the innocent, futile flirtation, even when Nelson was so officious about his right to a broad pendant. Certainly he understood the young captain's point then, and so did the Admiralty. As a result of Nelson's protestations, it was decided that, in future, shore bases such as English Harbour dockyard should become nominal ships, with a commanding officer on full pay with active seniority; and the system still exists.

For Nelson himself, the problem of seniority, afloat or ashore, ended on 20 March, when the Moutrays sailed for England. No one could any longer doubt that he was senior captain on the station. However, the need for consoling female companionship remained. A few weeks before the departure of his 'dear, sweet friend', Nelson began visiting Montpelier, the house of President Herbert of Nevis, who had generously offered to stand bail for him. He said goodbye to Mrs Moutray on 13 March, and either that same day or within forty-eight hours was at Montpelier again.

The visit changed his life. In Shakespeare's play *Much Ado About Nothing* the word 'benedick' is used. Archaic now, it was familiar to Nelson; it means a newly married man, especially a confirmed bachelor who marries. He did not quite get it right, but at the very end of another of his lengthy letters to Captain Locker – more than 1400 words long – he wrote a tantalizing twenty-five words: 'Most probably the next time you see me will be as a benedict. I think I have found a woman who will make me happy.'

7

'This Horatio is for ever in love'

SHE HAPPENED TO be in St Kitt's when first he came to Nevis, but she heard all about him in a letter from a cousin – a letter which shows both Nelson's local notoriety and the pressure he was under.

'We have at last seen the Captain of the *Boreas*, of whom so much has been said. He came up just before dinner, much heated, and was very silent; yet seemed, according to the old adage, to think the more. He declined drinking any wine; but after dinner, when the President, as usual, gave the following toasts, "the King", "the Queen and Royal Family", and "Lord Hood", this strange young man regularly filled his glass, and observed that those were always bumper toasts with him; which having drank, he uniformly passed the bottle, and relapsed into his former taciturnity.'

Evidently he was not a good guest during that first dinner: 'there was such reserve and sternness in his behaviour' that the writer, a young woman, could not make him out at all. Seated next to him, she tried 'to rouse his attention by showing him all the civilities in my power; but I drew out little more than "Yes" or "No".' She ended the letter in exasperation: 'If you, Fanny, had been there, we think you would have made something of him; for you have been in the habit of attending to these odd sort of people.'

On his second visit Fanny Nisbet was there, yet still did not see him: he arrived very early in the morning, chaperoning another of President Herbert's nieces – 'They trust any young lady with me', Nelson wrote, 'being an old-fashioned fellow.' The president was only half-dressed, but, coming down to greet Nelson, he found him being expertly entertained by the most junior member of the household. 'Good God!', Herbert said afterwards. 'If I did not find that great little man, of whom everybody is so afraid, playing in the next room, under the dining table, with Mrs Nisbet's child!'

Thus, by the time Nelson and Fanny first met a few days later, in the middle of March 1785 – just after he had said goodbye to Mrs Moutray – each had an idea of the other, and was predisposed to investigate a little further. Fanny saw much what she had been led to expect: a naval captain about her own age, slightly built, tanned, rather shy, very earnest, serious and polite, with a face not handsome but engaging, and an even more engaging ability to relax completely with her little boy. Nelson, to his surprise, saw a new incarnation of his 'dear, sweet friend', and wrote enthusiastically that 'her manners are Mrs Moutray's' – but without the encumbrance of a husband. Her accomplishments, too, were those of an elegant lady: she spoke French fluently (which, given his own difficulties with the language, would have impressed him); she sewed beautifully (some examples of her delicate needlework survive); she was said to be very musical (untrue, in fact); her eyes were dark grey, her features quite fine, her figure suitably feminine, and her complexion unusually fair for the tropics, for she was a creature not of the sun but of the salon, venturing outdoors only with a parasol and remaining always in the shade.

In short, she was a fairly ordinary woman of her time, class and place. But compared to the greater numbers of merchants' wives, prostitutes and black slaves (together, the majority of females in the Caribbean), there were not many like her; each had a rarity value; and presumably very few of the eligible women had an appealing young child. To many a young man like Nelson, then – lonely, affectionate and of fatherly disposition – the idea of an instant family is very beguiling, and there can be little doubt that Josiah, just five years old, formed a definite part of the attraction which Nelson swiftly felt. Within a few months, he was writing 'Give my love to Josiah', 'How is my little Josiah?' and 'My dear Josiah shall ever be considered as one of my own.'

There is great poignancy in that last remark. Nelson, child of a large and loving family, was obviously looking forward to having a family of his own, with children of his own blood as well as Josiah. But in the 'Sketch of my Life' which he wrote for his first biographers, this was all he felt able to say of Fanny, and of the years he spent with her:

'In March of this year [1787] I married Frances Herbert Nisbet, widow of Dr Nisbet, of the island of Nevis; by whom I have no children.'

*

However, the enormous private sadness compressed into those few words was, during the summer of 1785, unimaginable. Money, or the lack of it, was the only problem Nelson could foresee then, and in November he turned again to his uncle William Suckling with 'a business which perhaps you will smile at ... and say "This Horatio is for ever in love".' As he pursued his wooing, in a curiously formal fashion, Fanny responded likewise. The long interval between their meeting and their marriage was dictated by President Herbert. Uncle William learned that Nelson had admitted to Herbert, 'I am as poor as Job; but he tells me he likes me, and I am descended from a good family ... but he also says, "Nelson, I am proud, and I must live like myself, therefore I can't do much in my lifetime; when I die she shall have twenty thousand pounds; and if my daughter dies before me, she shall possess the major part of my property. I intend going to England in 1787 and remaining there my life; therefore, if you two can live happily together till that event takes place, you have my consent."'

Nelson ended his begging letter: 'Who can I apply to but you? Don't disappoint me, or my heart will break.' Uncle William, who had heard it all before, was somewhat put out by the emotional blackmail, for he was thinking of getting married again himself, and would need all his money for that. But family loyalty prevailed: he promised his help, and Nelson, reassured, was able to concentrate on his two favourite preoccupations, love and duty.

They had often conflicted before, but never so much. He proposed to Fanny in July 1785, and in mid-August he had to go to Barbados, and was not back until the end of the year. In March 1786 he had to cruise again, supposedly for three months; but apart from brief visits in July and October, duty kept him away from Nevis for most of the next twelve months, until the day he wed.

Duty always came first. From Barbados (which he nicknamed 'Barbarous Island'), he wrote to Fanny: 'Never, never do I believe shall I get away from this detestable spot. Had I taken your advice and not seized any Americans, I should now have been with you; but I should have neglected my duty, which I think your regard for me is too great to have wished me to have done. Duty is the great business of a Sea-officer. All private considerations must give way to it, however painful it is.' This meant that a very large proportion of the courtship was by letter, between two people who inevitably must have become almost imaginary to each other. It is probably not going too far to say that, instead of a flesh-and-blood woman, Nelson was courting an idea.

He did miss her, and when he received his first letter from her, he was as thrilled as a teenager: 'My dearest Fanny, What can I say? Nothing, if I speak of the pleasure I felt at receiving your kind and affectionate letter; my thoughts are too big for utterance. You may suppose that everything which is tender, kind, and truly affectionate has possession of my whole frame. Words are not capable of conveying an idea of my feelings ...'

Often the best love-letters are unplanned. They may end up disjointed, even incoherent, but if the writer begins without knowing what he is going to write and finishes without remembering what has been written, the result is at least authentic. Nelson's reply to Fanny's first letter has that authenticity of feeling – 'I have begun this letter, and left off, a dozen times; and found I did not know one word from another ... therefore expect nothing but sheer stupidity.' Writing from English Harbour in Antigua, fifty miles from Nevis, he rambles and gossips, telling her with touches of humour of things he has done, places and people he has seen, and ends: 'Although I am just away from salt water, yet, as I am in a hurry to get the *Berbice* away, that she may reach Nevis by the evening, I must finish this thing; for letter I cannot call it. I have a newspaper for Miss Herbert [the President's daughter]; it is all I have to offer that is worth her acceptance; and I know she is as fond of a bit of news as myself. Pray give my compliments to her, and love to Josiah.'

There are little intimacies here which carry echoes of conversations in Nevis, and a real sense of the closeness he felt to Fanny – an invitation from an islander 'made amends for his long neglect, and I forgot all anger: I can forgive sometimes, you will allow', while another islander 'says he understood and believed I was gone to England – Whistle for that! The country air has certainly done me service. I am not getting fat, my make will not allow it: but I can tell you, and I know your tender heart will rejoice, that I have no more complaint in my lungs, and not the least pain in my breast.'

So she had heard all his problems while he was in Nevis – his dislike of the station, his wish to get back to England, his health – and had teased and sympathized and warned him not to gain weight: all exactly the kind of things Mrs Moutray or any other well disposed woman would have done. But no other unmarried woman had been sufficiently well disposed; and since the only way Nelson seemed able to respond to a kindly woman friend was to fall in love with her, it followed that if she was unmarried, he was likely to propose to her. By the chances

75

of Dr Nisbet's death and President Herbert's position in Nevis, Fanny just happened to be the one. Many years later, in a love-letter to another woman, Nelson wrote that he had a 'fond heart – a *heart susceptible and true.*' He underlined the last phrase, and it was the single most accurate thing he ever wrote about himself.

Susceptible as ever, he had wasted little time in proposing to Fanny; but as the months away on duty lengthened, the spontaneous delight of that first enthusiastic response from Antigua vanished. Certainly, he wrote many expressions of esteem and affection; certainly, he was an inexperienced lover, and a busy man, and on both counts may have found it difficult to maintain, at a distance, the original authentic note of joyous confusion. Later, indeed, it did come back: 'You will not be surprised at the glorious jumble of this letter.' However, that was eleven years after his wedding, when he was writing to Lord St Vincent while sitting opposite Emma Hamilton. 'Were your Lordship in my place, I much doubt if you could write so well; our hearts and our hands must be all in a flutter.' When courting Fanny in the Caribbean, frequently hundreds of miles from her, his 'fond, susceptible heart' was indeed true; but only, it appears, in the sense of being unwaveringly loyal, which was a part of his nature anyway.

Even making every allowance, most of Nelson's letters on the way to the altar are pedestrian. 'The foundation of all conjugal happiness, real love, and esteem is, I trust, what you believe I possess in the strongest degree towards you', says one. 'I declare solemnly, that did I not conceive I had the full possession of your heart, no consideration should make me accept your hand.' (One wonders, had she proposed to him? Or was it a reference to the rumour that Admiral Hughes had offered another captain £5,000 to marry Rosy?) 'Separated from you, what pleasure can I feel?', another letter asks rhetorically. 'None, be assured: all my happiness is centred with thee; and where thou art not, there I am not happy. Every day, hour, and act convince me of it ... I daily thank God, who ordained that I should be attached to you. He has, I firmly believe, intended it as a blessing to me; and I am well convinced you will not disappoint his beneficent intentions.'

Correct, formal, stilted – ragged fragments of the Bible and Shakespeare – presumably he thought she would like this kind of letter, and presumably she did: at any rate, they did not put her off. It is hardly the stuff of romantic love, especially from a man who could be so headily romantic as he; but he specifically said, many times, that he did not love her in that way. What is more, other people – including

Prince William – said as much to him, and he agreed. The prince, now a captain, returned to the West Indies late in 1786. Spending more time with Nelson than Fanny could, 'his royal highness often tells me, he believes I am married; for he never saw a lover so easy, or speak so little of the object he has a regard for. When I tell him I certainly am not, he says, "Then he is sure I must have a great esteem for you, and that it is not what is (vulgarly), I do not much like the use of that word, called love." He is right: my love is founded on esteem, the only foundation that can make the passion last.'

There is something in that, indeed, but it is an observation one might expect more from a priest, a philosopher or a man already long and happily married. Yet whether he was showing an ominously intellectual approach to marriage, or an unusual degree of maturity for a twenty-seven-year-old, there is no evidence that he ever thought of changing his mind then – rather the contrary. A year after their first meeting, he said to Fanny: 'With my heart filled with the purest and most tender affection, do I write this; for were it not so, you know me well enough to be certain that even at this moment I would tell you of it.' And he would have done; he could never hide his feelings – 'I cannot carry two faces.' He knew himself as well as anyone can, and had found, in his own words, 'an amiable woman'. She and Josiah were what he wanted and needed, as he was for them, and he confidently expected a lifetime of contentment, slowly and surely building the bricks of esteem and affection into a happy household, unglamorous but solid, just as his parents' marriage had been. In this light, two unintended prophecies he made at the time are all the more painful. The first was in a letter to his brother William: 'The dear object you must like. Her sense, polite manners, and to you I may say, beauty, you will much admire; and although at present we may not be a rich couple, yet I have not the least doubt but that we shall be a happy pair – the fault must be mine if we are not.' And the second was to Fanny herself: 'How uncertain are human expectations, and how vain the idea of fixing periods for happiness!'

The months away from her were sometimes very busy, sometimes empty and dull. The duty he regarded as foremost was the continued enforcement of the Navigation Act. Once Admiral Hughes had realized Nelson's attitude was right – that is, once judgment had arrived from Britain – he had the grace to be grateful. Inviting Nelson to dinner, they soon became friends – 'I like the man,' Nelson wrote to Fanny, 'though not all his acts.' However, he also told Locker that, privately, he was very hurt that 'after the loss of health and risk of fortune, another should be thanked for what I did, and against his orders. I either deserved to be sent out of the service, or at least to have had some little notice taken ... But', he consoled himself, 'I have done my duty, and have nothing to accuse myself of.' Not knowing his private feelings, one of his junior officers – Lieutenant James Wallis – commiserated over the injustice, and for his pains earned a retort he never forgot: '"Pity!" exclaimed Nelson, "Pity, did you say? I shall live, sir, to be envied; and to that point I shall always direct my course."'

The remark sounds a little too 'Nelsonian' to be true; yet he certainly felt his judgment of a potential French threat had been exonerated, because shortly after his departure from Nevis in March 1786, a French man-of-war came snooping around. In Wallis's words, it was 'destined on a survey of our Islands, and had on board two General Officers and some Engineers for that purpose.' Wallis detailed the episode at length, describing how courteous and suspicious the two captains were – Nelson saying it was his duty to accompany them, to do honour to the king of France, 'which he was sure every Englishman in the Islands would be proud of an opportunity of doing'; the French captain as politely refusing to be followed; and Nelson, 'determined not to be outdone in *civility*', accompanying them none the less, until they gave up the project and returned to Martinique. Nelson's own account was more laconic: 'Going about with them so much in the sun has given me violent headaches.'

He was morose and despondent most of the summer of 1786. From his point of view, its major events were the departures of Cuthbert Collingwood; of Lady Hughes, with her mission accomplished – Rosy had become Mrs John Browne, wed to a more than usually brave army major; and of Admiral Hughes. Until another admiral arrived, Nelson was now senior officer on the station, and more lonely than ever. The antipathy between him and the islanders, still very resentful over their loss of trade, was such that none invited him ashore, and he invited none on board. 'At first I bore absence tolerably,' he told Fanny, 'but now it is almost insupportable ... I am alone in the commanding officer's house, while my ship is fitting, and from sunset until bed-time, I have not a human creature to speak to: you will feel for me a little, I think. I did not use to be over-fond of sitting alone. The moment old *Boreas* is habitable in my cabin, I shall fly to it, to avoid mosquitoes and melancholies. Hundreds of the former are now devouring me through my clothes ... The heat is intolerable.'

Midsummer brought a small but disturbing incident. On 20 June an able seaman named William Clark deserted from Wilfred Collingwood's sloop *Rattler*. After two weeks he was found in Antigua, drunk and unresisting, and confined pending a court martial. He was sure to be found guilty, and in peace or war, the mandatory penalty for desertion was death. Nelson found no pleasure at all in the prospect – he would have to preside over the court – but to his relief, not enough officers were available to make it up, and for the time being at least, Clark had to remain in confinement.

At the same time, though, there came to Nelson's attention another unwelcome discovery: corruption in the dockyards and customs houses. In the Caribbean islands, which should have been so heavenly, it seemed that something nasty crawled out every time a stone was turned. Nelson first became suspicious of public fraud when, as senior officer on the station, he was asked to sign bills for goods purchased. He insisted on written proof that the moneys claimed had actually been expended. There was no proof at all. None the less, the Admiralty advised him to authorize payment, and since he expected a new commander-in-chief to arrive any day, he did not pursue the matter at first. Gradually, however, he came to realize that almost every islander who could was cheating the navy somehow or other.

Meanwhile, illness, worry and the climate were wearing him down increasingly – 'to a skeleton', he told his uncle, adding to Locker that from June to the end of September, he was 'so very ill that I have only a faint recollection of anything which I did.' He became so thin his doctors thought he was dying of tuberculosis, 'and gave me quite up'; it must have been an immense relief when October came and he was able to go to Nevis. Loving care, friendly companionship and civilized surroundings restored him as thoroughly as could be – just in time for an event which completely altered his standing with the islanders. In November, accompanied by the frigate *Solebay*, Prince William arrived on the station in command of HMS *Pegasus*. The islands' English community was thrown into an instant ferment of nervous antici-pation. Everybody with any pretension to social status desperately wished to see the prince, better still to invite him to a ball or a dinner; yet since he had only recently been made post, every fawning invitation had to be approved by Captain Nelson.

In the event, Prince William refused for himself all invitations to private houses, but, being twenty-one years old and vigorous in every way, he made the most of the delightful opportunities ashore. The consequences were not always so pleasant – when he left the station in May 1787, he was undergoing a mercury cure for what he called 'a sore I had contracted in a most extraordinary manner in my pursuit of the *Dames des Couleurs*'. 'He is indeed volatile,' said Nelson discreetly to Fanny, 'but always with great good nature.'

In letters to Nevis he described the prince's social round from island to island. As senior officer he accompanied William everywhere. In Antigua before Christmas, 'there were two balls during his stay, and some of the old ladies were mortified that HRH would not dance with them; but he says he is determined to enjoy the privilege of all other men, that of asking any lady he pleases'. Moving on, 'I fancy as many people were as happy to see His Royal Highness quit as they were to see him enter St John's, for another day or two's racquet would have knocked some of the fair sex up. Three nights' dancing was too much, and never broke up till day.' January 1787 opened in another island with Nelson hoping 'to have remained quiet all this week; but today we dine with Sir Thomas, tomorrow the prince has a party, on Wednesday he gives a dinner to the regiment, in the evening is a mulatto ball, on Thursday we dine at Colonel Crosbie's brother's, and a ball; on Friday somewhere, I forget where; on Saturday at Mr Byam's ... If we get well through this, I shall be fit for anything; but I hope most sincerely the commodore will arrive before the whole is carried into execution: in many instances it is better to serve than command, and this is one of them.'

February was just as hectic, with engagements almost every night – 'Tuesday, please God, we sail.' Whenever they were at sea together, Nelson really enjoyed the prince's company, and William remembered later how 'we fought over again the principal naval actions in the American war' as they passed the various sites of battle. When he eventually succeeded to the throne, he was nicknamed the Sailor King, and always said it was these voyages with Nelson which gave his mind 'its first decided naval turn'. Yet with him, Nelson found professional problems as well as pleasure. The word 'martinet' is borrowed from the name of a notoriously strict French drill-sergeant in the time of Louis XIV, and was the only suitable term for Prince William's way of captaincy. The single most perplexing episode concerned his first lieutenant, Isaac Schomberg. Schomberg had purposely been chosen because of his long active experience, in the hope that he could keep a discreet rein on his inexperienced royal captain. Unfortunately he could not, and after an official reprimand from Prince William which he believed undeserved, he had written to Nelson asking to be court-martialled. When *Pegasus* arrived in the Leewards, the mood on board was already tense, and soon it became clear that other officers were also going to ask for courts martial in order to air their own grievances against the prince. Writing to Locker, Nelson seemed to support William – 'He has had more plague with his officers than enough. I have been obliged to put his first lieutenant under arrest . . . Our service has been so much relaxed during the war that it will cost many a court-martial to bring it up again.' However, he did not want to establish a court, because he was sure it would only harm everyone unnecessarily, and anyway he did not have enough suitable officers. Arresting Schomberg was the only solution he could think of; but that could only be temporary.

Eventually, in May, Nelson passed the buck by ordering *Pegasus* off his station to Jamaica, where the senior officer – a commodore – would be able to arrange a court martial. Just before then, with considerable reluctance, he had had to face up to the continuing case of William Clark, the deserter, who had been in confinement for the better part of a year. Under Nelson's presidency, Clark was finally tried on 6 April 1787, found guilty, and sentenced to death as naval law demanded. The entire process was gone through until the moment of execution, when Nelson could no longer bear it, and asked Prince William to grant a royal reprieve. William did so at once. Clark could hardly believe his luck, especially when Wilfred Collingwood supported his request to be discharged from the service. Nelson granted the request, saying that pardon made Clark a new man, and that there were plenty to replace him.

Weakness, clemency or common sense – there were different views on Nelson's way of dealing with the first lieutenant and the able seaman. He personally saw his method as common sense touched with mercy, but others did not. Those who had been harmed, or merely annoyed, by him, remembered; and it is possible that his naval career might have progressed more rapidly if he had been less punctilious about corruption, and harder hearted about discipline.

Prince William's tour of duty (if it can be called that) had another odd and very intimate effect on Nelson's life. After Nelson's somewhat priggish reply to the royal teasing about being married already – 'he never saw a lover so easy, or speak so little of the object he has a regard for' – William, in good-natured contrition, made an offer no one could possibly refuse. 'I can tell you a piece of news', Nelson wrote to Fanny. 'The prince is fully determined, and has made me promise him, that he shall be at our wedding.' What was more, since Fanny's father was dead, William had decided to stand in for him, and give her to Nelson himself.

Privately, Nelson may have felt the prince did not take his marriage as seriously as he should, but the honour was very great: William said explicitly it was the one and only time he would accept an invitation to a private house. However, it was also very inconvenient. No doubt President Herbert's family were highly excited at the prospect, but whether Fanny was or not, she did not have much choice. Worse, she had no idea when the day might come, for in spite of being senior officer, in practice Nelson's movements were dictated by the prince.

The royal offer was made early in December 1786. Telling Fanny about it, Nelson felt obliged to add: 'When I shall see you, is not possible for me to guess. So much for marrying a sailor.' Two months later, after much junketing around the Caribbean, he told her: 'We are at last out of English Harbour again, and so far I am on my way to be with you.' That was written from Montserrat, which with Nevis and Antigua forms an upside-down equilateral triangle, each island only fifty miles from the other. Seventeen days later, with the partying still in full swing, came another letter: 'It is possible his royal highness may stop at Nevis on his way up from Tortola.' Tortola lies 200 miles north-west of Monserrat; Nevis was to be bypassed on the outward voyage and visited on the return.

By then it was becoming embarrassing; the exact wedding-date of the future Captain and Mrs Nelson depended all too clearly on a royal whim, whenever the prince thought he might drop in at Nevis. 'We are most likely to be at Nevis about the 18th [of March],' Nelson wrote, 'but keep this to yourself.' How he thought she could, with all the preparations that would be necessary, is another matter; but less than a week after that letter: 'How uncertain are the movements of us sailors! His royal highness is rather unwell' – surely not a surprise – 'therefore I have given up the idea of visiting Tortola for the present ... I am feeling most awkwardly.' The surprise was that they were coming to Nevis direct. Fanny had five days to prepare for their wedding.

After all the uncertainties, she could be forgiven, in later years, for muddling the date. She said it was 12 March, but in fact the ceremony took place on Sunday 11 March 1787. Like most of the islands, Nevis possessed a small church and a rector, the former with the strange name of Fig Tree Church, and the latter with the humble name of the Reverend W. Jones. The church's register still displays the entry of Nelson's wedding, among many others which seem to be those of slaves of the sugar plantation. But the wedding was not in the church. It was in President Herbert's elegant mansion, Montpelier House, which was several miles away, but more suitable for a large reception in royal company.

Fig Tree Church is still there, and still in use. Montpelier House, however, has vanished. It was probably built of wood, and probably eaten in later years by ants. Nothing is left among the wilderness of abandoned sugar canes except the extensive foundations, which now have a deserted Caribbean shack on top, and a pair of stone gateposts, one of which bears a stone slab engraved with the words:

On this site stood
Montpelier House, wherein
on the 11th day of March 1787
Horatio Nelson,
Then Captain of HMS Boreas,
was married to
Frances Herbert Nisbet.

On Nelson's side of the gracious drawing-room were his officers and one relative, the young midshipman cousin Maurice Suckling. It may have been they who gave him a lovely silver model of a 28-gun frigate; certainly it was his 'people', the sailors of Boreas, who gave him a silver watch. Of course they had known about their captain's courtship for a long time, but he must have been very touched to realize they had clubbed their small resources together to present him with such a handsome gift.

On Fanny's side were all her relatives, and many friends and acquaintances of the president. Always a generous host, he was in his element. She wore a gown of Irish lace, and as the prince escorted her in, Nelson's colleagues thought her very comely – 'a pretty and attractive woman, and a general favourite.' The prince noticed that

Nelson, like many a bridegroom, looked sick with nerves, and 'more in need of a nurse than a bride.'

But all went according to plan; to much applause, Prince William made a speech congratulating Nelson on winning 'the principal favourite of the island'; there were many bumper toasts, and much dancing; and with his instant family joyfully and tearfully around him, Nelson prepared for a short honeymoon in the island.

'Until I married her,' he wrote to Captain Locker ten days later, 'I never knew happiness: and I am morally certain she will continue to make me a happy man for the rest of my days. I shall have great pleasure in introducing you to her.'

For Fanny, of course, it was a second marriage, and though naturally she did not mention it, she may well have thought back to that first union, eight years earlier in the same island, and the subsequent ill-fated voyage to England. She had already known loss, and financial hardship, and both had left their mark. Under the pale gown and fair skin was a frightened, dependent character. For Nelson, first time (and, he fully intended, only time) around, it was a great and satisfying adventure. From fellow officers, he knew the difficulties of reconciling marriage and naval service, but he was optimistic – during their courtship, he had once written: 'We are often separated, but I trust our affections are not by any means on that account diminished.' And in another letter, with exuberance: 'As you begin to know something about sailors, have you not often heard that salt water and absence always wash away love? Now, I am such a heretic as not to believe that faith; for behold, every morning since my arrival I have had six pails of salt water at daylight poured upon my head, and instead of finding what the seamen say to be true, I perceive the contrary effect.'

The image of the newly wed Nelsons, Horatio and Fanny, is charming. It is sad they could not have remained at Nevis for years, dancing minuets in Montpelier. But Nelson had always said firmly that duty must come first, and it did: when he wrote to Locker just ten days after the wedding, he was back in *Boreas*, escorting the prince to Tortola. By then, as always happens after the ceremony, the wedding guests had started discussing the new couple, with mixed reactions. Mrs Nelson was indeed pretty, said one officer, but personally he believed 'Captain Nelson has married a complexion' with 'a remarkable absence of intellectual endowment'. Thomas Pringle, a fellow captain and a friend of Nelson's since his days of convoy in the North Atlantic, was sure the new husband would remain captivated, and lamented the prospect – 'The navy, sir, yesterday lost one of its greatest ornaments, by Nelson's marriage. It is a national loss that such an officer should marry: had it not been for that circumstance, I foresaw that Nelson would become the greatest man in the service.' And in private, Prince William made a perceptive observation: 'Poor Nelson is over head and ears in love ... He is now in for it. I wish him well and happy, and that he may not repent the step he has taken.'

8

'I am fonder of the sea than ever'

THE CONTENTMENT OF marriage, Nelson told Locker, 'far makes amends for everything.' But he still detested the West Indies, and longed to leave his command – 'the wonder to me is that any independent man will accept it; for there is nothing pleasant to be got by it.'

The moment of release came at the end of May, after Prince William left the Leewards and was safely under the command of Alan Gardner, commodore on the Jamaica station. Early in June the Nelsons were able to set off for England, but they did not travel together: he went in *Boreas*, while Fanny and her boy travelled in a safer, more comfortable merchantman. This was not the only thing to surprise some of Nelson's officers. It was notable that, after three years in the West Indies, *Boreas* had not lost any member of her complement through illness: a remarkable testimony to Nelson's regime on board. Nevertheless, when the voyage home began, he himself was ill yet again, and – unusually among sailors – the idea of being buried at sea always filled him with horror. So, just in case, he had a puncheon of rum loaded for the express purpose of preserving his corpse if he died before reaching England.

But he recovered his health at sea, as always; the voyage passed off safely; and on 2 July 1787 – three years, six weeks and a day after she had left it – *Boreas* anchored at Spithead. After such a long absence, men were eager to return to their homes, and everyone on board expected that in a few weeks more at most, the ship would be paid off. But it did not turn out that way, for in Europe, great events threatened.

Holland was becoming politically divided between the traditional rule of the Stadtholder and a republican faction, supported by royalist French money. Pitt, Britain's youthful Prime Minister, interpreted this – probably correctly – as a route for France to gain control of the Dutch East Indies, which would constitute a direct challenge to Britain's position in the Far East. He, therefore, had been trying to create an Anglo-Prussian alliance, strong enough to counteract the French influence in Dutch politics; but the Prussians were not interested. All this happened while *Boreas* was away. However, about the time she returned to Spithead, Dutch republicans arrested the Stadtholder's wife, who happened to be the sister of the King of Prussia. They let her go quite quickly, yet as Lord Carmarthen, the British Secretary of State, remarked: 'If the King, her brother, is not the dirtiest and shabbiest of Kings, he must resent it.' So he did, instantly beginning preparations for an invasion of Holland. In spite of French subversion in Holland, those two countries were bound by a treaty of mutual defence in the event of invasion. If a Continental conflict developed so close to home, Britain would not stand idly by, and Nelson told Prince William succinctly: 'The Dutch business is becoming every day more serious; and I hardly think we can keep from a war.'

By the middle of August, *Boreas* and her crew were still at Portsmouth, being kept ready to return to sea at a moment's notice. For himself, in spite of being newly wed, Nelson did not mind – indeed, rather the contrary. 'If we are to have a bustle,' he told Locker, 'I do not want to come on shore, and I begin to think that I am fonder of the sea than ever.' He was fortunate in having a grasp of the implications of Europe's convoluted politics. For his men it was a different matter. No doubt most would fight bravely if they had to, but until they had to, being kept in readiness meant to them only that they were kept from home. As weeks of uncertainty passed in full view of a prohibited home shore, desertions began, and worse: the ship's cooper, James Carse, committed murder.

Boreas had been sent to Sheerness, on the River Medway, to fill the humiliating role of store and receiving ship for men pressed into the service. Filled now with a doubly unwilling crew, those who did not wish to join and those who did not wish to remain any longer, she could only be an unhappy ship. Carse too was morose and, since a bout of sunstroke in the West Indies, had become solitary. He was discharged early, with fifty guineas' pay. Shortly afterwards, in a seedy inn near the Thames at Shadwell, east of London, without having any apparent motive, he killed a woman. He was arrested without difficulty and it seemed certain that he would hang. Nelson was called to the Old Bailey as a character witness, and displayed good knowledge of

87

the man. Just as importantly, he explained to the court the nature of sunstroke: he had had it himself, saying 'I have been out of my senses; it hurts the brain.' When asked if he thought the killing had been intentional, he replied emphatically that he did not, adding, 'I should as soon suspect myself'. He was a convincing witness – a recommendation for clemency was accepted, and the cooper was sent to prison, but did not hang.

In other ways, however, the outlook was bleak. To be a receiving ship for pressed men, lying seven miles offshore as autumn gave way to another North Sea winter – everyone hated it, even Nelson, 'as much separated from my wife as if I were in the East Indies'. He did the duty, said one of his friends, 'with strict and sullen attention.' Another oppressive development was the Admiralty's refusal, for a variety of rather unconvincing reasons, to confirm any of the acting appointments Nelson had made while senior officer in the Leewards. The dismal work, the apparent neglect and lack of any official interest in him and his men would have disenchanted anyone. At the end of October, the French agreed to remain neutral in 'the Dutch business'; Prussian troops entered Holland briefly to confirm the Stadtholder's power; Prussia, Britain and Holland formed an alliance to try and uphold Europe's unsteady balance; and for the time being at least, the threat of a war with France evaporated. Even so, it was not until 30 November that *Boreas* was finally paid off, and in blunt terms, Nelson informed his commanding officer that he was finished with the navy – 'an ungrateful service . . . it is my firm and unalterable intention never again to set my foot on board a king's ship. Immediately after my arrival in town, I shall wait on the First Lord of the Admiralty, and resign my commission.'

Someone must have asked him: To do what? To which he might have answered: Farming – politics – I do not care what. Resigning would mean no income, not even half-pay, but he had a hundred pounds a year from his uncle, and Fanny had the same from hers; they would manage, if not in any great style, and anything would be more rewarding than naval work.

When he announced his intention to resign, he certainly meant it, and if Fanny ever heard of it, she must have been delighted. But for a man of Nelson's disposition, only a little attention and apologetic soothing was needed to make him change his mind back. Lord Howe was kind, and took him to a royal levée, where the king received him graciously; the Chancellor of the Exchequer and the Prime Minister again promised their support in sorting out not only the frauds he had exposed in the West Indies, but also the lawsuits that still followed him from disgruntled American traders. With his good humour restored, at last he was able to join Fanny at her uncle's house in London, just in time for Christmas 1787. The couple decided that after the festivities, they would make holiday for a while: rest, travel, find a school for Josiah, meet the rest of the family. In due course Captain Nelson would apply for another ship, this time a ship of the line – he had already put in one such application when the war-scare was on – and with luck would get one.

He put in many applications; but the Admiralty kept him on shore for five whole years.

In Burnham, there are still folk-memories of this miserable phase of Nelson's life. 'The Captain took his work to the bank on Saturdays' is a phrase that people remember. The Captain, without any doubt, was Nelson. The bank was the local name for the long embankment which shelters the creek of Burnham Overy Staithe from the sea: it is still a deserted and solitary place. But what work, and why Saturdays? The belief is that Saturday was the day the mail-coach came, and that the work, mysterious to the local people, was the official-looking correspondence which regularly came to him and to nobody else, the letters and navy lists, the movements and appointments of his friends – everything except the one letter he longed for, the news of his own appointment to another ship. One may still walk along the bank, two miles or so to the wide sandy beach between its end and the empty sea. Alone out there, one may still imagine the Captain's hollow longing to go further – to leave the land behind him and feel the deck of a ship beneath his feet again. Yet during those five increasingly desolate years, so far as he could tell, this was the end. He was exiled from the sea, the scene of all his experience and skill and companionship; there was nothing in his future except genteel poverty and the Parsonage House. Even that, his childhood home, was gloomy and empty now, with no children of his own to give it life – only his father growing old, and poor Fanny growing sickly, dissatisfied and querulous.

They had been happy enough to begin with. After their first Christmas together as a family, the Nelsons travelled down to the West Country. Josiah, escorted by Frank Lepée (one of Nelson's sailors, retained as a manservant), was placed in a suitable boarding school – the traditional trauma for a seven-year-old middle-class boy, who had never left his mother before, and now would see her only three times a year in the holidays. Settling Fanny for a while alone in Bath, Nelson, on the invitation of Prince William, went to Plymouth to take part in the celebrations marking the prince's safe return to Britain. Rejoining Fanny, he showed her the sights of Bristol before taking her on holiday to Exmoor. They gloried in the unexpectedly benign weather, infinitely welcome to Fanny in particular: already she was missing the warmth of Nevis. To a lesser extent she also missed the gracious company of Montpelier; and holidays, being expensive, could not continue for ever. Between them, the couple hatched two bright ideas: they would go back to London, where they could stay without expense at Fanny's uncle's house, while Nelson firstly applied to the Admiralty for repayment of his large out-of-pocket West Indian expenses, and secondly made use of his friendship with Prince William. William's younger sister Augusta, the Princess Royal, had recently turned twenty-one; it seemed likely that she must soon have her own household away from the royal palace. She would need ladies-in-waiting; how appropriate it would be for Fanny, the wife of a captain in the Royal Navy, to be one.

Both applications were made, as best Nelson knew how; and both failed. Here began the disappointments, the slowly growing distress that clouded Nelson's years on the beach and marred his marriage. No doubt Prince William replied to Nelson's tentative application. The reply is unknown, but whatever it was, William could not have helped: his parents, King George III and Queen Charlotte, simply would not allow Princess Augusta to have her own household. As for the naval authorities, Nelson wrote eleven years later that 'there was a prejudice at the Admiralty evidently against me, which I can neither guess at, nor in the least account for.'

All through those five shore-bound years, Nelson sensed he was out of favour with the Admiralty, but he did not understand why. His conscience was clear. He had always done his best to follow the 'radiant orb' he had imagined would lead him when he was a boy. Nobody, not even Captain Locker, told him what might be wrong, until one day in 1790, when he went to call on Lord Hood at his house in Wimpole Street. The Admiral who had promised him his friendship years before now frankly said he could not ask the First Lord of the Admiralty on his behalf for a ship. Astonished, Nelson asked why, and

Hood replied that the king 'was impressed with an unfavourable opinion of him'.

No answer could have shocked Nelson more. Whatever critics might say of his ability, he knew his loyalty was beyond question. 'His attachment to his king,' he knew, 'would never end but with his life.'

He might have understood (but never did) that too much zeal, too strong a conscience, might be nothing but a source of annoyance to his seniors. His insistence on the letter of the law, on exposing swindles high up in the naval administration, had irritated Admiralty officials who had to put the swindles right. He might even have guessed (but again, apparently never did) that his friendship with Prince William could be dangerous, for the prince had enemies and was often on bad terms with his father.

In the summer of 1788, puzzled, a little dismayed, but still optimistic, Captain and Mrs Nelson proceeded from London towards his old pastures in Norfolk: the time really was overdue when she should meet the family. She had already written, courteously and elegantly, to the Rector. With pleasure, he anticipated the return of his naval son, but the poor man was very nervous at the thought of his new daughter-in-law – her letters convinced him she would be a lady too grand for him, one who would bring her own lady's maid and look down on the country people who formed his simple staff. Accordingly, Horatio – or Horace, as his family always called him – took Fanny first to stay with his sister Susannah Bolton, her husband and their burgeoning offspring. Brother Edmund was there too, ill, possibly dying, no longer working for Mr Bolton or earning anything. Thence to Hilborough, thirty miles south of Burnham: brother William, after his brief experiment as chaplain of *Boreas*, had married a vicar's daughter. From their house, Horace went on alone to set his father's mind at rest, and learned that his other surviving brothers were enduring their own misfortunes: Suckling had tried to set up in business and failed, while Maurice, working in the Navy Office, was deeply in debt. In spite of his own meagre resources, Horace made a quick dash to London to bail Maurice out – quick, that is, in contemporary terms. Burnham is nearly 120 miles from London, and the fastest coach in Britain (which did not run in that part of the country) went at six miles an hour.

After rescuing Maurice from debt and Fanny from William's household, only Kitty, Horace's youngest and favourite sister, remained to be visited. She too had married, and well: her husband George Matcham was not only good-looking, energetic, enthusiastic and generally fun to be with, but rich as well. Everyone liked Matcham, and (as the Rector said, without jealousy) they lived in ease and affluence. Perhaps, with her sensitivity about money, that was why Fanny – alone of all the family – unfortunately did not take to 'G. M.' at all. But that same sensitivity had a good side to it: Fanny did not put on the airs and graces her father-in-law feared, and when at last they met, he found her entirely acceptable, and made her fully welcome in his humble home.

'I am as happy in domestic life as a person can be', Horace wrote. But he was still a sailor first and foremost, and when he heard in mid-October that Cornwallis was going to take a convoy out to the East Indies, he wrote at once asking if he could serve. The reply brought only another disappointment: knowing he had been in the East Indies before, Cornwallis had thought about him and would have liked to have taken him; but, he said, 'your fireside is so totally changed since that time, that I did not venture to name you'.

It had never occurred to Nelson that marriage could become, from his colleagues' misplaced consideration, an inadvertent bar to duty. However great his affection, respect and esteem for Fanny, this must have sown a little seed of resentment. Soon, though, he and she were considering another idea: they could go and spend the winter in France, for Horace still felt he ought to try to learn the language, and they did not want to outstay their welcome at Burnham. But at that point, the Rector invited them to make the Parsonage House their home for as long as they wished: with Kitty married and Anne dead, he wanted and needed company. There were good arguments in favour: Fanny was proficient in French – she could teach Horace, if he really wanted; there was also the matter of personal finances, and the possibility as well that, in his innocence, Horace may have spoken a shade too enthusiastically about Miss Andrews, the beauty of St Omer. At any rate, they soon abandoned the idea of France; and thus began their first winter in Norfolk.

It was as well they stayed. None of the inequality of French society had altered since Horace's last visit in 1784. In 1786, Second Lieutenant Napoleon Buonaparte wrote in his notebook: 'We are members of a powerful monarchy, but today we feel only the vices of its constitution.' In 1788, winter clamped itself over northern Europe with exceptional severity: in France, where trade had been bad all year, the Seine and other rivers froze, livestock died of the cold, men were laid off from work, prices of all food and products rose steeply, and before the spring, riots began as starving people fought for bread.

In Norfolk, at least there was food and firewood. But it was a deadly, bitter season. Fanny, brought up in the Indies, suffered particularly from the cold and discomfort of the Parsonage House, with its draughty windows and stone-flagged floors, and for many days at a time she stayed in bed. Both the men of the house suffered physically too – Horace from rheumatic aches, his father from failing eyesight and strength. Sometimes it must have been scarcely endurable, but they kept going; the Rector was saved by long habit and his own humility, Fanny by a sense of wifely duty – 'She does not openly complain', her father-in-law noted. 'Her attention to me demands my esteem, and to her Good Husband she is all he can expect.'

Unfortunately this was not entirely so. The Rector spoke of what he could see, and long after Nelson had abandoned her, Fanny remained a loyal, dutiful and pathetically hopeful wife. Even for those who are involved, it is hard enough to mark when the erosion of a marriage begins; for others, especially two hundred years afterwards and without written evidence, it is impossible to be certain. Yet one may fairly guess that for Nelson – whose hopes in marriage had been so modest – its decline began in this first ghastly winter on shore. Complaint does not have to be open to be felt. Indeed, it may be merely imagined, yet none the less real in its effect. Fanny may not have complained at all, but nor did she console. She could have been an excellent second wife to the Rector himself, a beloved comfort to an elderly, considerate man in his last years, a man whose heart was in his home and with his God. But to a man like Nelson – young, vigorous, energetic, who desperately wanted children of his own blood, and whose professional duty and fulfilment lay at sea – she could be associated, in the end, only with frustration and disappointment. Like most naval wives, she dreaded, quite reasonably, the day when he might have to return to sea; yet it seems she also resented his sense of naval duty – and that was unfair.

There was also the question of children. A freezing cold parsonage is unlikely to induce much physical passion, but by Christmas 1788 Horace and Fanny had been married for a year and three-quarters, and together almost all the time for a whole year. He was just thirty years old, she still under thirty-one, and any normal couple might justifiably have expected a pregnancy by then. There is no doubt about Nelson's desire or ability to become a father; but whatever happened or did not happen between Horace and Fanny, eventually he could bring himelf to write nothing more of her, and all the years of their marriage, than that one brief and tragic observation: 'I married Frances Herbert Nisbet, widow of Dr Nisbet, of the island of Nevis; by whom I have no children.'

Nelson, too, must have become increasingly difficult to live with. The life of an impoverished country gentleman was unbelievably dull and static. Only the rich had carriages; others, Nelson among them, could scarcely expect to travel at all, and when the day came – at the end of April 1790 – that he bought a pony, it was a red-letter day. But even that was spoiled. On his return home from market, he was so thrilled by his purchase that it took some time for Fanny to get him to listen to what had happened in his absence: two burly men dressed like Bow Street Runners had more or less forced their way into the house, made her identify herself repeatedly, then handed her a document for her husband. It was a writ for twenty thousand pounds' damages, issued by American traders in the West Indies, victims of his enforcement of the Navigation Act.

Nelson's reaction was explosive: his home had been violated, his wife frightened. He wrote at once to London, swearing that if he did not have the support he had always been promised in that matter, he would instantly emigrate to France. Probably referring to this occasion, Fanny said later that at one time he talked about joining the Russian navy. This was a prominent force which other western officers had joined, so it is quite plausible that the idea crossed Nelson's mind at least; but he did not have to do anything so drastic, for in little more than a week a reassuring answer arrived from the Treasury. In itself, the episode is not very important. However, as an indication of his state of mind, it is significant – the violence of his reaction was excessive, and shows how tense and strained he had become.

With no real work and not much money to enjoy his enforced leisure in any other way, he was obliged to fall back on hobbies and sports. He built a model warship, the traditional pastime of retired naval officers, and intended to launch it in his garden stream. That never came about: his brother-in-law Mr Matcham dreamed up a plan to improve the garden by diverting the stream, began but lost interest, and left a soggy marsh instead. Nelson learned something about farming, and much about gardening – his first biographers noted that he would dig furiously, 'as it were, for the sake of being wearied.' In the spring he went bird-nesting, as he had done as a boy, and tried to interest Fanny in it. In the autumn there was rough shooting, but he was not made welcome by family parties: from habit learned in sea-fights he always carried his gun fully cocked, and fired from the hip as soon as a target was seen. It was said he 'once shot a partridge', remembered ever after by his family as being 'among the remarkable events of his life'. He studied naval charts, and read (especially Dampier's *Voyages*, which he adored); but after a while even that pleasure was curtailed, for as the years on the beach mounted, his eyesight began to weaken – not through age, like his father, but because from the inner corner of each eye a film was beginning to cover the ball. Doctors noted it in later years – 'a film growing over both eyes', said one; 'a membranous substance', said another, 'seemingly spreading fast over the pupil' – and there was nothing they could do about it. Had he lived to be old, then even without the loss of the sight of one eye at Calvi, he would have gone blind.

Horace and Fanny endured one final winter in the Parsonage House, the winter of 1788–9, cold and childless as ever. A year later, wishing to afford them more privacy and to be closer to one of his churches, the Rector moved to a cottage in Burnham Ulph. But as they prepared to face the bleak months even more alone than before, there came an improvement in their surroundings: they were invited to stay with Horace's distant cousins Lord and Lady Walpole – by all accounts a boring couple, but with well stocked larders and cellars. It became an annual event, despite the tedious company, because any company was better than none, and (more importantly) it gave Horace a good address from which to beg the Admiralty for command of another ship.

By then it had become starkly plain to him, if not to Fanny and his father, that something had gone exceedingly wrong with his career. To be overlooked for a couple of years was unpleasant, but any number of reasons could be found which did not suggest an actual prejudice against him. However, when 'nearly the whole Service had been called forth' and he was still ignored, there could no longer be any doubt.

What drove it home, in the summer of 1790, was the sudden and serious possibility of war with Spain. The argument arose from the question of trading rights in north-west North America, a territory Spain had long claimed exclusively as its own. In the attractive natural harbour of Nootka Sound, on the western coast of Vancouver Island, some British merchants, and their ships, had been arrested. William Pitt did not accept the Spanish point of view; both countries made ready for war; and on 1 August, with the wind fair in the west-north-west, Lord Howe led a fleet of forty-six vessels, including thirty-one ships of the line, out of Torbay. Nelson had done all he could to be in command of any one of them ('even a cockle-boat', he pleaded), and told Prince William: 'My not being appointed to a Ship is so very mortifying, I cannot find words to express what I feel'.

Among those who had been 'called forth' were Midshipman Thomas Masterman Hardy, just twenty-one years old, under Captain Anthony Hunt in the 12-gun sloop *Tisiphone*, and Nelson's old friend Collingwood. He too had been on the beach since 1786, living in Northumberland and getting to know his family – 'to whom I had hitherto been, as it were, a stranger', he said wryly. When the 'armament was prepared against Spain', he was given command of the frigate *Mermaid*, and sent to the West Indies. Within a short time, however, the political problems were resolved, very much in Britain's favour; the ships were recalled and paid off; 'and', Collingwood wrote later, 'as I saw no prospect of my having any employment at sea, I went into the North, and was married.'

Pitt's success on this occasion had two causes: firstly, he had invoked the Triple Alliance of Britain, Holland and Prussia against Spain, and won his allies' support. Secondly, France, Spain's main ally, had declined to participate: for the Revolution had begun. Even in the depths of Norfolk people had read, during the previous summer, that the Bastille, Paris's notorious prison, had been stormed by a mob, and that though the king was still alive, a new popular government had curtailed the traditional privileges of nobility and clergy.

During the whole of 1791, his fourth full year on the beach, there is no direct evidence at all for Nelson's life, not a single letter of his own: by then he must have been sunk in the depths of frustration, making the best he could of the parsonage garden and the little round of social visits. But in France, for the first time, the nation was provided with a written constitution. Its introduction was powerfully resonant: 'Men are born and remain free and equal in rights. Social distinctions can be based only upon public utility . . .' Much later, the Poet Laureate Robert Southey (also one of Nelson's early biographers) tried to describe to a younger generation the feelings of that time. 'A visionary world seemed to open upon those who were just entering it', he remembered. 'Old things seemed to be passing away, and nothing was dreamt of but the regeneration of the human race.'

In Britain, the rapture of possibility affected two classes of people:

intellectuals and labourers. Nelson was neither, and he heartily disliked the 'great number of Clubs about the County and the City [of Norwich] who style themselves Resolution-men, alias Revolution-men.' Yet in a fundamental way he saw the justice of the Revolution's cause: four years on shore had provided ample opportunity to assess the grinding poverty of the working class, and to Prince William he wrote a detailed report on the subject. His own annual income (which he did not complain about) was £230 – a hundred pounds from his uncle, and his naval half-pay, minus some standard deductions. Fanny also had a hundred a year from her uncle; but with luck and health and energy, a typical Norfolk farm labourer could only earn twenty-three pounds and one shilling a year. With a deduction for clothing, and assuming the man had a wife and three children, this left 'not quite two pence a day for each person; and for drink, nothing but water; for beer our poor labourers never taste, unless they are tempted, which is too often the case, to go to the ale-house.'

The prince agreed with Nelson's aversion to revolutionaries, but ignored the report's implicit warning. Throughout 1792, 'a spirit of tumult and disorder' grew in Britain. Writing to Nelson from Northumberland, Collingwood observed 'the times are turbulent; and the enthusiasm for liberty is raging even to madness. The success of the French people in establishing their republic has set the same principle, which lurked in every state of Europe, afloat'. But the republic, established in September with the imprisonment of King Louis, floated on blood. There had been savage massacres in Paris, with many hundreds of innocents slaughtered indiscriminately by the mob; and with the New Year, the beginning of Nelson's sixth year on the beach, an event took place in Paris which changed the history of Europe – and the course of Nelson's life.

9

'Your most affectionate husband'

EARLY IN 1793, a report from Paris was published in the *Norwich Mercury*. Dated 22 January, it gave tragic but expected news: 'The unfortunate LOUIS is no more! He was beheaded yesterday morning in the Place de Louis Quinze. He died with the most heroic fortitude.' The poet William Cowper wrote to a friend, 'I will tell you what the French have done. They have made me weep for a king of France, which I never thought to do, and they have made me sick of the very name of liberty, which I never thought to be.'

Already, French troops had overrun Belgium (which belonged to Austria), captured Brussels and defeated the Austrians in battle at Jemappe. Now, as the revolution in France gathered energy from its excesses, a veteran French sailor, Comte Armand de Kersaint, was made Vice Admiral, and on the first day of the year told his country's new leaders that Britain too should be attacked – first through its maritime commerce, then through invasion, until terms of peace could be dictated 'in the ruins of the Tower of London.' In fact, some months later, Kersaint himself perished on the guillotine; but in Britain his challenge was taken seriously, and immediately it was reported, Nelson's hopes revived. He was thirty-four years old, mature, experienced, with fourteen years' seniority on the post list, and much of the last five years spent in pondering naval tactics; surely, at last, a new command must be given him. He took himself to London, and from the cold capital a letter dated 7 January came, full of joy, to Burnham Thorpe:

'Post nubila Phoebus! – your son will explain the motto – After clouds comes sunshine. The Admiralty so smile upon me that really I am as much surprised as when they frowned. Lord Chatham [First Lord of the Admiralty] yesterday made many apologies for not having

98

given me a ship before this time, and said that if I chose to take a sixty-four to begin with, I should be appointed to one as soon as she was ready; and whenever it was in his power, I should be removed into a seventy-four. Everything indicates war.'

Deep in the frozen wastes of Norfolk, Fanny Nelson was already dressed in black, mourning the death of her uncle, once president of Nevis. There is no record of how she received her husband's delighted message, but one may fairly guess it was with convulsing grief. As the sixth anniversary of her second wedding approached, her world had been transformed utterly: from the warmth of Nevis to the winters of Norfolk, from being hostess of the salons of Montpelier to mistress of the frosty parlour of the Parsonage House; and now both husband and son were going to leave her, for Josiah was twelve, and would be one of Nelson's 'servants'. 'One of our ships, looking into Brest, has been fired into; the shot is now at the Admiralty', she read. 'You will send my father this news, which I am sure will please him.' Nelson had been – still was – as good a husband to her as he could be, and despite all the privations of their limited lives, there must have been times in Norfolk when both were happy. In one of his letters from the days of their courtship, there is a hint that Fanny did not accept his view that duty was paramount: 'Had I taken your advice and not seized any Americans,' he had written then, 'I should now have been with you; but I should have neglected my duty ... the great business of a Sea-officer. All private considerations must give way to it, however painful.' Virtually all their married life, she had been able to ignore the full consequences of marriage to a sailor: true, they had been poor, but they had been together and on shore. Always a timid soul, Fanny could not avoid fear of the future, but on reading Nelson's letter she made one firm decision: she would not stay alone with the servants in the Parsonage House, nor would she live with her father-in-law the Rector. She would leave Burnham Thorpe.

HMS *Agamemnon* was, like her new captain, in the prime of life. She was twelve years old, constructed chiefly of New Forest oak, launched at Buckler's Hard on the River Beaulieu in Hampshire; and she was copper-bottomed. The technique was still quite new. Copper sheathing was first used in 1761, after the discovery that it reduced the growths of weed and shellfish which slowed ships down. But galvanic action between the sheathing and the iron bolts which secured it meant that from time to time, large sheets of copper could drop unnoticed from a hull; and it was not until 1783 that copper bolts began to be used throughout the Royal Navy. Gradually, other navies followed the lead; but in 1793 *Agamemnon* was, for her size, one of the fastest and strongest warships afloat anywhere.

Technically, her 64 guns made her a fourth-rate, one below the minimum rate for a ship of the line. But if necessary, she could stand in the line, and the promise of a 74, a third-rate warship specifically designed to stand in line of battle, overcame Nelson's first slight disappointment. He referred to *Agamemnon* as a ship of the line anyway, and soon he had decided that her size did not matter: far more importantly, she sailed well, and her strength and speed would offer opportunities a larger vessel might miss. She could outsail anything she could not outgun; she could outgun anything she could not outsail. But before anything else, she had to be manned and provisioned; and even before that, Fanny had to be settled.

To accomplish both, Nelson hurried back to Norfolk. As far as possible, he particularly wanted to choose his own men and to be chosen by them. The Admiralty agreed that no recruiting for *Agamemnon* would be done in London until his name could be officially published as captain: there would be a chance then of re-engaging men from his previous crews. He was also determined to recruit as many East Anglians as he could – men like himself who had grown up close to the sea, with familiar accents to their speech; men who might well know his name, and who would wish to serve under a captain from their own county. Most volunteers were better raw material for the service than pressed men, and, he said, an East Anglian volunteer was worth two from anywhere else. A lieutenant and four midshipmen were sent out to visit every sea port in the region, meeting with fair success, while Nelson himself coped with the inevitable stream of callers asking him to take their 'younkers' to sea. Apart from his own stepson Josiah (who, in the phrase of the time, he always called his son-in-law), the three boys he accepted were all, like himself, sons of Norfolk clergymen. One of them was, moreover, his sister's nephew by marriage; and since Nelson also took the chance of recruiting one of his Suckling cousins, *Agamemnon*'s gunroom and wardroom would have a distinct family atmosphere.

Meanwhile someone, perhaps Fanny herself, chose the market town of Swaffham as a suitable base during the indefinite absence of her husband and son. She had never come fully to terms with the flatness of Norfolk, the unending sky, the eternal hush; Swaffham, though less than twenty miles from Burnham Thorpe, would offer some distractions at least. The Rector knew he would miss her, and did not want her to go – 'there are good reasons against it; but as they please' – and in the midst of the bustle of naval business, Nelson tried to console her. 'Never fear,' he wrote to her later, 'I shall come laughing back one day.'

But he did not. On 4 February 1793, when he left the Parsonage House, the house of his birth, it was for the last time.

His commission for *Agamemnon* had been signed on 11 January. On 1 February, France had declared war on Britain and Holland. On 7 February, at Chatham, Nelson took formal command of his new ship and set about the task of making her ready for war – a considerable labour, for she was laid up in reserve, without even her masts on board. After five weeks they were ready enough to sail downriver to Sheerness, with orders to proceed to Spithead with all possible despatch. In a letter to Fanny, Nelson explained that 'we are wanted, Lord Hood writes me word, for immediate service; and hints we are to go a cruise, and then to join his fleet at Gibraltar: therefore I am anxious to get to Spithead. I never was in better health; and I hope you intend a new lease of your life.'

His eagerness to get going was not merely because he had been so long ashore: it was also because everyone predicted a short war, with limited chances of action, distinction and prize money. Actually, with one brief intermission, it lasted twenty-two years; but in the hasty spring of 1793, Nelson worried over every day spent fitting out – 'something might be done, if we were at sea, and I fear orders may come to stop us.' By mid-April they were 'getting into high order', and though they were still nearly a hundred men short of complement, he considered 'we shall be far from ill-manned, even if the rest are not so good as they ought to be.' He was satisfied with every officer in the ship, especially the surgeon – 'a very good sort', and potentially one of the most important members of the company. When at last they weighed anchor, Nelson was pleasantly surprised to find how fast *Agamemnon* sailed, but not at all surprised to find Josiah was seasick. Nelson would certainly have been sympathetic, if brusque, because he was probably likewise affected: later he admitted that despite sailing many thousands of miles in his lifetime, he was usually ill in the first few days of a voyage, and invariably so in rough weather.

After their arrival at Spithead on 28 April, brisk winds strengthened into a gale, preventing any further movement for several days, but allowing two latecomers to join the ship: Nelson's elder brother Maurice, and the last of Nelson's young 'servants' from Norfolk – William Hoste, a boy the same age as Josiah. Maurice, who had only come on board for a farewell visit, got rather more than he bargained for. The moment the weather moderated, Nelson put to sea; the moment he had done so, 'it blew so hard I could not land him'. Quite unexpectedly, Maurice found himself off the coast of France, taking part in a chase after two French frigates and two brigs, making a distant inspection of the fortifications of Cherbourg, and calling at Alderney before the final (and no doubt welcome) return to England. 'We had some blowing weather,' Nelson told Fanny, 'but nothing for *Agamemnon* to mind.'

He did not say what Maurice thought of the adventure. Young Hoste, writing to his parents, was frank – 'I was very sick both Thursday and Friday'. Nevertheless, he liked his situation 'very much' and thought it 'a very pleasant cruise'. Two items of special pride were that he had climbed to the foretop without going through the lubber's hole (an entrance to the final platform for the timid – experienced sailors swung out around the platform's edge); and that he had been ordered to sling his hammock in the captain's cabin. Ever after this early sign of favour, Hoste was absolutely devoted to his captain: eighteen years later, when he too was a captain leading ships into battle – at Lissa in 1811 – he made one simple signal which he knew would inspire his men more than anything else: *Remember Nelson*.

When Maurice tottered off *Agamemnon* at Spithead, Nelson 'rather expected' to find Fanny there. However, his brother-in-law had dissuaded her from the journey, saying 'There is no certainty in winds and waves', and Nelson did not blame her for the disappointment – 'Mr Matcham told you right'. Yet as time went by, husband and wife must have regretted the well meant advice: on 11 May 1793, *Agamemnon* sailed again, and it was not until September 1797 that the Nelsons were reunited.

But still, from ever more distant parts of the world, his letters continued to come – irregular but enlivening, sometimes two or three close together, perhaps out of order; sometimes a single long one composed over several days. Even before his departure from the Medway, he had said 'I know you wish to hear frequently from me'; and over the next four years – with Nelson writing occasionally from ports, but mostly at sea – their long correspondence returned Horatio and Fanny in an odd way to the days of their courtship.

To be sure, some of the first of his letters back contained testy complaints about items from home which had not been sent, or which had been badly packed and suffered in transit – the tone not of a lover but of a harassed, dissatisfied husband – yet even those also included the confidences he could only write to her. They were not letters of passionate romance; 'God bless you, and believe me your most affectionate husband' was a characteristic ending. However, when he said, 'How I long to have a letter from you: next to being with you, it is the greatest pleasure I can receive', there is no reason to disbelieve him. He would not have wanted Fanny on board; nor would he have wanted to be ashore until he felt his work was done. But he valued her; she was, he said, 'such a good woman ... and as I cannot here show my affection to you, I do it doubly to Josiah, who deserves it as well on his own account as on yours; for he is a real good boy'.

'What we have been sent out for, is best known to the Great Folks in London', he wrote wearily. 'To us it appears only to hum the Nation and make fools of us, for where we have been stationed no Enemy was likely to be met with.' In mid-May 1793, beating backwards and forwards between Scilly and the Channel Islands, he observed, 'this is not the first squadron sent out to do nothing, and worse than nothing.' There was not one enemy ship around, and every neutral they met told them how Nantes, Bordeaux and L'Orient were filling up with English prizes taken by French privateers and frigates. *Agamemnon* was one of a large force – eleven ships of the line and all their attendant vessels – under Lord Hood, 'but what his instructions or orders are, I cannot guess. I have not seen him since he joined us a fortnight tomorrow, nor even had a boat hoisted out. Our weather, although not bad, has been very unpleasant – foggy with drizzling rain.'

It was a salutary reminder of how morale could drop if the job in hand was unexplained and seemed pointless. But eventually all became clear. They were waiting to receive an inward-bound convoy of East Indiamen, which finally arrived safe and sound on 7 June; and to his enormous relief Nelson was allowed to turn *Agamemnon* south, through 'the finest passage and weather possible', to Cadiz.

The rivalry of Britain and France is a constant theme in eighteenth-century diplomatic history. When William Pitt the Younger was born, his father was directing the Seven Years' War against France. In the summer of 1793 – the latest round of an unfinished contest – the younger Pitt borrowed his father's strategy. Britain was strong at sea, weak on land; for France, it was the other way around. Britain, therefore, would subsidize Continental allies bearing the brunt of fighting on land, and at the same time would blockade the ports of France, attack its colonies in the West Indies, and keep the seas clear of French merchantmen. It had worked before.

Flying his flag in HMS *Victory*, Admiral Lord Hood had orders from the Admiralty to secure for 'his Majesty's subjects, and those of his allies, the free and uninterrupted navigation of the Mediterranean'. He accepted the orders with confidence – 'ready and happy', he wrote, 'to maintain inviolate the rights of sovereign and independent nations against the dangers with which they are threatened on the part of France.' Three weeks before declaring war against Britain, France had declared against Spain; now it seemed fortunate that Spain, covering the entrance to the Mediterranean, was allied to Britain. But France had changed since the Seven Years' War; Spain had not. The Revolution had destroyed many of the best French officers, naval or military: as emblems and usually supporters of the old royal regime, they fled abroad or died on the guillotine. Yet at the same time new leaders were able to emerge, by merit and skill rather than social connection, with the energy of missionaries eager to force change further, while the Spanish wanted only to keep things as they were – preferably with someone else doing the work. Nelson found them contemptible.

One month after leaving the Channel, he decided he knew everything he needed to know about the Spanish, and told Fanny, 'The Dons may make fine ships – they cannot, however, make men.' With her companions, *Agamemnon* had been made welcome in Cadiz. The British ships were able to stock up with all the provisions they needed, except wine, which they intended to take on at Gibraltar. While the loading went on, Nelson and other officers were entertained to dinner by an admiral on board the 112-gun *Concepcion*, and were allowed to visit every part of the dockyards and arsenals. There were four Spanish first-rates in harbour – 'very fine ships,' Nelson remarked, 'but shockingly manned. If those twenty-one sail of the line which we are to join in the Mediterranean are not better manned, they cannot be of much use. I am certain that if our six barges' crews, who are picked men, had got on board one of their first-rates, they would have taken her.'

Apparently Nelson did not know that in the years of peace, while British naval expenditure was low, there had been a kind of nautical brain-drain from Britain to other countries. In all the royal Spanish dockyards except Havana, most of the shipwrights and designers were British. If he had known that, his opinion of 'the Dons' would have been even lower.

It certainly appeared they could not work their ships, however fine. Sailing from Gibraltar in three columns, led by *Victory*, *Colossus* and *Agamemnon*, Hood's fleet included nineteen ships of the line and various frigates, all convoying fifty merchantmen. Ten days and 450 miles later, at dusk on 7 July, a strange fleet was sighted. At dawn next day twenty-four unidentified sail of the line were counted. Taking no chances, Hood's ships rapidly prepared for battle, and then watched in amusement as the other fleet tried to do the same. Their incompetence, apart from anything else, identified them as Spanish: 'The Dons did not, after several hours' trial, form anything which could be called a line of battle ahead.' An apologetic message came over saying that there were many sick in the fleet, for they had been sixty days at sea – an explanation which Nelson said 'to us appeared ridiculous'. The British ships had been longer at sea, and reckoned that was exactly why they were all becoming more and more healthy.

For Nelson the episode 'stamped in my mind the extent of their nautical abilities', and did nothing to improve another strong impression of the Spanish character which he had received on shore in Cadiz. There, he and his colleagues had been invited to see a bull fight; and the letter he wrote to Fanny afterwards shows that British people in Spain have changed little in two hundred years. They accepted because they were curious, and knew it was an honour – 'the better sort of people never miss one, if within reach of them; and the lowest will sell his jacket, or go without his victuals, rather than be absent.' There were 12,000 people in the audience, with ten bulls selected for the fight. By all except the small British contingent, it was rated 'a fine feast, for five horses were killed, and two men very much hurt: had they been killed, it would have been quite complete.' The whole thing seemed very unfair, especially for the bulls and horses – 'it would not have displeased me to have had some of the Dons tossed by the enraged animal. How women can even sit out, much more applaud, such sights, is astonishing. It even turned us sick, and we could hardly go through with it: the dead mangled horses with their entrails torn out, and the bulls covered with blood, were too much.'

If any of the British officers showed their feelings, their hosts would probably have been baffled. Leaving aside the horrible sights of naval death, when a man could be blown to pieces by a chance shot, naval life was hard, and often brutal; in the early stages of the voyage to Cadiz, even Nelson – never a captain of harsh reputation – had authorized five floggings for theft. One of the offenders was rated as a boy, meaning he was under fifteen years old, but he was given a dozen lashes none the less; another was given three dozen, which could lift the flesh off the spine. The Spaniards would have found it difficult to grasp how men who could face such sights with relative equanimity were sickened by a bull fight. Yet the hardness of naval life was inevitable, the occasional brutality usually necessary, and in battle each man took his chance with the rest: in its way it was all essentially fair, which the bull fight quite obviously was not. There certainly were unfair, sadistic captains in the Royal Navy, but they were the weak ones, and sadism was not elevated into a national sport. 'We have seen one bull-feast,' Nelson wrote to Fanny, 'and agree that nothing shall tempt us to see another.' And in another letter to her, after seeing the Spanish fleet at sea, he dismissed the inexpert allies: they were, 'I believe, glad we are arrived; and they mean to leave us the honour of keeping the French in order. I really expect never to see them again.'

Hood's fleet arrived off Toulon, one of the main ports of the French south coast, in mid-July; and there the majority of them stayed for a month, cruising to and fro in blockade. In Norfolk, Nelson's family hoped that he and Josiah might be back by Christmas, with *Agamemnon* and her crew 'either honourably discharged', the Rector wrote, 'or laid up for the winter in safety.' Nelson was optimistic: 'I hardly think the war can last: for what are we at war about?' Apart from its declaration of war, France had given comparatively little direct offence to Britain, and seemed to offer a diminishing threat, for every report from the interior suggested the country was on the brink of a civil conflict. Marseilles was in open struggle with the revolutionary Convention in Paris; 'if Toulon joins them, they propose offering themselves to our protection ... A peace with England is what they wish for; and Provence would, it is said, willingly put itself, as a separate republic, under the protection of England.'

While his servants studied – Josiah grappling with fractions and beginning on navigation as William Hoste applied himself to chronology – speedy *Agamemnon* was kept busy, scouting, reporting, bearing messages, and Nelson thought nostalgically of harvest-time at home. One of the warships in Toulon, *Commerce de Marseille*, flagship of Rear Admiral Trogoff, carried 136 guns ('the *Victory* looks nothing to her') and was reputed to have such thick sides that no shot could go through them. Overall, the French force was equal to the British; yet it would not come out. 'Our Jacks would be very happy to see it ... I dare say we should give a good account of them.' Life on board became routine and orderly, even dull. But on shore, they heard, 'the guillotine is employed every day'; and from the master of a ship escaping from Toulon came a vivid sketch of the reign of terror: 'There are now only two descriptions of people in France – the one, drunk and mad; the other, with horror painted on their faces, are absolutely starving.'

Hood and Nelson had become 'tolerably good friends' again, to the extent that the admiral offered Nelson the long-promised command of a 74-gun ship of the line. To Hood's surprise, Nelson refused. Presumably thinking of the long years of neglect on shore, and wishing to be quite certain he could keep a 74, he said he would prefer it to come direct from the Admiralty. When he also pointed out that he did not want to lose his chosen officers, 'Lord Hood approved of my reasons' – but one can imagine the admiral shrugging his shoulders and saying Nelson could have it his own way.

At the same time, Lord Hood exasperated his junior by refusing to take direct action against Toulon. Yet to Nelson's astonishment and honest delight, the approach worked. Towards the end of August, as Republican forces stormed Marseilles, the people of Toulon gave themselves, their city and the fleet in its harbour into British protection. 'What an event this has been for Lord Hood! Such a one as history cannot produce its equal; that the strongest place in Europe, and twenty-two sail of the line, etc., should be given up without firing a shot – it is not to be credited.' The Spaniards chose that moment to arrive. One official British judgment said they had 'done most fairly in joining.' Nelson was less charitable: 'The perseverance of our fleet has been great,' he observed, 'and to that only can be attributed our unexampled success.' His one regret was that because *Agamemnon* was so fast a sailer, he could not stay for the city's surrender. As soon as it became known there would be a treaty with Toulon, he was sent off with letters to the courts of Turin and Naples, asking for 10,000 troops to secure British possession of the port. 'I should have liked to have stayed one day longer with the fleet, when they entered the harbour', he told Fanny, 'but service could not be neglected for any private gratification.' By then she can hardly have needed reminding. Perhaps it was some consolation, though, to know that once again her husband was going to encounter royalty. Another officer would carry the letter to Turin, but the one to the King of Naples would be delivered personally by Captain Nelson.

It was likely that his task would be helped by the existing British influence in Naples. The Neapolitan prime minister was an Englishman; the British ambassador, Sir William Hamilton, was very friendly with the king; Lady Hamilton was close to the queen. Thus, during the night of 10–11 September 1793, as *Agamemnon* lay becalmed 'in sight of Mount Vesuvius, which shows a fine light to us', Nelson's worries were few. From his cabin windows the panorama of the Bay of Naples was splendid ('Nothing could be finer'), and he finished a letter home: 'My dear Fanny ... I have only to hope I shall succeed with the king'.

10

'A naval expedition'

'I HAVE PROMISED my people, as soon as we have taken Corsica, that I would ask for a month's rest for them.' In his cabin in *Agamemnon*, lying near Calvi on the northern coast of Corsica, Nelson was writing his first letter of the New Year to his wife. The date was 6 January 1794, and 'except to get provisions,' he observed, 'I have not been one hour at anchor for pleasure, since April 23rd; but I can assure you I never was in better health, as is Josiah.' The letter ended with a touch of homesickness – 'We will talk these matters over again in a winter's evening.'

In spite of his many letters, there would be much to tell; eleven months had passed since he last saw his wife, and one full year since his joyful letter informing her of his new command. 'Post nubila Phoebus!', he had written then – 'After clouds comes sunshine.' Now he looked out on 'nothing but hard gales of wind, and the heaviest rains I almost ever met with.' Even the Mediterranean, in its northern half at least, is harsh and inhospitable in the winter months; but the physical discomforts of his gale-tossed ship were the least of his worries. In the four months since Lord Hood's bloodless conquest of Toulon, much had happened, and much more seemed assured for the coming months.

Brief though it was, the diplomatic journey to Naples had been a notable success. The proper name of this unusual realm was the Kingdom of the Two Sicilies. Made up of the island of Sicily and the southern half of Italy, it was ruled haphazardly by Ferdinand IV, a Spanish Bourbon devoted to hunting, and more effectively by his queen Maria Carolina, daughter of the Empress Maria Theresa of Austria and sister of Marie Antoinette, whose execution in Paris was imminent. Both king and queen were wonderfully ugly.

Nelson did not meet the queen on that occasion: she was confined to bed, about to give birth. But through the good offices of the sixty-two-year-old British ambassador, and of Sir John Acton, the prime minister, he had immediate access to the king. With pleasure, he told Fanny that he had dined at the king's right hand, and that Ferdinand had promised to write personally in his praise to Lord Hood. The greatest satisfaction, however, was that six thousand Italian troops were to be sent at once to support Hood in Toulon.

For Nelson's young servants, Naples provided fun, and some embarrassment. Vesuvius was on show 'in all its glory,' William Hoste told his father, 'for now its irruptions are most splendid, the lava spreading from the top at a great distance and rolling down the mountain in great streaks of fire.' He and Josiah met Lady Hamilton ('wonderfully kind and good'), and were given tickets by Nelson to see the king's museum and the ruins of Herculaneum, near Pompeii, only to find that since they spoke no Italian and 'our conductors would not speak English or French', they did not know what they were looking at – 'a mortifying circumstance'.

For his own part, Nelson faced only one slight problem in Naples: he felt obliged to return the king's hospitality, not an easy thing to do in a man-of-war which had been five months at sea. Hamilton came to the rescue. Everything necessary for a royal entertainment was ferried out to *Agamemnon* from the embassy. At ten o'clock on Sunday morning, 15 September, the Hamiltons arrived for breakfast on board. The king was scheduled to follow three hours later for lunch, when he would be entertained with a cannonade and a demonstration of broad-sword fighting; but before this could happen, an urgent message came from Sir John Acton. A French man-of-war and three vessels in convoy were reported 250 miles away. There were seven Neapolitan warships and one 40-gun Spaniard in Naples Bay ready for sea, but none showed the least inclination to move, so Nelson 'had nothing left but to get to sea, which I did in two hours'. The Hamiltons were taken ashore, everything belonging to the embassy was hastily returned – with the exception of a butter dish, overlooked in the hurry – and in a manner which must have impressed all observers, Nelson and *Agamemnon* quit the bay.

Despite the effort, the Frenchman was not found. On the other hand, Sir William Hamilton's butter dish was, and twelve days later, at anchor in the neutral waters of Leghorn (present-day Livorno), Nelson wrote with thanks and apologies to Hamilton. Hamilton's reply was warm: he and his wife would always remember Nelson's visit with pleasure, hoped he would return, and promised him welcome at any time. This was more than a social platitude – the two men had taken to each other at once. Hamilton found the younger man's vigour and energy appealing; Nelson saw a man similar to his father, scholarly, kind and wise; and they continued to correspond until they met again, five years later. The first encounter had lasted only four days; after the second, the whole of the rest of their lives would become intertwined, with both men loving one woman, and all three, whenever possible, living together as one household.

In the autumn of 1793, however, Emma Hamilton and her already colourful past – blacksmith's daughter, artist's model, unmarried mother, cast-off mistress – made only a limited impression on Nelson. To Fanny, he mentioned her merely in passing as 'a young woman of amiable manners, who does honour to the station to which she is raised' – and he added that she had looked after Josiah very well. He did not think of her then as a possible lover; apart from anything else, he may have acquired one already, and certainly had done so long before he saw Emma for the second time. In Leghorn again in 1794, his colleague Captain Thomas Fremantle noted in his diary, 'Dined at Nelson's and his Dolly'. Her name was Adelaide Coregglia. A single note survives from Nelson to her, written (surprisingly) in French, and (less surprisingly) full of mistakes – 'Je suis partant en cette moment pour la Mere'. He came back to her: once more in Leghorn in August 1795, Fremantle 'dined with Nelson. Dolly aboard who has a sort of abscess in her side. He makes himself ridiculous with that woman' – which rings true, remembering his infatuations for Mary Simpson and Miss Andrews. Fremantle recorded two more evenings with 'Nelson and his Dolly', the last on 27 September 1795, adding grumpily, 'Very bad dinner indeed.' Even then the affair may have continued, for another year later, writing from Leghorn to Sir Gilbert Elliot in Corsica in August 1796, Nelson let slip an oblique reference – 'One *old* lady tells me all she hears, which is what we wish.'

There can be little doubt that 'Dolly' was Nelson's lover in that particular port, perhaps passing on information – even if it was only gossip, it could prove to be important. But at the same time, there can be no doubt it was nothing more than a diversion with some practical benefits. The response to the naval toast 'To wives and sweethearts' is always 'And may they never meet.' Nelson, like many sailors, left his marriage vows at Gibraltar, without loving his wife the less – after fifteen months apart, he could still write to her: 'All my joy is placed in you, I have none separated from you; you are present to my imagination, be I where I will.'

Adelaide, or 'Dolly', may not have been present in Leghorn in 1793, but there was another small diversion – a 40-gun French frigate in a state of mutiny. Being in neutral waters, Nelson could only place *Agamemnon* close at hand, and hope the other vessel would make a move. 'Last night', he told Fanny, 'the crew of my neighbour deposed their captain, made the lieutenant of marines captain of the ship, the sergeant of marines lieutenant of marines, and their former captain sergeant of marines. What a state! They are mad enough for any undertaking.'

Not mad enough, though, to shift out of the neutral area, and with some regret Nelson had to leave them: a return to Toulon was imperative, to acquaint Lord Hood with his success in Naples and receive further orders. His return coincided with the arrival of troops from Naples, and after only three days he was sent off to Sardinia, to place himself under the command of Commodore Robert Linzee. On the way, a letter arrived from home with the unwelcome news that Fanny was literally ill with worry about him. He wrote to her at once, 'truly sorry to hear that you were not perfectly well.' But there was a touch of curt irritation too: 'Why should you alarm yourself? I am well, your son is well, and we are as comfortable in every respect as the nature of our service will admit.' Once upon a time, Nelson had promised that Josiah 'shall always be considered by me as one of my own'; yet his letters show it was a promise he could not keep. He was as good to Josiah as to any other child on shore or on board; but unless Josiah is mentioned by name, in letters to Fanny he is always *your son*, and to others *my son-in-law*. There was more of a distance between them than would be hoped for between a father and a son; and before they returned to England, the distance would have grown to the point where Josiah wished aloud that his stepfather might fall and break his neck.

The rest of that letter cannot have done much to set Fanny's mind at rest. In his few days off Toulon, Nelson had had to take part in a court martial while a Republican shore battery was being bombarded by vessels further out – 'for four hours, the shot and shell going over us; which, extraordinary as it may seem, made no difference ... Such is the force of habit that we seemed to feel no danger.' He meant to be consoling; instead, he only fed the imagination of a timid and vulnerable soul. And a month later, from her brother-in-law Maurice, she heard confirmation of her most fearful thoughts: for the first time since he left her, Nelson had been in action against the French.

He called it a 'little brush' with the enemy, but it ended with one of Nelson's men dead – how easily it could have been him or Josiah – and *Agamemnon* 'cut to pieces'. At two o'clock in the morning of 22 October, off Cape Monte Santo, halfway down Sardinia's east coast, a squadron of five vessels had been sighted. Individually none was as strong as *Agamemnon*: the largest were three 44-gun frigates, the smallest a brig of 14 guns. But collectively they mounted 170 guns and carried 1,620 men, while *Agamemnon* had only 345 men healthy, effectively reducing her from 64 to 50 guns.

It was fortunate the enemy ships were widely separated. Concentrating on one, the fight began after a chase of three hours and continued for three or four hours more. By then the victim was disabled and apparently sinking, but *Agamemnon*'s rigging was shot away – the French always aimed for the rigging – and her main topmast was broken. Sailors used to observe that cannon-fire seemed to still the wind locally. It happened on this occasion, with the other ships approaching as the two antagonists lay becalmed and out of each other's reach. In consultation with his officers, Nelson found unanimous agreement that *Agamemnon* could not continue 'without some small refit, and refreshment for our people.' Accordingly, repairs were begun at once and wine and bread brought up. Throughout the morning the enemy had the option to engage; 'but', said William Hoste cheerfully, 'their courage failed them, for we had given their friend so complete a drubbing', and they sailed away to the north. *Agamemnon* continued south, 'being satisfied with offering them battle', and in his private journal Nelson showed something of why he was willing to offer battle even when outnumbered.

'When I lay me down to sleep', he wrote, 'I recommend myself to the care of Almighty God; when I awake I give myself up to His direction. Amidst all the evils that threaten me, I will look up to Him for help, and question not but that He will either avert them or turn them to my advantage. Though I know neither the time nor the manner of my death, I am not at all solicitous about it, because I am sure that He knows them both, and that He will not fail to support and comfort me.'

Many would envy such certainty of faith. It was essentially a private matter, but it coloured everything Nelson did; and after this novel experience of action, Hoste ended a long, enthusiastic letter to his father with an adoring remark: 'Captain Nelson is acknowledged to be one of the first characters in the service, and is universally beloved by his men and officers.'

The enemy ships had come out of Tunis, and it was from there that Nelson sent his account of the engagement, for with Commodore Linzee, his new task was another diplomatic expedition. The ruler of Tunis, the Dey, was being too friendly to the French. From time immemorial the inhabitants of the Barbary Coast – the north coast of Africa – had practised piracy, an agreeable occupation for people whose characters and country were unsuited to farming. European and American merchant ships were favourite targets, combining commercial attractiveness with a religion repugnant to Islam. Such ships had only two means of guaranteeing a peaceful voyage: either they must come from a nation with a strong navy, or else their national government must pay tribute to the pirate states – protection money. The British and French had strong navies; the Venetians, Dutch, Scandinavians, Austrians and Americans paid up. Now it appeared that the French had bought friendly neutrality, or possibly an alliance with Tunis, for the harbour was full of French men-of-war, hauled close in to the shore. Clearly they expected the British to attack, but Linzee followed his orders to negotiate with the Dey. He did so for five days, and absolutely nothing came of it. When he pointed out that the French were very undesirable allies, having killed their king, the Dey answered smoothly that if he remembered his history correctly, the English had once done the same. Nonplussed, Linzee decided to return to Toulon for further instructions, and, surrounded by scornful shouts and insults from the French, his ships departed.

Nelson's view was straightforward. 'The English seldom get much by negotiation, except the being laughed at, which we have been; and I don't like it.' He calculated the enemy shipping was worth at least £300,000, and that a bribe of £50,000 would have secured the Dey's allegiance to Britain. The enemy vessels would then be fair game; so Nelson was sure that a little firm action would have resulted in a net profit for Britain, as well as safety in the southern Mediterranean. 'My spirits are low indeed ... I should have taken every Frenchman here without negotiation. Even had negotiations taken place, I would have had the French men-of-war – and believe that the people of England will never blame an officer for taking a French line-of-battle ship.'

Lord Hood thought the same. Defending Toulon with 16,000 soldiers from five different countries against a steadily growing Republican army – its numbers already approaching 40,000 – he learned of the sea-fight off Sardinia. The confidence he had first felt in Nelson when they met in the west Atlantic was completely restored, and he showed it: Nelson was removed from Linzee's squadron, and put in charge of a squadron of his own – his first detached command. 'Very handsome', said Nelson, his spirits quite lifted again. He was ordered to find and defeat the ships he had fought before. Lord Hood expressed a flattering certainty in his success; and by happy chance, one of Nelson's new ships was his old friend *Lowestoffe*. Heading for Leghorn to refit and replenish, he wrote to Captain Locker, once his and *Lowestoffe*'s commanding officer, now comfortably governing Greenwich Hospital. Amongst other things, he assessed the main theatre of action: 'I think they will have a good deal of fighting at Toulon this winter. Shot and shell are very plentiful all over the harbour, and I wonder more damage has not been done. General O'Hara will, I hope, be able to drive the French from the heights above the harbour, or we shall be unpleasantly situated. Not that I think Toulon is in the smallest danger.' He was desperately wrong. Three weeks later, just after Christmas, two more letters were sent from Leghorn Roads.

'*Agamemnon*, December 27th. My dear Fanny: Everything which domestic wars produce usually, is multiplied at Toulon. Fathers here are without their families, families without their fathers. In short, all is horror ... Many of our posts [occupied by French royalists] were carried without resistance; at others, which the English occupied, everyone perished. I cannot write all; my mind is deeply impressed with grief. Each teller makes the scene more horrible.'

Writing to Prince William, Nelson spelled out the fall of Toulon: the Neapolitans had panicked, the Spaniards had been reluctant to destroy the French fleet, the royalist French had fled. 'Lord Hood is said to have attempted rallying the flying troops, but in vain ... The mob had risen, was plundering, and committing every excess; many – numbers cannot be estimated – were drowned in trying to get off; boats upset; and some put a period to their existence. One family, of a wife and five children, are just arrived – the father shot himself. Indeed, Sir, the recital of their miseries is too afflicting to dwell upon. Lord Hood was obliged to order the French fleet of twenty sail of the line, and as many other ships of war, together with the arsenal and powder magazines, to be set on fire: report says one half of that miserable place is in ashes.'

For the British, Toulon – which they had conquered without a shot, then lost amid scenes of blood and fire – was the best hope for a secure base in the Mediterranean and a swift end to the war. Its loss was an indictment of Pitt's unwillingness to commit British troops to France, and the first public success of the twenty-four-year-old artillery colonel whose name Nelson now learned, and learned to loathe – still, then, written in its Italianate form: Napoleon Buonaparte. Worst of all, the port and half the French fleet survived the flames. Lord Hood's ships must either find a new base, or quit the Mediterranean.

So it was that Nelson began the year 1794 off northern Corsica, in heavy seas and gales hard enough to blow *Agamemnon* off her station. The island seemed to offer the best alternative base for British operations, not least because its inhabitants were in active, though disorganized, revolt against French rule. It had, morever, a good harbour at Bastia on the north-east coast – well placed for attacks on France and French shipping, and for the defence of Italy if necessary.

Blockade was instituted. Whenever the gales moderated enough (and they continued off and on for weeks), the Agamemnons – as Nelson had begun to call his men – staged small, effective raids: the destruction of a mill ('the only one they have'), the burning and capture of ships loaded with wine, the taking of two forts. In one 'very smart contest', resulting in the seizure of a French courier-boat, William Hoste was at Nelson's side throughout, 'in high style', as the captain wrote in a complimentary letter to Hoste's father. Earlier, at the end of a long letter to Fanny, Nelson commented that 'Hoste is an exceedingly good boy, and will shine in our service.' He showed consideration towards her: knowing she would soon be going to Bath, a costly place to stay, he said, 'I desire you will not want for anything. My expenses are not very great, so don't be afraid of money.' This was thoughtful, but in neither of those letters did he mention her son. Perhaps Josiah was beginning to feel unable to match his stepfather's professional example; perhaps he was upset by Nelson's dalliance in Leghorn. He was still only thirteen, and had known no father but Nelson; one can only guess what teasing he might have received in the gunroom. Yet whatever the cause, he was becoming a severe disappointment and William Hoste a delight – 'Your son', Nelson wrote to the Reverend Dixon Hoste, 'is everything which his dearest friends can wish him to be; and is a strong proof that the greatest gallantry may lie under the most gentle behaviour.' The identical words could have been written to the Reverend Edmund Nelson; and that may be why the captain and his servant got on so well.

The shape of Corsica is like a pointing hand, the index finger – Cap Corse – directed northwards to France. On opposite sides of that mountainous peninsula (at the base of the index finger, so to speak) lie Bastia to the east and St Florent to the west, twelve miles apart. Thirty miles further west, where the knuckle of the little finger would be, lies Calvi – like Bastia, a well fortified town.

Beset from the sea by the British and harassed on shore by the Corsicans, the French troops in the island retreated to these places. St Florent (known then by its Italian name, San Fiorenzo) had a good harbour, but poor defences: its main protection was one enormous tower called Mortella. In mid-February 1794, after two days' bombardment by a combined force under Lord Hood and General Sir David Dundas, its garrison surrendered; yet the British were so impressed by the tower itself, they soon borrowed its design. The name became slightly changed; but all along the south coast of England, Martello towers were constructed to defend against possible invasion – and 140 years later, in the Second World War, they were still in use for the same purpose.

With Hood at St Florent, Nelson was off Bastia. He inspected the town's defences as closely as possible, exchanging fire with shore batteries, and during the night saw the mountains behind the town silhouetted with a red glow. He guessed correctly that Hood had taken St Florent and set the ships in its harbour ablaze, and in the morning was pleased to see British troops appearing on the mountains. Then to his astonishment, they left again without making an attack. 'God knows what it all means ... A thousand men to a certainty would take Bastia; with five hundred and *Agamemnon*, I would attempt it.' With that confidence in his men which they always returned, he added: 'My seamen are now what British seamen ought to be ... almost invincible; they really mind shot no more than peas.'

The more he thought of it, the more he was convinced that the Agamemnons could take Bastia. At last he 'presumed to propose it to Lord Hood, and his lordship agreed with me'; but before authorizing the action, Hood quite correctly asked for help from the army. It was not forthcoming. General Dundas told him he considered a siege 'with our present means and force, to be a most visionary and rash attempt, such as no officer could be justified in undertaking.' Hood replied, with spirit, 'To me it appears very much the reverse, and very much the right measure ... I am now ready and willing to undertake the reduction of Bastia at my own risk, with the force and means at present here'. 'Therefore', Nelson confided to Fanny, 'the naval service at Bastia is intrusted to my direction'. Yet again Hood had offered him command of a 74-gun ship, 'but I declined it. I shall stay by old *Agamemnon.*' Remembering Nicaragua, he added: 'Armies go so slow that seamen think they never mean to get forward'; but, he ended judiciously, 'I dare say they act on a surer principle, although we seldom fail.'

It took two months of unremitting effort afloat and on shore, and they did not fail. First they had been obliged to replenish their stores – 'We are absolutely without either water, provisions, or stores of any kind, and not a piece of canvas, rope, twine or a nail ... We are really without the common necessaries of life. The ship is so light she cannot hold her side to the wind ... Not a man has slept dry for many months.'

From other sources Hood managed to acquire eleven hundred marines and soldiers, and with them, at 10 a.m. on 4 April, 250 Agamemnons landed three miles north of Bastia. By noon they were in position a mile and a half from the citadel, below a steep, high, rocky ridge. To Nelson it looked a good place for a battery. To a British civilian observer on the spot, it seemed improbable that anyone could get a heavy cannon so high. He, the Corsicans and the French were all extremely surprised at the Agamemnons' solution: 'They fastened great straps around the rocks, and then fastened to the straps the largest and most powerful purchases, or pullies and tackle, that are used on board a man-of-war. The cannon were placed on a sledge at one end of the tackle, the men walked down hill with the other end.' It was simple but tough – 'Very hard work for my poor seamen,' said Nelson, 'dragging guns up such heights as are scarcely credible.' There were at least sixteen guns – one 4-pounder field-piece, three 12-pounders and five 24-pounders from the ship, a howitzer, four large mortars and some carronades – and it took a week to haul them to their positions. On 11 April, from *Victory*, lying south of the town, Lord Hood sent an officer under a flag of truce to offer the French an easy way out. He was abused and insulted; the red battle flag was hoisted at *Victory*'s main topgallant masthead; to the cheers of his men, Nelson had English colours raised above his tent on the rock; and 'in high health and spirits' they began the assault.

Sixteen days later they had advanced to 900 yards from the citadel,

The Reverend Edmund Nelson, Rector of Burnham Thorpe, painted in 1800 when he was seventy-nine years old.

Catherine Nelson (*née* Suckling) who died in 1767, aged forty-two, after the birth of her eleventh child. Nelson adored her memory, but said little about her except that she 'hated the French'.

An anonymous miniature, believed to be of Nelson at the age of eight or nine. That was when his mother died, and whether or not it is authentic, the sad, pensive but attractive portrait catches one side of his character well.

The Parsonage House where Nelson was born and grew up, and where he and Fanny endured five devastating winters. The building was demolished in his lifetime; despite the quantity of surviving memorabilia, not one of the houses that Nelson called home still exists.

Captain Maurice Suckling, Nelson's maternal uncle, who took him into the navy with the remark: 'What has poor Horatio done, who is so weak, that he should be sent to rough it out at sea?'

Captain William Locker, Nelson's lifelong friend and mentor: 'It was you', Nelson said, 'who always told me, "Lay a Frenchman close and you will beat him" ... and my only merit in my profession is being a good scholar.'

Left Fanny, Viscountess Nelson, painted by Daniel Orme in 1798: 'an amiable woman', Nelson wrote of her. 'I have not the least doubt but that we shall be a happy pair – the fault must be mine if we are not.'

Opposite Nelson, painted as a lieutenant by Rigaud in 1777: the captain's insignia and 'Nicaraguan' background were added in 1781 after he was 'made post' during his first tour of duty in the West Indies.

Below HMS *Boreas* off the mountainous, verdant, subtropical island of Nevis – as unlike Norfolk as possible – where Nelson and Fanny ('the principal favourite of the island') were married on 11 March 1787.

'Nelson's Patent Bridge for boarding First-Rates': on an improbably clean quarterdeck at the climax of the Battle of Cape St Vincent, 14 February 1797, 'the Spanish Captain, with bended knee, presented me his Sword . . .'

An enemy at anchor, seen from the shore: at about 6.30 p.m. on 1 August 1798, Nelson's fleet approached the French in Aboukir Bay. To the French, a night attack seemed unduly risky, but for Nelson his captains were 'a Band of Brothers; therefore, night was to my advantage.'

The HERO of the NILE.

Pub.^d Decr 1st 1798 by H. Humphrey N.º 27 St James Street

PALMAM QUI MERUIT FERAT

'Covered with stars, ribbons and medals, more like a Prince of the Opera than the Conqueror of the Nile' – cartoons like Gillray's could make an enemy seem inhuman, or cut a hero down to human size.

lowering and raising the guns from rock to rock – 'work of the greatest difficulty,' Nelson wrote, 'which never, in my opinion, would have been accomplished by any other than British seamen ... I have no fears about the final issue of the expedition – It will be victory, Bastia will be ours!' Of the soldiers and seamen commanded by him and a Colonel Villettes, he said 'there is not one but considers himself as personally interested in the event, and deserted by the general. It has made them equal to double their numbers.' But in fact he did have one worry. Dundas's officers in St Florent had derisively nicknamed him 'the brigadier', and 'my only fears are that these soldiers will advance when Bastia is about to surrender, and deprive us of part of our glory.'

They did. On 19 May, at 4 p.m., flags of truce from Bastia were borne towards the approaching *Victory*: the French were ready to surrender. An hour later, 'our troops from San Fiorenzo made their first appearance on the hills; and on the 20th ... the whole Fiorenzo army [four regiments] came on the hills to take Bastia.'

In the thirty-eight days of the siege, Nelson's force used 1,058 barrels of powder and fired 11,923 shot and 7,373 shells – 'often five shells in the air at once, all going to Bastia.' What he did not know was that news of the Fiorenzo army's advance had filtered through to the French in Bastia, and it was that, and their increasing fear of Corsican reprisals, that made them decide to surrender when they did. Yet the surrender would certainly have come later if not then, and since 'our boats prevented anything from getting in by sea, and [with] our sailors hauling up great guns, and then fighting them on shore', Nelson's remark to his wife was fair: 'I may say truly, this has been a naval expedition'.

11

'The Lion Sun'

'*Agamemnon*, BASTIA, MAY 30. I am just got on board,' Nelson wrote to Locker, 'after eight weeks' service on shore ... We are now taking on board shot, shells, powder, &c., for Calvi, which, although very strongly situated, will, I believe, soon fall.'

He did not trouble to tell Locker about a wound he received at Bastia. Nor did he tell Fanny about it, until the middle of August. Then he simply called it 'a sharp cut in the back', and said no more: such things were in the line of duty, and he knew better than to worry her unnecessarily. He did not even say exactly when it happened – it might have been on 12 April, when he was out reconnoitring under fire, and a fellow-officer was mortally wounded at the same time as their Corsican guide was killed; or perhaps it was a week later, when he went with Captain Thomas Fremantle for another close view of the enemy. On that occasion, Fremantle noted in his laconic way, 'a shot knocked him down and covered me all over with dirt. Determine never to go the short way again.' The point, which Fanny might have found difficult to cope with, was that in perspective they were trivial matters. Five of the Agamemnons had been killed during the siege – 'they are not the men to keep out of the way' – and he probably would not have mentioned his own slight hurt at all, if it had not been that in the high summer at Calvi he was much more badly wounded, and wrote a long letter of warning and consolation to her, trying to give her a sense of proportion about the risks of naval life.

In the middle of June 1794, preparations for the siege of Calvi began in storms of thunder, lightning, high winds and heavy seas. Again the Agamemnons were working alongside soldiers. This time, however, their general, the Honourable Charles Stuart, was as eager as Nelson – anxious to go on to the attack, he said, if Captain Nelson thought it right to proceed with the shipping. The crisp reply was 'I certainly do', and the two men decided at once that they could work together.

The only possible landing place was four miles west of Calvi, and it was a bad one at that. Though the water was deep even close in to shore, it was studded with uncharted rocks either awash, or almost invisible underwater; and it only took a breeze to set up such a swell that boats could scarcely land. There were more than forty pieces of ordnance to take ashore, and Nelson could provide no more than two hundred seamen – 'barely sufficient to move a twenty-four pounder.' Nevertheless, one month later, he reported to Lord Hood that they had done the equivalent of dragging a 26-pounder, 'with its ammunition and every requisite for making a battery, upwards of eighty miles, seventeen of which were up a very steep mountain.'

With the handicaps of weather and geography, Stuart's plan went ahead slowly. On 27 June, Nelson wrote to Fanny saying that in the ten days since their arrival, 'nothing particular has occurred. Dragging cannon up steep mountains, and carrying shot and shells, has been our constant occupation.' But all remained secret, and he was optimistic: 'The French here do not know what to make of us. They hear we have landed, yet have not seen us, nor have they any idea about our batteries, which, when they open, will be heavy on them. That we shall take Calvi in due time, I have no manner of doubt.'

The town had three batteries and a strong fort in its landward defence. Each was to have at least one battery directed against it. On the beach and through the hills, the seamen slaved away, soaked to the skin, filling sandbags, rolling casks, carrying platforms, dragging guns – only to see the construction of the batteries delayed time and again 'through the ignorance and laziness' of the sappers and engineers. Stuart grew more and more frustrated. He did not blame Nelson and the sailors – on the contrary: on 4 July he said apologetically, 'Every time I write *delay*, my dear Sir, I suffer more than I can describe; for it very little suits my inclination or disposition. I must, however, crave it for one night more ...' Nelson sympathized, for he liked Stuart's energetic attitude, but privately he still felt that army methods left something to be desired; the general was being too much a perfectionist. The first British battery, armed with three guns and named Royal Louis, had opened fire at dawn that morning, and as the siege proper began, Nelson wrote a discreetly tongue-in-cheek note to Admiral Hood: 'I cannot help feeling, my lord, that a happy degree of irregularity is sometimes better than all this regularity.'

Knowing the difficulties on shore, Hood was able to supply fifty seamen from *Victory*, along with two naval captains whom Nelson knew and liked, Benjamin Hallowell and Walter Serocold. During the next few nights, all, working in absolute silence, helped to construct another two batteries. By daylight on 7 July the second was ready for six guns. The fifth gun had been mounted when the enemy ('never thinking to look so near themselves for a battery') saw for the first time what was going on. At once they began a heavy fire of grape shot. 'The seamen did their duty', Nelson reported, with Captain Serocold cheering them on – until in mid-huzza he dropped dead, 'killed by a grape shot passing through his head.' Five other men lost their lives, including an Agamemnon, and as soon as he could Nelson scribbled a quick note to Fanny:

'It is possible you may hear that a captain of the navy has fallen. To assure you it is not me, I write a few lines; for if such a report should get about, I know well your anxiety of mind ... I am very busy, yet own I am in all my glory; except with you, I would not be anywhere but where I am, for the world.'

But only five days later, long before that note could reach England, another went to Lord Hood: Nelson had 'got a little hurt ... Not much, as you may judge by my writing.' In his private journal he was more explicit – 'At daylight on the 12th the enemy opened a heavy fire ... which in an extraordinary manner seldom missed our battery; and at seven o'clock I was much bruised in the face and eyes by sand from the works, struck by shot.' To Sir Gilbert Elliot, newly appointed viceroy of Corsica; he was more explicit still – he was 'a good deal wounded, and my right eye cut down; but the surgeon flatters me I shall not entirely lose the sight, which I believe, for I can clearly distinguish light from darkness.' Three weeks went by before he mentioned it to Fanny, and then he called it only 'a very slight scratch', ending his letter with a little joke: 'This day I have been four months landed ... I feel amost qualified to pass my examination as a besieging general.' He hoped, as much as anyone would, for a full recovery; but the eyeball had been pierced. Modern analysis suggests either it haemorrhaged inside, or else the retina was detached; and five weeks after it had happened, he finally wrote to Fanny in detail – 'As it is all past, I may now tell you.'

The wound had bled very badly, as head-wounds always do, 'yet I most fortunately escaped, having only my right eye nearly deprived of its sight ... As to all the purposes of use, it is gone; however, the blemish is nothing, not to be perceived, unless told. The pupil is nearly the size of the blue part, I don't know the name ... You must not think my hurts confined me: no, nothing but the loss of a limb would have kept me from my duty.' That would come; but meanwhile, though half-blind, he firmly believed that 'my exertions conduced to preserve me, in this general mortality.'

As the siege was pressed home, the French batteries were abandoned one by one, and at last the fort, the men retreating into the citadel of Calvi. On 20 July, in his daily report to Lord Hood, Nelson told him they had reached a crucial time: 'The siege is come to this point, either to go on, or to give it up.' And at that point, the constructive partnership with Stuart began to fray, as the general made impossible demands. Nelson acknowledged that Stuart had taught him much about land warfare – 'He is an extraordinary good judge of ground' – but now Stuart himself had to learn something unwelcome about sea warfare. The general wanted ships 'laid against the walls', and Nelson refused to allow it. The probability of their being attacked with red-hot shot was too great, and sea-borne guns were always less accurate than ones based on land. 'Our conversation was carried on with the greatest politeness, and he thanked me for my assistance', Nelson wrote, suggesting at best a professional but chilly discussion; and Stuart, tiring of naval explanations, repeated that 'it was necessary to come to the point, whether the siege should be persevered in, or given up? If the former, he must be supplied with the means, which were more troops, more seamen to work, and more ammunition.' Nelson ended the report there, with Stuart's implication plain: if the siege was abandoned, the general would regard it as the navy's fault.

The silent suggestion incensed Nelson. 'We will fag ourselves to death before any blame shall lie at our doors,' he wrote angrily, recording that all the mortars, and twenty-two of twenty-five guns, had been dragged into place, mounted and worked entirely by seamen. 'I trust the general will not forget our services.' But as the British dug themselves in only 650 yards from the centre of the citadel and negotiations started with the French, he had one still more serious worry: delay might bring it all to nothing, for 'the climate is the only enemy we have to fear; that we can never conquer.' As the full heat of a Mediterranean summer began to beat on besiegers and besieged, malaria broke out. Of course he fell victim – 'This is my ague day ... I hope so active a scene will keep off the fit. It has shaken me a good deal' – and, as he told Prince William, half the soldiers and sailors were struck down.

'It is now what we call the dog-days; here it is termed the Lion Sun. No person can endure it: we have upwards of 1000 sick out of 2000, and the others are not much better than so many phantoms. We have lost many men from the season, very few from the enemy. I am here the reed among the oaks; all the prevailing disorders have attacked me, but I have not strength for them to fasten upon: I bow before the storm, while the sturdy oak is laid low.'

One whose death upset him badly was James Moutray, son of the woman he had adored in Antigua in the days before he met Fanny. He told Fanny of the loss, adding that he had had a memorial tablet erected in the church at St Florent, and informing her too that, 'Poor little Hoste is also extremely ill ... I have great fears for him.' At least he and Josiah were healthy; indeed, Josiah had become 'a clever smart young man' – very far from the boy who had left home a year and a half before. In Nelson's letters, it is noticeable that during the period of the siege of Calvi, he wrote more often of Josiah than for some time before, and more happily: 'I have no fears but that he will be a good man ... His understanding is excellent. .... He is a seaman, every inch of him.' He added only one tactful criticism: Josiah was becoming 'warm in his disposition' – in other words, hot-tempered and argumentative. But that, he hoped, was a flaw 'which nothing can cool so thoroughly as being at sea, where nobody has entirely their own way.'

At last, on 18 August, he wrote a letter he felt long overdue: 'I left Calvi on the 15th, and hope never to be in it again.' On 10 August the siege ('which has been protracted beyond all bounds of calculation') had succeeded: the citadel capitulated, the garrison were permitted to march out with honours of war, and, with the sick and 'such inhabitants as chose', were embarked in British transports to be exchanged for prisoners-of-war in France. The island belonged to Britain, not only by conquest but by choice. 'George the Third is king of Corsica, chosen by the unanimous consent of the people themselves, the best of all titles; they are now our fellow-subjects. The first resolution of the parliament of Corsica was to declare that they were Englishmen' – something which Nelson found a little difficult to credit, for when he told Fanny about it, he added: 'They might have been mistaken for Irishmen, by their bull.'

He had never trusted them entirely; back in Bastia he had decided 'they may be good friends, if it is in their interest to be so; but I am rather inclined to believe they will always cry, Long live the conqueror!' Still, they were conquered, and seemed to like it, and the island would be very useful; and on 12 September Nelson wrote another letter long wished for. After twenty-five days of rest and refit in Leghorn, his ship's company were still very weak, but improving. They would have another three days in port before going to sea again, to 'attend Lord Hood in the *Victory* to Genoa, Porto Especia and Vado Bay; and then proceed ... I hope to Gibraltar and England.' Now he told Fanny confidently, 'I expect to see you in the fall of the year.' He had been away nineteen months, and as always his dreams were touchingly modest: 'I shall not bring with me either riches or honour, yet I flatter myself I shall bring an unblemished character ... I hope we shall find some snug cottage, whenever we are obliged to quit the Parsonage House.' Above all, he concluded, 'when Lord Hood quits this station, I should be truly sorry to remain; he is the greatest sea-officer I ever knew.' What he did not know was that, remembering his success at Naples and his attitude at Tunis, Lord Hood had selected him for another diplomatic mission, and intended that he should stay in the Mediterranean thereafter.

Thus, Nelson's thirty-sixth birthday, 29 September 1794, found him in Genoa, a city which was 'without exception, the most magnificent I ever beheld ... All the houses are palaces on the grandest scale.' The city-state, ruled by a Doge elected every two years, was neutral, but seemed likely to remain friendly – if not actually allied – to Britain: 'I do not think they can ever be mad enough to allow the Sans Culottes to enter Genoa; here would be glorious plunder for them.'

He noticed at once, though, that in addition to three English merchantmen, there were two French privateers in port. These, he learned, made occasional sorties, and had recently captured two vessels from Spain; but more important was his report on the mood of the Genoese court.

His intended mission had been simply to deliver despatches to a Mr Drake, British Minister at Turin, and to be on hand to provide supporting first-hand information if needed. However, Drake did not arrive on time, and Nelson was obliged to stand in for him. His experience with royalty, though limited, was invaluable. Internationally, the Doge was treated as a sovereign prince, and not only he but his entire senate assembled to meet the British naval captain, with the Doge himself advancing to greet his guest. To many people such grandeur could have been overwhelming, but Hood had chosen well. Joined with his professional confidence, Nelson's natural courtesy saved him from being tongue-tied, while honesty, respect for royalty and dislike of the French lent him the eloquence of a seasoned diplomat. After paying his formal respects, he assured 'His Serene Highness' that 'both by duty and inclination I should preserve the strictest attention to the neutrality of Genoa, and should be happy to do everything in my power to cement the harmony' between Britain and Genoa. Knowing as well as anyone how the Terror raged in France, the Doge was delighted, and promised a constant welcome to British warships; the provision of whatever supplies they might need; and to Captain Nelson personally, a constantly open door to his palace. This was not just a courtesy, but meant literally – when Nelson left, the order arrived before him at the gates, 'where the captain of the guard told me he had received the mandate for opening them at whatever time I pleased.'

There was only one embarrassment: on arrival he had hoisted a signal for a pilot. The Genoese mistook it for a vice admiral's flag, and fired a 15-gun salute, which Nelson felt obliged to return with an equal number. Apprehensively he reported the matter to Lord Hood, saying 'I shall probably hear more of it.' Knowing he was not entitled to such distinction, he feared he might have seemed presumptuous, and ever since his long years on the beach, the one thing that always made him nervous was the thought of Admiralty disapproval. However, nothing came of it; if the Admiralty were ever told, they must have recognized his small quandary and approved. He had carried himself well in Genoa, and as the worry faded, he could mark it down as one more mission accomplished – a satisfaction which was perhaps just as well, for within a fortnight a growing suspicion became a confirmed disappointment. Hood's expected departure for England took place on 11 October; but for Nelson, there was 'no chance whatever of going home. My ship's company are by no means recovered, and we are destined to keep the sea until both ship and crew are rendered unfit for service.'

It would have been no consolation to him to consider that those who do a job best always have more put upon them. 'The service must ever supersede all private consideration', he repeated despondently to Fanny. 'I hope you will spend the winter cheerfully ... Do not repine at my absence; before spring I hope we shall have peace, when we must look out for some little cottage: I assure you I shall return to the plough with redoubled glee.' But of course she did repine. He asked to hear often from her; in his dejected state it was his greatest comfort. Yet even her letters were comfortless – 'This winter will be another anxious one. What did I not suffer in mind, the last one!' she wrote. 'My mind and poor heart are always on the rack!' No doubt she meant well, and tried to express her love through conveying her fears; certainly she had not the strength of character to dissemble, and may have thought that happy letters would make her husband feel unneeded. But she only succeeded in irritating him – 'Why you should be uneasy about me, so as to make yourself ill, I know not', he answered, trying to moderate his impatience with a little humour: 'I don't know that I was ever so truly well; I fancy myself grown quite stout.'

There was a small, sad echo there of the letters of their courtship, when he had assured her he was not getting fat – 'my make will not allow of it.' Personally, and to his professional superiors, his demands were not great. What he needed from home was proud, optimistic, unquestioning support; what he needed from the navy, for himself and his men, was recognition, if not financial reward. But for close on two years both sources had failed. To his wife he had made every effort, with repeated assurances of his and Josiah's health; yet nothing he wrote could alter her absolute inability to face and accept the risks of his way of life. With his father it was quite different. The Rector's letters were full of touching pride in his son and faith in his God: 'It was an unerring power, wise and good, which diminished the force of the blow by which your eye was lost ... There is no fear that flattery can come from me; but I sometimes wipe away the tear of joy, at hearing your character in every point of view so well spoken of ... Accept, my dear good son, the usual but most hearty expressions of love and friendship from your affectionate Father.'

If only Fanny could have written with such simple confidence, such serenity and intimacy. 'Your lot is cast,' the Reverend Edmund wrote, 'but the whole disposing thereof is of the Lord ... a most comfortable doctrine.' So it was, and Nelson accepted it completely. Knowing Fanny could not, he did not blame her for being herself, but learned unwillingly to live with the disappointment.

At the same time, he had to bear the navy's lack of recognition for all in *Agamemnon*, though he believed they had given 'as hard service as a ship's crew ever performed.' The difference was that with professional matters he felt able to state his long-standing grievance bluntly. 'All we get is honour and salt beef', he wrote after the capture of Toulon. 'I believe the world is convinced that no conquests of importance can be made without us; and yet, as soon as we have accomplished the service we are sent on, we are neglected. If parliament does not grant something to this fleet, our Jacks will grumble; for here there is no prize-money to soften their hardships.'

The Corsican campaign brought 'nothing but honour' at first – 'far above the consideration of wealth', he added sententiously. 'Not that I despise riches, quite the contrary; yet I would not sacrifice a good name to obtain them.' However, when he did not even get the good name his efforts deserved, he really felt betrayed. After the fall of Bastia, Lord Hood's despatch said only that he had commanded the seamen in landing the guns, mortars and stores, and gave credit for the command of the batteries to Captain Anthony Hunt, who was not even there. Walter Serocold, later killed at Calvi, was so angered by the neglect of Nelson he swore he would publish the truth personally. He was only persuaded not to when it became clear that Hood knew exactly who should have the credit, but wanted to help Hunt, a good officer who (through bad luck rather than bad captaincy) had lost his ship. Though both Serocold and Nelson still felt it unjust, they accepted the explanation, hoping that someone would do the same for them one day.

Later, trusting that General Stuart would recognize his efforts at Calvi, Nelson was even more bitterly let down: in the public gazettes – the official accounts of outstanding military or naval action – Stuart's despatch ignored him entirely, to the extent that he, who had lost the sight of one eye, was not even named in the list of the wounded. 'One hundred and ten days I have been actually engaged, at sea and on shore, against the enemy', he wrote acidly. 'I do not know that anyone has done more. I have had the comfort to be always applauded by my commander-in-chief, but never to be rewarded: and what is more mortifying, for services in which I have been wounded, others have been praised, who, at the same time, were actually in bed, far from the scene of action. They have not done me justice.'

He had a shrewd idea of the cause: the successful siege had proved army doctrine wrong. In his own words, 'The taking of Bastia, contrary to all military judgment, is such an attack on them that it is never to be forgotten.' Still, he remained doggedly loyal to the greater cause, 'always happy, if my humble but hearty endeavours can serve my king and country'; and when he was feeling particularly low, a defiant streak emerged to pull him through. 'Never mind,' he told Captain Locker. 'I'll have a Gazette of my own.'

12

'We cannot spare you'

HOOD NEVER RETURNED to the Mediterranean, nor even to the sea. He was ill and old – his seventieth birthday took place on 12 December 1794, three days before his flag was struck in Portsmouth. But that was not why he had to leave the active service: he still possessed the mental vigour of a man half his age. Moreover, he quickly recovered his physical health and lived another twenty-two years, spending the last twenty of them as Governor of Greenwich Hospital. However, in April 1795, back in *Victory* and ready to sail for the Mediterranean once more, he stated in an official letter to the Admiralty the plain and unwelcome truth about the condition of the Royal Navy out there. It was this plain speaking which cost him his post. With long, hard duty, unrelieved and unrewarded, the crews of some ships were, he said, verging on mutiny, and without proper support from home, force might have to be used to restore discipline. His frank assessment was that 'no officer who looks to the honour and credit of his Majesty's Navy can venture to take upon him the charge and command of the Mediterranean Fleet ... without risk of becoming the instrument of disgrace to the nation.' Personally he was entirely willing to take that charge, if their Lordships would accept what he knew to be the truth and act accordingly, providing more ships, money and men. They did not. Instead, for his frankness, he was relieved of his command – in his own words, 'thrown upon the shelf for ever.'

Nelson heard the news in the middle of June: 'Oh, miserable Board of Admiralty. They have forced the first officer in the Service away from his command ...' He had rated Hood as 'the best officer, take him altogether, that England has to boast of', and since the chance to speak privately with professional equals was rare, he poured his consternation and resentment into his journal and personal letters.

A review of the past eight months offered him little comfort. In mid-March there had been one exhilarating moment which briefly made him feel that staying on was time well spent; but now it only increased the contrast with the rest. Hood's supposedly temporary replacement, Vice Admiral Sir William Hotham, was faced with all the problems which Hood had stated to the Admiralty – 'a fleet half-manned and in every respect inferior to the enemy; Italy calling him to her defence, our newly-acquired kingdom [Corsica] calling might and main ... all to be done without a force adequate to it' – and Nelson readily acknowledged that he 'has had much to contend with'. But Hotham's solution to the problems besetting him was to play safe, keeping his ships much farther from Toulon than Hood had ever done. Nelson did not like it. The Admiralty approved Hotham's prudence, and Nelson could understand the reasons, but all the same, it was exasperating. Soon he felt that, overall, the admiral 'heartily tires of his temporary command; nor do I think he is intended by nature for a Commander-in-Chief, which requires a man of more active turn of mind'. From Naples, Sir William Hamilton agreed, writing with his usual gentle perception that 'My old friend Hotham is not quite awake enough for such a command ... although he appears the best creature imaginable.'

When he took over from Hood, the French let it be known that 'they would eat their New Year's dinner in Corsica'. Hotham took the threat of reconquest sufficiently seriously to send Nelson to find out the state and numbers of the French fleet. Nelson counted twenty-two sail in Toulon harbour, without being able to tell whether they were ships of the line or not – there was a point of land between his ship and the enemy. Reporting to the admiral, he guessed they would send out small squadrons from time to time to interfere with British merchantmen; and he predicted they were enough 'to keep us in hot water the whole winter'.

Actually they did nothing of the sort: the weather that winter was far too severe for them to venture out. Outside the harbour, the entire British fleet was under storm staysails for up to twelve days at a time, and even Nelson reckoned he had never known such a long series of gales and heavy seas. 'In *Agamemnon* we mind them not', he said. 'She is the finest ship I have ever sailed in.' She also had a veteran crew, united by very varied experience under one captain. Nelson's prediction assumed the same standards for the French in Toulon. In fact, because of the Revolution, the shortage of naval officers was so bad that the Rear Admiral there, Pierre Martin, had been a lieutenant only three years before, and out of every hundred men in the fleet, sixty had never been to sea.

Nevertheless, by the beginning of March 1795, they did have 124 transport ships full of troops. 'Something they certainly mean to attempt', Nelson mused. Not knowing of developments in England, he added: 'I wish Lord Hood would make haste out.' And a few days later, on 6 March, he wrote a line obliquely showing his lack of confidence in Hotham: when the admiral made a sudden order for the fleet to go immediately to sea, Nelson's sceptical reaction was – 'I sincerely hope it is to some good purpose.' He would have felt no such doubt with Hood.

But Hotham did know what he was up to. Seventeen ships of the line and five smaller vessels had emerged from Toulon, bound for Corsica. Against them he had fifteen of the line, including one Neapolitan; and on 10 March Nelson found himself on the brink of his first fleet action. It could also be his last, so he wrote a hasty note to Fanny – 'We are just in sight of the French fleet, and a signal is out for general chase ... A glorious death is to be envied; and if anything happens to me, recollect that death is a debt we must all pay, and whether now, or a few years hence, can be of but little consequence. God bless you.'

Eleven days later, from the Italian haven of La Spezia, a dismissive letter was sent to Captain Locker. 'You will have heard of our brush with the French fleet – a battle it cannot be called, as the enemy would not give us the opportunity of closing with them.' Nelson's feelings were mixed: personally, he had distinguished himself and was pleased that both fleets recognized that, in their different ways. But professionally, he was profoundly dissatisfied, and considered that a prime opportunity had been wasted in anti-climax.

After that first contact, the French had made away. For the British, winds were so light that the fleets soon lost sight of each other, and did not make contact again until 12 March. This time – fifteen miles off Genoa, on a day so clear the town was plainly visible – the enemy turned, apparently to fight; but, said Nelson, 'they did not appear to me to act as officers who knew anything of their profession', for they changed course continually in their attempts to form a line. As the British formed up, their wind died again, and after a whole frustrating day in which each could see the other but neither could give battle, both fleets stood to the south throughout the night.

Dawn on 13 March found them twelve miles apart, the French sailing as fast as they could away, the British giving general chase, and *Agamemnon* – still, despite her two years out of dock, the fastest sailer in the fleet – pulling away from all her colleagues except Captain Fremantle's *Inconstant*, and closing on the enemy. The French might have escaped entirely, but at 8 a.m. one of their 84-gun ships of the line – the *Ça Ira* – ran foul of another, lost her fore and main topmasts, slowed and was caught by *Inconstant*. They exchanged fire and *Inconstant* withdrew, badly damaged; two other ships of the line – one of 74, the other of 120 guns – stood by to help *Ça Ira* while a frigate took her in tow; *Agamemnon* continued to close; and 'on looking round,' wrote Nelson in his official account, 'I saw no ship of the line within several miles to support me.'

Ça Ira opened fire with her stern chasers, 'so true ... that not a shot missed'. Nelson had intended to touch her stern before firing, and he meant that literally, for at half past ten, when *Agamemnon* did commence firing – 'a few minutes sooner than I wished' – the vessels were only a hundred yards apart. 'I ordered the helm to be put a-starboard, and the driver and after-sails to be brailed up and shivered, and as the ship fell off, we gave her our whole broadside, each gun double-shotted ... The instant all had been fired, braced up our afteryards, put the helm a-port, and stood after her again. This manoeuvre we practiced until one p.m., never allowing the *Ça Ira* to get a single gun from either side to fire on us'.

With pleasure, Nelson noted that through it all, his men worked their ship as calmly and precisely 'as if she had been turning into Spithead'. By half past one *Ça Ira* ('large enough to take the *Agamemnon* in her hold') was 'a perfect wreck', sails in shreds, rigging destroyed, virtually unmanoeuvrable – and then Hotham recalled him. In his official account, Nelson said simply: 'I instantly bore away'. Comments on the order had to wait for private letters.

Agamemnon had been struck a good deal, but there were no dead, and only seven men wounded, while 110 had been killed in *Ça Ira*. The chase continued during the night; in the morning, action resumed, with more ships on both sides involved than before; and at five minutes past ten, along with the 74-gun *Censeur*, *Ça Ira* surrendered. Both, Nelson told Prince William, 'defended themselves in a very gallant manner; the rest of the enemy's ships behaved very ill.' Lieutenant George Andrews, brother of the beauty of St Omer and 'as gallant an officer as ever walked a quarterdeck' was sent from *Agamemnon* to take possession of the defeated ships and take their captains, on Hotham's order, to his subordinate Vice Admiral Samuel Goodall; and that, in Hotham's view, was quite enough to be going on with.

This time Nelson really could not believe it, and urged the commander-in-chief to further action: the prizes could safely be left with two damaged British ships and some frigates to guard them, while the remainder were pursued. But 'absolutely in the horrors', he heard Admiral Hotham ('much cooler than myself') say: 'We must be contented; we have done very well.'

'Now,' he wrote to Fanny, pouring it all out back in St Florent, which he had hoped never to see again, 'Now, had we taken ten sail, and had allowed the eleventh to escape, I could never have called it well done. Goodall backed me, I got him to write to the admiral, but it would not do: we should have had such a day as I believe the annals of England never produced.'

He was quite sure of Hotham now, and quite sure of himself. For the first time he spelled out his own ambition – 'I wish to be an admiral, and in command of the English fleet. I should very soon either do much, or be ruined. My disposition cannot bear tame and slow measures. Sure I am, had I commanded our fleet on the 14th, that either the whole French fleet would have crowned my triumph, or I should have been in a confounded scrape.'

There were some consolations: to the rest of the fleet, his efforts against *Ça Ira* marked Nelson as a real fighting captain of great skill and seamanship. He enjoyed their approval, and was amused at the clownish praise of the French Royalists, who called him 'the dear Nelson, the amiable Nelson, the fiery Nelson'. They wrote bad but enthusiastic poems about him – 'in them I am so covered with laurels, you would hardly find my face' – and they presented him with a mistress. He told Fanny about this one, for it was 'no less a personage than the goddess Bellona', the Roman goddess of war. 'However nonsensical these expressions are, they are better than censure.' More importantly (for it carried extra pay, and prestige, being one of only four such appointments) he was made an honorary colonel of marines. This was particularly useful, because he had received nothing so far for the loss of his eye, and had been refused any extra pay for his work ashore in Corsica; and soon it appeared his talents as diplomat, colonel and naval captain would all be needed together. From a cruise off Minorca ('doing nothing ... out of spirits, though never in better health'), he was ordered at the beginning of July 'to co-operate with the Austrian General, Baron de Vins, in the Riviera of Genoa'.

De Vins and the armies he led – Austrian and Sardinian – were becoming peculiarly important to Britain. Britain, Holland, Austria, Spain, Prussia, Russia and Sardinia had joined in coalition against France, and surrounding it as they did, any one of them could (and did) assume that the thrust of revolution would be contained quite easily. So it would have been, if the coalition had been wholehearted. But none of those nations grasped that they were trying to cope with something which, at least within Europe, was an entirely new kind of national movement. The armies of France might be badly equipped, but they were well led, by men of talent rather than connection, and for those who were not victims of the Terror in France, it was a time of the utmost exhilaration: customs and habits overthrown, a novel and thrilling sense of power, success and infinite possibility – without, yet, any chastening burden of responsibility.

Against that wild energy – an enthusiastic, almost missionary vigour which they did not recognize and were not prepared for – the nations of the coalition failed one by one. Each had entered the war intent on two things: internally maintaining its own society unaltered, and externally increasing its power or dominion – even at the expense of an ally, if any one became vulnerable. Thus, one by one, they made peace with France, or fell prey to it; the coalition crumbled away; and by the summer of 1795, only three of its original members remained actively opposed to the original common enemy: on the land, Sardinia and Austria, and Britain on the sea. And the Royal Navy seemed to be doing little.

'Our operations are at a stand,' Nelson wrote to Fanny at the end of May, 'for the want of ships to support the Austrians ... and behold, our admiral does not feel himself equal to show himself, much less to give assistance'. Towards the end of June, Hotham was, nevertheless, prompted to act by a letter from de Vins. From this it appeared that the French fleet was back in Toulon; and although (as Hotham later said) 'the reports as to his success were extremely various', he decided to take de Vins' own report at face value. It stated that Vado Bay, to the west of Genoa, was in allied hands and would make a good base for the English fleet. So, on 4 July, with three frigates and a cutter under his command, Nelson and *Agamemnon* left St Florent across a supposedly empty sea, 'to give countenance to the general's operations'. Three days later they came rushing back, with the enemy's fleet – six frigates and seventeen ships of the line – hot on their heels.

'I was much surprised', Hotham admitted – and much embarrassed too, for the body of his fleet was in the middle of watering and refitting, and the wind was blowing directly into the anchorage: he simply could not move his ships out to help. But the French did not attack. Believing they must have been led into a trap, they bore away, and by the time Hotham's ships emerged, next morning, the enemy had vanished.

They were located again on 13 July, at daylight, south of the islands of Hyères – eighty-five miles from St Florent, and only thirty from their own base at Toulon. The action which followed was similar to the one in March, with the British trying to give general chase. They were plagued by light, very variable winds which sometimes died away altogether just as ships came in range; a French admiral 'undetermined', in Nelson's view, 'whether to fight or run away'; one ship, *Alcide*, beaten into surrender by *Agamemnon* and others of the British vanguard, only to take fire and blow up before she could be taken; and an English admiral who called off the action just as *Agamemnon* and the 74-gun *Cumberland* were closing with an 80-gun French ship. 'Those of our ships which were engaged had approached so near to the shore', Hotham explained, 'that I judged it proper to call them off.' And all they could do was to watch the French frigates and the sixteen surviving ships of the line scurry into the safety of Toulon.

'Thus has ended our second encounter with these gentry', Nelson wrote acidly to Prince William. 'In the forenoon we had every prospect of taking every Ship in the Fleet, and at noon it was almost certain we should have had the six near Ships ... To say how we wanted Lord Hood at that time is to say, "Will you have all the French Fleet, or no Action?" But', he concluded, 'the subject is unpleasant and I shall have done with it. I am now co-operating with the Austrian Army, under General de Vins, and hope we shall do better there.'

The higher the hopes, the greater the disappointment; lines from a few of Nelson's letters over the second half of 1795 put his dealings with de Vins in a nutshell, tracing the general's slowly revealed inertia, Nelson's declining faith in him, and the sudden overwhelming victory of the French.

In July, writing to Lord Spencer at the Admiralty, Nelson took General de Vins completely at face value: he 'appears to be an officer who perfectly knows his duty, and is well disposed to act with vigour on every proper occasion.' The General predicted that inside six weeks he would be in Nice, with the British fleet in Villefranche, and that Provence would instantly rise in their support. Certainly de Vins could talk; he had been a courtier all his life. Yet by mid-August Nelson's view was moderating: 'General de Vins has long been expected, but I fear in vain ... Some risk must be run'; a month later, 'I am not quite so well pleased as I expected with this army, which is slow beyond all description ... Week after week has passed, without his army having removed one foot to the westward of where I found them.' Early October: 'Our armies are very close to the French, every hour I expect an attack from them; as the General, from some cause or other, does not just now seem in the humour to begin'. On 9 November, 'General de Vins sent me word that he believed the French thought his position too strong to be attacked.' Nine days later: 'The two armies are both so strongly posted that neither is willing to give the attack: each waits to see which can endure the cold longest.' Finally, five days after that, on 23 November, the French did attack. In what became known as the Battle of Loano, the Austrians were routed; and as December began, the last of that series of letters described 'the futility of Continental Alliances'.

'The Austrians, by all accounts, did not stand firm', Fanny read some time later. 'The French, half-naked, were determined to conquer or die ... Retreat it could not be called ... it was the devil take the hindmost ... The Austrians ran eighteen miles without stopping, the men without any arms whatever, officers without soldiers, women without assistance. Thus has ended my campaign.' At about the same time, William Hoste's father learned from Nelson exactly where he thought the blame lay, and what the consequence would be:

'General de Vins, from ill health, as he says, gave up the command in the midst of the battle; and from that moment not a soldier stayed at his post: many thousands ran away who had never seen the enemy, some of them thirty miles from the advanced posts. We have established the French republic'.

Nelson had never liked Vado Bay, so warmly recommended by de Vins as a base for the British fleet; its water was deep, with a good clay bottom, yet it was only a bay by name, being nothing more than a bend in the shore, exposed in almost all weathers and difficult to land in. However, it had at least given a point of contact between the fleet and the Austrian army, and now even that was gone. At Loano, three of Nelson's officers and sixteen of his men had been captured on shore, and he was pleased later to hear that they were being 'exceedingly well treated ... because they belong to the *Agamemnon*, whose character is well known throughout the republic.' But that was almost the only spark of cheer he could find when he wrote to Fanny at the beginning of 1796: the future seemed clear. 'The French, I am certain, will this spring make a great exertion to get into Italy.' He estimated that by 1 February, there would be fifteen sail of the line, 140 transports and 200 flat boats ready in Toulon. Convinced he could work out their landing place, he also admitted it required great foresight to be positive; and the worst was that if their army was landed successfully, then their fleet would retire into Toulon, and the British would be unable to do anything more.

'If they mean to carry on the war,' he repeated, 'they must penetrate into Italy. Holland and Flanders, with their own country, they have entirely stripped; Italy is the gold mine, and, if once entered, is without the means of resistance.'

The roots of the recent disaster at Loano were equally clear. The elderly General de Vins, full of resounding phrases like 'All peace or all war', had turned out to be nothing but a windbag. Constantly finding excuses not to act, he put up one condition after another. Nelson complied with all that were in his power, but there was one he could do little about: de Vins began to ask for Admiral Hotham's direct assistance. Both Nelson and the British minister at Turin wrote to Hotham, sure that de Vins was preparing to blame any mishap on 'the non-cooperation of the British fleet' – 'The General', said Nelson, 'wants a loop-hole.' He got it. Hotham supported Nelson in everything except this, and would not come closer than Leghorn or St Florent.

There were few events in those months of 'co-operative' campaigning which Nelson could recall with pleasure. One that stood out, though, was an episode late in August, before he had become thoroughly bogged down with de Vins. On that occasion, his ships captured a French convoy of twelve supply vessels in Alassio, twenty miles south of Vado. The operation was entirely sucessful, with only one injury in the whole squadron: William Hoste, who was put in command of a small boat and told to cut out one of the enemy vessels. He did so, and when he found that it carried a great deal of ammunition, and sufficient arms for 1,700 men, he became so excited that he fell down a hatch and broke his leg. Typically, Nelson visited him every day during his recovery; yet when he was better, he re-enacted the exploit for his colleagues' entertainment, fell over, and broke the other leg. The captain 'strongly recommended him not to break any more limbs', but the reprimand was not very serious; everyone liked the boy, who sang songs as he hopped around on his crutches, and his perky attitude endeared him to the sailors. 'He has become such a favourite', another officer noted, 'that with a confidence of success little less than superstitious, they invariably ask that Hoste may command.'

There was nothing wrong with having a ship's mascot, and the comic relief was welcome; but the strain of 'pushing the Austrian general forward' took its toll on Nelson's health. His one good eye temporarily failed. Eventually he learned to wear a green shield above it, protecting it from the Mediterranean glare (and, incidentally, beginning the mistaken legend that he wore a piratical patch over his blind eye); but at one time, caught between de Vins and Hotham, he was nearly blind for more than a week. Later, he began waking at night unable to breathe properly, 'as if a girth were buckled taut over my breast'. Frequently he was in great pain – 'alive', he told one of his fellow-captains, 'and that's all.' And lying awake he would have had the unwelcome chance to ponder another source of stress: a serious problem, both personal and national, created by the Genoese.

Faced with the possibility of being engulfed by France, the authorities in Genoa resorted to appeasement, forgetting their neutrality so far as to permit the open recruiting of their citizens into the French army – recruits paid for with Austrian gold captured by the French. Worse, if anything, they began to supply the French by sea, under the guise of neutral trade. Mr Drake, British minister at Turin, requested Nelson to stop it. Nelson saw his point entirely, and agreed with it; yet there were two 'great obstacles', which he had to explain at length. Firstly, Admiral Hotham had issued an order specifically prohibiting his captains from doing anything to offend neutrals; secondly, 'as a captain in the navy', there was 'the being liable for prosecution for detention and damage'. It brought back ghastly memories of his time in the West Indies, trying to enforce the Navigation Acts. Nevertheless, on the strength of a guarantee of Drake's official support, he ordered his squadron to set about it, 'acting not only without the orders of my commander-in-chief, but in some measure contrary to them'; and as if to strengthen the West Indian memory, who should sail into the Mediterranean but Cuthbert Collingwood.

'I now thought', Collingwood wrote after his wedding, 'that I was settling myself in great comfort; but I was mistaken, for ... the French war broke out'. Nelson was delighted to know his old friend was close at hand, and told 'dear Coll' all about the Genoese problem. 'Our Admiral', he concluded, 'has no political courage, and is alarmed at the mention of any strong measure; but in other respects, he is as good a man as can possibly be.' To do him justice, Hotham soon approved Nelson's action, and issued to the fleet in general orders based on Nelson's own. However, being a good man was not enough. Every admiral may have one inconclusive action; but if it happens again, it may be time for him to go.

The way in which Nelson learned of Hotham's removal emphasized the problems of distant communication. In mid-November 1795 the two men's ships were little more than a hundred miles apart, and a change in command was an important matter; yet the first news to reach *Agamemnon* was an unofficial report. 'I believe it is true', Nelson said, hoping that under the temporary leadership of Admiral Sir Hyde Parker, his squadron of eight frigates ('certainly too small for its duty') would be strengthened with at least two 74-gun ships. Instead, the exact opposite happened: 'the moment Sir Hyde Parker took the command of the fleet, he reduced it [the squadron] to nothing, only one frigate and a brig'. The coast was almost literally clear; and whether by coincidence or design, that was the moment – 23 November 1795 – the French army chose to rout the Austrians at Loano and take possession of Vado Bay.

With a certain grudging admiration, Nelson observed that 'the French fight on shore like our seamen; they never stop, and know not the word halt.' Lucky or not, their timing had been impeccable; only four days after their resounding victory (which the Austrians called a mere check in their own advance), the new British commander-in-chief arrived on station, brought to the Mediterranean by the frigate *Lively*. It was an apt name: 'to the great joy of some, and the sorrow of others,' everyone in the fleet knew that Admiral Sir John Jervis would blow away the skulking in harbour, back-seat leadership and general inertia which had characterized Hotham's command. However, whether he would be in time to make any difference to events on shore was another question, and one which could only be answered in the spring.

He soon learned all that was necessary, including the news that by the first week of January the commander of his inshore squadron would have *Agamemnon* 'as fit for sea as a rotten ship can be.' For months Nelson had been saying that 'poor *Agamemnon* is nearly as worn out as her captain; we must both soon be laid up to repair', and he was not exaggerating – they had been almost constantly at sea for very nearly three years, often under fire, exposed to every kind of weather from blazing heat to freezing gales. When Nelson first wrote to Jervis, *Agamemnon*'s frame was only held together by huge hawsers tied around her hull amidships, and when eventually she was refitted, every single part of her masts, yards, sails and rigging had to be repaired or replaced.

She sailed a few days later than planned from Leghorn to St Florent, arriving on 19 January. That same day, captain and admiral met. Nelson said a little later that Sir John then 'was a perfect stranger to me', which was not absolutely accurate: some years before, at a brief chance encounter, their mutual friend Captain Locker had introduced the two. One may guess that Nelson did not presume to remind him, and whether Jervis remembered it or not, it was not the kind of connection that would count much on its own. What did count was that when they met in St Florent, both officers instantly recognized a like mind. Within minutes Jervis offered Nelson the choice of either the 74-gun *Zealous* or the 90-gun *St George*. Despite everything, Nelson still could not bring himself to give up *Agamemnon*, and said so. Jervis dropped the subject at once, instead asking Nelson all manner of questions about the fleet, its morale, the station, the state of the enemy, the prospects for the future and the best approach. Nelson was surprised no one else seemed to have told him, but gave his answers – whereupon Jervis asked if he would have any objection to continue serving under him if he, Nelson, became an admiral. Quite the contrary, Nelson replied; he would be proud to do so.

With that, he was sent at once on an independent command, directed to prevent any landing of sea-borne French troops on the coast of Italy. Writing home to Fanny, he said that Jervis 'seems at present to consider me more as an associate, than as a subordinate officer, for I am acting without any orders.' In another letter to her, he added: 'When I reflect that I have had the unbounded confidence of three commanders-in-chief, I cannot but feel a conscious pride, and that I possess abilities.' There are three key words: confidence, ability, pride. He knew he deserved the trust given him. Others in the fleet were surprised he was sent off so quickly, 'and', he told Fanny, 'I fancy there was some degree of envy attached to the surprise; for one captain told me, "You did just as you pleased in Lord Hood's time, the same in Admiral Hotham's, and now again with Sir John Jervis; it makes no difference to you who is commander-in-chief."' Without telling

Fanny his exact words (which was probably just as well), Nelson did say that he 'returned a pretty strong answer to this speech.'

Inside a month Jervis made his own view absolutely clear, though already there was no mistaking it. 'He asked me if I had heard any more of my promotion; I told him, no; his answer was, "You must have a larger ship, for we cannot spare you, either as Captain or Admiral."' Nelson was thirty-seven years old then, and Jervis sixty. Jervis survived to be eighty-eight; Nelson had only ten years of life remaining. But from the first moments of that January meeting in St Florent, each felt complete confidence in the other, and another enduring friendship began; and under those two men, the epic victories of the Mediterranean campaign were achieved.

13

'They live like brothers'

HE WAS LATE for the wedding. He was younger than the bride; she had been born, raised and married in the West Indies. Now, a widowed mother awaiting her new husband, her feelings were mixed, for she knew she did not love him much. Suddenly he arrived, and was angry to find that during the wait, the official who would marry them had fallen asleep. He shook the man awake, saying, 'Come on – marry us quickly.' The man struggled up and did as he was told, so quickly that it could hardly be called a ceremony.

'General Buonaparte, citizen, do you consent to take as your lawful wife Madame Beauharnais, here present, to keep faith with her and to observe conjugal fidelity?'

'Citizen, I do.'

'Madame Beauharnais, citizen, do you consent to take as your lawful husband General Buonaparte, here present, to keep faith with him and to observe conjugal fidelity?'

'Citizen, I do.'

'General Buonaparte and Madame Beauharnais, the law unites you.'

The date was 9 March 1796. After a two-day honeymoon spent reading six books on the military history and geography of north Italy, the twenty-six-year-old general left his new wife, boarded a light, fast carriage and began the journey from Paris to the Alps, there to take command of 41,750 underfed, underarmed, ragged and resentful men: the Army of Italy.

Thirteen years earlier, he had wanted to be a sailor, and had been recommended for the service. Pay was low, but his father had been short of money at the time, and it would ease the family finances; so with his schoolmaster's help, the young teenager had written and posted a letter asking to join the most successful navy in the world.

The letter duly arrived in London; but it appears the British Admiralty never bothered to reply.

At Leghorn, on the east side of the Gulf of Genoa, Midshipman William Hoste wrote a genial little letter to his family: 'Our Commodore does not like to be idle. I suppose your curiosity is excited by the word *Commodore* Nelson. It gives me infinite pleasure to be able to relieve it by informing you that our good Captain has had this additional mark of distinction conferred upon him, which, I daresay you will agree with me, his merit richly deserves. His Broad Pendant is now flying; therefore I must beg my dear father to draw an additional cork.'

The appointment was dated 27 March 1796. On the same day, 160 miles away at Nice, on the west side of the gulf, Napoleon issued his first order to the Army of Italy, a rousing challenge and appeal: 'The Government owes you much, but can do nothing for you. Your patience, the courage which has carried you among these rocks, do you honour ... I will lead you into the most fertile plains in the world, where you shall find great towns, rich provinces – within your grasp, glory, honour, wealth! Soldiers of Italy! Shall you be found wanting in constancy, in courage?'

Commodore Nelson, meanwhile, worked out what would happen next. In Genoa, 'the French, and not the Genoese, are masters of the country', and he was already certain that unless they meant to abandon the war, the French would move further into Italy. Leghorn, the prime source of British supply and main link between the allied sea and land forces, would become an obvious target. Yet even if French forces captured it, 'we are not to despair ... in fourteen days from their entry, if the allied powers unite heartily, we should take them all prisoners.' Both for the sailors of Britain and the soldiers of France, control of supply lines was a critical element of this stage of the war. If the Austrians could hold the land, the British navy could hold the Ligurian sea, covering Italy's north-west coasts; if not, it might have to be abandoned. By the same token, if the navy could prevent sea-borne supplies reaching the French when they began their advance, the Austrians – now under General Beaulieu – would be better able to resist. Much depended on the Austrian armies, and much on the British navy as well; and both spent much time in blaming the other for all that went wrong that summer.

On 11 April Napoleon's attacks began: victories in the foothills of the Alps, at Montenotte, Ceva, Millesimo and Dego; a hundred-mile sweep across the plain of Piedmont to the conquest of Lodi; and on 15 May, onward to Milan, where he was presented with the keys of the city. Less than five weeks after opening the campaign, he wrote proudly to the revolutionary government, the Directory in Paris: 'The Tricolour flies over all the towns of Lombardy.' To his pain and astonishment, their reply informed him that henceforward he must share the command with another general, François Kellermann. 'I am sure that one bad general is better than two good ones', he wrote back, and added: 'I cannot give the country the service it sorely needs unless you have entire and absolute confidence in me.' They gave it him: he retained sole command, and at once moved swiftly south, sending one division into the papal states and another, curving westwards through the Appenines below Florence, into the plains of Tuscany. Leghorn was only seventy miles ahead.

Hearing that, from every conquered city, the French demanded not only supplies and money but works of art as well, Nelson was disbelieving. 'What a race of people!', he snorted. 'But', he added honestly, 'they have done wonders.' The same could not be said of their opponents: Piedmontese, Sardinians, Austrians were all deeply disconcerted by the speed with which Napoleon's armies moved, by the Corsican's mountain-bred instinct for terrain, and by his inspirational power of leadership – a power he himself was only just discovering. Men fight best when they have a single leader and a simple purpose which everyone shares and understands. General Buonaparte inspired the Army of Italy with one of the oldest motives: greed, and the desire for conquest, masquerading as honour. It worked, and the more it worked, the more it went on working – 'Where or when', Nelson asked Jervis, 'is the progress of these people to be stopped? If the Emperor [of Austria] has not troops to stop them, peace seems the only alternative.'

Collingwood thought otherwise: 'So far from any prospect of peace, the plot seems to thicken, as if the most serious part of the war were but beginning.' Blockading Toulon with Jervis, the successes of the French army seemed to him 'quite miraculous ... the Austrians have failed everywhere'. But apart from the blockade of warships, the record at sea was little better. During May, Nelson patrolled the Gulf of Genoa in 'extraordinary weather – fogs, heavy swells, and calms'. Close inshore, sheltered by land batteries and shoal waters, French supply convoys of small merchantmen sneaked out of Toulon and scurried by with impunity. To his chagrin, Nelson found that 'because our fleet saw them', British allies on land assumed 'it was very possible for us to stop their course.'

Although he sympathized ('They know little of what a fleet can do, and therefore are in some measure excusable'), he also had to explain the limitations of his ships again and again. 'Our fleet is sent here to oppose the French at sea; and at the present time, should the admiral – in order to stop a tartan [the small coasters] or two, or a hundred – lose two or three sail of the line, or get them dismounted by a gun half a mile inland, the enemy would then be as much masters of the seas, as it appears they now are of the land, and Italy would be lost without a blow.' Without the Royal Navy there, 'Tuscany, Naples, Rome, Sicily, &c., would have fallen as fast as [the French] ships would have sailed along the coast: our fleet is the only protector at present of those countries.'

For those on land it was a difficult argument to understand or accept: they saw only sea-borne supplies passing almost unmolested, and heard from the interior only confused and frightening reports of lightning war. 'The Sardinians are worn out, and sue for peace,' Collingwood noted with dismay. 'Thus drop off our allies.' And on the day Napoleon entered Milan, Nelson – after more complaints from the allies on shore – put to Jervis a question that was starting to press at the back of every naval mind: 'Do you really think we are of any use here? If not, we may serve our country much more by being in other places. The Levant and coast of Spain cry aloud for ships, and they are, I fancy, employed to no purpose here; for unless the Austrians get possession of a point of land, *we cannot stop the coasting trade.*'

There was only one small success to cheer him and the allies: on 30 May, off Oneglia, his small squadron spied a convoy close inshore. Anchoring in less than four fathoms, his ships and boats attacked and captured it. The convoy was carrying brandy, cannon and mortars ('wonderfully fine, thirteen and a half inch') – and papers. 'I have got the charts of Italy sent by the Directory to Buonaparte,' Nelson told Jervis, 'also Mallebois' *Wars in Italy*, Vauban's *Attack and Defence of Places*, and Prince Eugene's *History*; all sent for the general. If Buonaparte is ignorant, the Directory, it would appear, wish to instruct him; pray God he may remain ignorant.'

Of course Nelson knew it would hardly make a scrap of difference overall, but it was a satisfying farewell to *Agamemnon*. The ship really had come to the end of her useful life without major refit – even he could no longer deny it. There was only one other 64 in the fleet,

Diadem, and when he left *Agamemnon* for the last time, he noticed with pleasure that in spite of all she had been through with him, *Agamemnon* was still the better sailer.

He could not avoid emotion at the end. Hardly anyone can, on leaving a ship, and he and *Agamemnon*, and the old Agamemnons, had voyaged many thousands of miles together, and endured much. Years later, he still spoke and wrote about her with affection; and by chance, she joined him again in his last battle, at Trafalgar. Now, though, he was embarking almost on a new life: the 74-gun *Captain* – a third-rate, a ship capable of standing in any line of battle.

The town of Leghorn dates from the year AD 891. It began to be used as a port in the thirteenth century, and had a chequered history of ownership, being sold by the Spanish to the Genoese and by them to the Florentines, until, in its eight hundredth anniversary year, 1691, it became a free and neutral port. So it remained for a further 105 years; and then, on 28 June 1796, 'the French took possession of the town about one o'clock, and immediately fired on the *Inconstant*'.

Nelson had heard of the French advance five days previously, in Genoa, and weighed at once: there was a large English contingent in the free port. Calm airs meant it took him two days to cover the hundred-mile distance, but, when he arrived on 25 June, he found that in spite of 'a most terrible bustle and noise – all packing up and getting on board the ships', those same calms had allowed the evacuation to proceed rapidly. Forty merchantmen, laden with property and civilians, were already moving out, shepherded by the frigate HMS *Inconstant*, and all under the able direction of Nelson's friend and junior colleague, Captain Thomas Fremantle, RN.

Over by Toulon, the ascetic Collingwood believed that 'if we are cut off from the flesh-kettles of Leghorn', it would be no bad thing. Too many sailors had fallen prey to its pleasures – including, of course, Nelson; it was Fremantle's Leghorn diary which contained the tell-tale notes of 'Nelson and his Dolly'. What became of 'Dolly' is unknown; but from the evacuation of Leghorn came a valuable legacy – the diaries of Betsey and Eugenia Wynne, two pretty and vivacious teenage girls temporarily on board *Inconstant* with their parents, their other sisters and a large number of naval men. Seventeen-year-old Betsey, who spoke French and Italian as well as she spoke English, had been annoyed that 'the French obliged us to run away,' But she was delighted with *Inconstant* – 'so fine, so clean and comfortable, so many civil persons' – and slowly, over the course of the summer, found herself much indebted to the French. The flight from Leghorn changed her life: she fell in love with Captain Fremantle, her rescuer, and he with her. For more than a year she remained with the Royal Navy in the Mediterranean and Atlantic, writing daily about the people she met, the places she visited and the events she saw, including the action in which Nelson lost his right arm; and when Captain and Mrs Fremantle returned to England in the autumn of 1797, they took with them the wounded admiral, who never expected to serve his country again.

In the last days of June 1796, however, while Commodore Nelson's squadron instituted a close blockade of Leghorn, the evacuees withdrew to Corsica. The Wynne family travelled in a merchantman, very uncomfortably. On shore at San Fiorenzo, Betsey began to get to know the service and officers who would form the framework and backdrop of the rest of her long life. Her upbringing had been erratic – she had four sisters, and her father, deciding he could never otherwise afford to marry them all off, sold his estate when she was small. Ever since, the family and their retinue had been engaged in a permanent tour of Europe. Suddenly, unexpectedly, and for the first time, Betsey found herself with people whose lives were disciplined and full of purpose, and she was enchanted: 'They live like brothers,' she wrote admiringly, 'and share all they have.'

The words are very close to Nelson's later, more famous phrase – 'I had the happiness to command a band of brothers.' Betsey may have been one of the first to put it into words, and one may easily imagine her saying something on those lines to Fremantle, or to Nelson himself, or even to an assembled group of officers at dinner. They would have listened, for being attractive, refreshing and very good company, she was popular. No doubt they would have been flattered; they would hardly have been embarrassed – later, after his first great victory, Nelson called his captains 'my darling children', and none was the least embarrassed by that. Coming in from outside, Betsey could see what was happening: under Jervis, the captains of the Mediterranean fleet were becoming a brotherhood, bonded by skill, experience, mutual respect and a common cause. Maybe they had not thought of it in quite that way before; but from about this time they all did, and Nelson most of all. And the concept – so suitable to his nature – became an important, conscious element in his conduct of the war.

*

Trying to forestall any further French advance, the island of Elba was taken over by British forces under Nelson's command on 10 July 1796. He admired its fine natural harbour, Porto Ferraio – 'for its size, the most complete port in the world.' Nearly eighteen years later, another British warship, the frigate *Undaunted*, anchored in the same bay and brought Napoleon to his first exile. His official title then was 'Emperor and Sovereign of the Isle of Elba'. On first sighting his new empire, all he felt able to say was: 'My island is very small.' So it is, a mere eighteen miles by twelve; but to Nelson it was a useful forward base for the protection of Corsica, and for the blockade of Leghorn which it was hoped might provoke a revolt against the occupying French. Yet as weeks of blockade went by, no revolt materialized. 'Sometimes I hope, as others despair of getting these starved Leghornese to cut the throats of this French crew', he wrote to Collingwood. 'What an idea for a Christian! I hope there is a great latitude for us in the next world ... With a most sincere wish for driving the French to the devil, your good health, an honourable peace, and us safe at home again, I conclude by assuring you, my dear Collingwood, of my unalterable friendship and regard.'

Summer wore on and concern grew that Spain – already at peace with France – might join actively in the war against Britain. Naples was the only remaining ally of consequence to the fleet, but as Collingwood remarked, 'If the French march on into the south of Italy, what can the Neapolitans do but make peace before they come?' Gloomily he added that if such events happened, he did not see how the British fleet could carry on the war single-handed – not because of the increased number of enemies, he hastened to say, but because of the difficulty of finding supplies. 'The moment there is a failure in that, we cannot stay here; for the French are equal to us in ships.'

Nelson was more optimistic. 'I have my doubts as to a Spanish war,' he wrote to Jervis, 'and if there should be one, with your management I have no fears. Their fleet is ill-manned and worse officered, I believe, and they are slow.' That letter was written on 16 August, the day after he received official confirmation of his rank as commodore, and he ended it on a note of cheerful, prophetic confidence. 'Should the Dons come,' he told his commander-in-chief, 'I shall then hope I may be spared, in my own person, to help make you at least a viscount.'

Three days later an intriguing letter began its journey from Commodore Nelson to Prince William. Nelson assumed that if the Spaniards declared war, they would send a naval squadron to the West Indies, to harass British possessions there. Further, he assumed that a combined French-Spanish fleet would have anything up to thirty-five ships of the line, against the twenty-two Jervis could muster. Nevertheless, 'I will venture my life Sir John Jervis defeats them; I do not mean by a regular battle but by the skill of our admiral, and the activity and spirits of our officers and seamen.' Yet it was more than that: 'This country is the most favourable possible for skill with an inferior fleet ... the winds are so variable that some time in twenty-four hours you must be able to attack a part of a large fleet, and the other will be becalmed, or have a contrary wind'. He does not say, in so many words, that a superior fleet might be deliberately divided by an inferior, and dealt with piecemeal, as he did before Trafalgar; perhaps he was still thinking of two opposing lines ahead, the traditional approach to battle, with part of the enemy line separated by weather and bad luck from the fray. But it is one of the first times that he explains how an inferior fleet can win; and if he did not learn it from Jervis, Jervis would still have agreed, for he never worried much about superior numbers.

In spite of the setbacks, other small things contributed to Nelson's good spirits. One, he admitted to Fanny, was 'all vanity to myself', but he felt it would amuse her. 'A person sent me a letter, directed as follows: "Horatio Nelson, Genoa." On being asked how he could direct in such a manner, his answer was "Sir, there is but one Horatio Nelson in the world." The letter certainly came immediately ... I am known throughout Italy; not a kingdom, or state, where my name will be forgotten.' By then he had been away from England for more than three years. 'You ask me when I shall come home? I believe, when either an honourable peace is made, or a Spanish war which may draw our fleet out of the Mediterranean. God knows', he added wryly, 'I shall come to you not a sixpence richer than when I set out.'

In addition to Elba, the tiny island of Capraia, halfway between Italy and Corsica's northernmost tip, was taken as a secondary base, and on 20 September, returning from its capture to the blockade of Leghorn, Nelson encountered and challenged two Spanish men-of-war. This was a striking example of the diplomatic difficulties, far greater than today, which could face a captain in a sailing navy. The frigates were just about the last warships he or any other British naval officer wanted to see, because nobody in the British Mediterranean fleet knew whether Spain and Britain were at war or not. Nelson suspected strongly that they must be: reports had reached him that English ships were being detained in Spanish ports, and that Spain and France had signed an alliance of offence and defence. But there had been no confirmation. If the reports were untrue and he opened fire, he would precipitate a conflict which, for all he knew, politicians might have otherwise avoided. Under the circumstances, that was a risk he did not want to take, and so he did the only other thing possible: he asked the Spanish captains.

Both protested vehemently that the two nations were not at war, or if they were, they (the captains) knew nothing about it, and wanted only to go into Leghorn. Refusing to allow them to do so, Nelson instead requested them to accompany him to Bastia, to speak to Sir Gilbert Elliot, the British viceroy there. This they declined, saying they would rather sail back to Cartagena, find out what was happening, and inform Nelson later.

In fact, Spain and England were at war, and had been since 8 September – four days after the Spanish captains alleged they had sailed from Cartagena. They may well have been telling the truth, but from the roundabout route they had taken, through the Straits of Bonifacio, it seemed quite obvious that they 'had cause for not wishing to meet any English ships of war.' However, Nelson had asked them to tell the truth, on their honour. With great misgiving, he assumed they had done so, and without firm information, there was little more he could do short of opening fire. So he let them return in peace to Spain – or at least in the general direction of Spain – and wrote to tell Jervis all about it.

The commander-in-chief approved his action, but both men felt it deeply when, just eleven days later, Jervis received confirmation of a state of war with Spain, with its starting date, 'I have orders to attack ships of war of that nation, in fleets, or singly, wherever I meet them', he told the Corsican viceroy. 'How unfortunate that Commodore Nelson could not have been put in possession of this in time!'

Late in September, Collingwood wrote again to his father-in-law, heading his letter, 'HMS *Excellent*, still off Toulon' – he had been on blockade for twenty-four continuous weeks. 'While we keep it,' he said, 'the Mediterranean is a sea only for our friends: yet I fear our friends will have nothing to do here soon, and if the war goes on, I have no doubt the French will assault the coasts of England, and we shall be wanted nearer home.' For all Nelson's personal optimism about the campaign, the evacuation of Leghorn had marked only the first step on a slow retreat down the Mediterranean. On his thirty-eighth birthday, 29 September 1796, he arrived in Bastia, and there found dejection: now the Spanish fleet was allied to France, the order had arrived from London to evacuate Corsica as soon as possible – and Nelson was to command the operation. He was bitterly shocked, remembering how the Agamemnons had slaved to capture the island; how Serocold and Mrs Moutray's son had died in the effort; how he himself had lost an eye, for which he had yet to receive compensation. 'We are all preparing to leave the Mediterranean, a measure which I cannot approve,' he told Fanny. 'They at home do not know what this fleet is capable of performing: anything and everything ... I lament our present orders in sackcloth and ashes.'

But there was little time for lamentation, and much to do: the viceroy and his family; other British civilians; troops; upwards of six hundred French and Corsican royalists; finally, some £200,000 worth of British property – all had to be removed to the comparative safety of Elba, or out of the Mediterranean altogether, as swiftly and secretly as possible.

It was a remarkably successful operation, in spite of gales which drove all the transports out of harbour, and Corsicans who suddenly decided they had better show as much support as possible for the French republic. Nelson was obliged to inform them twice that if there were any obstructions or delays, he would instantly batter the city down. Since all they really wanted (quite understandably) was to avoid being treated as collaborators by the next set of invaders, in the end he had only to promise 'a disagreeable visit, if I had any more complaints', and Bastia became more quiet and orderly than any of the British had ever seen it. 'It was clear', Nelson told Prince Willam, 'that dread of the French was more predominant in their minds than dislike of us.'

The actual loading of ships began on the morning of 15 October and continued day and night. On the 18th, French troops landed thirty-six miles from Bastia; at midnight on the 19th, the last British troops left the citadel; at 1 a.m. the first French troops entered it; at dawn on the 20th, 'not one man being left ashore', Nelson left the island; and as he wrote to Locker a few days later, 'I have seen the first and the last of Corsica.'

A Spanish fleet of twenty-six ships of the line entered the Mediterranean and approached Toulon. Its commander was Don Juan de Langara, and he had been there before – he was the man who, three years earlier, had arrived just in time to share the credit for its bloodless conquest with Lord Hood. Now he added his ships to those of the French, and the combination was the largest fleet of men-of-war Toulon had ever held – thirty-eight major vessels and their attendants.

When Nelson wrote that there would be twenty-two British liners to oppose them, he was including a squadron of seven, under Admiral Robert Man, whose arrival was daily expected; Jervis actually had only fifteen on hand. Now, at the beginning of December, Collingwood brought his father-in-law up to date with events.

'Our situation has been rather critical', he wrote, with some under-statement. 'The forces of France and Spain are very superior to ours, and after the evacuation of Corsica, we were left without a port, except Porto Ferraio, which was, of all places in the world, the most dangerous for us to be in. Few as we were, I think we could have managed them at sea well enough; but had they ever blocked us up in Porto Ferraio, our ruin, as it appears to me, would have been inevitable. But Sir John Jervis has excellent judgment at this game, and I never had an apprehension that he would offer them a checkmate, which such a move would have been if they had skill to take it.'

With the exception of Troubridge's *Culloden*, left to keep a distant watch on Toulon, Jervis had concentrated his fleet in San Fiorenzo. There they had waited 'with the utmost impatience' for Admiral Man. 'We wore our eyes in looking westward from the mountain tops, but we looked in vain ... No Man appeared; and as the enemy began to annoy us from the shore, we sailed on the 2nd of November.'

On 1 December the fleet arrived at Gibraltar, from where Colling-wood was writing – 'and', he continued indignantly, 'judge of our surprise to find that Admiral Man and his squadron had gone off to England ... The thing is incomprehensible, and God knows by what arguments he will justify it.' In fact he never did, or if he did, no record was made; yet although he knew the Spanish fleet was at large, and although Jervis had ordered him to rejoin, Man took a vote among his captains, and the result was that they all decided to go home. Less than forty years earlier, in 1757, Admiral Byng had been court-martialled, found guilty and (many felt unjustly) shot on his own quarterdeck for failing to drive off a French blockade of Minorca. Man was more fortunate; he was ordered to strike his flag, and was never recalled to service. Many again felt it was unjust, and that he deserved execution far more than Byng had done; for apart from anything else, there was not a single British ship of the line left in the Mediterranean, and now Napoleon was its master.

14

'A victory ... is very essential'

ONE LAST LONG voyage had to be made into the abandoned sea. Jervis had not intended to desert Elba, but to return as soon as Man's squadron was found. Apart from the consideration of British property and people (among them the Wynne family), several frigates were still there, including Fremantle's *Inconstant*. Without Man's ships, however, Jervis could not again take up his station, and from London the order came to evacuate the island, eleven hundred miles away. To oversee the operation, Nelson was his natural choice.

At the same time, the Spanish fleet and part of the French fleet left Toulon. De Langara's twenty-six ships of the line and ten frigates made their destination, Cartagena, without difficulty. The French ships, five of the line and three frigates under Vice Admiral Pierre Villeneuve, were ordered to go through the Straits of Gibraltar and on to Brest. Villeneuve did not know that fifteen British liners lay in Gibraltar Bay: he would pass within sight of them. But Nelson once observed of the French that, being the devil's children, they had the devil's luck; and as Villeneuve's squadron approached the straits a gale sprang up from the east, speeding them through, while Jervis watched in rage upon the Rock, unable to send his own ships out.

Three British ships were driven ashore by the gale. One was only slightly damaged; the second, much more severely so; and the third, *Courageux*, was totally wrecked – 464 of the 593 in her company were killed. It was a great misfortune that her captain, Ben Hallowell, was on shore attending a court martial when the gale blew up. Because of the weather, he was not allowed to return to her; yet his junior officers were not sufficiently experienced to save her. Nelson's 74-gun *Captain* could not now be spared from the reduced force, so, on 15 December, he shifted his flag to the frigate *Minerva*, and accompanied by the frigate *Blanche*, sailed back into the Mediterranean.

Minerva was a prize frigate, captured from the French. Her present captain, George Cockburn, had previously commanded the frigate *Meleager*, and had brought his tall, dour, heavily built first lieutenant with him: Thomas Masterman Hardy, now approaching his twenty-eighth birthday. From July 1795 to August 1796, *Meleager* had served in the Gulf of Genoa under Nelson's direct orders, and though there is no record at all of the place and time when he and Hardy first met, it is very likely that the event took place some time in those months. If it did not, Nelson must have heard Hardy's name then at least. Certainly, when preparing to transfer to *Minerva*, he would have learned the names of his new officers; and within four days of leaving Gibraltar, Hardy impressed himself on Nelson's mind.

They did not know of the Spanish fleet's presence in Cartagena, any more than Villeneuve had known of their presence in Gibraltar. Passing the enemy port during the night of 19 December, they made out two frigates, and attacked. After a three-hour battle both Spanish vessels were taken, and Hardy, with a fellow lieutenant, was put in charge of one, the 40-gun *Santa Sabina*. Her captain (who, everyone remarked, had fought extremely well), was found to be Don Jacobo Stuart, great-grandson of King James II, King of England a century before. Nelson rather enjoyed capturing people like that, and before long was able to make very practical use of his distinguished prisoner.

A few hours after the surrender, Nelson had suddenly to break off the report he was writing for Jervis. More Spanish vessels had been sighted. At first it was only one, which made away after a skirmish, but at dawn, two ships of the line and two frigates bore down. Both British frigates, partly crippled, had to cut their prizes loose. After some time attacking *Minerva*, part of the pursuit altered towards *Santa Sabina*; and both Hardy, his colleague Lieutenant Culverhouse and their prize crew were taken prisoner. 'An unpleasant tale', Nelson admitted to Jervis – rather than capturing two frigates, he had lost two officers and forty men, and for the time being could only leave them to their fate.

After that setback, the remainder of the voyage to Elba passed uneventfully; and in the island he discovered that despite his own troubled conscience about the affair, other people's view of it was quite different. The English population were delighted to see him, and even more so when they found he had been in action – any was better than none. He arrived on Christmas Day, and, carrying on as nearly normal a life as possible, the English were preparing a ball. Nelson was instantly invited to it; and when he entered the ballroom, the band (he told his brother William) struck up 'one particular tune'. Perhaps through modesty, he refused to name it; but a fair guess is that it was either 'Rule Britannia', or 'Hail, the Conquering Hero', which was a very popular tune – and one which he would hear played at his entrance many times in the future. But whatever the tune, he reflected that though he had lost Hardy, the fight 'was what I know the English like', and that he would be mentioned in the Naval Gazette.

Boxing Day brought unforeseen difficulties: Sir Gilbert Elliot, ex-viceroy of Corsica, was away on mainland Italy, trying to find out the intentions of those states which had not capitulated to Napoleon; and General de Burgh, commander of Elba's army garrison, refused to let the soldiers be evacuated without a military order. Nelson said his own orders were unmistakably clear, and he would proceed with the naval and civilian evacuation. As a first step he ordered Fremantle to go and collect Sir Gilbert from Naples. That voyage had the happiest of results, for the Wynnes sailed with Fremantle. Everyone knew that he and Betsey Wynne loved each other; yet Fremantle had no independent income, and without it her father would not consent to the match. They were in Naples only forty-eight hours, but in that time Fremantle (who could not trust himself to speak) wrote to Mr Wynne; Mr Wynne changed his mind, to the extent of giving the couple not only his blessing but also £8,000 (about thirty years' worth of Fremantle's pay); and Sir William and Lady Hamilton insisted that the wedding should take place in the Embassy, with Emma, very much in her element, taking charge of all arrangements.

'Sir,' Nelson wrote to the Captain General of Cartagena, 'The fortune of war put La Sabina into my possession after she had been most gallantly defended; the fickle Dame returned her to you with some of my officers and men in her.'

Don Jacobo Stuart had been well looked after, and now Nelson hoped to exchange him for Hardy, Culverhouse and the men. With the exception of Inconstant, left to protect the army garrison, the naval garrison was evacuated from Elba on 29 January 1797, proceeding on independent routes to lessen the risk of capture. Nelson took Minerva past Cartagena, to see what the Spanish fleet was doing. They were not there. He hastened on to Gibraltar, arriving on 10 February, and found that Jervis's fleet was not there, either. However, Hardy and the others were – the Spaniards had agreed to the exchange.

Swiftly welcoming them back on board, Nelson learned from them that the Spanish fleet had passed westwards, believed to be making for Brest, and that the day after he himself had sailed for Elba, Jervis had sailed to take station off Cadiz. There he could block the Spanish advance. Nelson wished to sail at once. Above all, he did not want to miss a fleet action – especially one which would be his first under a worthy commander-in-chief – but contrary winds forced him to wait a whole day. He could only hope he would not be too late.

A Spanish frigate and two ships of the line were lying nearby, just within their territorial waters. On 11 February they saw *Minerva* depart, and promptly began to chase. *Minerva* cleared for action, a process which Sir Gilbert, the ex-viceroy, and Colonel John Drinkwater, his aide-de-camp, watched with interest. Drinkwater was a successful author on military matters, and was taking notes on everything he saw: all Nelson's biographers are indebted to him for this last of his famous Mediterranean sketches. He asked the commodore if action was possible. 'Very possible', Nelson replied, and looked up at his broad pendant. 'But before the Dons get hold of that bit of bunting, I will have a struggle with them, and sooner than give up the frigate, I'll run her ashore.'

With this less than reassuring news the party adjourned for lunch. As they were eating and Drinkwater was asking Hardy about his imprisonment, a man fell overboard. Hardy jumped up, ran to a boat which was already being lowered, leapt in, and in minutes was carried far astern on the rapid eastward current, towards the pursuing Spanish ships. There was no sign of the missing man, and the boat's crew attempted to pull back to *Minerva*. But they could make no way against the current; the Spaniards were closing; and when the leading ship was nearly in gunshot of *Minerva*, Nelson exclaimed, 'By God, I'll not lose Hardy! Back the mizzen topsail.'

This slowed *Minerva*'s progress, enabling the boat to catch up. The Spaniards came closer too, and Drinkwater and Sir Gilbert were sure that battle must begin; but to their surprise, the Spaniards suddenly shortened sail as well, and fell back proportionately, while Hardy and his men were rescued for the second time.

The only explanation for the Spanish reaction was that Nelson's rashness made them think he could see the British fleet ahead; everyone in *Minerva* was lucky to have got away with it. Apart from that rashness, the other reason the story is always told is to show how fond

Nelson already was of Hardy. But it does not necessarily follow: in the two months in *Minerva*, he had lost Hardy once already, which was more than enough. He was not about to make a habit of losing anyone. If nothing else, though, the episode set the two men firmly in each other's minds, and Hardy knew at first hand that Nelson was a leader who would take risks, but who could be depended upon completely.

After her close shave, *Minerva* regained her lead, drew away, and with dusk escaped. The night became foggy, and a much stranger adventure began. One by one a multitude of large shapes appeared vaguely in the damp surrounding darkness. Drinkwater, sleeping lightly, and Sir Gilbert, sleeping very heavily, were in Nelson's cabin. He came in twice, and the second time Drinkwater asked him what was happening. Nelson replied that they were in the middle of either the whole Spanish fleet, or a convoy bound for the West Indies, and if the latter, they would have to make all speed to warn the British over there. Much excited, Drinkwater woke Sir Gilbert, and was somewhat disappointed at his response to the news – 'We are only passengers, and must submit to circumstances', he said, and fell asleep again.

It was indeed the Spanish fleet. With unusual skill and luck, Captain Cockburn traced *Minerva* through its centre without a single challenge. By dawn on 13 February they were far apart, and during the morning, Jervis's fleet was sighted at last. Nelson and Sir Gilbert were rowed over to *Victory*, where Jervis gave them dinner, with the flagship's captain Sir Robert Calder and Ben Hallowell, captain of the wrecked *Courageux*. The information they brought confirmed Jervis's expectations, and Nelson transferred back to *Captain* while Sir Gilbert pleaded with the commander-in-chief to be allowed to enter *Victory* as a volunteer. Jervis would not permit that, but let Elliot wait and watch in the frigate *Lively*, which soon would bear him and the result of the impending battle home to England. All day, there was brisk activity in the British fleet: 'grinding cutlasses, sharpening pikes, flinting pistols among the boarders, and fitting well-oiled gunlocks on our immense artillery by the gunners.' As the standard preparations went on, William Hoste noticed something else. Now battle was certain, everyone was eager and completely confident, and it showed. 'The men and officers', he said, 'seemed to me to look taller, and the anticipation of victory was legibly written on each brow.'

As night came on, the wind began to blow from the west. Gradually, on a misty sea, the fleet fell silent; and soon – like a long-awaited promise borne over the dark waters – the sailors in each patient, listening vessel could hear the signal guns of the Spanish warships.

Perched high on the main-yard ready for the dawn, the signal lieutenant of *Barfleur* was the first to catch a glimpse of them – looming out of the fog, he said, like Beachy Head. As it cleared he saw them better. 'By my soul,' he shouted down to the quarterdeck, 'they are thumpers! I can distinctly make out *four* tiers of ports in one of them, bearing an admiral's flag.'

From the quarterdeck, Midshipman Hoste heard a new cry echo through every part of the ship – '"Up all hammocks, ahoy!" . . . Some were sent to barricade the tops, while the remainder were stowed with unusual care as a bulwark around the upper decks.'

That day – 14 February, St Valentine's Day, 1797 – Admiral Jervis's fleet again contained fifteen sail of the line, as it had before the terrible gale in the Straits of Gilbraltar. But it had only been at that strength for eight days, for, after the gale, further disasters had befallen it. At Christmas, while Nelson was dancing in Elba, the rest of the fleet had celebrated the season in Lisbon – with the exception of *Bombay Castle*, impossibly hard aground at the mouth of the River Tagus. On the fleet's New Year return downriver, another ship suffered a similar accident and had to go back to Lisbon for repairs. With these losses, and the two gale-damaged vessels out of action, only ten were left to take their cruising station off Cape St Vincent, the south-west corner of Portugal. It was not until 6 February, following the unexpected, scandalous reappearance of Admiral Man's squadron in England, that Jervis finally received some of the reinforcement he needed so urgently, and then it was only five ships. But he was pleased with the Admiralty's choice of captains – 'I thank you very much for sending me so good a batch', he wrote. 'They are a valuable addition to my excellent stock.'

'Of all the fleets I ever saw,' Nelson had once observed, 'I never beheld one in point of officers and men equal to Sir John Jervis's, who is a commander-in-chief able to lead them to glory.' Few people would have envied the commander-in-chief's responsibility that morning: the stakes for which he was playing were very high indeed. The Dutch fleet had joined with the French in Brest, and had already attempted an invasion of Ireland. Admiral Lord Bridport, brother of Admiral Hood, was in charge of the Brest blockade, but his Channel fleet had been driven back to England by bad weather, and it was only the same weather which had prevented a successful Irish landing. If the Spanish fleet should also penetrate to Brest, it would make a formidable combination. Jervis was fully aware of the possibility – 'A victory', he remarked as the weather brightened, 'is very essential to England at this moment.'

Yet, like most of his officers and men, he had no more than commonsense worries; he had made his will the night before; and as daylight revealed his fleet in two perfect columns, he knew it could never be more ready to fight. The numbers and disposition of the enemy gradually became apparent, reported to him moment by moment as he walked with Calder and Hallowell on *Victory*'s quarterdeck, and his response has often been remembered as a classic illustration of a determined admiral.

'There are eight sail of the line, Sir John.'

'Very well, sir.'

'There are twenty sail of the line, Sir John.'

'Very well, sir.'

'There are twenty-five sail of the line, Sir John.'

'Very well, sir.'

'There are twenty-seven sail of the line, Sir John – near double our own.'

'Enough, sir, no more of that! The die is cast, and if there are fifty sail I will go through them.'

Ben Hallowell – Canadian by birth, hugely built, immensely strong and with the face of an experienced boxer – could not prevent himself crying out: 'That's right, Sir John, that's right!' Giving the commander-in-chief an ox-like slap on the back, he added with glee: 'And, by God, we'll give them a damned good licking!'

Determination, confidence, enthusiasm; and also that phrase – odd, considering the *Fighting Instructions* – 'I will go through them.' At the Saints in 1782, Rodney had ignored the convention of opposing lines ahead and had gone through the French line to win; at an inconclusive action against a Franco-Spanish fleet off Toulon in 1744, Hawke had left the line of battle, in defiance of orders, and taken the only prize of the day. Jervis knew all about these men, and liked their unconventional approaches: 'Hawke,' he said, 'when he ran out of the line, sickened me of tactics.' Today, as he understood the shape of the enemy, Jervis too, decided to ignore convention. Indeed, he had to, for two reasons. First was the disparity of numbers. Dividing the enemy, and engaging one part before the other was able to assist it, would reduce that.

Second was the simple fact that the Spanish were already in two distinct, loosely formed groups, nine ships in the van, eighteen in the rear. It would take them much time and effort to form a line ahead; he would save them the trouble. 'The circumstances of war in these seas', he commented judiciously, 'required a considerable degree of enterprise', and, forming his expert fleet into a single line ahead, he sent it straight towards the gap between the Spanish groups.

'We saw them very much scattered,' Collingwood told his wife later, 'while we were a compact little body. We flew to them as a hawk to his prey, passed through them … and then tacked upon their largest division.' Jervis and *Victory* were slightly forward of the centre of the line. In the van of the British attack was *Culloden*, commanded by Thomas Troubridge, who had known Nelson for twenty-five years – they had been to the East Indies together when they were still virtually children, and Troubridge was one of Jervis's favourite captains. As *Culloden* bore down, her first lieutenant pointed out that a collision with one of the Spaniards seemed imminent. 'Can't help that, Griffiths', said Troubridge. 'Let the weakest fend off.' Nelson and *Captain* were third from the rear, and in the rear was Collingwood's *Excellent*, a ship already renowned, under his captaincy, for its outstanding gunnery. This day's battle would show his skill again so well that the ship's name was given to the Royal Navy's gunnery school.

Yet though their crews had large numbers of soldiers and raw recruits, the Spaniards were not incompetent. Since Cartagena they had been under the command of Admiral Jose de Cordoba, in the world's largest warship, *Santissima Trinidad* – the 132-gun thumper picked out early in the morning. 'Four complete decks', wrote Collingwood enviously – 'such a ship as I never saw before.' De Cordoba swiftly understood Jervis's intention, and altered course to make his eighteen-ship rear group sail opposite and parallel to the British line. Jervis also altered, tacking his ships in succession: the line ahead began to form a wide V on the ocean, its left-hand arm being the leading edge. But, with the wind blowing across the top of the V, de Cordoba meant to bear over it to reunite all his ships. That was entirely possible, given the time it would take for the British line to re-form; and the Spanish intention, the risk of its success, and the only possible response all became clear in at least two British minds almost simultaneously.

'At 12.50 p.m.,' the log in *Captain* recorded, 'the Commodore ordered the ship to be wore [altering course by bringing the stern, rather than the bow, towards the wind] when she was immediately engaged with the *Santissima Trinidad* and 2 other 3-decked ships.' Nelson's dramatic move, breaking out of line in order to cut off the flight of the Spanish admiral, is often remembered as his first great disobedience: certainly it led directly to the 'very essential' British victory that followed, and began his national and international fame. But 'at 12.51 p.m.,' the log in *Victory* recorded, 'General Signal: Take out suitable stations and engage enemy as arriving up in succession.' The times were almost identical. Rather than an immense but crucial disobedience, Nelson anticipated and pre-empted Jervis's order by something up to one minute. This does not diminish the bravery and tactical brilliance of the act. It does show how closely he and Jervis understood each other in professional matters. Troubridge too: when the line had first tacked to follow the Spaniards around, *Culloden* had hoisted the repeating flags and was turning before the signal had reached *Victory*'s masthead. 'Look at Troubridge!' Jervis said then. 'He tacks his ship as if the eyes of all England were upon him!' When Nelson wore out of line seconds ahead of the order, Collingwood quickly followed him, and Calder, Jervis's flag captain, asked if they should be recalled. 'No,' Jervis answered decisively, 'I will not have them recalled. I put my faith in those ships. It is a disgrace they are not supported.'

That too was an odd phrase. Did he realize that a simultaneous turn, instead of a turn in succession, would have kept his whole line up with the Spanish? Did he mean that others should have been as prompt to act before they were ordered? Most of his captains would have known his impatience for convention, yet few would have been quite ready to presume or dare as far as Nelson did. But it did not matter, and does not now, for battle was joined and could no longer be escaped – 'We gave them their Valentines in style', said one of the British gunners. Between them, *Captain*'s immediate opponents carried 512 guns. *Culloden* rapidly joined her; *Excellent* engaged two other ships 'in a masterly style'; and within about fifteen minutes, as one report said, 'the engagement had become close and general' – in other words, utter pandemonium, as every ship found a target and added its own thunderous discharge, fire and smoke to the cataclysm.

Afterwards, everyone at home wanted to know what it had been like. 'Never, I believe, was such an action fought', William Hoste naively told his father, who wrote back asking for 'an accurate account of the action'. Apologizing, William said he could not write more, 'for at that time we were all hurry and confusion', and pointed out that he only wanted the family to know he was alive. Collingwood understood the problem: 'It is a very difficult thing', he said to his father-in-law, 'for those engaged in such a scene to give the detail of the whole, because all the powers they have are occupied in their own part of it.' Even Nelson had no idea how long he and Troubridge fought the leading ships – 'For near an hour, I believe,' he said when asked, 'but do not pretend to be correct as to time.'

To a generation brought up with radar and missiles as the weapons of surface warfare, the physical closeness of these sailing battles remains astonishing; but even at the time people found the sight impressive. Collingwood's first opponent was the 112-gun *San Salvadore del Mundo*; he was 'not farther from her when we began than the length of our garden.' She soon surrendered to his efficient fire, and *Excellent* concentrated on the next, *San Ysidro*, 'so close alongside that a man might jump from one ship to the other. Our fire carried all before it, and in ten minutes she hauled down her colours ... then making all sail, passing between our line and the enemy, we came up with the *San Nicholas* of 80 guns, which happened at the time to be abreast of the *San Josef*, of 112 guns; we did not touch sides, but you could not put a bodkin between us'. They were, in fact, about ten feet apart. It is worth measuring that distance from a wall and imagining the wall as the hull of an enemy ship, its great guns blazing and smoking. Firing directly into a hull virtually touching her own, there was so much power behind *Excellent*'s shot that it burst clean through one ship and into the next; and as they tried to escape, both Spaniards became inextricably entangled with each other. 'My good friend, the Commodore, had been long engaged with those ships,' Collingwood related, 'and I came happily to his relief, for he was dreadfully mauled.'

Nelson described the contest *Captain* and *Culloden* had been enduring as 'apparently, but not really, unequal'. Even so, *Culloden* was crippled and had fallen astern, while *Captain*'s fore topmast had been shot away, along with her wheel, and most of her rigging, 'not a sail, shroud or rope standing'. *Captain* could no longer chase or serve in the line; but Collingwood's intervention, and the collision of the two Spaniards, brought about an event which was never forgotten by anyone who saw it or heard of it: calling for boarders to make ready,

Nelson ordered his captain, Ralph Miller, to put the helm to starboard for another, deliberate collision. In moments all three ships were intertwined.

Edward Berry was the first to board *San Nicholas*, with enormous enthusiasm: it was the first time he had had something definite to do in the battle, for he had recently been promoted from being Nelson's first lieutenant to commander, and, as he did not yet have a ship of his own, was a passenger in *Captain*. Lieutenant Charles Pierson of the 69th Regiment then led his soldiers over; they were serving as marines, as they had done with Rodney at the Battle of the Saints. (Their part in the Battle of Cape St Vincent brought the regiment a second naval honour: the double distinction remains unique in the British Army.) Captain Miller tried to follow the boarders over, but Nelson prevented him – 'No, Miller, I must have that honour' – and all pushed through together, under fire through the internal windows of the Spaniard's cabin, breaking down the doors, swarming over the quarterdeck and poop. Under small arms fire from the next ship, *San Josef*, Berry hauled down the ensign; Nelson ordered men onward to board *San Josef*; and, as he himself leapt over, 'a Spanish Officer came upon the quarterdeck rail, without arms, and said the Ship had surrendered.'

Below decks, the Spanish admiral was dying. His captain knelt on the quarterdeck in front of Nelson and gave him his sword. Taking his hand, Nelson helped him to his feet and asked him to tell his officers and men 'that the Ship had surrendered, which he did; and', Captain Locker and Prince William read, in almost identical letters, 'on the quarterdeck of a Spanish First-rate, extravagant as the story may seem, did I receive the swords of the vanquished Spaniards, which as I received I gave to William Fearney, one of my bargemen, who placed them with the greatest sang-froid under his arm.'

Even Nelson found it a little difficult to credit at first, for in crossing from one defeated ship to another and accepting the surrender of both, he had done something no one had ever done before. His own reaction, and Fearney's phlegmatic gathering up of the swords like so much brushwood, are exactly what most people would have felt and done in the circumstances: hardly able to believe it, but carrying on just as if it happened all the time. Yet even as they were doing it, everyone realized it was something entirely new in naval history, something which would set that battle apart from all others. As soon as they were able, people began to write home about it, and when Collingwood wrote to his wife Sarah, he could have spoken for them all. 'Such a day', he said in dazed relief. 'It was indeed a glorious one, and it seldom falls to the lot of any man to share in such a triumph. First, my love, I am as well as I ever was in my life, and have pretty well got the better of my fatigue. Now for history.'

15

'I am ... useless to my country'

OF COURSE THE fleet loved it. One of Nelson's boarding party pushed his way through and shook the commodore's hand vigorously, exclaiming with apologetic, embarrassed delight that he might never have such a chance again. As *Victory* sailed by in pursuit of the enemy, her crew lined the rails and Jervis led them in cheers. Soon everyone was talking of 'Nelson's Patent Bridge for Boarding First-rates', and someone wrote it all down as a comic recipe from 'Nelson's New Art of Cookery' – the ingredients were a Spanish first-rate and an 80-gun ship, which had to be well battered and basted, without letting the fire go down, until they were 'completely dish'd, fit to set before his Majesty.'

By happy coincidence, Nelson's promotion by seniority from Commodore to Rear Admiral of the Blue was published in Britain a week later, though before anyone at home knew of the battle. With a simple pleasure, Fanny wrote to her husband, 'I never saw anything elevate our Father equal to this'; for the first time, with infinite pride, the Rector was able to address his son as 'My dear Rear Admiral'. A fortnight later, news of the victory reached England, and caused intense rejoicing – not so much because of its scale, which was actually quite small, but because it showed that victories were still possible, and because it removed (at least for a while) the genuine fear of invasion. Jervis was created an earl, with (on the king's suggestion) the title St Vincent, and an annual pension of £3,000; his two seconds-in-command, Vice Admiral Charles Thompson and Rear Admiral William Parker, were made baronets; all the flag officers and captains in the line received a gold medal; and Nelson was knighted. Drinkwater had predicted a baronetcy for him too, but Nelson made it clear to the colonel that he did not want one: he had not the means to support a hereditary title in what he considered the proper way. Drinkwater passed the information to Sir Gilbert Elliot before he returned home in the frigate *Lively* with Robert Calder, Jervis's flag captain, and Elliot contrived to put a word in the right place, so that no one was embarrassed.

In the space of a month, Nelson had gone from Commodore to Rear Admiral Sir Horatio. The Rector, on his winter retreat, was quite overcome: 'The name and services of Nelson have sounded throughout the city of Bath,' he wrote, 'from the common ballad singer to the public theatre.' Walking out in the town, he found that not only his friends but also complete strangers stopped him to congratulate him on his magnificent son; he had to go back to his lodgings before he shamed himself by bursting into happy tears in public. 'Joy sparkles in every eye,' he said, 'and desponding Britain draws back her sable veil, and smiles.'

Yet some unhappy notes sounded as well. One was from Calder. He was knighted too, if only for bringing the news to England. Most people in the fleet felt, like Collingwood, that it was an honour to have had a share in the battle, Calder, unfortunately, was one of the few who envied Nelson, and put it to Jervis that to have wore out of line as Nelson did was 'an unauthorized departure from the prescribed mode of attack.' Jervis, who had welcomed Nelson into *Victory* with open arms, agreed entirely with Calder, and then added crushingly: 'And if you ever commit such a breach in your orders, I will forgive you also.'

Rear Admiral Sir William Parker was another dissenter from the general joy. Calder's was the only name mentioned by Jervis (or St Vincent, as he now was) in the public gazette. Parker was irritated by that, and much more so when he read in a newspaper a vivid account of the battle which focused mainly on Nelson. That it should do so was not surprising: it was the account Nelson had written himself and sent to Locker, with the suggestion that if Locker thought it a good idea, it might be sent to the papers, 'inserting the name of Commodore instead of "I"'. Parker did not understand that for an officer without 'interest', the habit of self-publicity died hard, and he wrote a rude letter to Nelson on the lack of attention he himself was receiving.

The third note out of tune with the rest came from Fanny. As ever, she was filled with anxiety, 'far beyond my powers of expression ... Altogether, my dearest husband, my sufferings were great ... I shall not be myself till I hear from you again.' She called his actions 'wonderful and desperate'; but there was no congratulation. Instead, 'What can I attempt to say to you about Boarding? You have been most wonderfully protected; you have done desperate actions enough. Now may I – indeed I do – beg that you never Board again! *LEAVE IT* for *CAPTAINS*.'

Nelson was quite capable of coping with professional jealousies, but one can only guess at his thoughts when he realized that, of all people, his wife could not find words to praise him. Some have suggested she was being humorous, but she was not: the riskier his adventures, the more truly frightened she was, for him as her beloved husband, and for herself as his dependant. When she begged him never to board again she was utterly serious, and further than ever from understanding what drove him on.

The Battle of Cape St Vincent changed Nelson's naval life for ever: fame had come to him, at long last. He was thirty-eight years old, a rear admiral, a knight and a hero. He was hardly likely to change his way of doing things; even if he had wanted to, for Fanny's sake, he could not have done – it would have meant changing himself. In his professional life, the name 'Nelson' was beginning to mean something special and different, something new and exciting; it was beginning to acquire its sense of magic for the navy. The aftermath of that battle also shows something important in his personal life: namely, that it had not altered anything like as much as his professional life. This is made clear by his concern over the possible offer of a baronetcy. Josiah was not a male heir of his body, so would not have inherited any title of Nelson's. Eventually, his titles passed to his brother William, but only because special arrangements were made. In the spring of 1797 Nelson did not imagine such complications; clearly at that time he had not stopped hoping that he and Fanny might yet have children of their own. Before his knighthood was announced publicly, he told her of it in all secrecy, and ended his letter: 'Be assured, whether my letters are long or short, yet still that my heart is entirely with you.' She was timorous and tedious, he was ambitious and impatient; but however unsatisfactory the relationship was on either side, they were husband and wife, and whatever else changed, that, they both still believed, would not.

The port of Cadiz, which lies fifty miles north of the Straits of Gibraltar, on their Atlantic side, had been de Cordoba's original destination before he fell in with Jervis on St Valentine's Day. Thither the Spanish survivors fled, and there they remained, blockaded by the British fleet – 'parading under the walls,' said Collingwood, 'as we did last year before Toulon.' It was dull work, and he rather envied Nelson: 'My dear friend,' he wrote to the Rear Admiral on 13 April, 'How little you are with us; only just long enough to communicate with the Admiral, and away again ...'

The mild complaint was justified; Nelson had been away from the fleet for five weeks, and was on the brink of departure again. Collingwood guessed that, just possibly, he was searching for the legendary Spanish treasure fleet from South America, which was rumoured to have arrived, bulging with gold, in the Canary Islands. If rumour were true, who else could Earl St Vincent send 'but one whose name is poison to a Spaniard? Perhaps that is your service', Collingwood concluded gently. 'There or wherever you go, may your good fortune never forsake you.'

He was partly right. With one frigate and three ships of the line, Nelson had ranged to and fro between Cape St Vincent and the coast of North Africa, hoping to intercept the wealth of Spain. Success would bring many personal fortunes; more importantly, Britain would be enriched, the enemy impoverished, and peace would be an almost certain consequence. However, not a sail had been seen, and on his return on 11 April Nelson found he had been given charge of the inshore blockading squadron. At once he sent out orders to the captains under his command, and informed neutral authorities on shore that no shipping would be allowed in or out. At the same time, though, he was thinking of other things – the Spanish treasure, and the safety of the British army garrison in Elba, still under the protection of Captain Fremantle and *Inconstant*. The island's continued occupation could hardly be necessary, and after arranging the blockade, he wrote to Earl St Vincent offering to oversee its final evacuation. That evening, Thomas Troubridge came to dinner. He had been with Nelson in the fruitless five-week search for the treasure ships, and their whereabouts was much on his mind. During the day he had heard (as had Collingwood) that through fear of the British fleet, they had diverted from the direct route to Spain and were in Tenerife; and he had heard too that the commander-in-chief would welcome Nelson's thoughts on the matter. They talked late, and the following morning Nelson sent another long letter to his admiral.

What he now proposed was a detailed plan for an assault which Drake or Raleigh would have relished, and which had the beauty of doing two jobs at once. He remembered that twice, in 1656 and 1657, Admiral Robert Blake had captured Spanish treasure fleets, and that the second had actually been in Tenerife. 'I do not reckon myself equal to Blake', he said modestly – then added, with much more characteristic enthusiasm: 'Now comes my plan, which could not fail of success, would immortalize the undertakers, ruin Spain, and has every prospect of raising our country to a higher pitch of wealth than she ever yet attained.'

There were 3,700 troops in Elba, under General de Burgh. All should be evacuated, and used in a combined operation against Tenerife; he, Nelson, would command both operations. He foresaw many obstacles, natural and human. Santa Cruz, the port and capital of Tenerife, had never had to withstand a siege, so the hills around it were unfortified; but its harbour – the crater of an extinct volcano – was so deep that anchoring was only possible very close in. From the steep surrounding cliffs, violent winds could sweep down without warning; landing places were few and small. 'Here', Nelson warned St Vincent, 'soldiers must be consulted, and I know from experience they have not the same boldness in undertaking a political measure as we have; we look to the benefit of our country, and risk our own fame every day to serve her: a soldier obeys his orders, and no more.' He was thinking then particularly of General de Burgh, and suggested that if he was unwilling, General O'Hara, commander of Gibraltar, should be approached. But with army support, 'the business could not miscarry', and he urged St Vincent to put pressure on the soldiers as soon as possible. 'What a stroke it would be!'

The commander-in-chief liked the idea: after fifteen months in the Mediterranean fleet, he felt that if anyone could pull off such a stunt, Nelson could, and he wrote to the Admiralty for permission to proceed. First, though, the evacuation of Elba – Fremantle was about to begin it; de Burgh had been told to co-operate; Nelson could lend extra protection. On 13 April, the refurbished *Captain* weighed anchor once more, accompanied by two other ships of the line, and joined soon after by three frigates. As Collingwood pondered his friend's destination, Nelson, thirty miles south of Cadiz, passed a cape called Trafalgar, and shaped course for the Straits.

Evacuating Elba was a long enterprise – he did not return until 24 May – but it was almost completely painless. South of Corsica, his squadron met Fremantle's forty-ship convoy of transports and found it perfectly organized: 'It could not be in better hands; therefore I only overshadow them with my wings.' However, they also learned unsettling news of Napoleon's progress. In February he had entered the papal states, depriving Pope Pius VI of three of them, together with thirty million écus in gold; in March he invaded Austria. 'All is lost in Italy,' Nelson wrote to St Vincent. 'The whole state of Venice is actually French. Trieste is also said to be in their possession, and Buonaparte is within 150 miles of Vienna with 150,000 men ... There seems no prospect of stopping these extraordinary people.' Rumours and observation at sea brought more uneasiness. A French squadron of four liners, a frigate and a brig was reported off Minorca; a single French brig was sighted and ignored ('my charge was too important'). Such forays were only to be expected; but Nelson was much more worried by a report from a neutral Danish frigate. Apparently the Cadiz fleet had definite orders to come out and fight. 'I should seriously lament being absent on such an occasion', he said, encouraging Fremantle to chivvy the transports on with all speed to Gibraltar. No one could tell, but there might be the chance of another Cape St Vincent, so he was not surprised when the commander-in-chief postponed any attack on Tenerife. 'I must concentrate all my force of line-of-battle ships and frigates,' St Vincent told him, adding, 'I have written so strongly upon the subject of a reinforcement that I cannot entertain a doubt of its being sent.'

It was; but with it came the startling information of mutiny in the fleet at Spithead. Among the new ships from England was *Theseus*, which, the First Lord of the Admiralty warned St Vincent, was riddled with mutinous men. The admiral quickly confirmed that she was 'an abomination', and as soon as Nelson returned, ordered him to take command with the officers and men of his choice – Captain Miller, Midshipman Hoste, and several volunteers from *Agamemnon* days. 'They will soon put the *Theseus* to right', St Vincent decided; and within a fortnight a remarkable change had come about. Writing to Fanny on 15 June, Nelson proudly told her that a few nights previously, a paper had been found on the quarterdeck, clumsily written, but quite clear in its meaning. 'Success attend Admiral Nelson!' the stumpy letters said. 'God bless Captain Miller! We thank them for the officers they have placed over us. We are happy and comfortable, and will shed every drop of blood in our veins to support them, and the name of the *Theseus* will be immortalised as high as the *Captain*'s.' And it was boldly signed: 'SHIP'S COMPANY'.

At home, Prince William felt that such a thing as mutiny, bad enough at any time, was almost inconceivable during a war. Had it been politically motivated, the Spithead mutiny would indeed have been treasonable; but the mutineers' demands were pathetically modest. All they really wanted was decent food, without short weight; medicines to be more readily available, without being 'lost' by surgeons; and a review of pay, which had not altered for more than a hundred years. And they humbly promised that if the French fleet should take the chance of putting to sea, they would be ready to go and fight it immediately.

The demands at Spithead were substantially met, yet many officers, including Collingwood, were deeply suspicious. He did not see the concessions as reasonable rights, but as acts of favour, and heard that the men 'seem to be occupied, having felt their power, in considering what next may be demanded.' Nelson was a wise choice for *Theseus*. 'I am entirely with the Sailors', he said. 'We are a neglected set.' He was not soft on them; all the seemingly magical transformation in *Theseus* came down to was that, accompanied and aided by loyal men who knew him already, he provided his new ship's company with all the stores they lacked (there was absolutely nothing on board when he took her over), with purposeful activity, and with example. For men who had been so 'neglected' in the Channel, it was all they needed.

During Nelson's absence while evacuating Elba, an air of lethargy had settled on the inshore squadron. Mutual gallantries were commonplace then between active naval opponents, but, said Collingwood, 'Ours is a curious situation.' Almost every day, letters were exchanged with the Spaniards under flag of truce; local fishermen, finding a better price afloat than on shore, came out to the fleet to sell their fish; Spanish officers came to dine with Sir James Saumarez, Nelson's temporary replacement. The squadron even 'invited the Spanish ladies to a ball, but they did not come.'

St Vincent did not like the friendliness; nor did Nelson when he returned. The commander-in-chief provided him with ten ships of the line – half the fleet – and small craft, to provoke a Spanish sortie. Crews 'should assemble on board the *Theseus* between nine and ten o'clock every night,' St Vincent ordered, 'armed with carronades, pikes, cutlasses, broad axes and chopping knives ... and follow the directions of Rear Admiral Nelson for the night.' This promised the kind of activity any seaman would wish, and when action came on 3 June, Nelson gave the kind of example they all liked. He even impressed himself –

'It was during this period', he wrote later, 'that perhaps my personal courage was more conspicuous than at any other time of my life.'

That was how he put it to his first biographers, who printed it verbatim, without using any 'pruning-knife', as he asked them. It comes over as absurdly vain, boastful in a comic and vulgar way. If (as Nelson suggested to Locker after the Battle of Cape St Vincent) they had rewritten his notes in the third person, it would still have seemed improbably high praise; but it was true, and Nelson was only being honest about himself. Certainly he was vain – he was honest enough to say that too, and never managed to overcome either his vanity or his honesty.

The episode off Cadiz was small, but altogether characteristic: in reply to a heavy bombardment of the town, Spanish gunboats emerged. As a rear admiral, Nelson should not have been directly involved; a lieutenant, or possibly a commander, would have been quite senior enough. But there he was, accompanied by Captain Fremantle – two senior officers, together with his barge's ordinary crew of ten men and the coxswain – and picked out for a personal attack by the leading gunboat. 'The Spanish barge rowed twenty-six oars, besides officers – thirty men in the whole,' Nelson remembered. 'This was a service hand-to-hand with swords'. It was a vicious fight – eighteen of the Spaniards were killed; the remainder were wounded and their commander captured, while Nelson's life was twice saved by his coxswain. It was exactly the kind of situation Fanny begged him to avoid, but which he could not resist. Telling her all about it, he said he did not think it would lower him in the opinion of the world, and added frankly: 'I have flattery enough to make me vain, and success enough to make me confident.'

It was an exciting little adventure, and briefly livened up the fleet. But as an exercise in provocation, it did not work: after three nights of close bombardment, the Spanish men-of-war still refused to budge.

Nelson understood the distinction between civilians and combatants as well as anyone. The day after his first bombardment happened to be King George's birthday, an event usually marked by a 21-gun salute at 1 p.m. For once, though, the salute had to be delayed until eight o'clock in the evening, and Nelson wrote to warn the Spanish admiral, 'so that the ladies of Cadiz may not be alarmed.' An appreciative reply came back.

But in spite of the courtesies, life was not happy in the blockading fleet. Everyone became frustrated, trying vainly to goad or tempt the Spaniards out; and worse, back in England, Spithead was followed by further mutiny at the Nore. If the first had been a strong breeze, said somebody, the Nore was a full gale, and without the justification of Spithead. There had been some public sympathy for the sailors then; with the Nore there was none. As its political nature became clear, the mutiny collapsed, with ships 'returning to their allegiance' under fire from those which continued to resist. Courts martial followed; twenty-five of the ringleaders were hanged; and off Cadiz the mood of the time was felt. Mutinous thoughts were abroad in six different ships, including Nelson's old command, *Captain*. Four active ringleaders were identified, one in *Marlborough* and three in *St George*, tried, found guilty and sentenced to death. *Marlborough* was in such a state of indiscipline – the plot had been to capture her and sail her to Ireland – that her captain admitted to St Vincent he might not be able to enforce the sentence. At that, St Vincent had the ship surrounded, promising to sink her if his orders were not carried out. The threat was enough: at eight in the morning – the customary time – the execution took place.

The other three men died early in the morning too, but, contrary to custom, on a Sunday. Their trial had not ended until after dark the previous night, when St Vincent refused their request for five days in which to prepare themselves – in that time, he said, the condemned men 'would have hatched five hundred treasons.' Vice Admiral Thompson was so shocked by the desecration of the Sabbath that he wrote a public letter of protest; St Vincent promptly ordered him to leave the fleet and return to England. Nelson, of course, was a deeply religious man, and it might not have been surprising if he too had been offended by the Sunday executions. Far from it: 'Had it been Christmas Day, instead of Sunday,' he told St Vincent, 'I would have executed them.' No doubt he would have done. Religion was a basic element of his being, not a matter of outward form – he once said he could not understand an officer who would pray all Sunday and flog his men the rest of the week. But Cadiz was becoming a millstone of thankless, unpleasant work. Everyone from the commander-in-chief down wanted something more positive to happen.

The end of May brought one British success – small for the Royal Navy, but very great for Lieutenant Thomas Hardy. In the busy frigate *Lively* (now under Ben Hallowell), he looked into Santa Cruz and saw a French brig lurking there. There seemed a chance of cutting it out, and against strong opposition, Hardy did so. 'He has got it by his own bat', St Vincent growled with pleasure, and straight away made the lieutenant a commander, in control of the new little vessel *La Mutine*, 14 guns, 130 men – Hardy's first own command. From 'a sensible lad' in the same expedition, the commander-in-chief learned that 'Santa Cruz may be carried with the greatest ease.' Other intelligence revealed that because of their fear of his fleet, the treasure ships had not actually sailed from Central America, but that a rich merchant ship from Manila had taken refuge in the volcanic port. On 14 July St Vincent made his decision: Tenerife would be attacked. 'God bless you and prosper you,' were his last words to Nelson. 'I am sure you will deserve success. To mortals is not given the power of commanding it.'

Unfortunately, there were no soldiers available for the venture. Not only de Burgh but also O'Hara refused to commit any men at all – indeed, O'Hara countered St Vincent's request with a request for more naval protection at Gibraltar. However, with the exceptional natural hazards involved, the army's absence probably made little difference to the outcome. Perhaps St Vincent should not have ordered the enterprise; certainly Nelson should not have stuck with it as doggedly as he did. Yet though neither could command success, it is too simple now to say in reply that they did not have to invite disaster; better, instead, to think of the times they lived in and the men they were. To the generations born in Britain since 1940, their situation is difficult to imagine; but as in 1940, the British in 1797 faced a powerful Continental aggressor, without the support of any other nation. The Battle of Cape St Vincent had lightened but not obliterated the possibility of an invasion of Britain; the navy was the only force which could finally remove that threat. Inert as it was, the Spanish fleet remained in being; its removal from the equation was imperative, either through battle – but clearly, nothing would induce it to fight – or through peace between London and Madrid. It was only natural, then, that Nelson and Earl St Vincent should seek any means of bringing that peace closer. And when they assessed the risks, it may have been unsound to highlight the positive, to make so much of the solitary route to success and so little of the many routes to failure; but for men like them in times like those, that was only natural too.

From Cadiz to Santa Cruz is one thousand miles. At six o'clock in the morning on 15 July, with three ships of the line, three frigates, a cutter and St Vincent's blessing, Nelson sailed. He was away precisely one month. On the morning of 16 August, he sighted St Vincent's fleet again and requested permission to come on board the flagship to bid farewell for ever to his commander-in-chief – 'A left-handed admiral will never be considered as useful; therefore the sooner I get to a very humble cottage the better, and make room for a sounder man to serve the state.' Calvi had taken his right eye, and now Tenerife his right arm; he could imagine no future for himself at sea. 'I am become a burden to my friends, and useless to my country ... When I leave your command, I become dead to the world; I go hence, and am no more seen.'

Preparations had been as good as possible, from the construction of strong, light scaling ladders to the regular conferences between commanding officers on the outward voyage. A fourth frigate and a bomb vessel had joined en route, and all knew what they were to do. While the liners lay off out of sight, the frigates would close in after dark. Thomas Oldfield, captain of marines, and Thomas Troubridge (nicknamed 'General' for the operation) would lead ashore 250 marines, ninety named seamen and a further hundred volunteers, all in six boats rowed with muffled oars and tied in line together, to avoid being separated in the night. Without warning, they would attack the heights and batteries to the north-east of the town, while the bomb vessel opened fire on the town itself. At dawn the liners would close in, ready to fire on the town, when Troubridge would present its governor with an ultimatum, which he would be mad not to accept. All Nelson would require was for the ship from Manila to be surrendered, with all her cargo on board or on shore and all treasure or bullion anywhere in the town belonging to the Spanish crown. Alternatively, 'I shall destroy Santa Cruz, and the other towns in the island, by a bombardment, and levy a very heavy contribution on the island.'

But there was no alternative plan if, once the operation was started, any delay occurred and surprise was lost; and that was exactly what happened. The frigates met unexpected strong offshore currents and winds, and by dawn on 22 July had failed to get within a mile of their landing point. Inevitably they had been sighted, and Troubridge withdrew to consult with Nelson. The captain felt an assault on the heights might still succeed; Nelson agreed, and prepared to batter the town's defences. But now the weather was calm; the liners could get no closer in than three miles; and as for the heights, 'the enemy had taken possession, and seemed as anxious to retain, as we were to get them.'

Probably Nelson should have abandoned the whole business. But, 'thus foiled in my original plan, I considered it necessary for the honour of our king and country not to give over the attempt . . .' Self-confidence slipped, it seems, into over-confidence: he decided to repeat the night-time boat attack, and this time, to lead it himself.

He should never have done so, and that is not being wise after the event: as a rear admiral and commander of the whole squadron, he had no business in the vanguard. But again, he was incapable of doing otherwise, though he recognized the risks – 'Tomorrow', he wrote to St Vincent, 'my head will probably be crowned with either laurel or cypress.'

William Hoste and Josiah were with him in *Theseus*. During the Battle of Cape St Vincent, Hoste had contrived to make Nelson 'promise never to leave him again', as Nelson told Fanny. In the same letter, though, he had also said that he was sending Josiah into another ship. The blunt reason was that 'he must be broke of being at my elbow'. That night, however, Josiah was insistent. As the landing party was making ready, he appeared in Nelson's cabin kitted out with pistols and sword. A theatrical conversation took place: 'Should we both fall, Josiah, what would become of your poor mother?', Nelson is supposed to have said. 'The care of the *Theseus* falls to you. Stay, therefore, and take charge of her.' 'Sir,' Josiah apparently replied, 'the ship must take care of herself. I will go with you tonight if never again.'

Whether or not such a conversation actually occurred, he went, and both Nelson and he were glad of it, for it became Josiah's finest hour. But William Hoste had to remain on board.

Another who remained was Betsey Fremantle. After the evacuation of Elba, her husband had been given command of the frigate *Seahorse* – somewhat to his chagrin, for *Inconstant* needed a refit, and he had hoped to take her and Betsey home. The couple were cheered, though, when Nelson selected Fremantle for the Santa Cruz operation, and still more so when St Vincent said Betsey could go too. The commander-in-chief had liked her ever since their first meeting in *Victory*, when he demanded a kiss from her, and nicknamed her family 'the Amiables'. Off Santa Cruz, at one o'clock in the morning, she listened without worry to the gunfire ashore: 'Old Nelson' and her husband had assured her little could go wrong. But, she wrote in her diary, 'this proved to be a shocking unfortunate night.'

Hoste learned of the disaster before Betsey did. About 2 a.m., shocked beyond words, he saw Nelson ('whom I may say has been a second father to me') scrambling back on board *Theseus*, 'his right arm dangling by his side', with Josiah close behind him.

During the remainder of that night, charged with the sense of ghastly failure, Hoste heard from Josiah some of the details of disaster: how the defending batteries had opened fire when the boats were still hundreds of yards from land; how Nelson, in the act of leaping ashore, had been struck down, hit, with many others, in the right arm by a raking burst of grape-shot; how he had fallen back, gushing blood and gasping that he was a dead man; how Josiah had gripped his shattered arm and staunched the flow with a tourniquet of neckerchiefs; how one of the sailors had torn off his own shirt to make a sling for the rear admiral; how Josiah had taken command of the boat, taking it close in to avoid the deadly fire, then directed it back to the squadron. Hoste heard too how, when Nelson regained consciousness, he ordered as many men as possible to be gathered into the boat from the sea; how they had approached *Seahorse*, Fremantle's frigate, only to have Nelson refuse to go on board, saying he would rather die than alarm Betsey by appearing in such a state when he knew nothing of her husband's fate; and how, when at last they found *Theseus*, Nelson had refused any help – 'Let me alone,' the wounded admiral cried, with the anger typical of someone in a state of profound shock. 'I have yet my legs left, and one arm. Tell the surgeon to make haste and get his instruments – I know I must lose my right arm, so the sooner it is off the better.'

It was cut off high up, near the shoulder, and (on Nelson's order) thrown overboard. The knife seemed bitterly cold to him – ever after he made sure that surgeons in his ships warmed their blades before operating. The crude operation was over inside half an hour; then, but not before, he was given opium to ease the dreadful pain.

Throughout, the crackle and thunder of fire from the shore continued; and with daylight the completeness of failure became clear. Fremantle had been shot in the right arm too and taken back to *Seahorse* where Betsey demanded to tend him herself: he, at least, did not have to endure amputation. Lieutenant Weatherhead, Hoste's best friend, was mortally wounded. Nearly a thousand officers and men had set out; a quarter of them were killed. A further 240, under Troubridge, only returned because of Troubridge's own audacity and the gallantry of the Spanish commander. Separated from the others, their ammunition wet and useless, they had taken refuge in a convent, prepared bombs and grenades, and advanced into the town only to find themselves facing eight thousand troops. Troubridge announced that unless he and his men were allowed to retreat in an honourable manner, he would make every effort to burn the town; the governor of the island replied that an honourable retreat was entirely acceptable, and provided wine, bread and replacement boats. When he learned of the unwarranted courtesy, Nelson responded as best he could, with the gift of a cheese and a cask of English beer. Both were accepted, as was a third offer from the rear admiral: he himself would take the Spanish governor's despatches back to Spain, and become the herald of his own defeat.

16

'Where are they gone?'

IN THE CITY of Bath, on 2 September 1797, a letter addressed in an unrecognizable spidery scrawl was delivered to the house rented by Lady Nelson and her father-in-law. Whoever had written it was either extremely old or extremely ill, and when Fanny realized the strange handwriting was her husband's, she was too frightened to read his words. The Rector could not help: his eyes were too weak, and he had never wished to interfere with God's workings by wearing spectacles. Fortunately his daughter Susannah was visiting at the time, and to her small, apprehensive audience, she read out Nelson's first left-handed letter home, an unhappy message from a man much in need of comfort.

'I shall not be surprised if I am neglected and forgotten; probably I shall no longer be considered as useful,' it said. 'However, I shall feel rich if I continue to enjoy your affection. The cottage is now more necessary than ever.' Nelson was sure that Fanny would be as pleased with a letter from his left hand as from his right, 'and I know it will add much to your pleasure to find that Josiah, under God's providence, was principally instrumental in saving my life.' He begged that neither she nor his father should think much of 'this mishap' – he himself had grown used to it – and ended, in a postscript after he had rejoined the fleet off Cadiz, 'I think I shall be with you perhaps as soon as this letter ... the first you will hear of me will be at the door.'

Without Susannah, the letter might have lain unread until after its author's return. Barely twenty-four hours after she had steeled herself to hear the worst, Fanny heard the most welcome sound she had known in more than four years of waiting: her husband's voice echoing down the street, as he directed his coachman to the rented front door.

*

The voyage home had been painful in every way for everyone, with the solitary exception that Betsey confided in the surgeon, who, to her great pleasure, confirmed that she was pregnant. First, though, the ship had been blown far to the west, then endured contrary winds and flat calms before Scilly was sighted. Nelson called it 'a very miserable passage': all the worst wounded from Tenerife were on board, and, said Betsey, 'did nothing but groan from morning to night', with the two most senior being particularly bad patients. Captain Fremantle's arm was not improving and he seemed likely to lose it. Thinking of that, with the rear admiral in front of her, Betsey – stoic as she was – shuddered and thought, 'It looks shocking to be without one arm.'

How much more shocking it must have been to Fanny, who had never lived on board a naval ship. One can only imagine that reunion – the fluttering delight that her husband was back and alive, the awful strangeness of his first one-armed embrace, the realization that he had to turn his head to see anything or anyone on his right. Then, after the initial excited clamour, the most dreadful novelty: the actual stump. It needed dressing, and a doctor was called. But since a doctor would not always be available, Nelson insisted that Fanny should attend and learn how to do it herself. She did, finding quite soon that it did not disgust her and that she could do it well; and so began the happiest seven months of her whole life, and of their marriage.

There is no doubt that for that half-year, each was all the other wanted; jointly and individually they were satisfied and content in a way they never had been before. Nelson told St Vincent his domestic life was perfect, and added that: 'My reception from John Bull has been just what I wished'. He had achieved heroic recognition: as they would today, the newspapers dissected the failure at Tenerife in different ways, according to their political bias, but none blamed him at all, and one at least was so confident of his fame that it used only his surname, in capital letters – no Christian name or title, simply NELSON. Protected by such men, it said, 'we may defy the malignant threats of our enemies, and look with contempt upon the wild project of an invasion'. Fanny, 'his Lady', discovered a delightful, unfamiliar wifely fulfilment, caring for a husband who responded with warmth, gratitude and good humour – going to the theatre one evening, where Lord Lansdowne had lent them his box, Nelson remarked that 'his Lordship did not tell me all its charms'. Lansdowne had extended the loan to some of the most attractive women in Bath. 'and', Nelson complained lightheartedly, 'was I a bachelor I would not answer for being tempted; but as I am possessed of everything which is valuable in a wife, I have no occasion to think beyond a pretty face.'

There was, however, much occasion to think of professional matters in those months. In London, just four days before his thirty-ninth birthday, his investiture as a Knight of the Bath by the king in person was the highlight of his return, and gave him the chance of a graceful and useful compliment to a colleague. 'You have lost your right arm!', the sharp-eyed king remarked. 'But not my right hand,' Nelson replied, 'as I have the honour of presenting Captain Berry', and with his left arm pushed his pleased and embarrassed junior forward. They spoke, then King George turned to Nelson again and repeated his sympathy. 'But', he added, 'your country has a claim for a bit more of you.'

Nelson was entirely willing to give it, and said so one evening shortly afterward. Colonel Drinkwater came to dinner (nothing formal, Fanny warned him, just 'a family dinner') and had news of the naval war: in the North Sea, off the coast of Holland, Admiral Adam Duncan was about to engage the Dutch fleet in battle. Nelson's vigorous reaction surprised the colonel – 'Drinkwater! I would give this other arm to be with Duncan at this moment!'

The resounding victory at Camperdown on 11 October created a small but famous incident in the invalid's life. When it was announced, late on the 13th, the capital came to life with public and private illuminations – everywhere except on his house, for he was already in bed asleep, sedated with opium. An excited crowd came banging on the door to find out why this one building was unlit. Learning the reason, they shuffled off apologetically, saying, 'You will hear no more from us tonight.'

It was a pleasing compliment, but to have missed out on the battle only irritated him. Before he had left Cadiz, St Vincent had been looking forward to his early return, and wrote to the First Lord saying so. Each day in London, despite his pain, Nelson went to the Admiralty. At last he was to be examined to confirm the loss of his eye – 'Oh!', he said dismissively. 'This is only for an eye. In a few days I shall come for an arm; and in a little time longer, God knows, most probably for a leg.' However, it was worth the effort: he was awarded an annual pension of a thousand pounds. Better still, from his point of view, he was informed that in the New Year he would take command of the new 80-gun *Foudroyant*. Fanny knew she had to count the days.

After many medical consultations in Bath and London, an unusually wise doctor declared that time, nature and Fanny's care would heal Nelson's wound best. Until early December, when the last, very troublesome ligature fell away from his stump at a touch, Nelson was in constant, generally severe pain. Whether he and Fanny became physical lovers again is, of course, unknown; but to others they appeared very much in love. Countess Spencer, wife of the First Lord of the Admiralty, had them to dinner towards the end of this period on shore – so different from the five years on the beach – and later recalled frankly that on first seeing Nelson, 'a most uncouth creature I thought him ... he looked so sickly, it was painful to see him'. In fact, by then he looked as most people think of him today, but to the stern Countess, 'his general appearance was that of an idiot; so much so, that when he spoke, and his wonderful mind broke forth, it was a sort of surprise that riveted my whole attention.' Unimpressed by the appearance, then entranced by the character – hers was quite a usual reaction, and if she forgot that most people in love look idiotic, she was touched by his demand (awkward though it was for the dinner table seating) that Fanny should sit next to him. He saw so little of her, Nelson explained, that he did not want to lose a moment of her company; and there she sat, dutiful and glad, and cut up his food for him. The Countess beamed, and murmured: 'They look like lovers.'

Just as importantly, the couple put into action a long-held plan for their future together, and bought a house: Roundwood, close to Ipswich in Suffolk. They both visited it and liked it, though it needed redecoration, and with thoughts on how it might be further improved, Nelson arranged for Fanny and his father to be installed. 'I have not the least doubt', he had written in the days of their courtship, 'but that we shall be a happy pair – the fault must be mine if we are not.' That modest dream appeared to be working; and its material setting was grander than he had ever imagined. Instead of the 'very humble cottage' he had always spoken of, the home he now owned was a gentleman's residence of thirteen rooms, with sixty acres and an entire farm attached, eminently suitable for years of dignified harmonious retirement. But he never even slept there.

8 December 1797: 'To Captain Berry, RN – SECRET – My dear Sir, If you mean to marry, I would recommend your doing it speedily, or the to be Mrs Berry will have very little of your company; for I am well, and you may expect to be called for every hour. We shall probably be at sea before the *Foudroyant* is launched. Our ship is at Chatham, a

Seventy-four ... Ever yours most faithfully, Horatio Nelson.'

Two days after that letter was written – possibly at the same time as Berry, in Norfolk, was reading it – a public ceremony took place in Paris. A short distance south-west of the Cathedral of Notre-Dame, the Directory received from General Buonaparte the Treaty of Campo Formio, marking Austria's surrender; and it was recorded that no French general had ever been given such cheers before. Eight days after that, on 18 December, in St Paul's Cathedral in London, Nelson and Berry were among the huge congregation at a service of national thanksgiving for the battles of the Glorious First of June, Cape St Vincent and Camperdown, the three major naval victories of the war. It was a long service, but a happy one for all; Nelson was particularly touched when the queen and her four daughters gave him and other flag officers a graceful, impromptu curtsey. In and around the same building, barely eight years later, an even larger throng would gather in tears for the little admiral's funeral.

His new ship was the ten-year-old *Vanguard*, latest of an honourable name reaching back to the Armada. To Berry, as her future flag captain, fell the duty of fitting *Vanguard* out for war. Nelson took the opportunity to go with Fanny and his father to Bath again. At the same time, Napoleon arrived on the Channel coast of north-west France to inspect his new command, 'the army against England', and far away off Cadiz, Collingwood wrote of his certainty that England was fighting for its very existence. 'Considering how near the coasts are, the thing is practicable ... The question is not merely who shall be conqueror, but whether we shall any longer be a people'.

Berry's patience was sorely tried with the lengthy fitting-out of *Vanguard*, just as Nelson's had been with *Agamemnon* back in 1793. The new flagship was not ready until the end of March. In Portsmouth, on the 29th, the rear admiral's flag was broken out; in London, Fanny considerately visited Captain Berry's bride; and from London, on 30 March, Earl Spencer wrote to Earl St Vincent. 'My Lord: I am very happy to send you Sir Horatio Nelson again ... I believe I cannot send you a more zealous, active and approved officer'. On 10 April 1798, with the first fair wind and a convoy of merchantmen, *Vanguard* sailed for Cadiz.

By then, the port had been blockaded for thirteen wearisome months. On 1 May, St Vincent wrote gratefully to Spencer: 'I do assure your lordship that the arrival of Admiral Nelson has given me a new lease of life, you could not have gratified me more than in sending him; his presence in the Mediterranean is so very essential'. He had been the last British admiral to leave that hostile sea; now he would be the first to return. Writing home the same day – for Nelson had brought out many letters to the fleet – Collingwood explained. He did not know Napoleon's conclusion on a cross-Channel invasion ('Too chancy. I don't intend to risk *la belle France* on the throw of a dice'), but from some American ships he had learned that at Toulon and Marseilles a very large fleet was being equipped. Different rumours gave it different destinations – Naples, Sicily, even England, via the Straits of Gibraltar. 'If those people should attempt to pass the straits,' he said confidently, 'we shall certainly make a fine uproar amongst them'; and with the same relieved pleasure as St Vincent, he added, 'I never saw my friend Nelson look so well: he is really grown fat, and not the worse for losing an arm.'

There was no doubt about the enormous size of the French fleet: warships and transports together made it at least three hundred, possibly four hundred vessels. The problem which St Vincent gave Nelson immediately was to identify its target. *Vanguard* remained only two days off Cadiz; on 2 May, leading a squadron of one sloop, four frigates and two other 74s, she made course for Gibraltar and Toulon. St Vincent was refreshed and optimistic – 'The odds are that my gallant and enterprising rear admiral will lay hold of something'. Nelson was just as cheerful, telling the commander-in-chief, 'I will present you at least with some frigates, and I hope something better.' Nevertheless, there was initially at least one disconsolate man in the squadron: Alexander Ball, captain of the 74-gun HMS *Alexander*. He and Nelson had never actually met before, yet Nelson had seen him – he was the 'coxcomb' whom Nelson had jealously observed showing off his epaulettes in St Omer, fifteen years earlier. It is astonishing, but Nelson had neither forgotten that episode nor overcome the immature prejudice it left: in a way which made it clear he was not really joking, his first words to Ball were, 'What, are you come to have your bones broken?'

Nelson's perpetually youthful character had a strong positive side, giving him the enthusiasm and vigour people found so appealing. The incident with Ball was, in its way, just as typical, showing how unattractive that same youthfulness could sometimes be. However, it was the sequel which made it important. Within three weeks, he became firm friends with Ball, and (again typically) remained so ever after; but it took a near-tragedy to bring that about. In a vivid letter to Fanny, Nelson described what had happened.

'Figure to yourself a vain man, on Sunday evening at sunset, walking in his cabin with a squadron about him who looked up to their chief to lead them to glory, and in whom this chief placed the firmest reliance,' he wrote. A captured French corvette had informed them that Buonaparte himself was in Toulon. Fifteen sail of the line under Admiral François Brueys were ready for sea, with 12,000 cavalry embarked in the transports. But their destination was still secret, so Nelson took his ships towards Toulon. After dark on Sunday 20 May a ferocious gale blew up; and, Nelson continued, 'Figure to yourself this proud conceited man, when the sun rose on Monday morning: his ship dismasted, his fleet dispersed, and himself in such distress that the meanest frigate out of France would have been a very unwelcome guest.'

The storm blew them all the way to southern Sardinia, and, as *Vanguard*'s masts went by the board one by one, the ship was driven towards the shore, so close that the surf could easily be seen breaking on rocks – 'really alarming', said Berry candidly. Disaster was only avoided by Ball taking *Vanguard* in tow. Sure that both would be wrecked, Nelson ordered him to cast loose; Ball refused; and eventually, led by Sir James Saumarez in *Orion*, all three 74s found refuge. As soon as possible, Nelson visited *Alexander* to give Ball thanks as honest as his previous prejudice – grateful to be alive, and glad to include another in his circle of constant friends.

There were two other consequences to the gale. One was so fortunate that St Vincent could only see the hand of providence at work. The Toulon fleet – far larger than anything Nelson's squadron could handle alone – set sail on the day the storm began, and had it not been for the weather, it would almost certainly have found, fought and beaten the British ships. Returning to the main fleet to report events, Nelson's frigates enabled a reinforcing and protecting squadron to locate him easily. However, over the following weeks, the gale's second consequence caused Nelson extreme anguish. Believing *Vanguard* was so damaged she could not contemplate offensive action soon, the frigates did not return at once. In fact, after much hard work, the flagship was ready in three days, and promptly made sail. The frigates – 'the eyes of the fleet', Nelson called them – never caught up, and for eight weeks his ships sailed blind.

*

Only one light, fast vessel was present – *La Mutine*, still commanded by the bulky, stolid, utterly reliable Thomas Hardy, now twenty-nine years old. Writing to his brother in Dorset, Hardy showed his confidence in Nelson's command – 'You may expect to hear of something handsome being done very soon by his Squadron' – and expressed his private hope that 'Sir Horatio will have it in his power to do something for me before our Cruise is out.' Bringing orders from St Vincent and news of the impending reinforcement, he found the small squadron on 5 June. The orders were clearly and simply expressed, as always. This time, however, they were anything but simple to carry out: with his combined fleet, Nelson was to proceed 'in quest of the armament preparing by the enemy at Toulon and Genoa. On falling in with the said armament, you are to use your utmost endeavours to take, sink, burn or destroy it.' But, careful and very generous in his selection of extra vessels, St Vincent judged that, when completed, Nelson's force 'will consist of the ships which are really and truly the élite of the fleet under my command.'

He was right, for in addition to the 50-gun *Leander*, the reinforcement included ten 74-gun ships of the line, and the majority of the newly arrived commanders were friends of Nelson's, some of very long standing. Thomas Thompson in *Leander* was the youngest, at thirty-two. He had been in the navy twenty years, but for six of them had been on the beach – even longer than Nelson. Before then he had been on the African station, and among other things had helped to establish a British colony at Sierra Leone. His appointment in *Leander* dated from 1796, when he began work with the Baltic convoys, before being sent to St Vincent's fleet just in time to help Nelson with the evacuation of Elba.

Leading the captains of the ten new 74s, in *Culloden*, there was Thomas Troubridge, shock-headed, stern and, in St Vincent's judgment, as gifted a commander as Nelson. Nelson himself said more, calling Troubridge 'the very best sea-officer in His Majesty's Service.' They were the same age, had known each other for twenty-five years, and jointly had dominated the Battle of Cape St Vincent. Thomas Foley, in *Goliath*, was a little more than a year older, born in south Wales of an ancient family: their estate had remained with them since 1383. An uncle, after whom he was named, had sailed with Anson around the world; he himself had done duty in the West Indies and American waters, and had fought with Keppel off Brest in 1778. He had also had the slight misfortune to fall in love with Betsey Fremantle, before her marriage; she had rejected him vigorously and publicly. Luckily, he got over it, and became instead her devoted friend.

Alexander Ball – once the despised coxcomb, now the saviour and friend – was, like Foley, forty-one years old: with Sir James Saumarez they were the three oldest captains in the newly formed fleet. As a lieutenant, Ball had been present at the Battle of the Saints, where his bravery earned him an independent command. Though he was notably bookish (he read extremely widely, and became a friend of Coleridge) and in that way the opposite of Hardy (who loathed anything to do with paperwork and had a very loose grip on the spelling of almost every word), their temperaments were otherwise similar, reasoned and stable. Saumarez, in character, was more akin to Troubridge and Nelson – fretful, passionate, impetuous – but where they both revealed their feelings easily, he did not, and appeared aloof. His unusual name was of French origin (his family came from Guernsey) and he was exceptionally experienced and courageous. He had served in the American War of Independence; had fought the Dutch in 1781 and, under Kempenfelt, helped to capture a French convoy; had been one of Rodney's captains in 1782 in the victory over de Grasse; and in 1793 had earned his knighthood by capturing a French frigate without sustaining a single casualty in his own ship.

Another veteran of the Battle of the Saints was *Swiftsure*'s captain, Ben Hallowell, thirty-eight years old and a Canadian by birth. He had served in the Mediterranean during Admiral Hotham's ineffectual regime, and first met Nelson in 1794, when they worked twenty-four-hour turns in command of the advanced batteries during the siege of Calvi. He was a very large man, but though he looked like a boxer, people spoke mainly of his consideration for others and his generosity, and of his odd sense of humour – from which, in a short time, Nelson would benefit. Ralph Miller, commanding *Theseus*, was also from across the Atlantic. Born thirty-seven years before into a loyalist American family, he had fought on the British side in almost every action of the War of Independence, and had been wounded three times. He too had first met Nelson in Corsica; twice, Nelson described him as the only truly virtuous man he knew. With Troubridge, Hood and Thompson he had accompanied Nelson to Tenerife, and one might spare a thought, as St Vincent must have done, for him and the seamen in *Theseus* who had survived that ghastly night. 'We would shed every drop of blood in our veins', the once mutinous crew had said, and of course many of them had, following him and Nelson faithfully to disaster.

Zealous was commanded by the youngest liner captain to join Nelson's fleet – thirty-six-year-old Samuel Hood, a member of one of the most distinguished naval families of the eighteenth century. In 1777, his brother Alexander, four years older, had circled the world with Cook, and had been first to sight the Marquesas group of islands, one of which was named after him. He had been killed very recently in a victorious fight against a French ship off Brittany. The brothers were cousins and namesakes of Samuel, Viscount Hood, and his brother Alexander, Viscount Bridport, who was at that time directing the blockade of Brest. Samuel the younger (generally known as Sam) had served under both his cousins, and was yet another veteran of Rodney's Battle of the Saints. He had also been a member of Nelson's expedition to Tenerife, and of the inshore squadron at Cadiz. A further shared experience increased their mutual sympathy: both had endured Prince William's approach to naval life. Two particular evenings were lodged hazily in Sam Hood's memory: at one, he, the prince and eighteen other diners sank sixty-three bottles of wine between them; the other he described as ending with 'twenty-eight bumper toasts, by which time we were all in pretty good order. At nine o'clock a feu de joie was fired ... Those that could walk attended.'

For the first time, Nelson was in charge of a large independent fleet, and he began at once his miracle of command. These five captains of the reinforcing squadron, and many of their men, were personally known to him already. The other five captains – Peyton in *Defence*, Darby in *Bellerophon*, Westcott in *Majestic*, Gould in *Audacious* and Louis in *Minotaur* – were known to him by reputation, though not so well personally. Over the next two months, all became intimate friends, and by the end of the summer, a group of unequalled heroes; for these were the men of whom Nelson said, with pride and pleasure and truth, 'I had the happiness to command a band of brothers.'

But where were the French? 'You may be assured', Nelson wrote to St Vincent on 11 June, 'I will fight them the moment I reach their fleet, be they at anchor, or under sail.' On 8 July, an entry in the journal of Admiral Brueys's flagship *L'Orient* gave a concise account of those four intervening weeks. 'The English fleet has played with ill luck on its side: first, it missed us on the coast of Sardinia; next, it missed a convoy of fifty-seven sail coming from Civitavecchia, with 7,000 troops of the Army of Italy on board. It did not arrive at Malta until five days after we left it; and it arrived in Alexandria two days too soon to meet us ... We shall certainly meet it at last; but we are now moored in such a manner as to bid defiance to a force more than double our own.'

Time and again, with increasing despair, Nelson lamented his lack of frigates. Nothing else could scout and communicate as swiftly and efficiently; without them, like a gamekeeper probing a wood on a pitch-black night, his only aids were reason, instinct and familiarity with his ground. Whenever the weather was fine, he invited his captains over to *Vanguard* to dine with him. His dinner parties were almost always cheerful, but as weeks and thousands of sea-miles went by without any firm indication of where the French might be, the per-plexing strain told on the whole fleet. 'We are proceeding on the merest conjecture only', wrote Saumarez. His rank made him second-in-command, and he was grateful not to have to endure quite the same stress as Nelson: 'Should the chief responsibility rest with me,' he admitted privately, 'I fear it would be more than my too irritable nerves could bear.'

At the dinners in *Vanguard*, Nelson explained exactly what he meant to do when they found the French, whatever the situation they found them in, and he showed his captains he had perfect confidence in them to use their own discretion in doing it. The food on these occasions was simple, but the wine and conversation were good; and after them each captain was rowed back to his ship determined to live up to the Admiral's trust. The same confidence, reinforced by constant battle practice, spread down through all ranks in the fleet until the smallest boy knew exactly what Nelson expected of him, and felt sure he would achieve it.

They went to Naples and found only good wishes from Sir William and Lady Hamilton – 'God bless you, and give you the success which your talents and bravery in the good cause so richly deserve, and with such a chosen band under your command. Emma's most kind love attends you' – and news of a desperately fearful court and country. Beyond that, Hamilton could only confirm that Napoleon was with the armada in *Sans Culottes*, with a great number of scientists as well as soldiers. 'We hope in God to see you in this bay with the *Sans Culottes*, etc. – and that Buonaparte, with all his savants and astron-omers. Adieu, my brave dear friend.'

Sir William guessed that Malta might be the French target, and Nelson soon learned that they had indeed been there. The island had been reduced speedily, and all the treasure of the Knights of Malta embarked in *L'Orient*. The Admiralty's guesses had ranged from the Black Sea to the West Indies to Ireland; personally, Nelson favoured Egypt as Napoleon's objective, being a route to India. Agreeing with an intelligence agent in Italy ('the danger of losing half an army in crossing the desert from Egypt would be no great obstacle'), he found his captains felt the same. So, to Alexandria; but, said Saumarez, 'If we find we are upon a wrong scent, our embarrassment will be great indeed.'

Nelson did not need reminding; he knew the honour and responsibility placed on him. There were other admirals senior to him whom St Vincent had deliberately overlooked; one, Orde, was so angry he challenged the commander-in-chief to a duel. Earl Spencer assessed the Mediterranean situation as so critical that the fate of Europe depended upon success there, and Nelson was fortunate that, as the weeks passed with no news from him, he could not know of the rising calls in England for impeachment and court martial. And Alexandria was empty.

From there to Turkey, four hundred miles on; nothing. To Crete, another three hundred miles; nothing. Back to Sicily again, a further seven hundred miles; still nothing. Nelson's spirit was close to breaking point, and he sent a tortured letter to St Vincent. 'I recalled all the circumstances of this armament before me: 40,000 troops in 280 transports, many hundred pieces of artillery; wagons, draught horses, cavalry, artificers, naturalists, astronomers, mathematicians, &c. The first rendezvous, in case of separation, was Bastia, the second, Malta. This armament could not be necessary for taking possession of Malta. The Neapolitan ministers considered Naples and Sicily as safe. Spain after Malta, or indeed any place to the westward, I could not think their destination; for at this season the westerly winds so strongly prevail between Sicily and the coast of Barbary that I conceived it almost impossible to get a fleet of transports to the westward. It then became the serious question, Where are they gone?'

Before he despatched the letter, he showed it to Ball – an indication of how complete was the turn-around in his opinion of the captain. Ball advised him against sending it, urging him not to defend his actions until they were criticized. Nelson sent it all the same: expressing his anger and distress must have helped a little. 'The only objection I can fancy to be started', he wrote, 'is, you should not have gone such a long voyage without more certain information of the enemy's destination. My answer' – and he underlined it – 'is ready: *Where was I to get it from?*'

Yet they had to be somewhere to the east. Cyprus? The fleet weighed again, ready for another twelve hundred miles. Passing Greece, they captured a French brig laden with wine – the first enemy vessel seen for nearly two months – and from it and sources on shore learned, at last, the armada's destination: Alexandria. They had been right the first time, but had sailed so fast that they had overtaken the enemy – their own signal guns had been heard in Napoleon's ships as they passed by one night a month or more ago.

They had been sailing all the time at between five and six knots, close to their best possible speed. More than five hundred miles remained; they covered the distance in three days, going at a rate that liners scarcely ever achieved. Early in the afternoon of 1 August they approached Alexandria for the second time. The harbour was packed with shipping – but not a man-of-war among it, nothing but empty transports, the last evidence of a completely successful French voyage. The Army of Egypt was ashore; the conquest of Egypt must surely follow.

Nelson had scarcely eaten or slept in days. Now for the second time, and sick at heart, he turned his fleet eastward from the port. 'I do not recollect ever to have felt so utterly hopeless,' Saumarez wrote, 'as when we sat down to dinner. Judge then what a change took place when, as the cloth was being removed, the Officer of the Watch came running in saying, "Sir, a signal is just now made that the Enemy is in Aboukir Bay and moored in a line of battle." All sprang from their seats and, only staying to drink a bumper to our success, we were in a moment on deck.'

17

'Oh God, is it possible?'

As FEAR FED on ignorance, England was alive with rumours and recrimination. 'Where is Buonaparte?' the newspapers asked. 'Where is Admiral Nelson?' A story went around in mid-July saying the French general and five French warships had been captured. Two weeks later this was contradicted: seven British ships were lost. Out of France came garish prints announcing Buonaparte's victory over Nelson, and senior naval officers faced belligerent challenges – 'What is your favourite Hero about? The French Fleet has passed under his nose!' Writing to the First Lord of the Admiralty, the Secretary of War could only say: 'I am always in hopes we shall hear of Nelson doing something brilliant.' By the middle of September, the stories heard from Europe had changed again to 'extravagant accounts' of a decisive victory by Nelson; yet still the only definite information in London was that his ships had left Sardinia for the second time, en route to Cyprus. Without firm intelligence of some sort, no one knew what to believe. Not even Earl Spencer felt able to offer more than the thought that, whatever was happening in the Mediterranean, there would be 'a pretty good story to tell, at least.' Refusing to prepare to censure Nelson, Spencer admitted that like everyone else, he was 'in the greatest anxiety ... on the tiptoe of expectation'. Early in the morning of 2 October, authentic news at last reached the Admiralty. In the corridor outside his office, the First Lord heard it in silence, turned away, and fell to the ground in a faint.

'It began at sunset, and was not finished at three the next morning: it has been severe; but God favoured our endeavours with a great victory.' On 9 August Nelson was writing to the governor of Bombay: after 'this glorious battle ... fought at the mouth of the Nile, at anchor', one of his first thoughts was to pass the news to the East India Company and Britain's colonies in India – they could stand down their defences, for Napoleon's army would never reach them. 'I trust the Almighty God will, in Egypt, overthrow these pests of the human race. It has been in my power ... to take eleven sail of the line, and two frigates: two sail of the line and two frigates have escaped me.'

At the height of the conflict – wounded, nearly blind, thinking he might die, but already certain of the struggle's outcome – he had begun writing a report to St Vincent. Its text became famous all over Europe.

'My Lord: Almighty God has blessed His Majesty's arms in the late battle ... The enemy were moored in a strong line of battle for defending the entrance of this bay, flanked by numerous gunboats, four frigates and a battery of guns and mortars on an island in their van; but nothing could withstand the squadron your lordship did me the honour to place under my command. Their high state of discipline is well known to you, and with the judgment of the captains, together with their valour, and that of the officers and men of every description, it was absolutely irresistible ... I was wounded in the head, and obliged to be carried off the deck, but the service suffered no loss by the event: Captain Berry was fully equal to the important service then going on, and to him I must beg leave to refer for every information relative to the victory.'

Later, from Naples, Sir William Hamilton wrote to St Vincent too, comparing the victory to St Peter's Cathedral in Rome – 'It strikes you at first sight from its magnitude, but the more you examine into its dimensions and details the more wonderful it appears.' This was true, and when Berry and Miller published their accounts of the action, the books sold as quickly as they could be printed; yet the most remarkable aspects of the Battle of the Nile were not just its completeness, but its simplicity and directness. In being fought almost entirely after dark, it was extremely unusual – possibly unique, until modern times; Nelson claimed it was so. Nevertheless, everyone, outside or inside the navy, could picture it accurately: the crescent-shaped bay, ribbed with sandy shoals; the sun so low, it only lit the mastheads; the French ships anchored in a slightly convex line ahead, curving away from the dark desert coast, a few hundred yards distant; the British ships not bothering to form a strict line, but coming unexpectedly in for the attack at once, and their leading ships, *Zealous*, *Theseus* and *Goliath*, sweeping round the front of the French line, delivering raking broadsides as they crossed the enemy bows. They came to the fight cheering and laughing: 'When everything was cleared, the ports open, the matches lighted and the guns run out,' one of the seamen in *Goliath* wrote, 'we gave them three such cheers as are only to be heard in a British Man of War. This intimidates the enemy ... It shows them all is right, and the men, in true spirit, baying to be at them.' *Theseus* echoed the cheers, and, noted Midshipman George Elliot (son of the ex-Viceroy of Corsica), 'The French were ordered by their officers to cheer in return, but they made such a lamentable mess of it that the laughter in our ship was distinctly heard in theirs.'

Not only could everyone picture it, but almost everyone could easily grasp how and why it had worked. When the British fleet was first sighted, late in the afternoon, the French Admiral Brueys thought about putting to sea in anticipation of a traditional battle the next day with opposing lines ahead. His three largest ships – *Franklin* and *Tonnant* with 80 guns each, and the massive 120-gun *L'Orient* – had firepower equal to any four of Nelson's ships; overall, 1,196 French guns would oppose 1,012 British ones. But, as he made ready, he remembered that a third of his men were on shore digging wells; they could not be recalled immediately, and without them his crews would not be large enough to sail the ships and fight as well. However, shoals and shore batteries protected the French, who were the only people to have reliable charts of the bay. In their present positions, his own guns were, in effect, a very long shore battery, something every seaman knew was notoriously difficult to attack from the rolling deck of a ship in motion. All in all, therefore, Brueys thought a twilight attack, which would have to be carried through in the dark, was too risky for Nelson to consider; and with quite reasonable confidence, he stayed where he was.

In *Vanguard*, Captain Berry could see that Brueys's ships seemed to have 'the most decided advantages, as they had nothing to attend to but their artillery'. The French did indeed have the only up-to-date charts; in the whole British fleet, only Foley had a recent one, and that was twenty years old. Brueys's assessment was justified: even Nelson said later that if his fleet had been fresh out of Spithead, 'I would sooner have thought of flying, than of attacking the French in their position – but I knew my captains, nor could I say which distinguished himself most.' It was that shared, absolute confidence – and two bits of luck – which enabled him to give battle in such extraordinary circumstances. The luck was firstly that the wind was blowing perfectly for the entrance into the bay, and secondly that Brueys's ships were anchored only by the bow. This left gaps between the ships, making their defensive line less strong than it could have been. If they could anchor, Nelson reckoned, so could he; and in *Goliath*, Foley took the logic one step further, with an initiative as inspired as any of Nelson's. Single anchors meant the French ships had room to swing. If they could swing, he reasoned that there was sufficient water on both sides of them. No one had told him beforehand to take *Goliath* around and inside the French line, and hardly anyone (with the possible exception of Nelson) expected it. Sam Hood, following in *Zealous*, wrote that he 'expected to stick on the shoal every moment, and did not imagine we should attempt to pass within.' Nor had Brueys: on their landward sides, his ships' ports were closed, and the great guns were covered with furniture, barrels and pots of paint.

The first victim was a frigate, *La Sérieuse*. With great daring and rashness she stood out to challenge the 74s. 'Sink that brute, what does he here!' cried Foley, and both *Goliath* and *Orion* opened fire. The first French liner, the 74-gun *Guerrier*, was almost instantly dismasted: within pistol-shot, Hood gave her a broadside. Her foremast crashed overboard 'in about seven minutes.' Miller, followed so close he went under the French shot, opened fire when her rigging was only six feet from his jib-boom – 'a second breath could not be drawn before her main and mizzen mast were also gone.' He moved on past *Goliath*, now anchored inshore of the second French ship, and engaged the third, *Le Conquérant*, from her landward side at the same moment as Nelson in *Vanguard* attacked her from the seaward. Miller recorded that 'this was precisely at sunset.'

Thus, when it was quite dark, the head and centre of the French line was brought under concentrated fire at very short range on both sides, while the ships at the rear of the line, with the wind against them, could not move. The cannonading and slaughter went on all night, the flashes and thunder of more than a thousand guns in an area scarcely a mile long and two hundred yards wide. Each crash and flare gave a brief, stroboscopic glimpse of mounting carnage; slowly, the moon rose and cast its 'cold, placid light' on the fury below; and gradually, from about nine o'clock, a crackling orange glare began to light the whole scene – the giant *L'Orient* was uncontrollably on fire. Fuelled by fresh paint, newly tarred rigging, barrels of pitch and jars of oil, the blaze increased until every ship was clearly visible; the glow could be seen ('an immense illumination') sixteen miles away in

Rosetta. The heat was so intense that Ben Hallowell, anchored opposite her in *Swiftsure*, saw the pitch melting and running from his own ship's seams; and about ten o'clock, with an almighty explosion, '*L'Orient* blew into the air!!!'

No one in *Zealous* disputed the first lieutenant's rather un-naval note in the log: the roar was heard clearly in Rosetta; in both fleets, everyone thought his own ship had been hit; and every ship stopped firing, stunned into silence by the shock. In the sudden enveloping darkness, for several minutes – some said three, some as much as ten – the action ceased entirely, as scraps of corpses and flaming fragments of wood and canvas showered out of the sky.

Daylight showed *Bellerophon* with all her three masts gone: for more than an hour, she had engaged *L'Orient* alone, before drifting dismasted out of line, leaving a gap which was rapidly filled by two other British vessels. *Majestic* had only her foremast left. Of course there were casualties in every ship, although *Leander* had only fourteen wounded and no dead, and *Zealous*, astonishingly, had only seven wounded and one dead. But *Bellerophon*, *Majestic* and *Vanguard* suffered the highest casualties – between them, 129 killed (including *Majestic*'s Captain Westcott) and 366 wounded, including Nelson. Hurtling through the air, a fragment of shot struck him on the forehead above his blind eye and opened a gaping wound. The rush of blood, and the flap of skin hanging over his good eye, blinded him. As he fell into absolute darkness, he thought he was dying, and begged to be remembered to Fanny.

When his face was cleaned, an inch of his skull was visible, but there was no apparent fracture. Stitching the wound up, the surgeon said cautiously – for such things were never predictable – that the admiral was in no immediate danger, and urged him to rest in the quietest possible place, the bread room, deep down in the hold. Nelson did so, but not for long: neither his secretary, who was also wounded, nor the chaplain were able to take his dictation; so while the battle continued and the ship shuddered around him, he began writing his famous despatch himself, already quite certain that victory would come.

He had not finished when a message arrived from Berry saying *L'Orient* was ablaze. Pallid and bandaged, Nelson climbed up five decks to see the conflagration, and ordered *Vanguard*'s one remaining boat to make ready to pick up survivors of the inevitable explosion. But after such a blow to his head, he could not stay upright: sick and giddy, he was taken below to lie down in his cot, as, after *L'Orient*'s stunning end, the action picked up again and continued through the night. Perhaps he slept. Certainly, in other ships, after 'fighting for near twelve hours', officers and men dropped in exhaustion and slept where they fell – fourteen-year-old Midshipman Elliot fell asleep as he was hauling up a shroud hawser.

At dawn, the survivors saw clearly for the first time the devastation they had wrought. To those who had served below decks, it was particularly shocking. One of them, a cooper named John Nicol, had been stationed at the magazine, and spent 'the busiest night of my life' passing out gunpowder to boys and women – there were several women in the fleet: at least one died of her wounds, and in the middle of the battle, another gave birth to a son. Nicol had been at the Battle of Cape St Vincent, and 'saw as little of this action as I did of the one on 14 February'. In the morning, he went on deck to view the fleets, 'and an awful sight it was.' Everywhere there were ruined ships, and 'the whole Bay was covered with dead bodies, mangled, wounded and scorched ...' Nelson, 'weak, but in good spirits', could see the destruction from his cabin windows, and even he was a little overawed by what he saw and what he learned from his captains, as they visited and reported to him. Only thirteen of his fourteen 74s had been engaged: *Culloden*, to Troubridge's frenzied mortification, had run on to one of the sandbanks – everyone felt extremely sorry for him, and later Nelson made sure that, like all the others, he was awarded a medal. But neither the little *Mutine* nor a single one of the liners was irreparably damaged; and of the thirteen French liners, ten had been captured, one had exploded, and only two had escaped. 'Victory', said Nelson, 'is not a name strong enough.'

Berry left it on record that more than two months earlier, Nelson had worked out his plan of attack against a fleet at anchor, and that at the Nile it was 'minutely and precisely executed.' Foley's initiative in rounding the French line was exactly the kind of sensible independence Nelson encouraged: after outlining and discussing the master plan, he knew that when battle came, he could leave its details to individuals. Later he explained his confidence to some friends, saying he had no doubt each captain 'would find a hole to creep in at.'

From sighting the enemy to joining battle, he intended 'to throw what force I pleased on a few ships.' He was sure his captains would understand, and they did: 'This plan', he told Lord Howe, 'my friends readily conceived by the signals.' Yet he only had to send out four. The first was to prepare for battle and for anchoring by the stern. To his captains, it needed no explanation. Going in with the wind behind them, if the ships anchored by the bows in the usual way, they would swing to the wind and would be vulnerable while they did so. In each ship, they therefore made a cable fast to the mizzen mast, took the end out through one of the stern ports and along the outside of the hull to an anchor. When that anchor was let go and its own cable was slack, the ship would bring up by the stern cable and would not swing; and afterwards, by slackening one cable and hauling up on the other, she could be turned to bring her broadside to bear on any target. His other three signals – equally simple to such experienced men – were 'I mean to attack the enemy's van and centre'; 'Form line of battle as convenient'; and, at twenty minutes to six, the last one, for close action.

He had already announced that by dinner-time next day, he would have gained 'a Peerage, or Westminster Abbey' – the burial place for heroes. During the approach to battle (and while nursing a raging toothache), he 'could not help popping my head every now and then out of the window ... and once, as I was observing their position, I heard two seamen quartered at a gun near me, talking, and one said to the other, "Damn them, look at them – there they are, Jack, and if we don't beat them, they will beat us."' Other officers in other ships heard snatches of the sailors' talk, and it was all optimistic: 'There are thirteen sail of the line – a whacking lot of frigates and small craft. I think we'll hammer the rusk of ten of them, if not the whole boiling.' 'If we knock up a dozen of them – and why shouldn't we – damn my eyes, messmates, we'll have a breadbag full of money.' 'I'm glad we've twigged them at last. I want some new rigging damnably for Sundays.' 'So do I. I hope we touch enough for that and a damned good cruise among the girls, besides.' The admiral said happily, 'I knew what stuff I had under me, so I went into the attack'.

'Joy, joy, joy to you, brave, gallant, immortalised Nelson!' From the Admiralty, on 2 October, Countess Spencer wrote as the city shook with ecstacy and her husband lay prostrate, hardly able to believe the news. 'My heart is absolutely bursting with different sensations of joy, of gratitude, of pride, of every emotion that ever warmed the bosom of a British woman, on hearing of her Country's glory – and all produced by you, my dear, my good friend. All, all I *can* say must fall short of my wishes, of my sentiments about you. This moment the guns are firing, illuminations are preparing, your gallant name is echoed from street to street . . . I am half mad, and I fear I have written a strange letter, but you'll excuse it. Almighty God protect you! Adieu!'

Certainly a phenomenal victory deserved a phenomenal welcome, but the single most striking aspect of the nation's reaction was just that – it was national, not merely naval or governmental. 'It operated as an electric impulse', said one newspaper: the tidings were carried as fast as possible to every part of the land, and as they rippled out, people celebrated in every way they could think of – parades, volleys of musketry and field guns, ox-roasts, concerts, bunting, illuminations, ringing of church bells, impromptu balls; a new dance was devised 'called the *Vanguard*, or the *breaking of the line*', and as they got tired of 'God save the King, Rule Britannia, etc, etc,' they added new verses praising Nelson, wrote and sang brand new songs, and decorated their clothes with anchors, and Nelson's name, and 'The Hero of the Nile' picked out in gold spangles. Subscriptions were opened for the widows and orphans of the battle; someone, who would have made a fortune if copyright existed, realized that 'Horatio Nelson' could be turned into a Latin anagram, *Honor est a Nilo*; and in Drury Lane theatre, two members of the audience expressed it all – one called out for the singing of 'Britons, strike home', and another, in cheers and laughter, shouted back: 'Why, dammit, they *have*!'

'Every Briton feels his obligation to you. But', wrote Countess Spencer in wonder, 'if these strangers feel in this manner about you, who can express what *We* of this house feel about you? What incalculable service have you been of to my dear Lord Spencer!' Yet people who had never heard of Spencer, or the Countess, felt the same: Nelson had been of 'incalculable service' to all – even to the highwayman who waylaid one of the Admiralty's messengers, and then meekly apologized when he understood what news he was delaying. In her own rejoicing, the only thing that Countess Spencer missed was that, after the Nile, no one in the nation thought of Nelson as a stranger.

Neither was Hardy disappointed with the Mediterranean 'cruise': the morning after the Battle of the Nile, Nelson not only made him post-captain but also brought him into *Vanguard* as flag-captain, 'still on the sunny side of thirty'. It was a typical job for a new or very junior captain, enabling him to gain experience in commanding a large ship, while still having a more knowledgeable officer on hand to advise, instruct and if necessary take over. But very few people had the chance, after such a victory, to be the victor's flag-captain – the honour was great.

His first voyage in command of Nelson's flagship would be thirteen hundred miles to Naples: *Vanguard* was much in need of repair, and the only other safe dockyard in the Mediterranean was Gibraltar, another thousand miles on. Saumarez was to lead the least damaged liners there, with the surviving prizes; three were so battered they were not worth taking, and were burned in the bay. Berry was to carry the news home with Thompson in *Leander*. Besides Hardy's captaincy, there were other promotions: Thomas Capel, Nelson's signal lieutenant, was made post and given command of *Mutine*; William Hoste (not yet eighteen) was made an acting captain. Together, in case *Leander* did not get through safely, they took duplicate despatches to Britain's nearest and most important diplomatic representative, Sir William Hamilton. Sending duplicates was standard practice born of long experience, and its wisdom was proved again: *Mutine* got to Naples, but *Leander* had the misfortune to meet and be captured by one of the two French 74s which had escaped from the Nile. Berry and Thompson were soon freed in an exchange of prisoners, and for their spirited defence of the ship, both were subsequently knighted. But it was Capel who had the incomparable satisfaction of spreading the news overland through Europe, and from Naples he wrote tongue-tied to Nelson: 'I am totally unable, Sir, to express the joy that appeared on every countenance, and the bursts of applause and acclamation we received. The Queen and Lady Hamilton fainted ... They all hail you as the saviour of Europe.'

Today, one outstanding work still brings over the ecstatic spirit of the time. As messengers rode north, Franz Joseph Haydn was in Vienna, completing a new mass to celebrate the birthday of one of the Austrian princesses. Though it was sacred music, he intended it as a triumphant piece, full of exuberance and vigour. It had come to the point of rehearsal when, from Italy, the thrilling report arrived, and at once the music acquired a new name: the Nelson Mass. If the princess after whom it should have been named made any objection, no one listened to her. Birthdays – even royal ones – have a certain predictability, but to everyone who heard it, the exhilarating mass rang out for a real celebration which none had dreamed possible.

Vanguard's voyage to Naples was, meanwhile, extremely slow. After the climactic events in Aboukir Bay, Nelson was preoccupied with thoughts of their wider political implications, of his own deteriorating health, and of Josiah. Captain Nisbet – an officer whom few people thought really worthy of command – arrived at Aboukir in the sloop *Bonne Citoyenne* ten days after the battle, and was one of the first non-participants to learn of his stepfather's conquest. With him he brought orders from St Vincent and letters, including a sealed personal one from the commander-in-chief to Nelson. This contained an extremely unpleasant surprise: St Vincent's damning opinion of Josiah. 'It would be a breach of friendship', Nelson read, 'to conceal from you that he loves drink and low company, is thoroughly ignorant of all forms of service, inattentive, obstinate, and wrong-headed beyond measure, and had he not been your son-in-law must have been annihilated months ago. With all this, he is honest and truth-telling, and I dare say will, if you ask him, subscribe to every word I have written.' Nelson did not have to; he knew it was all true – he had often said similar things, though not quite so harshly. But to have them written by a man he respected deeply, and to read them in such a time and place, was bitter: he, who was so good with the sons of other families, could only acknowledge failure where he should have failed least, and wonder at the cause.

Moving to the orders, he learned that unless he had already found the French, he should leave the pursuit and return to assist in an attack on Minorca: a new British base must be won. Nelson agreed. He recognized the political and strategic implications of his victory – the night of battle had restored British naval dominance of the Mediterranean, and could lead to a new anti-French coalition – but it must be followed up, or the advantage would be lost. However, his next active part would have to wait; he was mentally and physically drained, still suffering from the head-wound, ill with a cough and fever. Nor would *Vanguard* be any better fit for active service until she was fully repaired, so, knowing St Vincent would understand, he turned to the letters from home. Naturally long out of date, they were pathetically inappropriate to the scene around him, speaking of far-off domestic life in Norfolk: gossip of new neighbours and the fine summer weather, anger at the thoughtless rumours circulated in the papers, problems with the orchard harvest, little worries over his health and comfort – 'Have you stockings enough?' Poor dear Fanny: 'I was determined', she said humbly, 'to see if I could write to you without tormenting you with my anxieties, every day produces hopes of hearing from you.'

On 16 September, four weeks after quitting Aboukir but still en route for Naples, he started his reply. 'My dearest Fanny: I hardly know where to begin.' While she and all in Britain wondered and worried, the tide of congratulation had begun to flood south from Italy. 'My head is almost turned by letters already, and what am I not to expect when I get on shore?' Lady Hamilton had described Queen Maria's display of frantic relief, and Nelson hoped he would not have to see it for himself. The letter became a long one, eventually sent on 25 September, three days after *Vanguard*'s arrival in Naples. With his inescapable frankness, he told Fanny all about it.

'Sir William and Lady Hamilton came out to sea ... Alongside my honoured friends came ... Up flew her Ladyship, and, exclaiming 'Oh God, is it possible?', fell into my arm more dead than alive. Tears, however, soon set matters to rights, when alongside came the King ... He took me by the hand, calling me his deliverer and preserver, with every other expression of kindness. In short, all Naples calls me *Nostra Liberatore*, for the scene with the lower classes was truly affecting. I hope one day to have the pleasure of introducing you to Lady Hamilton. She is one of the very best women in this world.' He must have realized that Fanny would find this hard to believe: she already knew Emma's early reputation as a mistress to the rich so well that Nelson immediately added: 'How few could have made the turn she has. She is an honour to her sex, but I own it requires a good soul. Her kindness with Sir William to me is more than I can express. I am in their house ... May God Almighty bless you, my dearest Fanny, and grant us in due time a happy meeting.' And he ended, as he always did: 'Ever your most affectionate husband, Horatio Nelson.'

Four and a half months later, he wrote again from sea. 'I think I shall run mad ... Last night I did nothing but dream of you, altho' I woke 20 times in the night. In one of my dreams I thought I was at a large table – you was not present – sitting between a Princess, who I detest, and another. They both tried to seduce me and the first wanted to take those liberties with me which no woman in this world but yourself ever did. The consequence was I knocked her down and in the moment of bustle you came in and, taking me in your embrace, whispered, "I love nothing but you, my Nelson." I kissed you fervently and we enjoyed the height of love.'

He was writing, of course, to Emma. Fanny never had inspired, never would inspire, such erotic passion – perhaps she was the anonymous other, or even the 'Princess, who I detest'. If so, did Nelson, in his dream, knock her down because he knew in conscience she must keep him from Emma? Because he was disgusted by the notion of Fanny as a physical seductress, her angular body mimicking the movements of Emma's voluptuous, sensuous shape? Because he was disgusted at his own delight, horrified to know this was one love affair he could not leave at Gibraltar?

His first biographers prefaced their three-volume work with the warning that they might show 'sometimes, perhaps, more minutely than the generality of readers may approve, the private feelings and motives of this extraordinary man'. But their courage failed them: Emma became 'this wicked siren'; Nelson's private journals were edited to leave her out – they applied 'the pruning-knife' there, indeed; they ignored his love-letters entirely, and could not bring themselves to mention his and Emma's daughter; and by the end of their second volume, with a whole book still to go, they simply gave up, saying that all the rest would be 'exclusively devoted to his more splendid public character.'

It could have been merely a decent reticence, but it seems not. The problem for those Victorian authors was threefold: firstly, Nelson did make a laughing-stock of himself; secondly, that and immorality did not square with the concept and the carefully developed image of a national hero; and lastly, they appeared unable even to comprehend, far less accept, that love may be superseded, honestly and without any intent or desire to deceive. So they made a sanitized champion, and for a while, though in a different way, Nelson was as fraudulent himself. Seduced by the image of his own heroism, he behaved as he thought a hero should; and embarrassed almost everyone who knew him.

18

'Ruined with affection'

IN THE SUMMER of 1800, in Leghorn, General Sir John Moore wrote a brief note in his diary. 'Sir William and Lady Hamilton were there attending the Queen of Naples. Lord Nelson was there, attending upon Lady Hamilton. He is covered with stars, ribbons and medals, more like a Prince of the Opera than the Conqueror of the Nile. It is really melancholy to see a brave and good man, who has deserved well of his country, cutting so pitiful a figure.'

Those four short sentences remain an accurate sketch of the two strangest years in Nelson's life: in sharp, simple words, Moore caught the central relationships, the admiral's pantomime appearance, and the dismayed thoughts of most who witnessed them. But he did not remark on the strangest facts of all – Rear Admiral Lord Nelson of the Nile and of Burnham Thorpe was returning home not by sea, as an admiral should, but by land, and he was taking his mistress and her husband with him.

Before his victorious arrival in Naples in 1798, Nelson's firm intention had been to stay no longer than it took to get *Vanguard* into shape again; he would then go to Syracuse. Five days after his arrival, as the city, the Hamiltons and the royal family engulfed him in a whirlpool of celebration and praise, he was still more determined – 'Nothing', he told St Vincent, 'shall again induce me to send the squadron to Naples, whilst our operations lie on the eastern side of Sicily; we should be ruined with affection and kindness.'

His instinct to be at sea again was sound, for given the peculiar combination of circumstances at the time, he was, on shore, a vulnerable man. It has been suggested that the wound to his head actually caused a psychological imbalance, since a concussive blow to the forehead, possibly damaging the frontal lobes of the brain, can bring about a prolonged loss of judgment and loosening of inhibitions. That interesting hypothesis fits many of the facts, yet perhaps sounds like a scientific excuse; and even without it, there were several simple but critical factors which, put together, must have had a profound effect on him. He had been away from home for eighteen months. Apart from a brief visit to the commander-in-chief in Cadiz, he had not been out of his ship for six months. In that time, he had endured extraordinary stresses: the chase around the Mediterranean, the climactic battle at Aboukir, the wound. There had been a long-drawn-out, abnormal degree of uncertainty, followed by much physical danger, all with a level of personal responsibility he had never had before. There had been no superior to turn to; no company except his officers and men; certainly none of the solace of a sexual partner; he had won an historic victory, and, as it happened, he was just now approaching his fortieth birthday. Brain-damaged or not, in Naples he was wide open to what today might be termed a mid-life crisis of appropriately large proportions. In a disciplined environment – at sea with his squadron, in the British dockyard at Gibraltar or, best of all, off Cadiz with St Vincent's comforting support – he would probably have adjusted to it all. Instead, he was surrounded by adoring civilians who looked to him as their guide, their guard and their hero; who competed to see who could honour him most lavishly; and who gave him, as senior naval officer present, no rest from responsibility.

'Between business and what is called pleasure', he wrote wearily, 'I am not my own master for five minutes.' He was willing to put up with it for a while, and did not deny the pleasure of seeing *Nelson and the Nile* and *Victory* picked out with three thousand lights. Emma, very much in her element, gave him a fortieth birthday party which (he told Fanny) was 'enough to fill me with vanity': every ribbon and button had his name on it; the entire dinner service was marked 'H.N. Glorious 1st of August!'; eighty people dined, a further seven hundred had supper, 1,740 came to the ball, and 'under a magnificent canopy' a decorated column was erected, inscribed 'Veni, vidi, vici' – 'never, Lady Hamilton says, to come down while they remain at Naples.' Unfortunately Josiah got extremely drunk, and had to be removed from the party when he started to say, loudly, that his stepfather was behaving towards Emma as he ought to behave towards Fanny. The next morning, sour and probably hung over, Nelson wrote tersely to St Vincent: 'I trust, my Lord, in a week we shall all be at sea. I am very unwell, and the miserable conduct of this Court is not likely to cool my irritable temper. It is a country of fiddlers and poets, whores and scoundrels.'

That week had not passed, however, when he met Queen Maria Carolina for the first time; and it was that meeting – far more than the Hamiltons' reception – which bound him to Naples for the foreseeable future. Sir William Hamilton's fortune came from his first marriage (he wed Emma in 1791 after nine years of widowerhood), and his first wife left a perceptive description of the Queen: 'She is quick, clever, insinuating when she pleases, loves and hates violently ... Her strongest and most durable passions are ambition and vanity ... The former, which I think is her principle object, makes her use every art to please the King in order to get the reins of government into her own hands in as great a measure as is possible.'

To a large extent she had succeeded. Ferdinand, her husband, was happy to spend his time slaughtering as many animals as possible in organized hunts, fishing (and selling his catch in the streets), and fathering children – he had seventeen legitimate ones, and no doubt even more elsewhere. Beyond her love of power and her offspring, Maria Carolina had one dominant passion: she loathed the French. Certainly she had good reason – her brother Leopold was Emperor of Austria; one of her daughters, married to Leopold's son, was Crown Princess of Austria. As if they had not suffered enough at French hands, Maria Carolina could not forget the fate of her sister Marie Antoinette, guillotined in Paris. She had no doubt the same would happen to her if revolution came to Naples; so, being royal and implacably opposed to 'the Jacobins', she impressed Nelson very much – 'She is, in fact, a great king', he said, and he meant it as a compliment.

A new alliance of Britain, Austria and Russia was being prepared against France. Technically, France and Naples were now at peace, but all the rest of Italy was under French control: the nearest Revolutionary army was in Rome, only three days' march from the Neapolitan border. Queen Maria Carolina did not believe for one moment that it would stay in Rome for ever, and wished for Nelson's advice on the matter.

It did not take long to persuade him. For one thing, he had already made up his mind. Within days of arrival, lamenting 'what precious moments the courts of Naples and Vienna are losing!', he declared that 'three months would liberate Italy; but this court is so enervated that the happy moment will be lost.' For another thing, there was no conflict with his orders from the Admiralty. Relayed through St

Vincent, they were to protect the coasts of Italy, blockade Malta, liaise with Turkey and Russia at sea, prevent communication between France and Egypt, and, if war became active in Italy, to co-operate with allied armies. Finally, as he wrote later, 'Who could withstand the request of such a Queen?'

Before Tenerife he had said that naval officers had to be ready to take political risks, and he did so now, with advice which was characteristically simple, urgent and aggressive: 'This country, with its system of procrastination, will ruin itself ... War at this moment can alone save these kingdoms.' Rome should be attacked at the earliest opportunity – 'The boldest measures are the safest.' His advice was taken, and within four months its results – the first practical political outcomes of the Battle of the Nile – were the flight of the whole royal family to Sicily, and the French conquest of all mainland Italy.

Autumn, however, had turned towards winter with almost unclouded optimism. Shortly after Nelson accepted the role of military advisor to the Neapolitan court, General Karl Mack von Leiberich arrived bearing promises of support from Austria, and declaring himself ready to march on Rome in ten days. 'He is active, and has an intelligent eye, and', said Nelson, 'will do well, I have no doubt' -- a surprisingly hopeful conclusion, given his experience of Austrian generals. Leaving shore preparations to Mack, he sailed in mid-October to commence the blockade of Malta. Although he predicted it would be a long task (and he was right – the French garrison held out for two years), it began promisingly, with the immediate surrender of the small neighbouring island of Gozo. Another good sign was the arrival of a Portuguese squadron, welcome because they showed that one more ally was becoming active again. The squadron, commanded by the Marquis de Niza, was not otherwise useful. Nelson could not agree with the nobleman's view that being a marquis made him the equivalent of an admiral, and that all his captains should be regarded as commodores with rights over any or all of the English captains, the veterans of Aboukir. Describing the Marquis as 'completely ignorant of Sea affairs', he thanked him for coming to Malta, sent him to Naples, and made it plain he should give orders only to Portuguese ships.

Leaving Alexander Ball with five ships of the line in charge of the Maltese blockade, he too turned for Naples again, and now began to hear gradually of his rewards for the Nile. In the end, they were immense, and he listed them all proudly. His captains had already pledged him a gold sword, with a crocodile at the hilt. Another sword came from the City of London, and a third, with a gold cane as well, from the little Greek island of Zante. 'From the East India Company, £10,000. From the Turkish Company, a fine piece of plate. From the emperor of Russia, a box set with diamonds, valued at £2,500 ... From the king of Sardinia, a box set with diamonds, valued at £1,200 ... From the city of Palermo, a gold box and chain, set on a silver waiter.' From the mother of 'the grand seignior', the ruler of Turkey, came a third diamond-studded box worth a thousand pounds, and from the grand seignior himself, the most unusual gifts of all: a pelisse – a fur-trimmed mantle – likewise valued at a thousand, and 'a diamond aigrette, or plume of triumph, valued at £2,000.' A fuller description than Nelson's own shows how garish this thing was. 'Crowned with a vibrating plumage', it had thirteen strands of diamonds – one for each of the French liners at the Nile – and in the middle 'a radiant star ... turning on its centre by means of watch-work which winds up behind'. He liked it very much, and sometimes wore it in his hat.

However, he could make still more show than that. To add to his gold medal for Cape St Vincent and his star as a Knight of the Bath, there would be a gold medal privately issued by his old friend Alexander Davison – the man who had stopped him getting married in Quebec, now a highly successful businessman and prize-agent for his whole fleet. There was a third medal – an official one – from King George, with an annual pension of £2,000 that would extend through the lives of his next two heirs; and there was a barony.

For Nelson to be raised only to the lowest rank of the British peerage annoyed everyone. Privately and indiscreetly, Admiral Lord Hood told Fanny that the Prime Minister intended her to be a viscountess at least. From Roundwood she wrote tartly to St Vincent that all of a sudden she was 'honoured with the notice of the great in this neighbourhood – truly I don't thank them: they ought to have found their way to the cottage before.' The Hamiltons were incensed – 'Hang them, I say!' Emma wrote to Fanny. 'If I was King of England,' she told Nelson, 'I would make you the most noble, puissant Duke Nelson, Marquis Nile, Earl Alexandria, Viscount Pyramid, Baron Crocodile, and Prince Victory ... Your statue ought to be made of pure gold, and placed in the middle of London.' Of course the statue was made, and placed in a new London square named Trafalgar; but it was not of gold, and not erected until 1843. In 1798, Emma gave the reason for her extravagant wish – it was in order 'that posterity might have you in all forms'. In her own way, she achieved exactly that.

In mid-November Minorca was captured by a force commanded by General Charles Stuart, who had worked with Nelson in the siege of Calvi, and afterwards ignored Nelson's share of the credit. There were no British casualties at Minorca, and Stuart was knighted. At the same time, in Naples, Nelson was trying to keep General Mack's enthusiasm alight – in addition to the ten days he had said he needed, three further weeks had passed, and he had not stirred. Discovering that Mack needed five carriages merely to move his personal luggage raised an uncomfortable memory of General de Vins' inertia. Thirty thousand Neapolitans had been armed, and a farcical review was held: exercising his troops ('healthy, good-looking', said Nelson), Mack allowed himself to be surrounded by the theoretical enemy. 'Wretchedly officered', was Nelson's opinion, but he seems to have been distracted: as he drove past the soldiers with the Queen and Emma, a disapproving eye noted how Lady Hamilton 'paraded her conquest over the victor of Aboukir, who, seated beside her in the same carriage, appeared fascinated and submissive to her charms.' As for the troops, a more professional military view came from a general who had served with the Russian army. Three-quarters of the Neapolitan soldiers were, he said, 'only peasants in uniform', scarcely able to perform the simplest manoeuvre.

That night it was agreed to start the advance in five days' time. Nelson's ships would take five thousand men and cavalry to Leghorn, attacking Rome from the north; the Austrians would come down the eastern side of Italy and attack from that direction; while Ferdinand would advance with the rest of his army from the south. The French army in Rome would be attacked from three sides. But then came news from Vienna: the Austrian army would only attack if the French did so first. Ferdinand, who was to lead the assault on Rome, began to have second thoughts. Nelson lost patience, and told the king straight out that he had two choices: either trust in God, advance and if necessary die sword in hand, knowing his cause was just, 'or remain quiet, and be kicked out of your kingdom.'

On balance, King Ferdinand decided it might be easier to attack Rome than to hold out against the combined force of Nelson and Queen Maria Carolina. At last, towards the end of the month, army and ships set out towards their respective targets. Leghorn was taken easily, and on 29 November (to Ferdinand's amazement) so was Rome.

Apart from five hundred soldiers shut in a strong castle, the French simply vacated the city as he approached, and he settled himself in an elegant palace.

Just over a week later, he and his army were in full flight back to Naples – Ferdinand, in civilian clothes, riding as close as possible to the Prince of Migliano, and gasping: 'Keep your knee stuck close to mine! Don't leave me alone!'

It might have been different with other men to fight and lead. As it was, outside Rome, the French had regrouped without interference and simply stormed back in. They did not stop there: by following Nelson's advice, Ferdinand had given them a perfect excuse for the invasion of his kingdom. At that, the Neapolitans – who had fled from an army one-sixth the size of their own – did begin to fight, defending their homes. Soon it became clear the capital would fall, and on 21 December the evacuation to Sicily commenced. Exactly three months had passed since Nelson's joyous reception. Now, in complete and awful contrast, on a windy, rainy, bitterly cold night, the royal family, their fortune, and the British residents of the city all tumbled pell-mell into his ships.

The flight, into a full gale, was dismal in the extreme. Even Nelson reckoned it was the worst weather he had known at sea. Sir William Hamilton, philosopher though he was, hated the idea of death by drowning so much that he prepared two pistols, and was ready to shoot himself if he felt *Vanguard* sinking. Quite reasonably, most of the passengers thought their last hour had come; and for one, it had. On the evening of Christmas Day, six-year-old Prince Alberto – the Queen's youngest and favourite son – had convulsions, and died in Emma's arms.

Throughout the terrible voyage, she was the only civilian to behave with courage. It was genuine, and Nelson could not fail to notice this unsuspected side of her character. Beauty and flattery he liked as much as anyone, yet they could be enjoyed and forgotten – anyone could flatter, and many women were beautiful; but he always respected courage. By showing she could be brave as well as beautiful, Emma – probably without intending it – earned his respect, and in his mind placed herself apart from most of the women he knew. 'Her head and heart surpass her beauty,' he thought, 'which cannot be equalled by anything I have seen.'

That winter in Palermo, the capital of Sicily, was unpleasant for almost all the evacuees. Their welcome had appeared good, but since the royal accommodation was hardly ever used, it was half-derelict, without carpets or fireplaces, and with doors and windows that would not shut against the freezing temperatures outside. Only King Ferdinand, who revelled in hunting the abundant woodcock, seemed unconcerned at the loss of the mainland half of his kingdom. The queen was so distraught at the same loss, and the death of their little son, that she took to her bed and was expected to die. Sir William was ill, and fell into a deep depression on hearing of the loss, near the Scilly Isles, of HMS *Culloden*: the most precious items of his famous collection of antiquities were on board when she went down. Anchored in the harbour, *Vanguard* effectively became the seat of Neapolitan government, and Nelson began the New Year in a fury. Despatches from the Admiralty informed him that Captain Sir Sidney Smith was being sent to the Mediterranean in two capacities – one, to liaise in diplomacy with his brother, Spencer Smith, British Minister at Constantinople; the other, to take command of naval operations off Egypt. A substantial slice of Nelson's command area, and one which he felt particularly his own, was being given to an officer junior to him. 'Could I have thought it, and from Earl Spencer?' he demanded. 'Never, never was I so astonished ... Sir Sidney writes to Sir W. Hamilton that he shall go to Egypt and take Captain Hood and the squadron under his command. He has no orders from you', Nelson reminded St Vincent, 'to take my ships away. Pray grant me your permission to retire.'

St Vincent wanted to go home too; approaching sixty-four years old, he was on the verge of a total breakdown in health. His reply to Nelson urged patience and tolerance, but from Palermo in mid-January came a letter saying, 'Things go from bad to worse ... Mack has disappeared. The few remaining cowardly troops are disarmed.' On the 23rd, Naples fell. Three days afterwards, writing to his brother-in-law in Dorset, Captain Hardy announced: 'There is little doubt but the *Vanguard* will soon go to England with the Admiral & Sir William Hamilton's family. If I can get a frigate in this country I shall not refuse; if not, I think you will see me in the course of three months.' It was the first letter he had been able to write since May. At once he and *Vanguard* were sent to visit the blockade of Malta; Nelson remained in Palermo. Three weeks later, when Hardy returned, he sent another letter home, with a surprising change of mood – 'I find the Admiral is not so anxious to quit this country as when I wrote you last.'

In that short interval, Nelson had bound himself to 'this country' –

or more specifically, to the two women in it who were closest and most important to him. First was the queen: at the beginning of February, building on his existing promise never to leave the coast of Naples unguarded, she extracted the promise of his personal protection – 'not to leave her, unless by her desire.' And second was Emma; for the night of 12 February was when she and Nelson became lovers.

This is a matter of deduction rather than recorded fact. Two years later, he wrote to her: 'Ah, my dear friend, I did remember well the 12th February, and also the two months afterwards. I shall never forget them, and never be sorry for the consequences.' He used the past tense ('I did remember') because he was telling her what his first reactions had been on the news of the birth of their daughter. By then, there had been only two 12 Februarys since the Battle of the Nile, those of 1799 and 1800. However, on 12 February 1800 he was at sea. On the same date in 1799 he was on shore in Palermo; and his first passionately erotic letter to Emma was written in early February 1799. 'The Princess, who I detest ... wanted to take those liberties with me which no woman in this world but yourself ever did.' One might say that such private moments are no one else's business; yet curiosity is inevitable, when a man alters his life for ever.

Once, shortly after his splendid fortieth birthday party in Naples, Nelson sent to St Vincent a message which would become famous: 'I am writing opposite Lady Hamilton, therefore you will not be surprised at the glorious jumble of this letter. Were your Lordship in my place, I much doubt if you could write so well; our hearts and hands must be all in a flutter: Naples is a dangerous place and we must keep clear of it.'

Though no one else was such an intimate as Nelson, many other officers were fond of Emma: Alexander Ball called her 'the Patroness of the Navy', and in February 1799 told her, 'I find you fascinate all the Navy as much at Palermo as you did at Naples.' It was not Naples that was dangerous, but Nelson's own nature, and hers. 'Do not let your fascinating Neapolitan dames approach too near him', St Vincent warned her, 'for he is made of flesh and blood and cannot resist their temptations.' The commander-in-chief half-expected that some affair might develop on shore; his main concern was that it could interfere with professional duties, and he told Nelson how pleased he was that that had not happened. But friends and colleagues did begin to worry

Lady Hamilton, painted in 1800 when she was pregnant with Nelson's first child. A frank acquaintance said, 'She is indeed a Whapper! and I think her manner very vulgar', but the artist, Schmidt, tactfully concealed her size and created Nelson's favourite portrait of 'Santa Emma'.

'Paradise Merton' on its eastern side, looking towards the Canal. Within fifty years of Nelson's death, 'those beautiful pleasure grounds and gardens' were all gone, replaced by a Victorian suburb.

Nelson's little angel of paradise: his daughter Horatia visiting Merton, unaware who her parents were, but always happy to play with 'my dear, dear Godpapa ... Give my love to him every day when you write, and a kiss.'

Cuthbert Collingwood, Nelson's
second-in-command at the Battle of
Trafalgar: 'My friendship with him
was unlike anything I have left in the
navy – a brotherhood of more than
thirty years.'

Thomas Masterman Hardy,
Nelson's flag-captain at
Trafalgar: although the
portrait (unlike some
painted when he was an old
man) does not convey
Hardy's great physical size,
here he is much as Nelson
would have known him.

Sailors in a Fight: 'When they had given us one good duster, and I found myself snug and tight, I bid fear kiss my bottom, and set to in good earnest . . . How my fingers got knocked overboard I don't know, but off they are, and I never missed them till I wanted them.'

An enemy at anchor, seen from the sea: on 2 April 1801, with the towers of Copenhagen in the background. Nelson's fleet sailed in to give battle against 'the brothers of Englishmen, the Danes'.

Hoisting the most famous signal in British naval history, 'England expects . . .' – With some people busy and others simply waiting, the painting conveys Victory's slow, orderly and solemn approach to battle.

'Oh *Victory, Victory,* how you distract my poor brain!' Devis's painting is one of the best, and certainly the most famous, of Nelson's last hours, but it has some curious inaccuracies: Hardy (standing with his hand above Nelson) was well over six feet tall and, with only 5′ 8″ of headspace, must have been half-crouched in the cramped orlop deck; and Nelson's exposed shoulder shows no trace of the fatal wound.

when Nelson moved from his flagship, to live with the Hamiltons in Palermo.

Already, Fanny's daily concerns were deepening. Nelson's letters were even less frequent than usual. Though they still ended with his habitual formula of affection, they contained too many flattering remarks about Lady Hamilton; and Emma too was writing to Fanny saying how well she and Josiah were getting on together – 'I love him much and, although we quarrel sometimes, he loves me and does as I would have him.' Nelson confirmed this: 'The improvement made in Josiah by Lady Hamilton is wonderful. She seems the only person he minds ... your and my obligations are infinite on that score.' Whatever was intended, Fanny could only read this as criticism of her ability as a mother. 'She is in good health,' Davison told Nelson, 'but very uneasy and anxious, which is not to be wondered at ... She bids me say that unless you return home in a few months, she will join the Standard at Naples. Excuse a woman's tender feelings – they are too acute to be expressed.'

Nelson's reply was both cryptic and clear: 'You would, by February, have seen how unpleasant it would have been ... I could, if you had come, *only* have struck my flag and carried you back again, for it would have been impossible to set up an establishment at either Naples or Palermo.' He protested, in what should have been an unnecessary way, that 'nothing but the situation of affairs in this country has kept me from England'; and Fanny, forbidden to leave home, could only pray he meant political affairs.

These were indeed complicated. During March, Austria belatedly declared war on France; Napoleon and his stranded army penetrated through Egypt into Palestine and conquered Jaffa; in Tripoli the Bashaw was discovered to be negotiating with the French government; and, evading Lord Bridport's blockade for the second time, twenty-five French ships of the line in Brest escaped and made for the Mediterranean. St Vincent, seriously ill, was on shore in Gibraltar. His second-in-command on the Cadiz blockade, Vice Admiral Lord Keith, gave chase to the Brest fleet, and in so doing allowed seventeen Spanish ships to slip out. Meanwhile – as 120,000 Austrians and Russians began marching to Italy and a Russian naval squadron began operations in the Adriatic – a counter-revolution gained strength in Naples, led by Cardinal Fabrizio Ruffo, a warrior-cleric of the crusading school with 17,000 irregulars ('the Christian Army of the Holy Faith') under his command.

One of St Vincent's last acts before going ashore had been to sort out, in a way satisfactory to all, the problem posed by Captain Sir Sidney Smith, which had sprung from the captain's (admittedly wilful) misunderstanding of ambiguous Admiralty orders. Smith was sent to relieve Troubridge on the Alexandria blockade, as the orders had stated, but placed firmly under Nelson's command. (To the very ruffled rear admiral, St Vincent said gently: 'I am sure you will mortify him as little as possible.') Troubridge in turn blockaded Naples, while Hardy was sent to Tripoli in *Vanguard* to convince the Bashaw that an alliance with France would not be in his best interests. The Bashaw, a notoriously truculent and devious man, returned a flowery letter to 'Admiral Nelson, Capitan Pasha of the King of England' and carried on as before. Nelson sent back an equally ornate reply and a larger force, which, after fruitless discussions with the Bashaw, opened fire on his palace, 'upon which everything was adjusted'.

Troubridge had quicker success: early in April he captured the islands of Capri and Ischia, commanding the bay of Naples. 'Your Lordship never beheld such loyalty', he wrote to Nelson. 'The people are perfectly mad with joy and asking for their beloved Monarch.' On the other side of Italy, Russian ships blockaded Ancona and took Brindisi and Bari; and in between, the approach of Cardinal Ruffo's holy irregulars squeezed all but five hundred of the occupying French out of Naples again. However, there were still some twenty thousand Neapolitan Jacobins in the city, and Troubridge discovered the viciousness of Latin revenge: 'Everyone has his marked Jacobin to stiletto.' One morning a basket of grapes was delivered to him, at sea, with a parcel and a covering letter from a proud loyalist. Troubridge ate the grapes, read the letter, endorsed it with the words 'A jolly fellow', and sent it on to Nelson. He threw the parcel overboard: 'the weather being very hot', he thought he should not forward it to Nelson too, for it contained the severed head of a rebel.

In Palermo, the Nelson–Hamilton household was becoming progressively odder. Sir William's name for it was the motto of the Knighthood of the Bath, *Tria Juncta in Uno*, Three Joined in One. He was no cuckold; he knew perfectly well what was going on between Emma and Nelson, but he was happy, for he had always predicted that something of the sort would happen – that he would be 'superannuated' while Emma was still young – and he both liked and admired

Nelson. But Nelson was starting to display one of his least attractive characteristics: if he thought someone did not know his name and heroism, he told them himself. This happened to a visiting Scottish major. 'Have you heard of the battle of the Nile?' Nelson asked him, and without waiting for an answer told him that it was the most extraordinary battle ever fought, unique for being at night, at anchor, and won by a one-armed admiral. The major bowed courteously three times, and thought to himself, 'Had the speech been made *after* dinner, I should have imagined the hero had imbibed an extra dose of champagne.' Emma's behaviour that evening was a great deal worse. To receive a Turkish messenger, Nelson dressed up in his furry scarlet pelisse and diamond aigrette with the clockwork star. Deeply impressed, the Turk announced he had decapitated twenty French prisoners in one day. He drew his sword to prove it, and showed off the bloodstains. Emma, said the Scottish soldier, took the sword, 'beamed with delight, and ... looking at the encrusted Jacobin blood, kissed it ...!' One woman fainted; some people clapped; 'but many groaned and cried "shame" loud enough to reach the ears of the admiral, who turned pale, hung his head, and seemed ashamed ... Poor Nelson was to be pitied – never was a man so mystified and deluded!'

By the end of April the reconquest of Ferdinand's capital seemed imminent; but at that point Nelson learned of the new naval threat from France and Spain. In the end this came to nothing at all – the combined fleets ranged around the northern Mediterranean, chased but unchecked by Lord Keith, until the end of July, when they slipped back into the Atlantic with Keith still in pursuit. Yet their presence brought much confusion, and (unhappily, from Nelson's view) coincided with the least welcome event of his professional life that year: the departure, in June, of St Vincent. Keith, twelve years older than Nelson and three years his senior as an admiral, became commander-in-chief. As usual, Nelson could not mask his feelings – after an impassioned appeal to St Vincent to stay ('Give not up a particle of your authority to any one; be again our St Vincent, and we shall be happy'), he wrote sarcastically to Troubridge: 'We of the Nile are not equal to Keith in his estimation, and ought to think it an honour to serve under such a clever man.'

His open contempt for the new commander-in-chief was not really justified, and in his letter to the outgoing commander he had given as good a reason as any for tolerance: 'It must take a length of time ...

to be in any manner a St Vincent.' But now he was a hero, accustomed to free rein, perilously certain that his judgment was correct. To a man, the 'band of brothers' agreed with him, and in the tense and torrid, contradictory atmosphere which surrounded him that summer, acts which seemed strange and drastic to outsiders became usual. From Ben Hallowell, he accepted with pleasure the gift of a coffin, especially made for him out of the mainmast of *L'Orient*. Before having it taken to his cabin (where he stood it up behind his chair), it lay for a few days on *Vanguard*'s deck. 'You may look at it, gentlemen, for as long as you please', Nelson remarked to some curious junior officers. 'But depend upon it, none of you shall have it.' Nor did they, for his body lies in it today.

Even to those who had never seen the Mediterranean, fought in it, or been called upon to defend a corrupt court, this seemed an appropriate eccentricity. But the same outsiders found other events much more difficult to accept: in June, Nelson's abrogation of an armistice between one of his own captains and Cardinal Ruffo on one side and the French on the other; his execution of King Ferdinand's senior naval officer; and in July, his outright disobedience of Lord Keith.

At the first scare of an advancing Franco-Spanish fleet, Nelson had concentrated his ships near Sicily, leaving only a flotilla under Captain Edward Foote in Naples bay. Returning at the head of his fleet to Naples on 24 June, Nelson found that Ruffo had persuaded Foote to sign an armistice with the French and rebellious Neapolitans. 'As you will believe,' said Nelson later, 'the cardinal and I have begun our career by a complete difference of opinion. He will send the rebels to Toulon. I say they shall not go.' Both the Hamiltons were present, Emma virulently opposed to any form of threat to the royal family, and Sir William suspicious that Ruffo was preparing to usurp Ferdinand. After a frigid interview with the cardinal, who had certainly exceeded his authority, Nelson allowed the rebels to embark in small boats, but would not permit them to sail until he had firm instructions from Ferdinand. These came in the form of a letter from Queen Maria Carolina to Emma; unconditional surrender, followed by an example of some of the leaders, male and female alike. 'France will be none the better for all these thousands of rascals; we shall all be better off without them.'

The first man to be executed, Commodore Prince Francesco Carraciolo, had turned coat to the French side to the extent of attacking the ships he had once commanded. There was never any doubt of his guilt – he admitted that himself, though he pleaded for clemency – and after trial, he was hanged at the yardarm of a Sicilian frigate. This was the penalty for a common mutineer, not a nobleman; but it was the speed of the process which aroused criticism in Britain. Arrested in the morning, Carracciolo was tried by a Neapolitan court martial in the early afternoon, and on Nelson's confirmation of the sentence, hanged that evening. When the corpse was cut down the fleet watched, without much interest ('only an Italian prince, and an admiral of Naples ... a person of very light estimation compared with the lowest man in a British ship'), and Nelson dined in his cabin with the Hamiltons, assured he had done the right thing.

The British Admiralty agreed with him; but it soon became apparent he had cleared the way for a brutally vengeful monarch. Ferdinand returned to his kingdom soon after Carracciolo's death. In the castle of St Elmo, the French troops – who had not trusted Ruffo's armistice enough to leave their stronghold – were besieged. On the quarterdeck of *Foudroyant*, Nelson's new flagship, the king had dinner while Emma played the harp and heavy artillery thundered at St Elmo; and on shore, summary trials and public executions began in earnest. They continued, without interruption, for ten months.

In his brief autobiography, Nelson spoke of Hood, St Vincent and even Hotham, but he never mentioned Keith. 'In June and July, 1799,' he wrote, 'I went to Naples, and, as his Sicilian Majesty is pleased to say, reconquered his kingdom, and placed him on his throne. On the 9th of August I brought his Sicilian Majesty back to Palermo ...' Of course this was only 'a sketch of my life', but among other things he left out were the orders of Lord Keith to send 'all, or the greater part of your force' to Minorca. During July, the combined Franco-Spanish fleet of forty or forty-two liners still threatened, and Keith, with only thirty-one to oppose them, feared an attack on the island base. Nelson knew the force available to each side, and simply refused to support his commander-in-chief. 'I have no scruple', he told him bluntly, 'in deciding that it is better to save the Kingdom of Naples and risk Minorca, than to risk the Kingdom of Naples to save Minorca.' Eventually he sent four of his twelve ships, but grudgingly, and only after Keith had repeated his order three times. Each regarded the other's preoccupation as a sideshow to the main event, and on this occasion the Admiralty sided against Nelson, as they were bound to do: it was not his business to make such a decision, and his disobedience risked not merely the island, but the major part of the British Mediterranean fleet. The misjudgment and loss of perspective showed how disproportionately important the court of Naples had become to him; and when the Admiralty issued a stern reprimand, he remained unimpressed: 'My conduct is measured by the Admiralty by the narrow rule of law, when I think it should have been done by common sense.' Coming from one who used to lie awake in fear of offending their Lordships, the dismissive reaction showed how far he had moved in spirit.

It was his great good fortune that the battle of Minorca never took place. As the combined enemy fleets headed for the Atlantic and Keith gave chase, executions continued in Naples, and, ignoring the audible hubbub from the shore, those in *Foudroyant* celebrated the first anniversary of the Battle of the Nile. The celebration was spectacular enough to prompt a letter to Fanny – 'the beauty of the thing was beyond my powers of description', he said, but gave a good description none the less. Ferdinand drank Nelson's health as all the Neapolitan warships and castles fired a 21-gun salute; one large vessel was fitted out as a Roman galley, with lights fixed on all the oars, a rostral column bearing Nelson's name, two angels on the stern supporting his picture, over 2,000 coloured lights hung around, and an orchestra with 'the very best musicians and singers. The piece of music was in a great measure my praises, describing their distress, but *Nelson comes, the invincible Nelson, and we are safe and happy again.*' Did he think it would make her happy to know what scenes he was forbidding her? It did occur to him that his letter might sound vain, but he hoped not – 'so far, very far from it, and I relate it more from gratitude than vanity.'

This was nonsense: he would have been superhuman to have avoided being vain. 'You are now as near the pinnacle of fame as any mortal ever reached', one of his admirers wrote. 'God grant you health to enjoy the admiration and gratitude of your country, and strength of mind to bear the adoration you will receive; for it is almost too much for the mind of a mortal to support.' And King Ferdinand had still greater gifts in store: on 13 August he created Nelson Duke of Brontë. (People have sometimes wondered how this very un-English name came to be one of the eminent names of English literature, when, from the parsonage of Haworth in Yorkshire, the Brontë sisters began producing their novels. Their father's name, originally Irish, was Patrick Prunty or Brunty; he changed it in honour of Nelson.) Unsure whether he should accept before having King George's permission to take a foreign title, Nelson hesitated – briefly – but could not resist a dukedom, even an Italian one. The name Brontë meant thunder, aptly derived from the cyclops who made Neptune's trident and Jove's thunderbolts. Though it sounded fine, in practical terms it was not actually a very generous gift; the attached 30,000-acre estate, on the slopes of Mount Etna, was supposed to produce £3,000 annually. As generous as ever, Nelson promptly decided to give his father £500 a year from it, and worked out how he would bequeath the rest. The reality was disappointing, for the estate was desolate; it had not produced any income for a very long time, and would not without a large investment, which is probably why Ferdinand gave it to him. Before he learned that, however, Nelson enjoyed himself, practising his new signature and trying to decide what title he should use. *Brontë Nelson of the Nile* seemed cumbersome, so he settled on the more modest *Nelson and Brontë*. Emma called him 'My Lord Thunder', which he did not mind; and naturally the occasion provided an excuse for another stupendous party. The centrepieces this time were, firstly, a firework display representing the Battle of the Nile, culminating with the explosion of *L'Orient*, and secondly, the unveiling of a Greek temple with an allegorical trumpet-blowing statue of Fame on top, and inside, life-size statues of Nelson, Emma and Sir William. (A disrespectful midshipman remarked aside that Emma was quite statuesque enough already.) The obligatory 'Rule Britannia' and 'See the Conquering Hero Comes!' were played, and when nine-year-old Prince Leopold crowned Nelson's image with a laurel wreath inlaid with diamonds, it all became too much for the duke: he embraced the small boy and burst into tears. The other naval officers present whisked out their handkerchiefs, apparently likewise overcome. So they were, but not with tears – one of them, busy stifling hoots of laughter, noticed that most of his colleagues were doing the same.

19

'Unfit for command'

IN THE MIDDLE of August 1799, with a certain degree of satisfaction, Nelson informed his second-in-command that 'Lord Keith is gone, and all my superior officers; therefore I must now watch from Cape St Vincent to Constantinople.' From the 17th of that month to the beginning of December, when Keith returned, Nelson was commander-in-chief Mediterranean, but only in an acting capacity – though the Admiralty gave him the authority, he was not granted the permanent rank. All the same, it was agreeable to be in undisputed charge, not least because of Palermo's central location: flying his flag in a transport, he could remain there with Emma, and with a clear naval conscience as well.

Instructing his officers to distribute the fleet between Oporto, Lisbon, Cadiz, Minorca, Naples, Sicily, Malta and the Levant, he allowed them the latitude of experience which he always did allow, and which, under St Vincent, he had learned to expect for himself – 'in short, to act in the best manner for his majesty's service. In giving this command I know to whom I trust, and that it is not necessary to enter into the detail of what is to be done.'

To be able to delegate so freely and confidently shows either a commander who is certain of his subordinates, or one who is shirking responsibility. Nelson and his captains knew which he was, and personally he was sure he gave a good example to anyone. On a visit to Minorca in October, he took time to write the 'sketch of his life', and he ended it with an uplifting moral: 'Perseverance in any profession will most probably meet its reward. Without having any inheritance, or having been fortunate in prize-money, I have received all the honours of my profession, been created a peer of Great Britain, etc. And I may say to the Reader, GO THOU AND DO LIKEWISE.'

Unfortunately, some of those readers were beginning to hear scandalous gossip about his private life. One year earlier he had been instrumental in causing an identical embarrassment to his greatest enemy: French despatches, intercepted and sent to England after the Battle of the Nile, had included an agonized letter written by Napoleon following his discovery that Josephine, his wife, was having an affair. On 24 November 1798 the letter had been published in the London *Morning Chronicle*. Copies reached Paris before the end of the month, making the young general, trapped in Egypt, a laughing-stock. Now, in the late autumn of 1799, Troubridge wrote to Nelson from Naples: 'I fear, my lord, that some person about Sir William Hamilton's house sends accounts here; as I have frequently heard things which I knew your lordship meant to keep secret.' And from aged Admiral Samuel Goodall in London came a discreet warning: 'They say here you are Rinaldo in the arms of Armida' – Armida being a legendary Saracen princess who lured Christian knights, including Rinaldo d'Este, into her magic garden. 'To be sure,' Goodall continued, ''tis a very pleasant attraction, to which I am very sensible myself. But my maxim has always been *Cupidus voluptatum, cupidior gloriae* [Be eager for pleasure, more eager for glory]. Be it as it will, health and happiness attend you.'

Making ready to take over from Spencer Smith as Minister in Constantinople, Lord Elgin was in Gibraltar. Newspapers there had started to run 'unpleasant paragraphs' on Nelson, as Lady Elgin reported to her mother in Scotland: 'They say that there never was a man turned so *vain glorious* (that's the phrase) in the world as Lord N. He is now completely managed by Lady Hamilton.' On their eastward journey, the Elgins had to stop at Sicily, and could not politely refuse an invitation. Emma's outstanding beauty was in her face: she had always tended to plumpness, and in Naples had become quite fat. Lady Elgin (all of twenty-one years old) confirmed this in astonishment: 'She is indeed a Whapper! and I think her manner very vulgar. It is really humiliating to see Lord Nelson, he seems quite dying and yet as if he had no other thought than her.'

Sir William was beginning to complain of the expense, which, he said, 'I can by no means afford, as it is now a year that Lord Nelson has lived with us and, of course, the numerous train of officers that come to him on business'. To make it worse, Emma adored gambling. 'Her rage is play,' wrote an English visitor, 'and Sir William says when he is dead she will be a beggar.' (He was right: twelve years after his death, and nearly ten after Nelson's, she died of drink, alone and in poverty.) Rumours said Nelson and Sir William had quarrelled and even fought over the costs. This is inconceivable: Nelson would certainly have contributed to the expenses. But it is possible that he could not fully pay his way; and the mere rumours of illicit love and late-night parties were enough to do him great harm. In trepidation and deep concern, Troubridge wrote again:

'Pardon me, my lord, it is my sincere esteem for you that makes me mention it. I know you can have no pleasure sitting up all night at cards; why, then, sacrifice your health, comfort, purse, everything, to the customs of a country where your stay cannot be long? ... Your lordship is a stranger to half that happens, or the talk it occasions; if you knew what your friends feel for you, I am sure you would cut all the nocturnal parties; the gambling of the people at Palermo is talked of everywhere. I beseech your Lordship, leave off. Lady Hamilton's character will suffer ... a Gambling Woman in the eyes of an Englishman is lost.'

Only one fact could remotely excuse his dalliance: 'All our Mediterranean operations are pretty nearly at a standstill, for the enemy have no fleet at this moment'. There were only two areas of active operation against the French – Ball's blockade of Malta, and Sir Sidney Smith's of Alexandria. Earlier in the year, after conquering Jaffa, Napoleon had led the Army of Egypt further north and laid siege to Acre. A combined garrison of Turkish soldiers and British sailors under Smith's command defended it for six weeks, until, in May, reinforcements arrived at the same time as several hundred of Napoleon's men caught bubonic plague, the Black Death. Raising the siege, the French retreated across the Sinai desert – almost all, including Napoleon, on foot – in temperatures reaching above 130° Fahrenheit, until they came again to Aboukir Bay. There they encountered the same force, ferried across the sea from Acre by Smith. Another battle of Aboukir took place, but on land, and between the Turks and French; and this time the French won – 'a victory', said Napoleon, 'that will hasten the return of the army to France.'

He was wrong; but it did hasten his own return. Opening negotiations for the exchange of prisoners, he sent a young officer out to Smith's flagship. On board, all was courtesy. The officer was given some English newspapers with news of Europe; and as he departed, Smith, in perfect French, remarked in an off-hand manner: 'Lord Nelson understands the Directory desires your Commander-in-Chief to return at once to France.'

It was true. It is galling to find out your enemy knows more of your affairs than you do yourself, but Smith did not mean to tease: he hoped to tempt Napoleon into sailing, then capture him at sea.

Hearing of the defence of Acre, Nelson wrote Smith a warm and honest letter: 'The bravery shown by you and your companions is such as to merit every encomium which all the civilised world can bestow. Be assured, my dear Sir Sidney, of my perfect esteem and regard, and do not let anyone persuade you to the contrary. My character is that I will not suffer the smallest tittle of my command to be taken from me; but with pleasure I give way to my friends, among whom I beg you will allow me to consider you.'

On 18 August – the day after Nelson assumed the acting role of commander-in-chief – Napoleon put to sea without saying a word to the men he was deserting. On 22 August he transferred to a new Venetian-built frigate. By the end of September he was in his native Corsica. On 6 October he embarked again, and as dusk was falling that evening sighted English ships. On 9 October, while Nelson was sailing from Palermo to Minorca, Napoleon landed in France. One month later, in Paris, he masterminded a coup against the Directory; and on 12 December he became First Consul of France.

To go from refugee to national leader in less than four months was a brilliant transformation. If Smith's plan had worked fully and Napoleon had been captured, no doubt Nelson would have been the first to hail his ingenuity; and of course the history of Europe would have been very different. Instead, Napoleon had escaped across nearly two thousand miles of sea supposedly under Nelson's command. It was perhaps the greatest single misfortune of his distraction in Palermo.

A commander-in-chief is entitled to the credit, and should accept the blame; yet no one appears to have blamed the admiral directly, and that was fair – even today, the sea is a very good place for one small ship to hide. However, Nelson did lose his command, and not just a tittle of it, but the whole thing; for Lord Keith returned to the Mediterranean.

His first order to Nelson was to report to him at Leghorn and give an account of the past few months. After hoping that he might be granted the full permanent rank of commander-in-chief, Nelson was very disappointed, suggesting with heavy sarcasm that 'Greenwich Hospital seems a fit retreat for me, after being *evidently* thought unfit to command in the Mediterranean.' To Emma he was bitterly realistic: 'I cannot command, and now only obey.'

The meeting of the two admirals was chilly and correct, Keith formal, distant and disapproving, Nelson transparently resentful. At its end Keith informed his junior they would travel together to Palermo. Nelson could not refuse, but to have a quiet, dour, old-fashioned Scot inspecting his blowsy base was the last thing he wanted. It went as badly as he expected. After 'the *long* eight days I was at Palermo', Keith concluded: 'The whole was a scene of fulsome Vanity and Absurdity . . . I was sick of Palermo and its allurements, and much as I was made up to (their hours are beyond belief) I went to bed at ten.' Wanting some action, he decided they would go to Malta to inspect the blockade. Nelson agreed with reluctance: he had not been there for over a year, and knew he was at fault. In the decadent regime of the Sicilian court, he seemed to be ageing prematurely – he had lost his upper teeth, and the dimming films were spreading visibly over both his good and his blind eye. Nevertheless, as Alexander Ball said with a thrill, in that voyage Nelson showed again that he was 'truly . . . a heaven-born Admiral, upon whom fortune smiles wherever he goes.'

It was, indeed, pure good luck that Keith forced Nelson to put to sea, for it led to two outstanding episodes which showed that despite all, the old Nelson – the decisive commander and considerate mentor – still existed. The first took place at sea, six days after his unwilling departure from Palermo. Related in detail by Midshipman George Parsons, this was the capture, on 18 February, of *Le Généreux*, one of the two surviving liners from the Nile. South of Sicily, *Foudroyant's* look-out sighted a strange ship.

'Deck there! The stranger is evidently a man-of-war – she is a line-of-battle ship, my lord, and going large on the starboard tack.'

'Ah! An enemy, Mr Staines. I pray God it may be *Le Généreux*. The signal for a general chase, Sir Ed'ard. Make the *Foudroyant* fly!'

Northumberland began to gain on *Foudroyant*. 'This will not do, Sir Ed'ard,' said Nelson briskly. 'She is certainly *Le Généreux* and to my flagship she can alone surrender. Sir Ed'ard, we must and shall beat the *Northumberland*.'

As Berry did everything possible to speed his ship along, people noticed the stump of Nelson's right arm twitching violently. They called it 'working his fin', and knew it was a sign of agitation. Sure enough, the admiral turned angrily to the quartermaster at the wheel and burst out: 'I'll knock you off your perch, you rascal, if you are so inattentive! Sir Ed'ard, send your best quartermaster to the weather-wheel.' Another strange sail was seen, and Nelson turned to Parsons. 'Youngster, to the masthead!' In his haste, Parsons forgot to take a telescope. 'Be damned to you!' Nelson cried. 'Let me know what she is immediately.'

She was a British fifth-rate, *Success*. 'Signal to cut off the flying enemy,' Nelson ordered. 'Great odds, though – thirty-two small guns to eighty large ones.'

'The *Success* has hove-to athwart-hawse of the *Généreux*, and is firing her larboard broadside. The Frenchman has hoisted the Tricolour with a Rear Admiral's flag.'

'Bravo, *Success*! At her again!'

'She has wore, my lord, and is firing her starboard broadside. It has winged the chase, my lord.'

As *Le Généreux* opened fire with her much stronger broadside, everyone in *Foudroyant* 'stands aghast, fearful of the consequences. The smoke clears away, and there is the *Success*, crippled . . .'

'Signal for the *Success* to discontinue the action and come under my stern', said Nelson. 'She has done well for her size. Try a shot from the lower deck, Sir Ed'ard.'

'It goes over her.'

'Beat to quarters, and fire coolly and deliberately at her masts and yards.'

The French warship turned its fire on *Foudroyant*, its first shot passing through the mizzen staysail. Nelson asked one of the 'younkers' how he liked the music, and when he saw the boy was frightened, patted him on the head and told him: 'Charles XII of Sweden ran away from the first shot he heard, though afterwards he was called "the Great", and deservedly, from his bravery. I therefore hope much from you in the future.'

The battle was short; 'amidst the thunders of our united cannon', *Le Généreux* was quickly defeated. There are few authentic glimpses of Nelson in action, and Parsons's is one of the most vivid, with its indication of the admiral's provincial accent, his agitation and irritation during the chase, his encouragement of the young and his complete composure after battle was joined.

Six weeks later, at the end of March, came the other episode which showed that Nelson had not changed entirely. After returning to

Palermo on grounds of ill-health, he was flying his flag in a transport vessel there when Berry and his ships captured *Guillaume Tell*, the final fugitive liner of the Nile. Thirty-year-old Captain Henry Blackwood, in the 36-gun frigate *Penelope*, intercepted the 80-gun enemy at night and fought her single-handed till morning, when she fell prey to Berry. Blackwood, as it happened, had never met Nelson. He had a right to expect some formal praise from his admiral, but what he got was a delightful letter – 'My dear Blackwood: Is there a sympathy which ties men together in the bonds of friendship without having a personal knowledge of each other? If so, (and I believe it was so to you) I was your friend and acquaintance before I saw you. Your conduct stamps your fame beyond the reach of envy: it was like yourself – it was like the *Penelope*. Thanks; and say every kind thing for me to your brave officers and men.'

This was the warmth of personality which none could resist, and which made the 'Band of Brothers' irresistible. Of course Blackwood became another devoted friend; and Berry could not help telling Nelson how much he had missed him. 'My very dear Lord,' he wrote, 'Had you been a partaker with me of the glory, every wish would have been gratified. How very often I went into your cabin, last night, to ask you if we were doing right; for I had nothing to act upon!' This showed Berry's dependence on Nelson: he would turn to him for advice on things which, the admiral remarked privately, 'excellent Captain Hardy takes entirely from me.' But Nelson would not have been there for anything, and in a buoyant (but not altogether tactful) letter to Lord Keith, he said why: 'It would finish me, could I have taken a sprig of these brave men's laurels. They are, and I glory in them, my darling children; served in my school; and all of us caught our professional zeal and fire from the great and good Earl of St Vincent.'

He decided he wanted to stay no longer. Lord Keith had been fore-bearing, far more than he need have been, to his disobedient junior, but Nelson was set on going – 'My task is done, my health is lost, and the orders of the great Earl of St Vincent are completely fulfilled.' There were other reasons too; Sir William Hamilton, disgraced by his part in the fall of Naples, was recalled to England. The first that Hamilton knew about it was in January, in an out-of-date copy of the *Morning Chronicle* – official notification, polite but curt, did not reach him until the end of March. Of course Emma would go as well; and Queen Maria

Carolina, seeing that she was 'neither agreeable nor necessary' to her husband, wished to visit her son-in-law and daughter, the Emperor and Empress of Austria, in Vienna, to place some anti-French steel in their backbones.

Added to the imminent departure of Nelson's personal and political friends was the dispersal of his professional supporters, the band of brothers. Miller had been killed in an accidental explosion at the siege of Acre; Hallowell was taking part in the continued blockade of Cadiz; Hood and Foley had had to return to England; Louis was serving directly under Keith; Ball, still trying to starve the French garrison out of Valletta, had become military governor of the island, and was no longer under naval command. Troubridge had also been ordered to go back to England, and Nelson viewed his removal with mixed feelings: during the blockade of Naples, he had made the captain up to commodore, and King George had made him a baronet. Both officers were pleased by the double recognition, but their friendship had been breached: Troubridge's candid written criticisms of Emma, her behaviour and the damage both were doing to Nelson's public reputation could not be answered; Nelson did not try to answer them; and Troubridge felt he was being spurned, which hurt him deeply.

Hardy had gone too, superseded when Berry returned, knighted and healed after a long illness in Britain, in time to participate in the captures of *Le Généreux* and *Guillaume Tell*. Contrasting the two flag-captains, Nelson missed the steady, imperturbable Dorset man. 'How is it', he asked Hardy once, 'that you and I never disagree, while my other captains never let me do a thing without at first resisting?' Hardy replied: 'It is, Sir, from my being always first lieutenant when you like to be captain, and flag-captain when you have a fancy for being admiral.' The frank answer amused Nelson; he could not deny Hardy was right, and anyway he had asked. Hardy did not like the affair with Emma, any more than Troubridge, but he did not presume to offer uninvited criticisms, however well meant: it was the admiral's private business. Nelson was grateful for that; moreover, he respected Hardy's refusal to be swayed by Emma on professional matters. The crew of one of the boats, sentenced for some offence to a dozen lashes each, asked Lady Hamilton to intercede with Hardy on their behalf. She did so, and next day each of the offenders got two dozen lashes – one for their offence, and the other for trying to get off it. The flag-captain informed her abashed ladyship that that would be the standard for any future interference in the running of his ship; and Nelson did not complain.

Before he left, King Ferdinand took the opportunity of investing him with another knighthood, that of the Order of St Ferdinand. Previously the king had overcome Nelson's apparent hesitation about accepting the dukedom of Brontë by saying it would be unfair if posterity remembered him, Ferdinando Bourbon, as ungrateful to his saviour. But its estate was barren, and so was the new knighthood: like the ducal title, which had never existed before, Ferdinand had only just made it up, along with the special privilege that its members (that is, the royal family and Nelson) could keep their hats on in his presence. As it happened, the sultan of Turkey had done the same sort of thing: there had never been an Order of the Crescent before, but there was now, and Nelson was its first member. Both orders provided him with large splendid stars to wear on his coat alongside that of the Order of the Bath. The first showed St Ferdinand dressed very like King Ferdinand, surrounded by six bright rays alternating with fleur-de-lys; the Turkish one, biggest of all, had a crescent and star on a red field in its centre, with a positive burst of beams around it. Such were the honours of the time, and though dreaming up new titles which carried no practical benefit might seem a cheap and easy way for a ruler to express gratitude, it would be foolish to deride them now: in the remaining monarchies of the world, there are probably few citizens who would reject a public distinction, and for republics it is much the same.

The only problem with decorations, medals, ribbons, stars and titles is that unless they are accepted by others they become meaningless. All the stars awarded Nelson, British or not, were designed to impress the onlooker and give pride to the wearer; and eventually they worked in both ways. From the start he took great pleasure in them, wearing them on every public, official or service occasion until the day he died – and there must be a particular pleasure in displaying decorations created especially in honour of one's own deeds. But for at least the first year after he had won them, the noble trinkets – the foreign ones, that is – brought discomfort to others ('more like a Prince of the Opera ... so pitiful a figure') and humiliation to himself.

The band of brothers lamented his departure. In England, Sam Hood, who had looked forward 'with the greatest happiness' to serving under his flag again, realized he might never do so. 'I have seen him in the hour of danger and difficulties,' said Ball, 'and I can never forget his great and immortal traits.' Louis was miserable, and promised to join him, if possible, wherever he might be; Troubridge wished he could be Nelson's flag-captain on the voyage to England. Berry hated 'the smallest idea of leaving you – tho' only for a short time'; even Blackwood, who had scarcely come to know him, said his greatest regret was that 'we are so soon to lose a valuable friend, under whom we can never fail to succeed'. And it was not only the officers; the sailors loved him as much as always, and in a letter which has become famous, some of them told him so.

'My Lord – It is with extreme grief that we find you are about to leave us. We have been along with you (though not in the same ship) in every Engagement your Lordship has been in, both by Sea and Land; and most humbly beg of your Lordship to permit us to go to England as your Boat's crew, in any Ship or Vessel, or in any way that may seem most pleasing to your Lordship. My Lord, pardon the rude style of Seamen who are but little acquainted with writing, and believe us to be, my Lord, Your most humble and obedient servants – Barge's Crew of the *Foudroyant*.'

If Nelson could have had his own way, no doubt he would have taken them – though he might not have wanted Troubridge as flag-captain. But he could not go by sea. On 14 June, the day they landed at Leghorn, French forces under Napoleon defeated the Austrians at Marengo, and Lord Keith refused to let *Foudroyant* go. 'Bored by Lord Nelson for permission to take the Queen to Palermo, and the prince and princesses to all parts of the globe', his private opinion was that 'Lady Hamilton has had command of the Fleet long enough.' He offered Nelson and the Hamiltons passage to England in either a frigate or a troopship; but suddenly Emma refused to travel by sea at all. If she would not, clearly neither Sir William nor Nelson would. Queen Maria Carolina was heading for Vienna, anyway, so when Emma added that she would like to visit the courts of Germany, it was decided: overland through friendly countries, with only the short sea crossing from Hamburg at the end.

Emma had two good reasons, not merely curiosity, for wishing to travel overland. One was uncertainty surrounding her and Sir William's future in England: a European tour would postpone what could be an unhappy return. Perhaps she spoke of that with him. As for the second reason, however – the wife of a diplomat gains experience in discretion. In their last voyage together, she had been violently ill, quite unlike her brave demeanour in the flight from Naples. She cannot have been sure, and may not have told anyone; but in July 1800, when the combined party made ready to leave Leghorn, she was two months pregnant with Lord Nelson's child.

20

'My Lord Nelson's letter of dismissal'

HARDY WAS A very private man where service matters were concerned. He did his job well and expected the same of others: he was not interested in their personal business, and did not pry; he did not want others to be curious about his, and did not invite inquiry. But in his own way he would show if he felt something personal was wrong. He got back to the delightful Dorset village of Portisham (which he always called Possum) on Christmas Eve 1799. He spent only two weeks at home before going to London; and there he visited Lady Nelson. To do so was not unusual: as outgoing flag-captain he could tell his admiral's lady much of what had happened to her lord, more than any letter could express; the wife of any naval officer long absent was always glad of news of her husband, and officers returning home generally tried to give it. However, he and Fanny became good friends, for – although it is inconceivable that either actually said as much – both loved Nelson, and both wished for nothing other than his safe and happy return: whatever had passed in the Mediterranean could be ignored, forgotten, forgiven, if he came back as he had left, cheerful and affectionate, and above all, alone.

But at the beginning of April 1800 the *Morning Chronicle* was adding sharp spice to the titillating gossip in town: 'Of all the seeds lately sent home by Lord Nelson, that of "Love lies bleeding" was sown and gathered at Naples.' Later, from Vienna, it reported more blatantly: 'The German State Painter, we are assured, is drawing Lady Hamilton and Lord Nelson *at full length together*. An Irish correspondent hopes the artist will have delicacy enough to put Sir William *between* them.'

Fanny was being made ridiculous, as Napoleon had been when Josephine was unfaithful to him; and on 8 November, a Saturday, writing to his brother-in-law, Hardy came the closest he ever had to

233

putting his personal views of private matters on paper. 'Dear Manfield – Notwithstanding all the Newspapers, his Lordship is not arrived in town & when he will, God only knows. His Father has lost all patience, her Ladyship bears up very well as yet but I much fear she will also despond. He certainly arrived at Yarmouth on Thursday last & there has been no letter received by anybody. Should he not arrive tomorrow, I think I shall set off for Yarmouth, as' – and he underlined the rest of the sentence – '*I know too well the cause of his not coming.*' And before sending it, he added a postscript to the letter: '$\frac{1}{2}$ past 5 – No News of Lord Nelson.'

The first part of the overland journey had become a flight from increasing danger: at one point the travellers passed within a mile of advanced French units. But after a long stay in Vienna, their journey turned into a kind of triumphal tour; and with the defiant gaiety of a group of Royalists about to face Puritan execution, they made the most of it.

At first Nelson spoke more of *Foudroyant* than anything else, wishing aloud he were back in her. It was not only being ashore that rankled; his companions probably did not know of a chilly letter he had received from Earl Spencer. 'It is by no means my wish or intention to call you away from service,' the First Lord had written, 'but having observed that you have been under the necessity of quitting your station off Malta on account of the state of your health, which I am persuaded you could not have thought of doing without such necessity, it appeared to me much more advisable for you to come home at once, than to be obliged to remain inactive at Palermo'. The phrase must have caught Spencer's mind, for he repeated it: 'I am joined in my opinion by all your friends here, that you will be more likely to recover your health and strength in England than in an inactive situation at a Foreign Court, however pleasing the respect and gratitude shown to you for your services may be'.

Nelson never learned how to be courteous and barbed at the same time, but he knew when it was happening to him. Spencer's letter hurt much and promised little; Vienna and Germany, however, allowed the dream to continue for a few months more. Lord and Lady Minto, his old friends from Corsican days, were in Vienna, and Lady Minto described how, outside the house Nelson stayed in, there was always a crowd waiting for a chance to see him. They would applaud him in the street; people brought their children to touch him, as if he were a saint. In spite of that, she said, 'I don't think him altered in the least.

He has the same shock head, and the same honest simple manners; but he is devoted to *Emma*; he thinks her quite an angel ... and she leads him about like a keeper with a bear.' She admitted he was 'a gig from ribands, orders and stars,' but added firmly: 'He is just the same with us as ever he was.'

However, as her husband pointed out, the public problem remained unsolved: 'He does not seem at all conscious of the sort of discredit he has fallen into, or the cause of it, for he still writes, not wisely, about Lady Hamilton and all that'. And in an unhappy letter to Lord Keith, Lord Minto remarked: 'I, who am a lover of naval merit and indeed a sincere friend of the man, hope we shall again hear of him on his proper element'.

After a tearful farewell with Queen Maria Carolina, all the foreigners they encountered from Vienna to Hamburg – with one exception – treated them as royally as they could; but other British expatriates, less charitable than the Mintos, sharpened their talons. The British Consul in Leghorn (who never got on with Sir William) had already said that the *Tria Juncta in Uno* 'all sit and flatter each other all day long'. In Vienna, while confirming Lady Minto's view that Nelson was still basically unaltered, 'open and honest', Lord Fitzharris found Emma 'without exception the most coarse, ill-mannered, disagreeable woman I ever met.' In Dresden, where Minto's brother Hugh Elliot was British Minister, one of his guests observed: 'It is plain that Lord Nelson thinks of nothing but Lady Hamilton ... She puffs the incense full in his face; but he receives it with pleasure and snuffs it up very cordially.' Elliot despised Emma's singing: 'She acts her songs, which I think the last degree of bad taste.' A Swedish diplomat held exactly the opposite opinion – 'In her are combined voice as well as method, sensitivity as well as musical knowledge, so as to bewitch the listener', adding frankly that Emma was 'the fattest woman I've ever laid eyes on, but with the most beautiful head.'

Of Emma's many well known talents, the one most acceptable to British people was the performance of what she called her 'Attitudes'. With a few simple accessories – shawls, vases, flowers and a tambourine – she could strike poses depicting almost any of her husband's antique statues. Later on this too was lampooned as something more akin to a striptease; but the parody was unjust. Even the Elliots' disapproving lady guest was impressed: 'She does it so quickly, so easily and so well ... Each representation lasts about ten minutes. It is remarkable that, though coarse and ungraceful in common life, she becomes highly graceful, and even beautiful, during this performance.' But the barbs still followed – 'It is also singular that, in spite of the accuracy of her imitation of the finest ancient draperies, her usual dress is tasteless, vulgar, loaded and unbecoming.'

It was also in Dresden that the travellers had their sole experience of coldness from a foreigner: the Electress of Saxony would not receive Emma. 'If there is any difficulty of that sort,' Nelson declared, 'Lady Hamilton will knock the Elector down.' All three proceeded to stagger their hosts, the Elliots, with their behaviour. Emma 'declared she was passionately fond of champagne', and drank more than anyone thought possible; Nelson 'called more vociferously than usual for songs in his own praise'. After another performance of the 'Attitudes', Emma went on to act and dance 'intolerably ill', while Nelson 'expressed his admiration by the Irish sound of astonished applause'. Emma then asked again to go to Court, 'and Mrs Elliot assured her it would not amuse her, and that the Elector never gave dinners or suppers. – "What?" cried she, "no guttling!" Sir William also this evening performed feats of activity, hopping around the room on his backbone, his arms, legs, star and ribbon all flying about in the air.'

It did not occur to the Elliots that their guests might have decided to make fun of the censorious hosts, and were simply enjoying themselves by acting up to the part given them. When they had gone, 'Mr Elliot would not allow his wife to speak above her breath, and said every now and then, "Now don't let us laugh tonight; let us all speak in our turn; and be very, very quiet."'

Elliot had another gloomy thought. It seemed to him probable that his dreadful visitors would get on very well in England. Emma would 'captivate the Prince of Wales, whose mind is as vulgar as her own, and play a great part'. Nelson had spoken with pleasure of the many dinners he, Fanny and the Hamiltons would enjoy together. Afterwards, while the Hamiltons 'went to their musical parties, he and Lady Nelson would go to bed.' Perhaps Elliot felt it was unjust that, merely by winning the greatest sea-victory ever known, a man could gad about as much as he pleased with the most outlandish companions, before all returned to positions of national honour and importance and sound domesticity, which none could criticize. Like many of Nelson's contemporary critics (and their numbers were growing) he may have been jealous that one man should have it all, fame, glory, glamorous romance – and a faithful, loving wife; but unfair or not, that was what Elliot foresaw for the flamboyant admiral. And so, apparently, did Nelson.

The night of 9 November 1800 became memorable for two reasons. London was battered by a thunderstorm so violent that trees were uprooted by the wind, and for the first time, Fanny and Emma came face to face. In an evening of bleak antipathy, each found every prejudice confirmed. Even if they had met in normal circumstances, neither would have liked the other. In these highly abnormal circumstances, each already feared the other, and under a brittle veneer of courtesy, the instant, inevitable dislike was deep and mutual. Of course anyone could have foreseen that: quite apart from human nature, eighteen hundred years of religious tradition confirmed that any other reaction was impossible or wrong. That same evening forced Nelson to stop pretending to himself that all could be well: as the two women faced each other, he too was obliged to face, at last, the conflicting realities of culture and heart; and so began the final, most traumatic weeks of Fanny and Horatio's life together.

One part of him, however, still stayed in a dream world. The voyage from Hamburg had been accomplished not in a frigate, as he had expected, but in a mail boat: no Royal Navy vessel was waiting, and none appeared. It must have been an obvious signal of official disapproval, but for a little longer he was able to delude himself. From the party's arrival on 6 November, the public greeting had certainly been all he wished: escorts of cavalry and militia, his carriage unhitched from its horses and pulled by willing volunteers, cheering crowds applauding him as he appeared on balconies with Emma at his side. But then, on 11 November, alone, he attended a royal levée, wearing all his gorgeous foreign decorations, with the diamond aigrette and its clockwork star pinned in his hat. It was an absurd thing to do, and showed how much he had forgotten British courtly manners: he was not yet authorized to wear a single one of the foreign devices in his own country. Yet despite that and everything else that was rumoured about his conduct, he was shocked and amazed when the king publicly snubbed him. His Majesty merely asked if he was well again, and then, before he could answer, turned away and began a long conversation with an undistinguished general.

That evening, Earl and Countess Spencer invited the Nelsons to dinner, and the Countess – who, three years earlier, had dimpled with pleasure at the sight of the loving couple – now stared aghast: 'He treated her with every mark of dislike and even of contempt ... Such a contrast I never beheld!' The tense atmosphere peaked when Fanny hesitantly presented Nelson with a glass of walnuts she had peeled for him: he thrust it aside so hard that it fell and shattered. As the Countess maintained a steely calm, Fanny began to weep. Later, when they withdrew to leave the gentlemen with their wine, Fanny could contain herself no longer: all that she had feared was true, but she had not voiced her fears. Now, in Lady Spencer's stately phrase, 'she told me how she was situated.'

In the weeks leading to Christmas, the public activity of the Nelsons and the Hamiltons – and much of their private activity – was closely observed and reported. It was a hectic time: after business at the Admiralty and the Navy Office in the Strand (with the by now customary hordes of admiring folk following every step), there were banquets, dinners, presentations, civic receptions, visits to the theatre, and Nelson's introduction to the House of Lords. He might have thought with irony of his youthful hopes for a political career: no one would have him then; now he was in Parliament as of right, unelected, when any constituency in the nation would have fought for the honour of electing him as its member. But in all the busy glitter, he and Fanny never once appeared as a couple. If she was there, so were the Hamiltons; otherwise he performed on his own. All four went to the theatre together, which guaranteed a full house, whatever the play. At one, *Pizarro*, Fanny screamed and fainted. As it happened, one of the leading ladies was an old friend of Emma's, but what made Fanny pass out was hearing from the stage: 'How a woman can love, Pizarro, thou hast known ... How she can hate, thou hast yet to learn ... Meet and survive – an injured woman's fury.'

Despite the nightmarish contrast of public adulation and private trauma, Nelson, a few nights later, insisted that he and Fanny should have the Hamiltons to dine at home. Emma was seven months pregnant by then, but because she was so fat anyway, and because of her billowing clothes, she concealed it well. This evening, however, she said during the meal that she felt ill, and left the table. The others remained until Nelson rebuked Fanny for her lack of consideration to their guest. She followed Emma out and found her, and the most pathetic and grotesque single incident of Fanny's dutiful life took place: whether or not she guessed the reason for this sudden illness, the betrayed wife held a basin while her husband's pregnant mistress vomited into it.

Even when Christmas came and the Hamiltons left the capital for a holiday, still Fanny felt no relief; for Nelson went with them. Passing through Salisbury, where Fanny's first husband lay buried, Nelson – amid the usual scenes of rejoicing – was presented with the Freedom of the City, and met old Agamemnons, including one who had been present at his amputation. On to their destination, the mansion of Fonthill Splendens; and there, apart from the weather, the environment they joined brought back some of the dream of Naples, opulent, bohemian, untouched by the outside world. The place was owned by a fabulously wealthy and suitably eccentric gentleman who had recently built in his park a bogus medieval abbey with a tower 278 feet high; the company he had invited included artists, satirists (one of whom, using a pseudonym, had written about Nelson and Emma) and opera singers, as well as the President of the Royal Academy. Their host was inclined to refer to 'Lord Nelson's Lady Hamilton – or anybody else's Lady Hamilton', but on 23 December, in the setting of the phoney abbey, she performed one of the best 'Attitudes' of her life. For an encore, apparently without seeing anything incongruous about it, she portrayed an abbess greeting novice nuns into a convent.

The party disbanded on Boxing Day. On the same day, a hundred miles away in Greenwich, Captain Locker died.

The cartoons of the trio sold as briskly as the heroic engravings. The laurel-wreathed 'Victor of the Nile' stood framed alongside 'Dido in Despair', an obese matron in a nightgown weeping fat tears as the fleet stood out to sea and a skinny old man snored on the bed beside her. There were the songs too, such as the new London version of the National Anthem:

> Also huge Emma's name,
> First on the roll of fame,
> Now let us sing.
> Loud as her voice, let's sound
> Her faded charms around,
> Which in the sheets were found –
> God save the King.
>
> Nelson, thy flag haul down,
> Hang up thy laurel crown,
> While her we sing.
> No more in triumph swell,
> Since that with her you dwell,

But don't her William tell –
Nor George, your King.

For those who did not choose to be scandalized, it was all great fun; the hero was fallible and very human. It did not hurt anyone to be laughed at, after all, and it certainly did not stop him being a hero. But for those involved, the crisis was imminent. Nelson sold Roundwood, the 'cottage' of his earlier dreams, and spent some undated sleepless night roaming the streets of London alone, before turning, in the small hours, to the haven of Sir William's house. In the morning he returned to the house Fanny had rented for him, and went in silence to her room, where she was in bed. Reaching out to him, she asked if she had ever done anything to give him cause for complaint. He replied that she had not, and left the room. On 1 January 1801, he was gazetted Vice Admiral of the Blue. Twelve days later, in preparation for a pending lawsuit on prize money, he and Fanny had a guest for breakfast, one William Haslewood, a solicitor. Much later, Haslewood described that breakfast.

'Lord Nelson spoke of something which had been done or said by "dear Lady Hamilton". Lady Nelson rose from her chair and exclaimed with much vehemence, "I am sick of hearing of dear Lady Hamilton, and am resolved that you should give up either her or me." Lord Nelson, with perfect calmness, said: "Take care, Fanny, what you say. I love you sincerely; but I cannot forget my obligations to Lady Hamilton, or speak of her otherwise than with affection and admiration." Without saying one soothing word, but muttering something about her mind being made up, Lady Nelson left the room, and shortly after drove from the house. They never lived together afterwards.'

The description was made forty-five years after the event, and cannot be entirely accurate. Moreover, Haslewood clearly took Nelson's side – although it is difficult to see why Fanny should have soothed any longer. But the gist of it is probably correct, and that evening Nelson wrote Fanny a letter: 'Southampton, January 13th, 1801. My dear Fanny – We [his brother William was with him] are arrived and are heartily tired; and with kindest regards to my father and all the family, believe me, your affectionate Nelson.'

That was all. Still affectionate, but no more 'your husband'. And Haslewood did not go far enough: not only did Fanny and Horatio never live together afterwards, they never even saw each other again.

*

240

'Poor fellow!' St Vincent sighed. 'He is devoured by vanity, weakness and folly; was strung with ribbons, medals, etc., and yet pretended that he wished to avoid the honours and ceremonies he everywhere met with on the road.'

A part of the old team was reunited, and an expedition was being prepared for the Baltic. After a splendid, speedy recovery in England, St Vincent had been given command of the notoriously ill-disciplined Channel Fleet. His first action in March 1800 had been to call for his Mediterranean order books: he would repeat in the Channel the process which had perfected the Mediterranean fleet. Fremantle's convalescence, following his wound at Tenerife, had been very long and painful, but eventually he had also recovered. Joining the fleet that August he found it greatly improved, with 'as much respect and obedience in every ship as at any period of my service.' St Vincent would not go as far as that, but did admit that 'This fleet, which when I came to it was at the lowest ebb of wretched and miserable discipline, is now above mediocrity.' In his flagship *Ville de Paris*, Troubridge was Captain of the Fleet; and with Hardy as his own flag-captain, Nelson's new command was the 120-gun *San Josef* – the ship which had become his 'patent bridge' at Cape St Vincent. Foley and Saumarez were there too; and so was Collingwood, now a rear admiral.

It took Nelson two days to get from Southampton to Plymouth, where *San Josef* was moored. Members of the band of brothers had congratulated Hardy on 'the happyness' of being with Nelson again, and in such a large ship. Deeply but discreetly pleased, he was much concerned for Nelson, who told him that on the journey down he had felt so dreadful he thought he might die. Collingwood was also very low in spirits: after a short visit home, he had been with the Channel Fleet for a year and three-quarters and was missing his family badly, especially as he realized that his daughters hardly knew him; so it was with particular pleasure that he met his old friend again, and found someone to share troubles with. He noticed it was becoming more difficult for the one-armed admiral to get in and out of ships, and heard all about his humiliation at Court. He did not record if Nelson spoke of his separation from Fanny, but Collingwood probably spoke of his own wife Sarah; for after so long apart, the intrepid woman had decided to make the four-hundred-mile journey, in winter, from Northumberland to Plymouth. She was bringing one of their daughters, also called Sarah, and now they were expected any day, to take rooms, on Collingwood's advice, in the Fountain Inn.

On 27 January, Nelson and Collingwood were sitting together at dinner when the arrival was announced. Insisting that Nelson should come too, Collingwood 'flew to the inn', and the evening was transformed: 'How surprised you would have been', the happy husband told another old friend, 'to have popped in to the Fountain Inn and seen Lord Nelson, my wife, and myself sitting by the fireside cosing, and little Sarah teaching Phillis, her dog, to dance.'

That letter was written to Mrs Moutray, whose care had given such comfort to the two lonely young officers all those years before in the West Indies. Her husband had died shortly after their return to England. Had he not died there, but in the West Indies, it is possible Nelson might have been her second husband – the age difference was not great – and she could have been an ideal wife, combining Fanny's decorum and social acceptability with Emma's warmth and cheerfulness. The Collingwoods' charming unconscious display of family serenity must have been, to Nelson, bitter-sweet, knowing that it could never be his. But on or about that same evening, an event took place secretly in London which, when he learned of it five days later, threw him into a delirium of happiness – he had a child of his own, a little baby daughter.

Soon after, a terse note was addressed to Lady Nelson. 'Josiah is to have another ship, if the *Thalia* cannot soon be got ready. I have done *all* for him, and he may again, as he has often done before, wish me to break my neck, and be abetted in it by his friends, who are likewise my enemies; but I have done my duty as an honourable, generous man, and I neither want nor wish anybody to care what becomes of me, whether I return or am left in the Baltic. Living, I have done all in my power for you, and if dead, you will find I have done the same; therefore my only wish is to be left to myself; and wishing you every happiness, believe that I am your affectionate – Nelson and Brontë.'

Fanny was, in her own word, 'astonished': she could not bring herself to believe the utter finality of the letter. But Nelson firmly intended it should be his last direct contact with her; and much later, she gave way to the inevitable, and wrote on the paper: 'This is my Lord Nelson's letter of dismissal'.

21

'I think I can annihilate them'

To BEGIN WITH the tale of the turbot: the whole fleet, including fifteen liners, two 50-gun ships, frigates and brigs, were passing near the Dogger Bank when, late in the afternoon of 14 March, Nelson ordered William Layman, one of his lieutenants, to try his hand at fishing. Earlier, Layman had remarked that he had once caught a very fine turbot in that area, and the admiral wished him to do so again. He succeeded, and in spite of a rising sea and gathering darkness, the fish was immediately taken over from Nelson's ship, *St George*, to the flagship of the commander-in-chief. Something had to be done to gain his confidence, and knowing his fondness for fine food, Nelson thought the fish might do the trick. A message of thanks was returned, but nothing else; and two days later, the rigging white with frost as they sailed from one snowstorm to another, Nelson wrote: 'I have not yet seen my Commander-in-Chief, and have had no official communication whatever. All I have gathered of our first plans, I disapprove most exceedingly'.

There had been many changes in recent weeks, including Nelson's move from *San Josef* to *St George*, a ship of shallower draught; and now an ill-led fleet was sailing towards an improbable war. After eighteen uninterrupted years as Prime Minister, Pitt – whom Nelson thought 'the greatest Minister this country has ever had, and the honestest man' – had resigned. Under the new administration, St Vincent became First Lord of the Admiralty. Most officers agreed with Collingwood's opinion: 'The navy, I doubt not, will be ably directed by Lord St Vincent ... No man is more capable of conducting the Naval department than he'. And most agreed with his view of St Vincent's successor as commander-in-chief, Admiral Sir Hyde Parker: 'In the little I have seen of him I could only discover a good-tempered man, full of vanity, a great deal of pomp, and a pretty smattering of ignorance.'

The sketch was probably not meant to sound unpleasant; it was simply accurate. Before his death in the East Indies, Parker's father – also called Sir Hyde – had amassed a considerable fortune through prize money in a long and distinguished naval career. The present Sir Hyde was another matter. He had always been a competent officer, but not destined by nature for the rank he now held. Apart from anything else, he had recently married (at the age of almost sixty-four) a plump lady of nineteen, known to St Vincent as 'batter pudding', and had been noticeably unwilling to lead his ships from Yarmouth, where Lady Parker was preparing a grand ball. Nelson jealously understood: 'Consider how nice it must be', he wrote, 'laying in bed with a young wife, compared to a damned cold raw wind.' Neither he nor St Vincent liked anyone other than commanders-in-chief to write to the Admiralty, but against his own principles he did so: 'If a Lord of the Admiralty – and such a Lord – had not told me that the Baltic fleet had orders to put to sea, I would not have believed it ... There is not the least appearance of going'. The answer came by express, and in an unexpected hurry, the fleet weighed anchor and the ball was postponed.

Their target, the Baltic, seemed unlikely. As far as anyone could recall, the last time there had been any serious fighting between Britons and Scandinavians was about a thousand years ago. For them to be at war now was an aberration rather than a habit, but its causes were clear enough: they were the fate of Malta, the rights of neutral shipping in wartime, and the continuing conflict between France and Britain.

Malta came into it because Tsar Paul of Russia was Grand Master of the Order of St John, the Knights of Malta, whose treasure had been stolen by the French and now lay scattered at the bottom of Aboukir Bay. With Alexander Ball still besieging the French garrison in Valletta, Napoleon tried to woo the Tsar by promising that if the garrison held out, he could have the island. However, in September 1800 the garrison gave up at last; the British government, who naturally saw no plausible connection between Malta and the Tsar, took control and kept Ball as governor. Tsar Paul left the second coalition against France.

At the same time, the neutral Baltic states were much annoyed by the principle that warships of belligerent nations could stop neutral merchantmen and search their cargoes for contraband enemy supplies. For the navies of both France and Britain, the Baltic was an irreplaceable source of essential stores – tar, flax, hemp and above all, timber: the tall straight pine trees made superb masts and spars. If one belligerent waived the right of stop and search, as Napoleon now did, it seemed unreasonable if the other would not; and the British did not. So in December 1800 Tsar Paul revived the Armed Neutrality of the North, which had been used to protect Baltic shipping from British searches during the American War of Independence; in February 1801, by the treaty of Lunéville, the Austrians made peace with France again; and King Ferdinand felt obliged to conclude an armistice prohibiting British warships from his ports.

The Napoleonic Wars are sometimes compared to World War II: in both, men of obscure origin – Napoleon and Hitler – rose to lead their countries in a new social order, dominating continental Europe by force of arms in struggles which eventually became world-wide and in which, for a time, Britain was the only surviving opponent. The implication of this comparison still irritates French people immensely. No one suggests that Napoleon, given the technology, would have instituted extermination camps; but the notion that he took devious, belligerent initiatives is almost as unwelcome, since he was, in the French view, a man of peace. This is clear from the fate of the second coalition against France: like the first, it fell apart, and the war would not have carried on if Britain had not insisted.

The British saw it otherwise, and generally still do. There, the offer of Malta was viewed as a hollow bribe and the waiving of the right of search as a red herring. Nevertheless, both were critically effective: Portugal became the only remaining British ally; the command of the Mediterranean was once again in doubt; the shortage of supplies from Scandinavia threatened to cripple the fleet more thoroughly than battle; and if the navies of Russia, Sweden and Denmark (which then included Norway) joined actively with the French, it would all be over. Hence the British Baltic fleet, which, on 19 March 1801, rounded the northernmost tip of Denmark with Nelson, its second-in-command, as much in the dark as ever about Sir Hyde's intentions.

Seeing a frigate sent on ahead, Nelson guessed that diplomacy with Denmark was going to be tried first, which he thought a worthless idea without a display of force to back it up. At a meeting on his initiative with Sir Hyde the following day, he learned little except that his guess about diplomacy was right, and he began to think that if it failed, the commander-in-chief had no plan of action ready at all. This too turned out to be right; on 23 March the unsuccessful diplomats returned, reporting that the Danes were more scared of the Russians than of the British, and had prepared formidable defences for Copenhagen. A message came from Sir Hyde to *St George*, and Nelson wrote to Emma, 'now we are sure of fighting, I am sent for. When it was a joke I was kept in the background'.

The conference, with other senior officers and the diplomats present, was not a happy one. Nelson found that Parker was still very unsure of fighting, although his orders from the Admiralty were clear: if the Danes could not be persuaded to leave the Armed Neutrality, they must be forced to do so, after which the fleet must proceed six hundred miles to Reval (now Tallinn) at the mouth of the Gulf of Finland, reduce the Russian naval strength there, and if necessary penetrate a further two hundred miles to Kronstadt at the end of the Gulf and do the same again. The Admiralty's orders included an escape clause, and Sir Hyde was inclined to take it. Faced with the reality of a Baltic winter and the possibility of opposition from more than eighty Russian liners, he found his position very unwelcome – as most people would – and thought it best to keep his ships where they were, effectively blockading the entrance to the whole Baltic Sea.

Nelson's own view was exactly contrary. A blockade would enable the Baltic fleets to combine, with a total of over 120 sail of the line. Imagining the 'Northern League', as he called it, like a tree, he saw Tsar Paul as the trunk, and Sweden and Denmark as the branches. Closely anticipating the US Navy's leap-frog strategy in the Pacific in World War II, he argued that if the trunk was hewn down, the branches must follow. Parker, though, focused on Copenhagen: bypassing it would leave a hostile fleet in his rear, which he would not accept. Nelson managed to control his temper (it took him such an effort that he mentioned it in a letter) but found Sir Hyde almost unbearably haughty towards him. The commander-in-chief – who Nelson had noticed privately was 'a little nervous about dark nights and fields of ice' – clearly suffered as his second-in-command quizzed the diplomats closely. From them it emerged that the defences of Copenhagen were strongest to the northward; Nelson promptly suggested the possibility of an attack from the south. This would mean a long approach. Copenhagen lies on the isle of Zealand, separated from Sweden by the narrow Sound to the east and from the rest of Denmark by the Great Belt, to the west. Either would do, said Nelson – 'Let it be by the Sound, by the Belt, or anyhow, only lose not an hour.'

Parker gave way; probably he was already considering how best to let his junior have effective command. That evening Nelson dictated a long, reasoned letter, setting out the options in detail, calling on British honour and emphasizing that it was far safer to act than to lie passively waiting. 'They will every day and hour be stronger; we shall never be so good a match for them as at this moment. The only consideration in my mind is how to get at them with the least risk to our ships.' Warning Sir Hyde that he must 'expect the natural issue of such a battle – Ships crippled, and perhaps one or two lost,' he added: 'Such a measure may be thought bold, but I am of opinion the boldest measures are the safest.' He had said exactly the same to King Ferdinand, when recommending the pre-emptive attack on Rome which lost Ferdinand his kingdom. Here he was on safer ground, or water: he was not advising untrained Latin armies, but preparing to lead highly trained sailors. And yet tragically, the preparation and the battle which ensued were all unnecessary; for on 24 March, when Nelson's letter was delivered to Admiral Parker, Tsar Paul, the trunk of the Northern league, was strangled. His son, Paul II, did not share his optimistic view of Napoleon, and in just a few weeks would send Nelson an invitation (which Nelson could not accept) to visit him in St Petersburg. But by then many Danes and many Britons – 'the brothers of the Danes', said Nelson – would be dead.

'I have just been reconnoitering the Danish line of defence,' he wrote to Emma on 30 March. 'It looks formidable to those who are children in war, but, to my judgment, with ten sail of the line I think I can annihilate them; at all events I hope to be allowed to try.'

Fifteen hundred miles south, L'Orient remained a sunken testimony of his ability to annihilate, and in the last days of a freezing north European winter, the Danes' defences were similar to those of Admiral Brueys, off the desert of Aboukir: shoals and shallows protected an anchored line. But at Copenhagen there were important differences. The natural hazards were even greater than at Aboukir, and made worse by the Danes' sensible removal of all navigational buoys. The artificial hazards were also considerable. Foremost among these was the powerful Trekroner fortress, to the north of the harbour entrance. In the entrance itself were two two-decker hulks; close by, two small brigs, a large frigate and two 74-gun ships, all rigged; and in the narrow channel between shore and shoal, a line a mile and a half long of eighteen low-lying floating batteries, hulks and men-of-war. All were heavily armed, and had in their rear the shore batteries of the capital; this time there would be no chance of mooring between the land and the line and battering it from both sides at once.

There was also a real difference in mood. After a short time, any naval battle pressed home with vigour on both sides inevitably became similar to any other, at least for the individuals involved: the billowing smoke, deafening noise, shrieks and screams of men and shot, urgent activity and general confusion as men carried out their jobs and hoped only to survive. But the approach to battle is different every time, and the British did not come cheering and laughing to their conflict at Copenhagen, as they had done at Aboukir. There was not the same joyous release in locating the enemy after long frustrating weeks of chase, nor was it the same enemy. Anyone could understand fighting the French, half-hereditary antagonists, and if the Danes were so foolish as to aid the French cause well then, they too must be fought. Yet no one felt any particular hatred for the Danes; there were no popular cartoons making them seem stupid and vicious. Indeed, there were quite a number of Danish sailors in the British fleet, and when a group of them – explaining they remained loyal to the Royal Navy – asked permission to go to another part of the fleet in Britain, so that they would not have to fight their own countrymen, they were allowed to do so; and no one thought any the worse of them, or doubted their word at all.

But without the delicious tribal urge, it was more a job that had to be done, and the quicker and more efficiently the better. Admiral Parker's indecisive leadership had already lost much time: after saying they would pass west of Zealand, and setting course that way, he began to wonder about the chance of accidents – the Great Belt was notoriously tricky for large vessels. He called in Nelson and Captain William Murray (who knew the Baltic well) for another consultation. Murray favoured going by the Sound; Nelson simply said, 'I don't care a damn by which passage we go, so that we fight them!' The Sound it was, but Parker, wanting one more try at diplomacy, began negotiations with the Governor of Kronborg Castle, which defended the Sound's northern entrance. This produced nothing except further delay. At last, out of range of the castle's guns, the fleet sailed past and, twenty miles or so later, anchored north of Copenhagen. Then came the distant inspection of its defences, which, as predicted, had been much strengthened since the first diplomatic sally; and the following day, 31 March, Parker showed himself (at least to Nelson) as a child at war. He called another conference, and as his own uncertainty affected the assembled captains, they began to worry again about the size of the various Baltic fleets they might encounter. 'The more numerous the better', said Nelson. 'I wish they were twice as many; the easier the victory, depend upon it.' Not everyone was convinced. Parker's chaplain, Alexander Scott (who later became one of Nelson's faithful followers), was not expected to advance his opinions on martial matters, but privately he shared the view of several commanders: 'I fear there is a great deal of Quixotism in this business'.

However, it was then that Parker took his only real decision, and gave Nelson command of the close attack. The fleet would be divided in two parts; shifting his flag from *St George* to the shallower-draught *Elephant*, Nelson would have not the ten liners he asked for, but twelve, and would attack from the south. The rest (which drew too much water for the channels involved) would stay with Parker to the north, and hope to silence the powerful batteries of Trekroner. Much – even more than usual for a sailing fleet – would depend upon the wind. Blowing from the north, as it was, it could take Nelson's ships down to the point where they would want to turn around the largest shoal, the infamous 'Middle Ground', and come back to assault the Danish defence's weakest section. It could also take Parker's ships down towards Trekroner. But if it stayed in the north and Parker was not successful, he would not be able to escape, and Nelson would be unable to attack.

There was no point in worrying about something uncontrollable, and Nelson did not: on 1 April, swiftly taking his dozen liners and their attendant vessels to a point south of the Middle Ground, he anchored and announced he would fight as soon as the wind came fair. In the meantime he had to tell his captains what to do, and this gave another marked contrast with the Battle of the Nile. All then had been perfectly prepared for anything by the weeks of pursuit; now the same readiness had to be achieved with perhaps only a few hours' grace. He set to work at once in a characteristic way: his second-in-command, Rear Admiral Thomas Graves, and the captains were invited to dinner. It was a convivial evening – Nelson, 'in the highest spirits', drank a toast to a leading wind and a quick victory, and it had exactly the effect he intended: Foley was there, and Hardy, and Fremantle, who could all be expected to be enthusiastic, but even the officers who had not previously fought alongside Nelson went back to their ships fired with vigour. After they had gone he started dictating their written orders, at first pacing his cabin, and later (on his manservant's insistence) lying down in his cot. He finished about 1 a.m., when six clerks began making the necessary copies – more than thirty – for distribution to the individual ships; and at the same time, by extraordinary luck, the wind was gradually shifting to the south. He slept very little; battle would almost certainly begin in the morning.

Given full charge of his own plan, the public face was all confidence, and the prospect of action crowded out other concerns. At the start of the voyage, he had been irritable and interfering – 'Lord Nelson *would* give the orders'. On one occasion, he mistimed a tack and lost the wind. 'Upon this,' a member of his company recorded, 'he said rather peevishly to the master, or officer of the watch, "Well now, see what we have done. Well sir, what do you mean to do?" The officer saying with hesitation, "I don't exactly know, my Lord. I fear she won't do", Lord Nelson turned sharply towards the cabin and replied, "Well, I am sure if you don't know what to do, no more do I either." He then went in, leaving the officer to work the ship as he liked.' Playing at captain again, Hardy would have said; and people put the irritability down to Parker's lack of drive and organization. But the personal letters Nelson wrote at the same time – some never meant to be seen by anyone except Emma – show the confused private background he brought to Copenhagen: guilty, joyous, jealous, deceived and self-deceiving. The most important relationship of his life, which brought him the greatest happiness he ever knew, was hedged around with dreams, pretence and lies.

As far as the social aspects went, the pretence was inevitable. It was not that irregular unions were uncommon – Nelson's own brother Maurice lived happily unmarried with a woman called Sarah Ford; Prince George, heir to the throne, was flagrantly adulterous; Prince William, as Duke of Clarence, lived in great domestic contentment with the actress Mrs Jordan, fathering a long series of Fitzclarences. But Maurice was not important enough to be endangered by scandal, and the princes were too important. The very thought of Prince George put Nelson into a spin of fierce jealousy: hearing that Emma had caught the prince's fancy, which was true, he thought in horror that they might have an affair, which they did not. Panic-stricken, he wrote to Emma: 'Don't let him touch you, nor sit next to you; if he comes, get up. God strike him blind if he looks at you – this is high treason and you may get me hanged by revealing it. Oh God, that I were! ... Does Sir William want you to be a whore to the rascal?' Yet his own position in conventional society was vulnerable – the king's snub made that obvious – and though he had brought it on himself, Nelson badly wanted public respectability, as well as private happiness and international fame. He must have known that he could only have two of the three; so self-deceit was almost equally inevitable.

Perhaps Emma's deceit was inevitable too. 'Now, my own dear wife, for such you are in my eyes and in the face of heaven, I can give full scope to my feelings ... You know, my dearest Emma, there is nothing in this world I would not do for us to live together, and to have our dear little child with us. I firmly believe that this campaign will give us peace, and then we will set off for Brontë ... I love, I never did love anyone else. I never had a dear pledge of love till you gave me one, and you, thank my God, never gave one to anybody else.'

It was the same dream as ever, the victorious sailor home from the sea, settled on shore with a happy family; yet further from reality than ever, with the cottage exchanged for the Italian dukedom, a 'wife' whom no earthly authority would acknowledge, and a child he thought was Emma's only one. Horatia, whom he had seen just once, may have been one of twins – there is a hint to that effect in one of his letters. When Horatia was a few days old, Emma took her to be looked after at a secret address, and it has been suggested that a second child was given, for some reason, to a foundlings' home. But Emma never revealed to him that she already had a child by another man. At some time, she must have wondered whether to tell him or not, but if she was still uncertain, his beautiful phrase for their baby – 'a dear pledge of love' – would have decided her. She could not risk telling him.

Except in letters delivered by mutual friends, he used a childish little fiction when writing to Emma about Horatia. He would write as if on behalf of an illiterate sailor, Thomson, whose wife had had a baby under Emma's protection; not a very plausible idea at best, and made quite implausible both by the number of letters supposedly written by the vice admiral for the lovelorn seaman, and by the muddle he got into – Thomson was sometimes Thompson, his wife was often a friend, married to her own uncle. Yet there was no mistaking the feeling: 'Poor dear Mrs Thompson's friend will go mad with joy. He cries, prays and performs all tricks, yet dare not show all or any of his feelings ... he has only me to consult with. He swears he will drink your health in a bumper this day and damn me if I don't join him ... he does nothing but rave about you and her.' No one could have been taken in by the code, but in a time of chaotic emotion, it gave a small sense of security – almost the sole security he had. 'No, the thought of Horatia cheers me up. We will yet be happy ...' He had to believe it. 'You, my beloved Emma, and my country, are the two dearest objects of my fond heart – a *heart susceptible and true.*' For them both, he worked towards peace and happiness in the only way he knew – through the calming discipline of command, and battle.

During the night, as Nelson dictated his orders, Hardy was rowed in to sound the channel as close as possible to the Danish line. Using a pole rather than a lead and line, so that he would not be heard, he found that the closer he went, the deeper the water became. He managed to go undetected right around the nearest ship, and reported his findings to Nelson. In the morning, though, the pilots were extremely nervous, with (said Nelson angrily) 'no other thought than to keep the ships clear of danger, and their own silly heads clear of shot', and it took more than an hour to find one who would lead the fleet in. At 9.30 the advance began, in almost complete silence: the only sounds on board the van ship, the 74-gun *Edgar*, were the voices of pilot and helmsman, giving and echoing commands. Listening to the chant-like orders and responses, one man in the hushed warship suddenly felt as if he was in a cathedral service, and reflected that the occasion was certainly solemn enough.

Broadly, the plan was for the British line to move down the Danish, firing as it advanced, until each ship anchored in succession opposite a Dane. As each Dane was battered into submission, the British vessels would move on down, passing outside their colleagues and engage the next available Dane. Only the first broadsides could possibly be co-ordinated; thereafter, it was bound to become a series of thunderous duels. And it began with calamity: despite their care, two British ships ran aground, and a third – Nelson's beloved old *Agamemnon* – turned too soon, could not regain the wind, and was obliged to anchor. Thus one quarter of his fleet was effectively out of action, able only to fire random shots at extreme range. As the others were rapidly redisposed, the battle began at about 10.40, and soon after 11 o'clock became general. Of all the fights Nelson was ever in, Copenhagen had the least finesse: 'Here was no manoeuvring,' he said afterwards. 'It was downright fighting.'

It was also the tightest position he had ever taken a sailing fleet into; for without another magical change in the wind, Parker's ships could conduct only a limited assault on the Trekroner batteries, and if Trekroner was not silenced and the wind remained the same, Nelson's ships had no safe escape route. But he had no intention of seeking an escape. He expected the wind to remain constant, and it did. Once his ships were in, with a determined opponent on one side – reinforced throughout the day by men and supplies from on shore – shoals on the other side and batteries at the end, 'downright fighting' was the only way out; and that was just what he wanted. When a shot crashed into *Elephant*'s mainmast, he observed aside to a companion: 'It is warm work, and this day may be the last to us at any moment.' Then a moment later, he turned and added firmly: 'But mark you, I would not be anywhere else for thousands.'

It was half past one when the episode occurred which lodged this battle permanently in popular memory. Four miles away, all Parker could see were clouds of smoke pierced by the flare of guns. The struggle seemed to be turning out as badly as he had feared: the Danish resistance appeared as strong as ever; Nelson's force was cut by a quarter from the start; by now he must be in serious difficulties. 'For Nelson's sake', Parker decided to make the signal of recall. Both his flag-captain and the Captain of the Fleet objected. 'If he is in a condition to continue the action successfully,' Parker explained, 'he will disregard it; if he is not, it will be an excuse for his retreat, and no blame can be imputed to him.' His flag-captain, Robert Otway, asked and received permission to be rowed the four miles to *Elephant* to find out exactly what was going on before the recall was made; but before he reached the battle, Parker could bear it no longer. 'The fire is too hot for Nelson to oppose,' he declared. 'A retreat must be made.'

Frederick Langford, one of Nelson's lieutenants, was first to see the signal. When he shouted it across the quarterdeck to Nelson, the admiral did not seem to hear. He repeated the message, and received a scolding rebuke: 'Mr Langford, I told you to look out on the Danish commodore and let me know when he surrendered; keep your eye fixed on him.' The lieutenant asked if he should pass the signal to the rest of the fleet first. Nelson replied tersely: 'No, acknowledge it', and reminded Langford to keep the signal for close action flying. Pacing swiftly this way and that, twitching his stump, he suddenly stopped and faced the senior officer of his marines. 'Do you know what's shown on board the Commander-in-Chief?' he demanded. 'Number 39!' The lieutenant colonel asked what it meant. 'Why, to leave off action!' Nelson exclaimed. He paused a moment and said again. 'To leave off action!' There was another pause; he added, more quietly, 'Now damn me if I do', and turned to Foley. 'You know, Foley, I have only one eye. I have a right to be blind sometimes.' Picking up a telescope, he put it to his blind eye and announced cheerfully: 'I really do not see the signal!'

22

'I shall live at Merton'

OFF THE ISLAND of Bornholm, between Sweden and Poland, Fremantle penned an indignant letter to his home in the Buckinghamshire village of Swanburn. Surrounded by their growing family – they had three children in the first three years of their marriage – Betsey read eagerly of Lord Nelson's flattering attentions to her husband, and then, with dismay, of Admiral Parker's fate: 'The insult of the Admiralty to my friend Sir Hyde is scarcely to be named ...' On 5 May 1801, barely a month after his signal recalling Nelson, Parker himself was recalled to England 'in such a way', wrote Fremantle, 'as *Treason only* could have rendered necessary.' Parker never served again. And though Nelson consequently became an official commander-in-chief for the first time in his life, he too was unhappy about the circumstances: 'They are not Sir Hyde Parker's real friends who wish for an enquiry', he wrote to Alexander Davison. 'His friends in the Fleet wish everything of this Fleet to be forgot, for we all love and respect Sir Hyde; but the dearer his friends, the more uneasy they have been at his *idleness*, for that is the truth – no criminality.'

When Parker gave in to his fears for Nelson and hoisted signal Number 39, he was aware (and said so at the time) 'of the consequences to my personal reputation'. His reasoning was that of a decent man, fair and honourable: 'It would be cowardly to leave Nelson to bear the whole shame of the failure, if shame it be deemed.' But in naval terms it was ill thought through. He could not see clearly what was happening; expecting failure, he thought it was already taking place. Putting the onus of disobedience on Nelson, Parker apparently did not consider that ships closer to him must obey the recall; and with the wind still southerly and the Trekroner batteries still in full cry, he might have realized that – whatever the conditions in the battle – obeying his order would be suicidal. Such was the fate of the frigate *Amazon* and her captain, Edward Riou. At the head of the British line, closest to Parker, he could not ignore the commander-in-chief's signal. 'Grieved at being thus obliged to retreat', his first reaction was 'What will Nelson think of us?' As *Amazon* turned away and her stern faced Trekroner, the batteries' fire continued. One shot killed Riou's clerk, standing at his side; another slaughtered several marines. Already wounded in the head, Riou called out, 'Come then, my boys, let us die all together!' The next shot cut him in half.

Writing about Parker's signal afterwards, the reaction of Rear Admiral Thomas Graves, Nelson's second-in-command, was definite. 'If we had discontinued the action before the enemy struck, we should have all got aground and been destroyed.' Responding to a summons from Nelson towards the end of the battle, he was rowed over to *Elephant*, and thought on the way that 'it was beautiful to see how the shot beat the water all around us in the boat.' It may have been a curious sense of beauty, and one which Sir Hyde would not have shared, but it was a useful attitude under the circumstances. Graves considered himself very lucky – less than a month after gaining his flag, he had served with the 'enterprising little Hero of the Nile' in an action rated the hottest of the war ('I am told the Battle of the Nile was nothing to this'); he had survived; and in the king's Birthday Honours list, he was knighted for his service. The ceremony took place on 14 June, with as much style as possible, on the quarterdeck of *St George*; and by special authority of the king, it was performed by another beneficiary of the same Honours list, Viscount Nelson.

Knighting Graves was Nelson's last public duty in the Baltic. Eleven weeks of depressingly routine naval work passed between his disobedience at Copenhagen and his departure from the northern sea, now swimming in summer, its waters blue and still and calm in long bright windless days and ever-shortening nights. The contrast with the bleak, bitter afternoon of 2 April was immense. As one Danish ship after another had caught fire or exploded, efforts to rescue survivors were impeded by continued shots from the shore, while those vessels which did not surrender were constantly reinforced. At last, about half past three, he decided that only two alternatives remained: 'Either I must send on shore and stop these irregular proceedings, or send in our fire ships.' Quickly writing a letter headed 'To the brothers of Englishmen, the Danes', he gave them the choice with a dreadful threat – 'Lord Nelson has directions to spare Denmark, when no longer resisting; but if the firing is continued on the part of Denmark, Lord Nelson will be obliged to set on fire all the Floating batteries he has taken, without having the power of saving the brave Danes who have defended them.'

Delivered by a Danish-speaking officer personally to the crown prince (who acted as regent for his mentally unstable father, the king), the letter achieved its effect: after being reassured that 'Lord Nelson's object in sending the flag of truce was humanity', the firing stopped. 'Certainly as convenient to *us* as to the Enemy,' Fremantle told his wife honestly, 'as we had several ships on shore [aground] and most of the Ships engaged crippled so completely that it was with difficulty they could sail out.'

The immediate sequel followed the pattern Sir Hyde had set. As commander-in-chief, he should have conducted negotiations for peace; but, well aware of his own inadequacy and Nelson's greater fame, the honest, unfortunate appointee directed Nelson to be the diplomat. Hardy accompanied him and was profoundly impressed: 'The more I see of his Lordship the more I admire his great character, for I think on this occasion his Political management was *if possible* greater than his Bravery ... He was received with as much acclamation as when we went to the Lord Mare's show ... We dined with all the Court, and after Dinner he had an audience with the Crown Prince for more than two hours; and I will venture to say that his Royal Highness never had so much plain trooth spoken to him in his life.'

Nearly a thousand Britons had been killed or wounded, while the Danes, unable to count their wounded, estimated they had lost three thousand dead. 'I have been in a hundred and five engagements,' Nelson wrote that evening, 'and today is the most terrible of them all.' His own opinion of his persuasive powers was low ('a negociator is certainly out of my line'), but even before the battle was finished he had been thinking of the wider political implications of success, explaining to captured Danish officers (as Fremantle saw) that he 'longed to see the Russians down'; and although it took a week, he succeeded with the prince. On 9 April, an armistice of fourteen weeks was agreed upon. Nelson had hoped for sixteen weeks, which was the time he reckoned it would take to deal with the Russian fleet and 'hew down' Tsar Paul, 'the trunk of the Northern League'. But that night, just after the agreement was reached, news came at last to Copenhagen that Paul was already dead.

On 17 May the Armed Neutrality of the North was officially disbanded. By then, Parker had been recalled – he left on 6 May – and Nelson had taken the fleet as far as Reval: until he had definite news to the contrary, he had to assume a threat still existed. Off the coast of Egypt, William Hoste heard of his progress and remarked, 'If I am not mistaken, he will find the climate too cold for him.' Hoste was not mistaken, for, as happened so often after action, Nelson had fallen ill. Parker, when still in command, outraged the fleet by ordering them to burn all their prizes except one, which was to be used as a hospital ship. With his inherited wealth, he had no particular need of prize money; but this decision, effectively depriving his officers and sailors of the fruits of battle, damaged his standing with them more than any indecision had done. Supervising the operation while Parker proceeded into the Baltic, Nelson was informed the Swedish fleet had made a sortie. He could not sail, for the wind was against him; but though night was falling, determined not to miss a battle, he called for a boat, and without a greatcoat or cloak, was rowed to the squadron. It took more than five hours, and though Foley welcomed him back into *Elephant* (pleased and astonished at hearing the familiar Norfolk accent asking to come aboard), Nelson admitted that 'a cold struck me to the heart'. This brought on 'one of my terrible spasms of heart-stroke' – possibly angina – and such a bad cough that 'I brought up what everyone thought was my lungs'. Soon, though, it became obvious the Swedish fleet was not coming out at all, and for Nelson the last weeks of Parker's inert command were improved only by a party marking Emma's birthday ('My dear Fremantle, If you don't come here on Sunday to celebrate the birthday of Santa Emma, Damn me if I ever forgive you') and by the care of others for him. 'All the fleet are so truly kind to me that I should be a wretch not to cheer up', he wrote to Ball. 'Foley has put me under a regimen of milk at four in the morning' – the time he usually started the day – 'Murray has given me lozenges and all have proved their desire to keep my mind easy, for I hear of no complaints or other wishes than to have me with them.'

But by the middle of the summer, as commander-in-chief of a completely peaceful Baltic, all he really wanted was to go back to England, and any boat returning home carried at least one letter from him asking to be recalled. Nelson found it odd writing to the Admiralty these days, for when St Vincent became its First Lord, Troubridge was made one of its Lords Commissioner, though he was not yet an admiral.

Since their breach in Palermo, he and Nelson had both tried to patch up their friendship, but it was still touchy – 'Sir Thomas Troubridge has the nonsense to say, now I was a Commander-in-Chief, I must be pleased', Nelson told Emma. 'Does he take me for a greater fool than I am?' It seemed to Nelson that, for reasons he could not fathom, he was being left to fester; but at last a message arrived from the First Lord. 'To find a proper successor, your Lordship well knows, is no easy task', he began, and proceeded to explain why. He had come to the conclusion that Nelson was simply unique. In addition to his 'other talents and habits of business not common to naval characters', Earl St Vincent went on to say: 'I never saw a man in our Profession, excepting yourself and Troubridge, who possessed the magic art of infusing the same spirit into others, which inspired their own actions ... Your Lordship's whole conduct, from your first appointment to this hour, is the subject of our constant admiration. It does not become me to make comparisons: all agree there is but one Nelson.'

This letter remains one of the best descriptions of the aura, or charisma, surrounding Nelson; and remembering how highly he respected St Vincent, the generous praise must have given him great pleasure. Best of all, though, was its accompanying news – with difficulty, a successor had been chosen, and was already on his way. With happy gratitude, the commander-in-chief prepared to relinquish his command, and told Hardy that he would never look for naval employment again.

Hardy did not believe it for a moment. In his private opinion, at such a time of domestic crisis and war abroad, it was 'as much impossible for him to remain at home as it is for him to be *happy* at Sea.' In a letter to his brother-in-law, Hardy added that he was very comfortable with the new commander-in-chief of the Baltic squadron, Admiral Charles Pole, 'but I am not anxious to remain with him or any other Admiral (except Lord Nelson)'. Knowing that Nelson still hankered after the Mediterranean command, he expected to hear soon 'that he is gone to Egypt, & I shall be ordered to follow him in the best way I can'. Part of his prediction quickly came true – for though they were not in the same ship, captain and admiral served together again sooner than either expected, and in a place that neither had thought of: the eastern end of the English Channel.

When Nelson wrote from the Baltic that out of respect for Parker, 'his friends ... wish everything of this Fleet to be forgot', he meant everything to do with Parker's shame, and expected everyone else to be accorded the same kind of honours which had followed the Nile. Copenhagen had been a longer, harder action, closer to home, and Captain Thompson, veteran of the Nile, had lost a leg; but to Nelson's disgust all that came as public recognition was his own viscounty and Graves's knighthood. On 1 July there was a pleasant welcome at Yarmouth, and, after visiting the wounded in hospital, a garlanded carriage to take him to London; and then nothing. No grateful award from the City; no royal gold medals; not even, though he suggested it to St Vincent, a gracious message from the king to the House of Commons 'as a gift to this Fleet'. Indeed, when he met the king again at St James's, His Majesty's greeting was merely: 'Lord Nelson, do you get out?' – meaning, in the phrase of the time, was he sufficiently healthy and leisured to join in social events. Nelson only just managed to keep back the reply that sprang to his lips: 'Sir, I have been out and am come in again. Your Majesty perhaps has not heard of the Battle of Copenhagen?'

The lack of recognition never ceased to rankle. Certainly he would have loved another medal, but what he most wanted was 'justice to the brave officers and men who fought on that day', and who, after Parker burnt their prizes, got nothing at all. It was desperately unfair, but since the assassination of Tsar Paul, no one could be sure that the Armed Neutrality would not have been dissolved anyway. Moreover, though the Danish commander at Kronborg had fired first, neither country had formally declared war on the other, and now most people in Britain wanted to forget it had ever happened, and concentrate instead on their habitual foes in France.

Only the Hamiltons gave him the joyous welcome he hoped for, and with them, briefly, he tried to forget about the war. At Yarmouth, meeting a sailor who had lost an arm at Copenhagen, he said, 'Well, Jack, you and I are spoiled for fishermen'; but now he decided to try the sport again, on holiday. In his youth he had enjoyed it, and Sir William loved it; so the trio left London, first for an inn in Surrey, then for another on the banks of the Thames. With them as Nelson's aide-de-camp was another Parker, Edward, a junior captain who had come under the admiral's wing and filled the emotional vacuum left by Josiah and William Hoste. More than ever, Nelson needed the love of a substitute family: his own seemed to shrink every time he went to sea. While he had been away in the Mediterranean, his uncle William Suckling had died; so had one of his own nephews, coming out to serve as a midshipman; so had his younger brother, Suckling; and while he was in the Baltic his elder brother Maurice died too. Visiting Mrs Ford, Maurice's common-law wife, Nelson found her very poor and half blind. He and Maurice had often helped each other out of debt, and now Nelson helped again, providing 'poor Blindy' with a pension. But of the Rector's eight sons, only two were still alive: Horace and his large, crass brother William. William had joined in the Hamilton's welcome, and joined in the holiday too; and despite his canonical pretensions, he did nothing to hide his glee at Horace's continued success. Because of it, he reckoned on getting a deanery at least, and found nothing disagreeable in the idea that if he outlived his father and sole surviving brother, he would inherit Horace's titles.

Nelson could tolerate that, with Emma at his elbow, privately considering how they might outlive Fanny and Sir William, marry and have a son; and where would greedy brother William be then? A bishop, no doubt, and that would have to do. Then into the happy atmosphere came two letters. One bore congratulations on his victory and safe return; and for the first time he wished he had not received such a message. 'My Dear Husband,' it said, 'I cannot be silent in the general joy ... This Victory is said to surpass Aboukir. What my feelings are, my own good heart will tell you. Let me beg, nay intreat you to believe no Wife ever felt greater affection for a Husband than I do, and to the best of my knowledge I have invariably done everything you desire. If I have done anything, I am sorry for it ... What more can I do to convince you that I am truly – Your Affectionate Wife, Frances H. Nelson.'

Rashly, naively, he showed it to Emma. Perhaps he could not avoid doing so; she must have known the letters had come. The reaction was explosive – Emma, as insecure as Nelson, instantly assumed he was deceiving her, and nothing, not even his own rising fury, could convince her otherwise. All he could do was respond to the second letter: a command to lead a squadron 'on a particular service'. In rage and accusation, the holiday broke up.

Since the Franco-Austrian Treaty of Lunéville in February, reports had been crowding in to Britain of ominous preparations across the Channel. Troops were said to be massing, and transports in readiness: invasion loomed. In this century only people born by 1930 or so can remember what it was like when, in 1940, German troops and transports gathered in the same place for the same purpose; but anyone in Britain can imagine the alarm their forebears felt at the thought of enemy armies landing. The threat, in 1801 as in 1940, united the country as nothing else could. The nation armed its defenders on both occasions with absurdly obsolete weapons, and on both occasions the people as a whole were determined, or said they were, to repel the invaders with pitchforks and kitchen knives, or anything else that came to hand. They frightened each other with rumours of secret weapons, and encouraged each other with stories that the invasion had already been tried and had failed. Men dressed up in unfamiliar uniforms, which made some of them feel brave and some ridiculous. They drilled on village greens, and laughed at each other's clumsiness or their own; and they earnestly manned the same stretches of the coast, and nervously patrolled the seas offshore in fishing boats which had been hastily armed.

This was the work that Nelson had to oversee. His father was told that it was the most important and honourable task that any naval officer had had 'since the Armada business', but from the start Nelson thought it was an odd little job he had been given. His flagship was a frigate; his fleet was mainly composed of luggers – sound and weatherly vessels, but small, flat-bottomed, and generally used for fishing, smuggling or privateering; and his senior colleagues were another one-armed admiral and an army commander with one leg. That amused him – 'I expect we shall be caricatured as the *lame* defenders of England'. He found that apart from regular seamen, he had Sea Fencibles – the ancestors of today's Royal Naval Reservists – in his command area, the Channel coast from Orfordness to Beachy Head. Like modern reservists, they were all volunteers, but unlike most of those of today, they felt extremely cautious about going to sea; a very disconcerted Nelson had to stand up in front of curious crowds and harangue them 'like a recruiting serjeant', speaking of 'our glorious ancestors', 'our undoubted right to the Sovereignty of the Narrow Seas', and the like, at the same time promising that no one would be forced to go to sea for more than two days. It was unfamiliar and rather embarrassing work; but, he remarked to St Vincent, 'everything must have a beginning, and we are literally at the foundation of the fabric of our defence.'

Though the threat of invasion was real, St Vincent and most professional naval men rated its chances of success as nil. 'I do not say the French cannot come', he observed with splendid aplomb. 'I only say they cannot come by sea.' Nelson saw one way they could, and pointed out that 'in very calm weather, they might row over in 12 hours', while his sailing ships would be more or less immobile. In that case, he added, 'if a breeze springs up, our ships are to deal *destruction*; no delicacy can be observed on this great occasion.' He also felt that passive defence, merely sitting and waiting, was not enough. On 1 August, the third anniversary of the Battle of the Nile, he took his frigate *Medusa* and some bomb-vessels over to 'look into Boulogne', checking its defences and dispositions, and lobbing a few shells in for good measure. It was a useful exercise, but back off the English coast, young Edward Parker noticed Nelson looked gloomy, and tried to cheer him up by reminding him what date it was. The admiral had not realized how transparent his feelings were, but he could not tell Parker that he was missing Emma desperately. 'My heart is ready to flow out of my eyes', he wrote to her that night, and suggested that she and Sir William should come down to the south-east and find lodgings somewhere close by.

A few days later, Hardy returned from the Baltic. Uncertain of Nelson's whereabouts, he went to visit the Hamiltons, and left a tiny, touching glimpse of the occasion. Emma knew that, though he was too discreet to say so, he disapproved of her relationship with Nelson, and after conversing for a while, she went out of the room. Then to his surprise, she came back with an infant in her arms, and said with pride, 'Look what a pretty baby I have got.' She did not explain whose it was, but wanted to show the child Nelson loved most to the captain he trusted most; and whether or not Hardy allowed himself to guess at the parents, he must have been a little disarmed.

From Portsmouth, on 20 August, Hardy wrote to his brother-in-law: 'I embark on board the *Vesuvius* Bomb at 12 o'clock this day for the Downes, but strange to tell, I have no orders from the Admiralty – nothing but a private letter from Sir Thomas Troubridge desiring me to go to the Downes as fast as possible ... I very much fear that my little friend Parker has lost his thigh.'

It was true. During the night of 15 August, Nelson sent a force of fifty-seven luggers and naval boats over to Boulogne, armed with howitzers and carronades, and manned by sailors and marines with boarding weapons. For once, he recognized that his rank was too high for him to be directly involved, and he had to grapple with the unpleasant sensation of sending others into danger, instead of leading them. 'My dear Emma,' he wrote from *Medusa*, 'my mind feels at [that] which is going forward this night; it is one thing to order and arrange an attack, and another to execute it. But, I assure you, I have taken much more precaution for others, than if I was to go myself ... If our people behave as I expect, our loss cannot be much.'

In the same letter, his mind was on very different things: would the Hamiltons like to come to Margate or to Deal? And so that the Three Joined In One might never be dissolved, where might they all live thereafter? 'From my heart I wish you could find me out a good comfortable house, I should hope to be able to purchase it. At this moment, I can command only £3,000; as to asking Sir William, I could not do it; I would sooner beg.'

But, as he dreamed and worried and planned, his attack was going disastrously wrong. Currents were faster than expected, and the French defences stronger: a line of twenty-four ships lay across Boulogne harbour entrance chained together, moored with chains instead of hawsers, and surrounded by netting. Of his fifty-seven boats, twelve were lost, and none of the French; and as the night wore on and the survivors straggled back, Nelson, heavy-hearted, prepared a list of losses to forward to St Vincent. Forty-four officers and men were dead, and 128 wounded, including 'dear little Parker, his thigh very much shattered; I have fears for his life.'

St Vincent was all consolation: 'It is not given to us to command success; your Lordship and the gallant officers and men under your command most certainly deserved it.' He had said almost exactly the same thing after the assault on Tenerife, and must have recognized the similarity between that and Boulogne: both were boat attacks by night, and both were savage defeats. However, Boulogne was Nelson's last defeat.

Naturally he accepted full blame for the tragedy, but it was hard – especially when he learned that in the coastal towns, posters were stuck up telling seamen to refuse 'being sent by Lord Nelson to be butchered'. A courtly message which, at any other time, would have given him unalloyed pleasure, now seemed incongruous: he was given official permission to use his Italian title in Britain. Edward Parker was touchingly loyal – 'To call me a Nelsonite', he said, 'is more to me than making me a Duke: I would lose a dozen limbs to serve him.' Yet the young man's wound was turning gangrenous; amputation was his only hope, and if he survived, he would never be able to serve at sea again.

'Heavy sea, sick to death – this sea-sickness I shall never get over.'

With even the weather against him, the newly recognized Duke of Brontë was utterly wretched. There was 'nothing to be done on the grand scale', and he could see no reason for having a vice admiral in personal charge of the area. However, late in August, two very welcome events occurred: within a few hours of each other, travelling respectively by sea and by land, Hardy and the Hamiltons both arrived. On shore, the Hamiltons lodged at the Three Kings inn, where Nelson speedily joined them. 'I hope he will not remain long', Hardy commented.

He should have known better. The visitors stayed for more than three weeks, and Nelson was with them most of the time. There were two consuming topics of conversation – Parker's health, and the news that Emma brought: she thought she had found a house that Nelson would like. It was one hour's drive from London, at Merton in Surrey, and would cost £9,000, which was more than Nelson could afford in cash; he would have to have a mortgage. A surveyor had looked it over, and delivered a firm report. In the grounds was 'a dirty, black-looking canal ... which keeps the whole place damp'; the grounds themselves were 'worn and out of condition', with 'not the least privacy', while the house was 'an old paltry small dwelling of low storeys ... very slightly built ... altogether the worst place, under all circumstances, that I ever saw pretending to suit a gentleman's family.' Nelson told Emma to buy it the moment she got back.

At the end of September, a week after the Hamiltons had left, Parker died in delirium and extreme pain. Early in the month, his leg had been sawn off, close to the hip. It was a long, difficult operation – 'his groans could be heard far off' – and afterwards, from his lonely frigate, Nelson told Emma how the young captain 'got hold of my hand, said he could not bear me to leave him, and cried like a child ... I came on board but no Emma. No, no, my heart will break. I am in silent distraction ... Good God, what a change! I am so low I cannot hold up my head.' He wrote again to the Admiralty requesting to be relieved of his command; his presence there seemed more than ever unnecessary, for in diplomatic and political circles, great changes were imminent. After more than eight years of unremitting war, peace negotiations between France and Britain were under way. In the Mediterranean, Lord Keith and General Sir Ralph Abercromby had finally defeated the army Napoleon had abandoned in Egypt; off Algeciras, in the Straits of Gibraltar, one of Nelson's Nile brotherhood, Sir

James Saumarez, had won an outstanding victory against a Spanish fleet. 'Saumarez's action has put us on velvet', St Vincent purred; but he was deaf to Nelson's plea for release. 'The public mind is so much tranquillized by your being at your post', he explained, 'that it is highly desirable that you should continue there', and added a flattering but unwelcome reminder of 'how very important it is that the enemy should know that *you* are constantly opposed to him.'

There could be no arguing with this, so Nelson reluctantly turned to another difficult task. He learned in a letter from his father that Fanny had rented a house in Somerset Street, near Portman Square in London. When Nelson had been far away, the Rector had always stayed with her over the winter; now, Nelson told Emma, 'he seems to think he may do something I shall not like. I suppose he means going to Somerset Street. Shall I, to an old man, enter upon the detestable subject; it may shorten his days. But I think I shall tell him that I cannot go to Somerset Street to see him ... If I once begin, you know, it will *all out*, about her ...' Day after day, he put off replying, but on 4 October it was announced that preliminary articles of peace had been signed in Paris. The Rector wrote again – an unusually cool letter – asking if he might know where, under the happy new conditions, his son intended to reside. Nelson had to answer, yet, prolific letter-writer as he was, he found this one of the most difficult he had ever had to compose. After many drafts, he was still dissatisfied, but felt he had to send it. There was a warm invitation to come and stay with cheerful society at any time, but the central message was blunt: 'I shall live at Merton, with Sir William and Lady Hamilton.'

If peace had been signed, he must be able to go. Yet on the morning of 6 October, packed and ready, he was astounded to receive notification from the Admiralty that he should remain at his post until the treaty was ratified. A suspicion which he had held ever since taking up the job now crystallized: the Admiralty, particularly St Vincent and even more particularly Troubridge, were deliberately keeping him away from Emma. Hardy felt it might well be true, telling his brother-in-law, 'They seem determined to oppose him in everything he wishes. I begin to think Lord St Vincent wishes to clip his wings a little, & certainly has succeeded in the affair of Boulogne. Troubridge, like a true Politician, forsakes his old friend (who has procured him all the Honor he has got) & sticks fast by the man who is likely to push him forward hereafter.'

After another week, still seasick and suffering from toothache, Nelson tried to entertain a distinguished visitor – William Pitt, the only politician he admired, whose example had once inspired him with thoughts of a political career of his own. Each knew the other's reputation well, but Nelson cannot have been a very good host: he told the ex-prime minister his woes, and found with gloomy satisfaction that 'he thinks it very hard to keep me now all is over.' However, very soon after came news from Troubridge that hostilities would cease on the 22nd: then, but not before then, Lord Nelson could quit his station – and have ten days' leave.

On 16 October, he wrote to Emma the most bitter letter of his life: 'My dearest friend, Tomorrow week all is over – no thanks to Sir Thomas. I believe the fault is all his, and he ought to have recollected that I got him the medal of the Nile. Who upheld him when he would have sunk under grief and mortification? Who placed him in such a situation in the Kingdom of Naples that he got by my public letters *Titles, the Colonelcy of Marines, Diamond Boxes* from the King of Naples, 1000 ounces in money for no expenses that I know of? Who got him £500 a year from the King of Naples? and however much he may abuse him, his pension will be regularly paid. Who brought him into public notice? Look at my public letters. *Nelson*, that Nelson that he now *Lords* it over. So much for gratitude. I forgive him, but my God I shall never forget it . . . I shall never forget it . . .'

And he never did. But on the same day, in HMS *Barfleur*, 'blockading Brest as closely as ever', Collingwood was happier than he had been for many months. 'I cannot tell you', he wrote to his father-in-law, 'how much joy the news of the peace gave me.' He had heard it only three days earlier, on the brink of leaving England. Now 'the hope of returning to my family, and living in quiet and comfort among those I love, fills my heart with gladness. The tidings came to us at the happiest time. I was to take leave of my wife after breakfast, and we were both sad enough, when William came running in with one of his important faces on, and attempted to give his information in a speech; but, after two or three efforts, which were a confused huddle of inarticulate sounds, he managed to bring out "Peace! Peace!", which had just as good an effect as the finest oration he could have made on the subject . . . I hope by Christmas to have the pleasure of embracing you all.'

On the same day again, from Surrey, Sir William Hamilton wrote an equally engaging letter. He had always enjoyed arranging the interior decoration of his own houses, and was bemused when Nelson gave Emma an entirely free hand not only in selecting Merton but also in fitting it out. Yet to his surprise and pleasure, it had worked: 'We have now inhabited Your Lordship's premises some days & I can now speak with some certainty. I have lived with our dear Emma several years. I know her merit, have a great opinion of the head & heart that God Almighty has been pleased to give her; but a seaman alone could have given a fine woman full power to choose and fit up a residence for him without seeing it himself. You are in luck, for in my conscience I verily believe that a place so suitable to your views could not have been found ... If you stay away three days longer I do not think you can have any wish but you will find it completed'. Better still, though it had taken all Nelson's money and more, Hamilton now reckoned it was a bargain: the rumours of peace began to circulate just three days after the deal had been struck, and property prices were rising rapidly; if Nelson sold the next morning, he could probably get an extra thousand for the place. The location was first class, close to the capital, yet entirely secluded – 'two points beyond estimation' – and Nelson would find he had 'a good mile of pleasant dry walk around your own farm.'

In every way possible, Emma was bringing the dream to life: apart from the house, she was 'fitting up pig-sties and hen-coops, & already the Canal is enlivened with ducks, & the cock is strutting with his hens about the walks.' Everything was completely delightful; and so, Sir William said happily, 'You have nothing but to come and enjoy immediately.'

23

'The Eyes of his Country are upon him'

WHEN THE HAMILTONS showed him around Merton for the first time, Nelson exclaimed again and again with boyish pleasure: 'Is this, too, *mine?*' In one sense it was not entirely, for in establishing himself in what he considered to be a suitable way for an admiral and a lord, he was mortgaged to the hilt: without unexpected help from Alexander Davison, who lent him £6,000 – two-thirds of its cost – he would not have been able to buy Merton Place. There is nothing left of the house now; less than fifty years after Nelson's death, a man who had been a gardening boy there lamented the loss of 'those beautiful pleasure grounds and gardens ... the trees and shrubs all cut down ... nearly all the ground covered with unsightly bricks and mortar; and if this is not sufficient to disfigure and transform the place, they are going to make a railroad right through the centre of it.'

In the last days of October 1801, however, even fastidious Sir William could find no fault with Emma's work, and Nelson, unaccustomed to ownership, was thrilled beyond measure: 'Oh, Sir William!' he cried in delight. 'The longest liver shall have it all!' He meant, of course, that whoever lived longest would keep it, and told Emma that she would be 'Lady Paramount of all the territories and waters of Merton, and we are all to be your guests and to obey all lawful commands.'

She had done exactly what most people today would want to do when taking over a big old run-down house: she brought the kitchen up to date with new stoves, installed plenty of lavatories and made sure each main bedroom had its own bathroom. To brighten the interior and make it seem more spacious, she also gave the reception rooms French windows (though Nelson would certainly not have called them that) to the gardens, and covered their inside doors with mirrors. Many pictures of Merton Place survive: one, by Edward Locker, Captain Locker's youngest son, shows a frock-coated gentleman who must be Sir William (he has two arms) fishing in 'the Canal' – 'Your Lordship's plan as to stocking the canal with fish is exactly mine', he had written. 'I will answer for it, that in a few months you may command a good dish of fish at a moment's warning.' Other paintings, pretty watercolour sketches, show the Canal – which was much more attractive than the name suggests – curving around from the west side to cross the north-facing front of the house, approached by a drive over a Roman-arched bridge. Lawns, paths, shrubs and mature trees separated the pediment and decorative urns of the front door from the water, and spread out gracefully around the eastern side, where two bow exteriors were sheltered by verandahs. There was an orchard, an ice-house, a kitchen-garden and paddock; under the house were good cellars, kept cool (and no doubt damp) by the proximity of the water; and the property extended to the other side of the road, with a barn, a dairy and an artificial mound, possibly of pre-Roman origin. Indoors, in addition to kitchens, cloakrooms and two halls, the ground floor had a dining room, drawing room and west-facing library, while upstairs were a second drawing room, five best bedrooms and eight servants' rooms.

It was Emma's court, as much as Nelson's domain, and she brought to it all the exuberance of her own nature and her Neapolitan past. 'Not only all the rooms,' said Lord Minto, 'but the whole house, staircase and all, are covered with nothing but pictures of her and him, of all sizes and sorts, and representations of his naval actions, coats of arms, pieces of plate in his honour, the flagstaff of L'Orient, etc. – an excess of vanity which counteracts its purpose. If it was Lady H.'s house there might be a pretence for it; to make his own a mere looking-glass to view himself all day is', the astounded Minto ended with a sniff, 'bad taste.' So it was, or would have been, if Nelson had set it all out himself. He could have reduced the show, but saw no need to: firstly, he had given Emma a free hand, and would not go back on that; secondly, if the pictures and trophies were not displayed, they would have to be stored, and an unnecessary expense laid out in buying different ones; and finally, there was no earthly reason why, in their own private world, they should not indulge and be indulged.

It used to be said of Emma that she seduced Nelson for the sake of reflected glory. That was uncharitable. Nobody can know how much she loved him: he destroyed most of her letters to him, but she carefully preserved most of his to her. It should be sufficient to know that she had qualities – skill as a lover, shrewdness and common sense, a sailorly sense of humour, and her capacity for giving admiration – which made him devoted to her until he died. Had they been man and wife from the start, no one would have criticized them – except perhaps for Emma's gaudy taste, and even that might have been less. As it was, said Minto, 'nothing shall ever induce me to give the smallest countenance to Lady Hamilton. She looks ultimately to the chance of marriage, as Sir W,. will not be long in her way, and ... she may survive Lady Nelson; in the meanwhile she and Sir William and the whole set of them are living with him at his expense. She is in high looks, but more immense than ever. She goes on cramming Nelson with trowelfuls of flattery, which he goes on taking as quietly as a child does pap.'

His love for her forced him inevitably into the only notable unkindness of his life, his rejection of Fanny. A week before Christmas 1801, in a final, heart-rending letter to him, she made one last hopeless effort to win him back.

'My dear Husband, It is some time since I have written to you; the silence you have imposed is more than my affection will allow me, and in this instance I hope you will forgive me in not obeying you. One thing I omitted in my letter of July, which I now have to offer for your accommodation, is a comfortable warm house. Do, my Dear Husband, let us live together. I can never be happy until such an event takes place. I assure you again I have but one wish in the world, To please you. Let everything be buried in oblivion; it will pass away like a dream. I can now only entreat you to believe I am, most sincerely and affectionately, your wife, Frances H. Nelson.'

He was always an assiduous, conscientious correspondent: in his days off the Downs he had sometimes had as many as a hundred letters a day to answer, and replied to them all by return, even the dotty ones – someone who tried to blackmail him with the threat of exposing the Boulogne disaster in the press was told, 'I have not been brought up in the school of fear and therefore care not what you do. I defy you and your malice.' But he never replied to Fanny's last poignant appeal; it went back to Somerset Street with a note signed by Alexander Davison: 'Opened by mistake by Lord Nelson, but not read.'

He had provided well for Fanny, giving her £1,800 a year, paid quarterly. Later he increased the sum to two thousand, which was maintained after his death by a parliamentary pension; emotionally she was destitute, but financially she was never poorly off. If it was true that he never read her last letter (though he must have recognized the handwriting), it may have been the best he could manage under the circumstances. Ensuring her income was the least and the most he felt able to do; reading of her distress would only have pointlessly revived his own.

Like most of the people who knew them, people ever since have tended to take sides with either Emma or Fanny. Nelson's surviving brother William took Emma's part, and so, one by one, did all his sisters and their families. As Horatia grew up, she heard often, both from Kitty's family and Susannah's, that the separation was Fanny's fault: in their words, 'However beautiful and fascinating Lady Hamilton was, it would have had no effect upon Lord Nelson, had not his affections been chilled, and thrown back, as it were, upon himself.' Horatia added to this: 'He was treated with coldness by his wife. His home was not made happy ... He felt the want of someone to love, and be loved by in return.' Emma was venomous about Fanny. Writing that Viscountess Nelson was 'a very wicked, artful woman acting a bad part' (which was preposterous) 'who rendered his days wretched and his nights miserable' (which was probably nearer the truth), she nicknamed her bird-like rival 'Tom Tit', and Josiah 'the Cub'. On one occasion, she reported spitefully how Sarah Nelson, William's wife, 'saw, *met* the Cub, but he looked as if he were going to be hanged, but did not speak to her. The precious couple are fit for each other.' The unnecessary sneers were taken up even by Nelson's favourite sister Kitty, who wrote to Emma in March 1805: 'I have seen Tom Tit once. She called in her carriage at Lady Charlotte Drummond's, who lives next door. The lady was not at home, but she got out of her carriage, walked as stiff as a poker about half a dozen steps, turned round, and got in again. What this Manoeuvre was for, I cannot tell, unless to show herself. She need not have taken so much pains if nobody wanted to see her [any] more than I do. She is stiffer than ever.'

For William and his sisters to enrol themselves firmly on Emma's side was not surprising. Fanny had never liked Kitty's husband, George Matcham, though the rest of the family did; she was ill at ease with her sisters-in-law; and William, always on the look-out for preferment, wished to keep in with his brother. One by one, they all took a natural, fairly easy but unpitying way out. Only two people, in their different ways, realized it was possible to accept the new arrangement without recrimination, and they were the two men who, apart from Nelson, were most intimately involved: his father the rector, and Sir William.

Many people assumed then, and have done since, that if Nelson was guilty of loving Emma and hurting Fanny, he was also guilty of deceiving Sir William. But Hamilton was a man of the world, urbane and wise, who perfectly understood the problem he had foreseen so long before: himself growing old and his wife remaining irrepressible, buoyant and ambitious. He still loved her, although he sometimes found her exasperating, and he loved and respected Nelson. From his point of view, nothing could have been better than for her to fall in love with the man he esteemed most in the world. All his life, he was a contented non-Christian, but he used religious terms to express his personal creed, and one day put his tolerant wisdom into three short, memorable sentences:

'My study of antiquities has kept me in constant thought of the perpetual fluctuation of everything. The whole art is really to live all the days of our life; and not with anxious care disturb the sweetest hour that life affords – which is the present. Admire the Creator, and all His works, to us incomprehensible, and do all the good you can upon earth; and take the chance of eternity without dismay.'

That gentle philosophy made deception unnecessary, and jealousy impossible; and when he died, in April 1803, he bequeathed a favourite portrait of Emma to Nelson, 'my dearest friend, the most virtuous, loyal and truly brave character I ever met with. God bless him,' he ended firmly, 'and shame fall on those who do not say amen.'

For the Rector, with his deep-rooted Christian beliefs and long-standing affection for Fanny, accepting the breakdown of Nelson's marriage was difficult – so difficult that he feared he might never feel able to see his son again. Invitations went each way, from Burnham to Merton and vice versa, but the Rector seemed to be unexpectedly busy, and Nelson had no intention of returning to the Parsonage House: happy childhood memories were long overlaid by the shade of Fanny and five years on the beach. So there was a certain irony when, in November 1801, the Rector hesitantly agreed to come to Merton; because he did so on Fanny's insistence that he should not break relations with his son. It is possible that at that time she had some faint hope he might change Nelson's mind, but there is nothing to suggest that the Rector tried to do so when he was at Merton. To his surprise he found a 'Mansion of Peace' – Emma must have restrained herself considerably – and an agreeable new companion in Sir William. Though Emma found him rather a bore, and very prone to falling asleep at odd times, Nelson wanted him to stay permanently – 'I must become one of the inhabitants', said the Rector shyly. For Nelson's sake, he and Emma would have tried it, but it is difficult to imagine him tolerating for long the rowdy parties Emma so enjoyed, or her curbing her tempestuous nature indefinitely. However, it did not come to the trial. As winter approached, the old man could not refuse the habit of many years, and moved to the milder climate of Bath; and there he died, late in April 1802. He was nearly eighty years old by then, and of course would have preferred Fanny and Horace to be together; but he had seen that his son at least was happy, and he still loved them both, and that was well.

Nelson's ten days' leave was repeatedly extended by a fortnight, until a formal arrangement was made for his flag to remain flying until the peace treaty was ratified, while he, on full pay, lived at Merton: it was close enough to the Downs station for him to be on board at short notice. Hardy remained on duty in the Downs, missing his admiral, and irritated not to hear any news of him except through the papers. On 29 October Nelson took his seat in the House of Lords, where Hardy hoped he would be guarded in his speeches – 'we poor Sailors are quite out of our element when on shore'. Two weeks later, disappointed and emphatic, Hardy growled: 'I see almost by every paper that Lord Nelson has been speaking in the House. I am sorry for it, and I am fully convinced that Sailors should not talk too much.' So were the other peers. Nelson's maiden speech should have been simple – he seconded a vote of thanks to Saumarez for the victory off Algeciras – but he filled it out with naval words and ideas which nobody understood, and everyone found deadly dull. When he ended with an apology for having taken so much time, there was a nearly unanimous 'Hear hear!' Nelson, hurt though not completely put off, admitted the speech was 'bad enough, but well meant', and soon after, joined in a debate on the terms of the peace treaty with France. Confining himself to its naval aspects, he knew what he was talking about, and Emma (who supportively declared that he sounded like an angel) was told by others that 'he spoke well, firm, distinct and audible.' Sighing with admiration ('He succeeds in all he does ... I am quite Nelson mad again for him as an orator'), she did not know that members who were not sailors – that is, most of them – could not grasp his arguments, and simply laughed at him. 'How', asked one, 'can Ministers allow such a fool to speak for them?'

Nevertheless, Nelson enjoyed himself, with 'gardening, attending the House, and eating, drinking and hurra-ing', and he did not forget Hardy: his plan was to go back to Naples when peace was certain, and he wanted his captain to live there too. 'Lord Nelson has given me one hundred acres in any part of his estate at Brontë that I choose', Hardy wrote, 'with apartments in his house, a knife & fork &c . . . The former part I have accepted and intend to keep, but the latter I have not yet determined on, nor shall I till I know the Company that will attend him there.'

He was one of the few people to maintain good relations with Nelson and with Fanny. After breakfasting with Lady Nelson one summer's morning in 1802, he decided he was 'more pleased with her if possible than ever; she certainly is one of the Best Women in the World.' She must have been grateful for his continuing unfeigned friendship. He always found it more difficult with Emma. She never entirely won him over, though she tried: a few weeks before his visit to Fanny, he 'stole three hours to go to Merton, where I saw his Lordship, Sir Wm & Lady Hamilton. They are all extremely well, & her Ladyship was quite *angry* that I could not stay longer.' It is perfectly possible she was sincere; but knowing how close Hardy and Nelson were, it is equally possible she was pretending, in an effort to be fully accepted by Hardy.

While Nelson lived at Merton, this was the only time that Hardy and Emma met; but it seems that they never quite trusted each other, and that there was a tacit rivalry between them for Nelson's affection. For Emma this was in the most personal way possible; for Hardy it was both personal and professional: he feared that at some crucial time, Emma might induce Nelson to neglect his duty again, as she had done in Palermo. Much later, after Nelson was dead, another naval captain wrote to Emma: 'Hardy may have spoken his mind on former occasions more freely than you could have wished; but depend upon it that the last words of our lamented friend will influence his conduct.' And whether it was because of Nelson's dying words, or because the final victory had been won, or because at last the rivalry was over and only grief was shared, Hardy personally delivered to Emma an unfinished letter he had found open on Nelson's desk. Beginning 'My dearest beloved Emma, the dear friend of my bosom,' Nelson knew, and said, that his last writing before battle would be to her. So it was; and the final words he wrote to Emma, who had brought him so much turbulence and joy, were: 'May God Almighty give us success over these fellows, and enable us to get a Peace.'

*

On 27 March 1802, the peace for which he eventually died seemed to have been achieved already: on that day, the Treaty of Amiens was signed, and the war between Britain and France came to an end; and Napoleon, in recognition of the one man who had done his country's cause most damage, placed a bust of Nelson on his dressing table.

During the preceding winter months, while negotiations were still carrying on, the newspapers often reported that Nelson was about to be sent to some new command. The idea worried Hardy at first – 'I think he would at least have given me a hint' – but by Christmas he was sure: 'It is all humbug, as I heard from him a day or two ago & he says he will not be employed if he can possibly help it.' On the other hand, he added, 'I am of opinion that Old St Vincent will not let him remain at home if *he* can possibly help it.' There was some brief talk of sending him to sort out a mutiny which flared up in Bantry Bay, but that quickly faded, and there was no other place the Admiralty could reasonably send him; and when, with the spring, peace came, Nelson – for the first time in his life – realized he could actually relax on shore, confident that, whatever else the future held, he would not be ignored in an emergency again. No more wandering lonely to 'the bank' on Saturdays, reading bitterly of his friends' appointments; no more searching for hobbies to fill out empty hours.

It was then that his father died. Some men find a sense of liberation in the death of a powerful father, and the Rector's very humility had made him a powerful man to Nelson. Yet there was no sense of freedom, only of loss. To the end of his own life, on occasions of particular strain when he most needed someone to turn to, he would still cry in private, because he was all alone.

Perhaps he might have felt stronger at those times if he had bidden his father farewell; but he was not present either at the dying man's bedside in Bath or at the funeral in Burnham. Fanny had got to Bath before him, and he feared she might appear at Burnham too.

'Our dear Lord Nelson is noble, generous, open and liberal to all', Hamilton wrote, 'and I wish to God he could afford it.' Throughout 1802, both men had serious money worries. Partly for the sake of a moral appearance and partly to be close to the Royal Academy and British Museum, Sir William decided to keep up his own rented household in Piccadilly; and despite Nelson's protests, he insisted on paying one-third of the Merton bills whenever he and Emma were staying there. Visits were long, frequent and filled with entertainment. Hamilton knew only too well the cost, and the cause: 'It is not my fault', he told Emma, 'if by living with a great Queen in intimacy for so many years that your ideas should so far outrun what my means can furnish.' With an estranged wife and an extravagant mistress, Nelson also had the problem of supporting two households. Pondering his own finances, he calculated his assets in property, plate and furniture at £20,000; his debts (the mortgage and the costs of fitting out both for the Baltic and the coastal command) at £10,000; his income at £3,418; and his outgoings (the voluntary alimony to Fanny, the pension to 'poor Blindy', help with his nephews' education and interest on debts) at £2,650. 'Therefore,' he concluded, writing it all down formally and referring to himself in the third person, 'Lord Nelson is free of House-rent, but has to pay charities necessary for his station in life, taxes, repairs, servants, and to live upon £768 per annum.'

Emma was very generous with her own money, such as it was; the difficulty was her generosity with other people's too. Nelson could never refuse her anything, though he suffered for it; Hamilton rebuked her – 'You do not think of Shillings and Sixpences that in time make up a great sum' – but even he could not get a grasp of money into her head. Yet though none of them had enough to get by on properly, in the summer they made up their minds to go on a splendidly expensive holiday together: a ten-week tour of southern England, south Wales and the Midlands, which in the end cost almost five hundred pounds.

It started because Hamilton and Nelson had been awarded honorary doctorates in civil law by Oxford University. News had also come recently from Bavaria that Nelson had been created a Knight Grand Commander of the Order of St Joachim, which (after British royal permission) entitled him to wear the Order's laurelled cross – the fourth and last of his stars. Never averse to any bit of public praise, he was keen to attend the degree-giving ceremony in Oxford: apart from a change of scene and the opportunity of having some work done on Merton, it offered the chance of showing off all four stars and dressing up in a new kind of outfit. Many years before, Sir William, for his part, had inherited an estate in Wales from his first wife. Now he felt he should inspect it, to make sure that his nephew Charles Greville – Emma's previous lover – was managing it well; and so, in the latter part of July, in humid, thundery weather, the party set off.

The weather seems to have been the same across the whole country, for at the same time up in Northumberland, Cuthbert Collingwood, travelling from Newcastle to Morpeth, found the heat so oppressive he preferred to take off his coat and get 'well wet' in the rain. He had not been home for Christmas – he had not been allowed to strike his flag until 7 May – and like Nelson, had refused any peacetime service. Now he was engaged in the favourite occupations of most naval officers on shore: enjoying his family and improving his property, pulling down walls and building others, making plans for interior alterations and 'jaunting about a good deal'. He found this all rather costly, but Sarah, his wife, liked the changes, which gave him great pleasure. She, he wrote charmingly, 'has become languid and relaxed', and they had a modest seaside holiday at Newbiggin, just eight miles from home. 'Here we are a set of happy creatures.'

Most of the officers Nelson knew well were doing the same: Louis in Devon, Berry in Norfolk, Thompson newly settled in a Hertfordshire manor, Saumarez in Guernsey, Foley in Wales and Fremantle in Buckinghamshire – all had either returned home or bought houses. Fremantle stood unsuccessfully for Parliament, but was consoled by Betsey's producing another child and by the purchase of a 70-acre farm; Foley, who had been in love with Betsey, married Lady Lucy Fitzgerald ('very plain indeed', said Betsey, 'but seems affable and agreeable'). Four accepted peacetime naval employment: Ben Hallowell went to be commodore on the West African coast, Alexander Ball remained as a very popular governor of Malta, Sam Hood sailed to the West Indies to be Commissioner in Trinidad, and Hardy, after taking the Duke of Kent to Gibraltar, ferried Sir Robert Fitzgerald to his new post as British Minister in Lisbon. 'The weather was not the most pleasant in the world', he said of that voyage. 'At least Lady Robert Fitzgerald did not think it so, for she talked of departing this Life more than once, but we landed her safe at last.'

All, in other words, remained within their own society, well satisfied with the diversions of home and business, perhaps making occasional visits to London: Thompson, Berry and Louis do not appear even to have left their estates. Nelson's decision to tour the country was an extraordinary thing to do, and it resulted in something he had not thought about at all. Of course, after the battles of St Vincent, the Nile and Copenhagen, everyone knew his name, and most people had an idea of what he looked like – with his starry coat and empty sleeve he was the easiest officer in the navy to portray, at least in a stylized way. But outside London, Portsmouth and the navy, very few people had actually seen him for themselves. Without intending it – for the tour simply grew of its own accord, as one town or borough or city after another issued formal invitations – his six-hundred-mile journey showed him to the people, just as effectively as the carefully planned royal progresses that Queen Elizabeth had made two hundred years before.

From Oxford, the travellers went to Gloucester, Ross-on-Wye and Monmouth; all the way through south Wales to Milford Haven, then back to Monmouth via Swansea; up to Ludlow, Hereford and Worcester; and finally to Birmingham, Warwick and Coventry, before paying a visit to Lord Spencer at Althorpe and returning, on 5 September, to Merton. With one exception, they were magnificently fêted everywhere they went. The exception was at Blenheim Palace near Oxford: the Duke of Marlborough was there, but would not receive them – he had enough scandal in the family already, for his son was carrying on in a much publicized way with Lord Bridport's wife. In Wales there was a smaller hiccup: like the Duke of Marlborough, Captain Foley's sister-in-law did not want Emma in her house. Her husband overruled her, and 'Lord Nelson's tourists' probably did not know they had caused any awkwardness. Those incidents aside, it was all festivity, as people who had never thought to see Nelson in the flesh celebrated his presence with bell-ringing, fairs, dinners, triumphal arches and bands. Approaching Monmouth by water, rowing down the pretty river Wye ('a little gut of a river', he called it), they could hear the music from a long way off: 'See the Conquering Hero Comes!' Everywhere, from Merton to Milford Haven, it was echoed; and in Monmouth, he delivered a graceful speech of thanks:

'It was my good fortune to have under my command, some of the most experienced Officers in the British Navy, whose professional skill was seconded by the undaunted courage of British Sailors; and whatever merit might attach itself to me, I must declare that I had only to show them the Enemy, and Victory crowned the Standard ... The same success would have crowned the efforts of any other British Admiral, who had under his command such distinguished Officers and such gallant Crews. And here let me impress it on the mind of every Officer in the Service, that to whatever quarter of the Globe he may be destined, whether to the East or West Indies, to Africa, or America – the Eyes of his Country are upon him ...'

On his second visit to Monmouth, returning from the west, he spoke again, this time in praise of civilians: 'If ever war was again to take place, I would send every ship, every regular soldier out of the kingdom and leave the nation to be protected entirely by the courage of her sons at home. Suppose the French were to land in England, they might plunder and destroy a village, they might burn Monmouth, but I will engage for it they never advance as far as Hereford, for they would always find Britons ready to receive them.' Whatever Emma thought, he was not a great orator, but he was learning, and everyone who heard him felt a little braver, and much prouder.

London newspapers were astonished at the warmth of his reception, reporting the 'singular fact that more *éclat* attends Lord Nelson in his provincial rambles than attends the King.' They should not have been surprised: the capital might be full of famous men, but the provinces were not. No doubt the cities and county towns of south Wales, the Borders and the Midlands would have been pleased to play host to any hero; but Nelson of the Nile was already uniquely famous, and in each place people felt uniquely honoured to have him as their guest, for no one like him had made such a journey before. If he had never done it, his eventual death would still have been mourned, but only in an abstract way. After this trip, however, he became the people's admiral. Merely by distant association, ordinary sailors and undistinguished officers became slightly special. Even folk who had never been in a ship heard of naval deeds with greater interest, and of Nelson's achievements with added pride; and when he was killed they mourned him sincerely, because once they had seen him for themselves.

24

'Miracles of passive valour'

SOMEWHERE OUTSIDE THE north door of St Paul's Cathedral, in an ummarked grave, there lies a skeleton with a severed neck, the skull separated from the bones of the body. These are the mortal remains of Colonel Edward Despard of the Liverpool Blues, hanged as a traitor, beheaded after death in front of a crowd of twenty thousand, and buried on 21 February 1803. 'We went to the Spanish Main together', Nelson remembered. Called to the colonel's trial as a character witness, he described to the court the Nicaraguan expedition of 1780. 'We slept many nights together in our clothes upon the ground; we have measured the height of the enemy's wall together. In all that period of time, no man could have shown more zealous attachment to his Sovereign and his country than Colonel Despard did.' Yet since then, Despard had changed radically, and in the autumn of 1802 he master-minded a conspiracy to kill the king and destroy the government. Betrayed, the conspirators were arrested and the plot came to nothing. There was no doubt of the colonel's guilt, and he was sentenced to the full medieval penalty for treason – hanging, drawing and quartering. That involved the condemned man's being hanged, but not until dead. Still living, he would be taken from the gibbet, his guts drawn out and burned in front of his face, and his body cut in four pieces 'at the king's disposal'. But Nelson spoke for him so well that the court recommended mercy. It was granted, though not to the extent of letting him live; and Despard declared that if his tomb had any inscription at all, he wanted only Nelson's testimony.

The new year started grimly in every way. After hosting a musical evening for a hundred guests in Piccadilly, Sir William Hamilton was taken ill, and sensed that he was dying. At the same time a change greater than any individual death was in the air, with fears of betrayal abroad: Napoleon and the British government accused each other of dishonouring the Treaty of Amiens, and a renewal of war seemed imminent. While Nelson prepared his support of Despard, the recommissioning of British warships began, and from HMS *Amphion* in Portsmouth, Hardy told his brother-in-law: 'We get men so fast that I almost despare of seeing you.' At the end of March he wrote again: 'We are ordered to be fitted for Foreign Service, & what follows is yet to be learnt ... I rather think Lord Nelson will hoist his Flag in this Ship for a passage to the Mediterranean'.

A week later, 'fitted for Foreign Service as full as an egg', he had sad news – Hamilton was dead. So as not to leave a distressing memory at Merton, Sir William had chosen to live his last days in Piccadilly, where Emma, her mother and Nelson nursed him, and watched him quietly fade away 'as an inch of candle'. He died in Emma's arms, holding Nelson's hand, as serenely as he had lived; and in a private letter, Hardy voiced the obvious question. 'How her Ladyship will manage to live with the Hero of the Nile now, I am at a loss to know, at least in an honourable way.'

Nelson was well aware that he and Emma could not decently remain alone under one roof, and on 6 April 1803 – the day of Sir William's death – he moved from the house in Piccadilly to another, four doors away. One month later, any thoughts he may have had on the problem of setting up an illegitimate family home were abruptly shelved: early in May, he was advised to prepare for a swift return to active duty. In a sudden whirl of arrangements and rearrangements, Horatia was christened on 13 May, without either of her parents present; on the 14th Nelson's appointment to the Mediterranean command was announced; on the 16th war was declared against France; on the 18th, early in the morning, he left London; later that same day, his flag was hoisted in HMS *Victory*; and at about 10 a.m. on the 20th, accompanied by Hardy in the frigate *Amphion*, he sailed from Portsmouth with a northerly wind, but without any idea when fate and the Admiralty might allow him to return.

Since the Baltic campaign two years before, Hardy had often said how much he wanted to serve with Nelson again. Now, to his pleasure, he was, and he knew that if all went well, he would soon transfer to *Victory* herself, and work directly under his favourite admiral once more: Nelson had requested it, and told him so himself. But the admiral never breathed a word on one private matter. In naval life, Hardy's personal loyalty and professional dependability made him invaluable. The price was his completely conventional attitude. If he had not already guessed that Nelson and Emma had a child, he must have done so when he saw the prominence given to two portraits in Nelson's cabin. That was past, and had to be accepted as a matter of fact; but the dour captain would have been shocked to the core if he had known that Emma was pregnant again, and that Nelson's second child was conceived about the time of Sir William's death.

The precise date of the conception is uncertain, but it was either in the two weeks before or the two weeks after Hamilton died peacefully beside them, and since Nelson did not stay in Piccadilly again, it is more likely to have been in the last few days of Hamilton's life. The idea of Nelson and Emma making love while Sir William lay dying in the same house may still sound strange and hypocritical. It was not: Nelson could not dissemble so much, and Emma loved her husband honestly. Hardy would have found it grotesque. But however difficult it would have been (and may still be) for others to understand, that was the reality of the Three Joined in One; and if Nelson and Emma comforted each other in a time of great strain for both, it would have been without any thought of deceit, and in the certainty that Hamilton had always been happy they should love each other.

The largest squadrons of Napoleon's fleet were in Toulon and Brest. Two English squadrons, under Rear Admiral Sir Richard Bickerton and Admiral Sir William Cornwallis respectively, were already outside the ports. Nelson had never met Bickerton, whose command he was to take over, but he knew Cornwallis well – it was he who, as captain of HMS *Lion* in 1780, had nursed Nelson back to England from Jamaica, after the Nicaraguan expedition. Passing Brest, Nelson left *Victory* with Cornwallis as a temporary reinforcement, and proceeded to the Mediterranean in *Amphion*. After a bad passage across the Bay of Biscay, south of Lisbon the wind came fair, and on 3 June he brought news of the outbreak of war to Gibraltar. He paused only one night and a morning before shaping course along the Barbary coast for Malta, Sicily, Naples and – eventually – Toulon.

The long route was designed both to give and gather intelligence, and on the way three small prizes were captured; it was not unusual, either for merchantmen or individual warships, to learn of a declaration of war only when an enemy pounced upon them. The war was news to Alexander Ball in Malta too, and Nelson revised his opinion of the island's value. In the House of Lords he had dismissed it as a possible base against Toulon, and still felt the same on that score. Now, though, he realized it gave great influence over southern Italy and Egypt, and was even 'a most important outwork to India'. His view on Sicily altered as well: it was 'almost as bad as a civilized country can be ... No troops fit to be called such ... a scarcity of corn never known ... The lower classes are discontented. The nobles are oppressors and the middle rank wish for a change' – all, in short, the same as when he and Emma had passed 'days of ease and nights of pleasure' there. But the romance had gone out of it, and now he recognized the island for what it was, and always had been. In the Bay of Naples, the sight of Vesuvius brought back so many memories he felt almost overpowered. He longed to go ashore and wander again through the streets and buildings, clearly visible from *Amphion*'s deck, but decided against it: although the kingdom was neutral, Taranto, Otranto and Brindisi were already occupied by the French, and he did not want to provoke another flight of the royal family. Just in case, though, he promised Sir John Acton – still the Neapolitan prime minister – that a British man-of-war would always be on hand in the Bay, 'on some pretence or other'.

Finally heading for his war station off Toulon, he wrote a long report of all he had seen to the British prime minister, Henry Addington. At last, on 8 July, he joined the blockading fleet: two sloops, another frigate, three fourth-rate 64-gun ships, six 74s, and one third-rate 80-gun vessel – Bickerton's flagship, HMS *Gibraltar*. The news Nelson brought, of Britain's declaration of war against France, was a shock – the whole fleet were overdue for refit and replenishment, for in their peacetime patrol of the Mediterranean, they had been at sea for six months, and were expecting to return home. Now they learned from the vice admiral that 'unless the French will be so good as to prevent us', they must prepare for 'a winter's cruise' of indefinite length; but after the first disappointment, they did so willingly. Bickerton particularly requested to be allowed to remain as Nelson's second-in-command. Nelson agreed, but refused to oust him from *Gibraltar*, because HMS *Victory* was expected at any time. He remained in Hardy's frigate for three more weeks, commanding the fleet from her cramped quarters.

On the morning of 30 July 1803, *Victory* came in sight: three decks, one hundred guns; a first rate, and one of the best anywhere – over two hundred feet long, displacing more than two thousand tons, with a crew of 847 men. At half past five in the afternoon, accompanied by Captain Hardy, Nelson went on board the ship which he had first seen on the day he joined the navy, thirty-two years before, and in which, two years, two months and three weeks later, he would die; and apart from one interval of twenty-five days, he never stepped off her again.

*

> Baby, baby, naughty baby,
> Hush, you squalling thing, I say;
> Hush your squalling, or it may be
> Bonaparte will pass this way.

This was the song which, according to Hardy's biographers, Dorset nursemaids would sing to infants.

> Baby, baby, he's a giant,
> Tall and black as Rouen steeple;
> And he dines and sups, rely on't,
> Every day on naughty people.

> Baby, baby, he will hear you
> As he passes by the house,
> And he, limb from limb, will tear you,
> Just as pussy tears a mouse.

One difference between the two most recent invasion threats to England, Hitler's and Napoleon's, was their length. Hitler's lasted for a single hectic summer, but Napoleon's lasted from 1797 to 1805, with only the brief uncertain pause of the Treaty of Amiens. That treaty afforded Nelson the happiest eighteen months of his whole life, living mainly at 'Paradise Merton' with the woman he adored, seeing and playing with their daughter in her foster home; but at the turn of the eighteenth and nineteenth centuries, almost a whole generation of English children went to bed every night with the fear of Frenchmen lurking in the dark.

A further difference was that, in 1940, there could be no doubt whatever that the German threat was real; but in the war against France and Napoleon, the 'mighty project for the invasion of England' lasted so long that no one was certain whether it was all a bluff or not. Hardy was sceptical yet cautious. 'I think it necessary that every step should be taken in England to prevent the Enemy landing, but in my own opinion the Corsican never intended an invasion'. Writing from HMS *Victory* off Toulon, in September 1803, he used the past tense; yet the great blockade of France's naval ports had barely begun. In command of the Mediterranean station, Nelson, like everyone else, hoped for a short and profitable war – 'just long enough to make me independent in pecuniary matters' – but at the same time made a terrible vow: 'Never to go into Port until after the Battle, if they make me wait a year.' Collingwood's assessment of invasion was that it would be tried if possible, but via Ireland; and he expressed that thought in July 1805. By then, nearly two years had passed since Hardy had written his own view, and yet the blockade was still in force; in the Mediterranean, Nelson was still commanding the fleet off Toulon; and in all that time, true to his word, he had never been on shore.

Off Brest, Cornwallis's tactic was to remain as close as possible to the Isle of Ushant, the westernmost point of France. There he covered both the western mouth of the Channel and the approaches to Brest; and this was perhaps a harder blockade than that of Toulon. The northern part of the Bay of Biscay is a notorious stretch of sea, foggy, cold and stormy, where strong tides set through the rocks of Ushant. 'Mariners must exercise the greatest caution', the modern Admiralty Pilot says of it, still with the studied elegance of eighteenth-century style. 'This island is surrounded by dangers; rocks are numerous and some lie far from the land; fogs and thick weather are not uncommon; the tidal streams are strong, and the extent of their influence seaward undetermined ... Sailing vessels, except those bound from western French ports should not, as a rule, pass in sight of Ouessant [Ushant] but, even with a fair wind, should make a good westing, bearing in mind that the prevailing winds and currents have a tendency to set towards Ouessant and into the Bay of Biscay when southward of that island. To get well westward is therefore of the greatest importance.'

No such options existed for the blockading fleet. Among outsiders, the difficulties of a naval blockade – especially a prolonged one – were not well understood: Collingwood complained that 'city politicians' imagined it was as easy as standing guard at a door. 'So long as the ships are at sea they are content,' he said morosely, 'little considering that every one of the blasts which we endure lessens the security of the Country.' To keep the approaches to Brest under close observation, they had to sail in constant sight of this lethal shore, or at least with their frigates in sight of it; and in the prevailing south-westerly winds, it lay to leeward, so that the fleet was constantly blown towards it. By modern standards the ships were unhandy, slow to go about and slow to windward; and probably no modern mariner would dare to explain exactly how they were able to stand off and on, estimating the tidal streams and currents, night and day, summer and winter, constantly solving the problems of navigation and ship-handling – and this not merely in one ship, but in a whole fleet. The achievement astonished the French, who looked out every morning and saw the sails still there, and it is just as astonishing now. So is the crews' toughness: anyone, seaman or not, can imagine this life in ships with no shelter on deck and no warmth below, exposed to the rain and fog and to seas with a fetch of several thousand miles. They only relaxed in settled westerly gales when the French could not conceivably have left the harbour: then they could run for shelter in Plymouth Sound, a hundred and fifty miles across the Channel.

In this one respect, Cornwallis's fleet had the advantage over Nelson's off Toulon: their weather was worse, but they had a home port within reach. They never went in there unless they were forced to, and when they did they were seldom allowed ashore; but at least they could land their sick and ask for dockyard repairs, and perhaps hear some news of their families and the world. An inspection of Collingwood's ship 'began by discovering slight defects ... and the farther we went in the examination, the more important they appeared'. It turned out she was 'so completely rotten as to be unfit for sea. We have been sailing for the last six months with only a sheet of copper between us and eternity.' But he was able to ask for, and receive, a sounder vessel from home. Nelson's fleet had no such luck. Their nearest ports under British control were Malta and Gibraltar, each between six and seven hundred miles away – much too far to be any use as bases. So they had to depend entirely on themselves: cure their own sick, repair their own ships, and find their own provisions where they could.

Another serious difficulty which few people on shore considered was that after a time, the interminable sailing to nowhere became almost unbearably dull and uncomfortable. Almost all sailing ships are beautiful, being blends of art and science, and one cannot quite avoid a romantic picture of these blockading fleets, investing them on their ceaseless watch with qualities of gallantry and splendour. But remembering their beauty, it is easy to forget their other qualities. The beauty of a ship is external, and comes mostly by chance: the functional shape of a hull, and the natural shape of a sail filled with wind, make spacious curves which please the human eye. The naval ships of Nelson's time had less beauty of line than many others: they were bluff, square, solid, built for seaworthiness and fighting strength. Still, they had the rough beauty of master-craftsmanship and fitness for their purpose, and no doubt their size, slowness and silence gave them a stately air when they were under way. But not many artists who painted them had also lived in them. People who had knew only too well that they were damp, insanitary and overcrowded, with no provision whatever (except in the officers' cabins) for any physical comfort. Every description of them ought to evoke a smell – of tar, bilge water, sodden timber, old salt meat, rum, gunpowder and closely packed human bodies.

It was extremely difficult to describe these things to friends and family, and compared to Wellington's soldiers, Nelson's sailors wrote very few letters home. Staying at sea, hardly touching the land, for months – eventually years – on end, the crews were turned in on themselves. From each other they had no privacy whatever, but from the outside world they suffered the isolation of hermits. They received their orders from the flags the admiral hoisted. Sometimes they came within hailing distance of another ship. In calm weather, captains were rowed from ship to ship, and the boats' crews had a chance to hear the gossip of the fleet. But news of events in the world only reached them as distant rumours long out of date, and news of home was rare, especially on the Mediterranean station, where it could take six months to receive a reply to a letter. Soldiers could, and did, write of their marches: they saw foreign places and met strange people, and their life was something most people at home could comprehend. But sailors saw nobody but their shipmates, and nothing but the sea and other ships, and distant shores; and their work and daily life could only be described in sailor's language. There were tens of thousands of men at sea in the blockade, but none of them wrote very much about it. Perhaps they felt that no one else would be interested in what seemed to them so tedious; perhaps they sometimes found a pen, or a pencil and paper, and a corner of a bench to put the paper on, and then found their minds a blank at the problem of telling land-lubberly relatives what they were doing. Except after a battle, they had virtually nothing to tell. At all events, only the most literate of them, with the strongest family ties, wrote letters at all, or hoped to receive them. The majority lost all touch with their families while they were at sea. Whether they liked it or not, the ship became the only home they had.

Even Nelson sometimes found himself at a loss: 'Our days pass so much alike that having described one, you have them all . . . We cruise, cruise, and one day so much like another that they are scarcely distinguishable.' At the same time, Hardy, like everyone else, was looking forward to the French coming out and making 'a Dust during the winter . . . This is so barren a spot for the pen that I really have nothing to say but that we are anxiously waiting for the French fleet, as there is no prospect of going into port until they have been beat' – and that was after only three months on the station, in the autumn of 1803. A year later, he wrote plaintively to a friend in Malta: 'I have not seen a female face these sixteen months', and admitted he would even be prepared to pay attention to a certain 'Old Maid' they both knew.

Almost every man in the fleet had to endure the same frustration. There were a few lucky ones, Bickerton amongst them: his wife had come out to Malta, and Nelson kindly allowed him every opportunity to see her there. For most of the officers and all of the men, there was no such pleasurable diversion, and Nelson felt the lack as much as anyone; going to bed about nine and rising at five, he told Emma that each night he would 'dream of what is closest to my heart'. She suggested she could come out and join Lady Bickerton, or even come and live in *Victory*. A few years earlier, Nelson might have agreed; now, however, he scotched both ideas gently but firmly: he was more likely to see Merton before Malta, and as for Emma living aboard, 'Imagine what a cruise off Toulon is! Even in summer time we have a hard gale every week, and two days heavy swell. It would kill you, and myself to see you. Much less possible to have Charlotte [his niece], Horatia, etc. on board ship! And I who have given orders to carry no women to sea in the *Victory* to be the first to break them!'

In this monotonous, monastic world, keeping up the fabric of the ships, and the health, morale and discipline of their crews, became a constant preoccupation. Fortunately one of the captains knew of, and had charted, 'a beautiful little bay, or rather harbour' inside Maddalena Island, north-east of Sardinia. Only two hundred miles from Toulon, it had two entrances, but no name; so Nelson called it Agincourt Sound, after the ship from which it had first been charted, and gratefully made it his operational base. The island supplied wood and water, sheep, bullocks, some fruit and vegetables, and a convenient central location. Judging the three most critical areas to be the heel of Italy, Toulon and the Straits of Gibraltar, he lessened the tedium by rotating the ships between them. Scurvy was avoided by distributing as many as thirty thousand Maltese oranges a week; dull food was given more flavour with plenty of onions; stocks of fresh water were kept as sweet and abundant as possible; during the summer, the alcohol ration – the sailors' only lawful pleasure – was all wine, and in the winter half wine and half grog.

Fully replenished, *Victory* carried four months' worth of supplies for nine hundred men, and Nelson and his officers would breakfast together off tea, hot rolls, toast and cold tongue. From seven o'clock they would work at the business of the day until two, when a band began to play on deck; at 2.45 the admiral's dinner was announced with drums and the tune of 'The Roast Beef of Old England'. Dinner lasted for an hour and a half, or two hours, with three courses, each accompanied by a different wine, and ending with fruit, coffee and liqueurs. The band played again, while the diners walked on deck until six, when tea was served; and this very sociable part of the day ended at eight in the evening with a rummer of punch, and cake or biscuits. Nelson's dinners were well known among the officers of his fleet: the food and drink were better than their own, and he was a host of unequalled charm. Whenever the weather was fine, the flag which signalled his invitations was hoisted and eagerly acknowledged by his guests. He did not care very much what he ate personally, he drank comparatively little, and he was often on a self-imposed, mainly vegetarian diet; but he liked to give pleasure, and his hospitality was part of his technique for keeping the fleet happy and efficient. Captains led lonely lives with great responsibility and frequent physical hardship, often remaining on deck all night in bad weather, sometimes unable even to change their clothes for a week at a time; many, in their quieter hours, devised odd little diversions for themselves. One kept an aviary; another brewed spruce beer in his cabin; a third took to growing mustard and cress on his quarterdeck. But after an invitation to Nelson's flagship each was rowed back to his own ship revived by an afternoon of good living and conversation, and spell-bound afresh by the admiral's friendship. His secretary noticed how they were all 'wonderfully attached to him, and as contented as men can be. Those that had been a long time in this country before we arrived and were anxious to get home have forgot that entirely'; and from the captains, the same feeling percolated down through their own ships' companies.

Of course it was not always so agreeable: the navy's iron-hard discipline was never allowed to relax, and even in *Victory* there were floggings; foul weather, especially during the winter, could isolate all the ships from each other for weeks on end, and the sources of fresh supply could not always be relied on. When they failed, everyone, officers and men alike, could find themselves drinking water as dark as pear-bark, with small things swimming in it, and eating beef that had been preserved for ten years or more, and biscuits so full of cold jelly-like maggots that when they swallowed, their throats were quite chilled. Sometimes they did not bother with the beef, but carved it into boxes and models, for it was as hard as wood, and took a polish well. Generally, however, the system worked well: it became unusual to find more than ten or twenty men sick throughout the whole fleet, and for all their discomfort, hard work and boredom, the only real resentment anyone felt was against the French, who would not come out and fight, and let everyone get it over with and go home. As much as anything else, Nelson's officers admired his tenacity and patience, and one of them wrote with confidence: 'If the enemy venture out, we are sure of a victory over them. If they continue in port, we may expect the continuance of [Nelson's] victory over himself, the hardest victory of all! For a high heart like his, to endure a destiny where there is nothing to display but the melancholy miracles of passive valour!'

Nelson's own view was more prosaic. 'Well,' he wrote to Emma, 'this is an odd war – not a battle!' In the interminable cruising there was often time to dream and worry of home. He knew that Horatia must be learning to talk, and wished he could be there to hear her – 'I dreamt last night I heard her call "Papa"' – and though of course she could not read, he wrote to her, telling her that he was her father, and that he had provided for her in his will. Coincidentally, that letter – his first to her – was written on 21 October 1803, exactly two years before his death. One evening late in March 1804 he learned that both Emma and Horatia were ill, and that 'dear little Emma' – his second daughter, whom he had never seen – had died. 'It all together upset me. But, it was just at bedtime, and I had time to reflect ... I was so agitated, as it was, that I was glad it was night, and that I could be by myself.' He decided that Horatia should come and live permanently at Merton; Emma would have to fence off the Canal so the little girl did not fall in. He kept these matters entirely to himself, not speaking to his colleagues of home life: 'Dear domestic happiness – my only boon – never abstracted his attention', wrote Edward Codrington, one of his young captains, to his own wife. It is possible that at least once Napoleon knew more than the English captains of Nelson's private thoughts, for in April 1804, a despatch of Admiralty and personal letters was captured and forwarded to the First Consul. Nelson told Emma that he was worried at what the Admiralty papers might reveal, but added, 'From us what can they find out? That I love you most dearly and hate the French most damnably.' And he did not mind their knowing that.

Some sense of humour was essential, but not everyone could bear the strain of constant patrol: one of Nelson's officers, Rear Admiral George Campbell, suffered a nervous breakdown and had to be sent home. The strain told too on at least one of the French officers in Toulon, Louis de La Touche-Tréville, the rear admiral commanding the port. From his defence of Boulogne, he was a rarity in the French navy, for he could (and did) claim to have beaten Nelson's men. Nelson's policy in the Mediterranean, off the port which his sailors aptly called Too-Long, differed from Cornwallis's off Brest. With Brest so close to the English Channel, its blockade was intended to keep the French ships in harbour, which it did. But Nelson's intention, indeed his burning wish, was to lure the French out of Toulon and beat them; so he kept out of sight. His frigates watched the port, and he noted sarcastically that 'my friend Monsieur La Touche sometimes plays bo-beep in and out of Toulon, like a mouse at the edge of a hole.' Occasionally he would send a squadron, deliberately weak and tempting, to trail their coats across the harbour mouth; and on 14 June, 'Monsr. La Touche came out with eight sail of the line and six frigates, cut a caper off Sepet, and went in again.' Nelson took five liners in for an attack, although he 'did not believe anything was meant serious, but merely a gasconade', and was not at all surprised at the French retreat. However, a few weeks later he found that La Touche had published a letter 'of how he chased me, and how I *ran*. I keep it; and, by God, if I take him, I shall make him *eat* it.' He never had the chance: on 18 August La Touche died. According to French papers, it was from walking so often up to the signal post to watch the English, and Nelson, dissatisfied, said he had always thought that would happen.

In a general promotion during April 1804, when he was forty-five, Nelson became Vice Admiral of the White – the rank he died in, eighteen months later. His new opponent in Toulon, appointed in November, was Pierre Villeneuve – only forty-one years old, yet already an admiral. The navy had been his career since childhood, but he was young to have reached so high in his profession. During the Revolution he had escaped the fate of many naval officers – flight or execution –

because he sincerely believed in the Revolution's ideals; and in the shortage of officers afterwards his promotion had been quick. He was sensible enough to understand that, and also to understand why he was put in command at Toulon: as commanding officer of *Guillaume Tell*, he had escaped from the disastrous Battle of the Nile. Some said his escape was ignominious, but Napoleon then considered him a lucky admiral, the right man to place against Nelson; and Napoleon's word was now effectively law, for in May the French Senate declared him Emperor. 'A very extraordinary change', Hardy remarked, adding that he thought it might bring about a peace – 'altho' I fear a good one cannot be made with Bonaparte.' Collingwood saw no prospect of peace, good or bad. In his assessment, there was no power on the Continent left to resist France – 'Russia cannot; Prussia will not; Austria dare not.' The whole of continental Europe was either ruled or overawed by France; but every port which held French warships, from Texel in the North Sea to Toulon in the Mediterranean, was blockaded by the Royal Navy. The British could not make war on land; nor could the French at sea. To Collingwood, it seemed the stalemate ('this dilatory war') could continue for years, and there Hardy reluctantly agreed with him: 'It is not necessary to fight with every Rascal one meets, but to be on our guard is incumbent upon us.'

Nelson shared their view of the future and found it stupefyingly dull. As always when he was bored, his health declined: nervous anxiety and the constant exposure to the elements, winter and summer, gave him rheumatism, followed by fever, and a cough which made his old wound from the Battle of St Vincent hurt terribly; he became even thinner than usual ('my rings will hardly keep upon my fingers'), and every month he found 'a visible (if I may be allowed the expression) loss of sight.' Altogether, he found himself in a sad dilemma. He did not want to leave his command; he thought it the most enviable in the world, and in spite of the tedium was very happy with his fleet. But if he stayed, it seemed very likely that his health would be so ruined he would have to go home anyway, perhaps never to serve again.

About the time that La Touche-Tréville died, he made up his mind and applied for a few weeks of sick leave, recommending Bickerton as commander-in-chief while he was away. Then as soon as he had sent the request, it occurred to him that the Mediterranean was such a sought-after command he would not be allowed to return. Suddenly wishing he had not sent his request, he could only wait and see what response it would bring; and while he waited, three events took place which set him firmly against a return to England. On 2 December he learned that Vice-Admiral Sir John Orde had arrived off Cadiz with four ships of the line. On the same day, in Paris, Napoleon crowned himself Emperor; and ten days later, on 12 December, Spain declared war against Britain.

New Year's Eve found *Victory* still off Toulon and Hardy busy writing a letter to his brother-in-law. 'I myself have given up all idea of returning to England,' he said, '& it is by no means clear to me that his Lordship will, but he has by no means given up the idea.' Mentioning Orde's arrival, he added: 'It is conjectured that he is to have the command here, but it is quite unknown to our good Admiral. I think since the thoughts of a Spanish War our Commander-in-Chief looks better, & I conclude as troubles increase, he will mend ...'

However, Nelson had not told Hardy the news he had received from the Admiralty. His request had been granted – but not in the way he wished. He could go home and Bickerton could take over; but the command area was reduced. Orde, senior to Nelson, had been jealous of him ever since he had been given the command which resulted in the Battle of the Nile. Now, in spite of being confined to his cabin with gout, he was to have the approaches to the Mediterranean – the waters from Gibraltar to Cape St Vincent, sure to be the most profitable source of prize money, with Spain in the war – and Nelson further suspected that if he left, Orde would soon take over the rest of the Mediterranean station. So, without telling anyone, Nelson decided to ignore the Admiralty's permission to go home – after all, it was not an order – and took the fleet to Agincourt Sound.

At the same time the Emperor of France was ready to send his fleets to sea. On New Year's Day 1805, the squadron at Rochefort escaped from its blockade and vanished westward; and on 19 January, Nelson's two look-out frigates came hell for leather into Agincourt Sound. Admiral Villeneuve had come out of Toulon, and eluded the look-outs in a gale. Now the Emperor's lucky admiral was loose with eleven ships of the line and eighteen frigates; and no one knew where he was.

25

'We won't part without a battle'

'I AM IN a fever! God send that I may find them!' Six days had passed since the first news of Villeneuve's escape. For five of those days Nelson had scarcely eaten, drunk or slept; for three days he had had no further news of the enemy. The last information had been of a single French frigate sighted off southern Sardinia. Unremitting westerly gales suggested that Cagliari, the island's capital, might be the French target. The same foul weather forced Nelson's ships to struggle down the eastern side at only thirty miles a day; yet when they arrived in the Gulf of Cagliari, there were no other warships there at all, and none had been seen. A report came next morning, 26 January, of a French first-rate dismasted and driven into the Corsican port of Ajaccio, little more than 150 miles out of Toulon, and Nelson tried to divine the French emperor's plan. He thought of what he knew of Napoleon's character, and decided that 'the orders given by him, on the banks of the Seine, would not take into consideration winds or weather; nor could the accident of three or four ships alter, in my opinion, the destination of importance; therefore such an accident did not weigh in my mind'. Whatever the plan was, it would be proceeding. His own first duty was the defence of the Mediterranean; he had always considered that the best defence was to defeat the French at sea. 'The port of Toulon has never been blockaded by me, quite the reverse', he once wrote to the Lord Mayor of London. 'Every opportunity has been offered to the enemy to put to sea'. Now that they had, not only the shape of the war, but his public reputation and professional career depended on finding them; and he could not. The wind was fair for any part of the sea's eastern half; once before, he had defeated French ships there. It seemed very likely that Napoleon, thwarted before in the east, was aiming there again.

The 3,000-foot volcanic peak of the tiny island of Stromboli was blazing furiously when, on 31 January, he led his fleet through the narrow Straits of Messina, between Sicily and the toe of Italy. Half a dozen frigates had been sent carrying warnings of a possible French presence in all directions north, south and west; a seventh, followed by the fleet, was flying eastwards towards Greece. No news there; on to Alexandria. Perhaps the Battle of the Nile would have to be fought again. But Egypt held no sign of activity of any sort, not even Egyptian. At once the fleet reversed its course for Crete. That too was empty. The ships turned west again, towards Malta. On 18 February, they anchored in Valletta Bay; and there, after sailing close on three thousand miles in one month, Nelson learned Villeneuve's whereabouts at last: he was back in Toulon, and had been ever since 21 January.

The first gale, between Toulon and Corsica, had proved too much for the French. To the Minister of Marine, Admiral Decrès, Villeneuve wrote a vivid and pathetic explanation: 'My fleet looked well at Toulon, but when the storm came on, things changed at once. The sailors were not used to storms; they were lost among the mass of soldiers; these from seasickness lay in heaps about the decks; it was impossible to work the ships; hence yardarms were broken and sails were carried away. Our losses resulted as much from clumsiness and inexperience as from defects in the materials supplied by the dockyard.' But Napoleon, accustomed to achieving the nearly impossible with armies on land, was furious – 'What is to be done with admirals who allow their spirits to sink,' he demanded, 'and hasten home at the first damage they receive?' He refused to accept it could not have been done as he wished: the Rochefort fleet, under Admiral Missiessy, had got away to the West Indies; the Toulon fleet should and could have done the same. 'All captains ought to have had sealed orders to meet off the Canary Islands. A few topmasts carried away, some casualties in a gale of wind, are every-day occurrences.' So they were, and Nelson, at the same time, was able to report his fleet in 'excellent good health' – 'the Ships, although we have experienced a great deal of bad weather, have received no damage, and not a yard or mast sprung or crippled, and scarcely a sail split.'

'The great evil of our navy', said Napoleon viciously, 'is that the men who command it are unused to all the risks of command.' As a youth he had wished to join the navy; as a young officer commanding artillery he had taken part in the recapture of Toulon from Admiral Hood; as a general he had sailed across the Mediterranean to Egypt in defiance of the British, capturing Malta on the way, and later escaping past Nelson's own ships back to France. There was nothing his admirals could tell him about the navy, and Decrès wrote unhappily to him: 'It is grievous to me to know the naval profession, since this knowledge wins no confidence, nor produces any result in Your Majesty's combinations.' Napoleon frequently said that becoming Emperor had not changed him, that he was still the same Republican of modest origins, and he may have been right; but it changed everyone else. The British saw him not only as threatening but as comically pretentious; the French saw him and behaved towards him as commoners to a crowned head of state. To that extent his admirals' attempted obedience to soldierly orders was their own fault, but they tried their best, and his harsh judgments were unfair and wrong. Villeneuve knew it; Decrès knew it; and so did Nelson. 'Buonaparte has often made his boast', he wrote to Collingwood, 'that our fleet would be worn out by keeping the sea, and that his was kept in order and increasing by staying in port; but now he finds, I fancy, if Emperors hear truth, that his fleet suffers more in a night than ours in one year.'

'I think upon the whole the Emperor will not have much to brag of', Hardy chuckled. 'How fortunate it is for us that he cannot cast sailors in a mould.' Napoleon, however, continued to behave as if he could do just that, and as if he could control the elements as well. Villeneuve's first destination, which Nelson never guessed at, had been the West Indies. There, Napoleon intended him to join Missiessy in raising havoc among British possessions, while the Brest fleet under Admiral Ganteaume would attack Ireland. Since Villeneuve had returned to Toulon and Ganteaume had not even been able to get out of Brest, Missiessy was recalled – an order which he obeyed with alacrity. But as he sailed eastwards, Napoleon sent another set of orders, telling him to stay where he was. The time had come for the execution of the Emperor's greatest plan. For months soldiers had been massing near Boulogne – 175,000 of them, according to some reports – with two thousand flat-bottomed boats ready to transport them across the Channel. All that was required was two or three days' control, perhaps even a few hours' control, of the Straits of Dover. That could be achieved by mustering the naval squadrons of France, linked with those of Spain, in the West Indies, and descending from there in overwhelming force upon the Channel.

To achieve this concentration of force seemed, on paper, simple. Ganteaume's six frigates and twenty-one ships of the line would escape, avoiding action by coming out invisibly at night or in thick weather. They would then sail four hundred miles across the Bay of Biscay to Ferrol on the north-west corner of Spain, and there liberate a small French squadron and some Spanish ships before proceeding nearly three thousand miles to Martinique. Villeneuve, meanwhile, would take his six frigates and eleven of the line out of Toulon, evade Nelson again, free a further French liner and whatever Spanish ships were ready from Cadiz, and also head for Martinique. Missiessy's force was supposed to be waiting there, augmented by another half-dozen ships which had been on the station already; and thus an enormous fleet would be assembled, with at least a dozen frigates, forty or more French ships of the line, and perhaps twenty or thirty Spanish.

There were some drawbacks. Leaving aside the glaringly obvious inability of any man to command the weather, one thing which Napoleon did not know was that Missiessy started back from the West Indies the moment he received his recall, and the order countermanding it missed him. Another, which Napoleon did not grasp, was that the relief of a blockaded sailing fleet was not the same as the relief of a besieged castle or town. Besieged land forces could actively assist a relieving force, sandwiching the besiegers between them; blockaded sailing ships could not, for the same wind which helped a relieving force in would prevent them from coming out. A third drawback, which Napoleon simply dismissed, was the Royal Navy: he seemed to think the British Admiralty, and the fleets at its command, would only sit back and gasp, dazzled by the scope and audacity of the plan. More than a century later, a member of the French army general staff found its premisses quite embarrassing: 'Such a plan would be unworthy both of Napoleon and his genius, if we could discover nothing deeper in it.' All that even the analytical Colonel Desbrière could discover 'deeper' in the plan was that if it went wrong, as it was almost bound to do, the Emperor could place the blame on the navy, while he went on to further glittering conquests on land. This was only half the truth, and despicable as it was, it still seems easier for a French soldier to acknowledge than the other half: namely, that Napoleon was an undisputed genius on land, but when it came to matters of the sea, he did not have the faintest idea of what he was talking about.

Nevertheless, following this order, on 30 March Villeneuve and his squadron left Toulon to brave the open sea once again; and once again, Nelson lost them.

*

After the futile chase to Egypt, Hardy had told his brother-in-law: 'Our good Commander-in-Chief's great zeal and activity pushed us in rather too fast; however, the error was on the right side (at least I think so) for by every account we can get, they were certainly bound to Alexandria, and', he added with ponderous wit, 'had they not been *Taylors* instead of *Sailors* it is more than probable that we should have fallen in with them'. Of course they could never have done so, since Villeneuve had never been bound for Egypt, but within the limits of their certain knowledge it had been a sensible guess; and to guess sensibly was the only thing to do, for they had hardly any certain knowledge at all. In trying to imagine what the ensuing weeks of search were like for Nelson, his officers and men, one central thing to remember is that, at all times, their only positive information came verbally, from their own observation, or in writing from other ships. Messages which today could be received in minutes took months, and sometimes just did not arrive: because the sloop *Raven*, bringing him Admiralty despatches, was wrecked en route, Nelson heard nothing from England from 2 November 1804 until 7 March 1805. Similarly, it was not until the middle of March that he heard Missiessy's fleet had left Rochefort; and then he was told that the date they left was 19 January, when in fact it had been New Year's Day.

Early in April, his own watchful frigates brought him news of Villeneuve's second sortie. By then, the outline of Napoleon's grand plan was known in London; but without any inkling of it, Nelson still considered that the east was Villeneuve's target. 'I must leave as little as possible to chance', he wrote: 'I have taken everything into my most serious consideration.' Believing that the French would probably expect him to go straight to Egypt, leaving Sicily, Sardinia and Naples wide open to them, he disposed his ships south of Sardinia, preparing to ambush the enemy; and there, with growing unease, he waited, and waited.

By then he had been in *Victory* for twenty months, and in the Mediterranean for twenty-two, always anticipating that his battle with the Toulon fleet would take place somewhere in that sea. The one thing he never considered was that the enemy might wish to leave it, and, with luck, might do so. As days passed, and one scout after another left and returned without anything to report, he felt sick with impatience and growing worry. On 12 April, 'very, very miserable', he began to suspect the truth; on the 16th it was confirmed. A fleet had been sighted nine days previously, seven hundred miles from him and only two hundred from Gibraltar, heading for the Straits with a fair wind. 'Sorely vexed at the ignorance in which I am kept', he learned too that a special expedition of four thousand crack troops, sent from Britain for the reinforcement of Malta, was even then approaching the Mediterranean, expecting his protection. His miscalculation – 'It kills me, the very thought' – might deliver them directly to the French. 'If this account is true, much mischief may be apprehended.'

Villeneuve had had extraordinary luck. The weather had favoured him; he had managed to shake off a shadowing British frigate; and best of all, a neutral ship told him where Nelson was. Yet he was horribly afraid that at any day, any hour, the eastern horizon might show Nelson's fleet approaching, so he pressed on as fast as he could, alerting but not waiting for the Spaniards in Cartagena, and, on 8 April, entering the Bay of Cadiz. One part of the grand plan had worked so far: but it was the only part. Instead of waiting in the West Indies, Missiessy was on his way back to Rochefort; and Admiral Ganteaume was stuck in Brest. He could have fought his way out, and told Napoleon so, but the Emperor forbade it: he must escape unseen and unscathed. That was impossible. He tried to, but in Bertheaulme, the outermost bay of the harbour, he was seen and challenged. So he went back – and there he stayed, prompting a Frenchman of the time to write him a sarcastic epitaph, which may be translated:

> Here lies the Admiral Ganteaume,
> Who, when the wind was in the east,
> Sailed out from Brest towards Bertheaulme;
> And, when the wind was in the west,
> Turned round, and sailed back into Brest.

A strange thing happened in Cadiz Bay: when Villeneuve arrived there, he surprised Sir John Orde's ships, five of the line, as they were taking in stores. Forming line of battle, Orde's small squadron sailed slowly out as Villeneuve's, more than twice as large, sailed in; but to Orde's astonishment, the French ships ignored him completely. Wondering what they were up to, he knew what he should do, and stood away to the north.

Meanwhile, Nelson checked on Toulon for the last time, making sure that Villeneuve had not doubled back yet again. When he was positive, he too knew what his next act must be, and shaped course for the Straits.

Without needing specific orders, both British admirals were conforming to a system of naval defence worked out over the previous hundred years or more. If an enemy escaped from a given command area, its commander-in-chief should either follow with or send enough of his force to ensure the security of the threatened area; and if there was any doubt where the threat might be aimed, all would rally in the western approaches to the Channel. It was a simple enough system, but it was tested, trusted, and so familiar and instinctive that, in just such an emergency, everyone knew how to respond. Details did not matter: unless the threat was certainly elsewhere, defence of the country meant defence of the Channel.

That was where Nelson meant to go, and where Orde was going; and in his passage across Biscay, Orde became the first English admiral afloat to work out Napoleon's grand plan. Knowing that Villeneuve and Missiessy were out and that Ganteaume had tried to escape, he sent an urgent assessment to the Admiralty: 'I am persuaded the enemy will not remain long at Cadiz, and I think the chances are great in favour of their destination being westward, where, by a sudden concentration of several detachments, Bonaparte may hope to gain a temporary superiority in the Channel, and, availing himself of it, to strike his enemy a mortal blow.' Napoleon could not have put it better himself; the plan might be grandiose, but it was not impossible, and even if the French never reached the Channel, they could cause immense damage and loss in the British West Indies.

At home in London, the crisis was temporarily compounded by a sudden political hiatus. One year earlier, returning to office as Prime Minister, Pitt had replaced Earl St Vincent with Lord Melville as First Lord of the Admiralty. Now a financial scandal forced Melville to resign. His hurriedly sought successor was, like St Vincent, a professional sea-officer, Admiral Sir Charles Middleton, hastily raised to the peerage as Lord Barham, and already eighty years old. It sounds, at first hearing, like a recipe for disaster, an appointment made only on the basis of seniority; yet in spite of Barham's age, even one of his rivals for the post said he was 'indisputably the fittest man that could be chose to occupy it'. And here it is important to remember something which, ever since Trafalgar, has been easy to forget: Nelson was only one flag officer among many, and did not direct the naval war against Napoleon's fleets. That responsibility lay with the First Lord. As highly dangerous possibilities increased, Barham was stately in his calm. Orders were issued in bursts, as intelligence came in, and naturally they varied, which prompted Napoleon to read 'uncertainty and confusion' in the First Lord's actions: 'Orders and counter-orders and the greatest indecision – that is the actual state of things', he said to Decrès. It was not so: Barham never strayed from the central system. And because the naval commanders at sea understood it, he knew that at the end of each thread – except one – there was an officer who would respond to each tug, comprehending the whole pattern as well as the individual part.

The exception was Nelson, the vice admiral commanding the Mediterranean fleet, the officer whose seeming obsession with the east had let Villeneuve escape to the west. Throughout April and halfway into May, the Admiralty had no news of his position or intentions, and accepted the general verdict that he was somewhere off Egypt. 'They are out of humour with him,' remarked a fellow-admiral, Lord Radstock, 'and I have my doubts whether they would risk much for him, were he to meet with any serious misfortune.' His son was with Nelson's fleet, and in the fatherly hope that a letter might arrive before disaster, Radstock wrote: 'Where are you all this time? for that is a point justly agitating the whole country more than I can describe ... The cry is stirring up fast against him ... You may readily guess that your chief is not out of our thoughts at this critical moment. Should providence once more favour him, he will be considered our guardian angel; but, on the other hand, should he unfortunately take a wrong scent, and the Toulon fleet attain their object, the hero of the 14th of February and of Aboukir will be – I will not say what, but the ingratitude of the world is too well known on these occasions.'

They could have trusted him a little more, for as well as anyone else, Nelson knew the defence system and his place in it; but 'the cry stirring up against him' shows both how frightened people in England were, and how readily they imagined him giving in to the lure of Egypt. It took his ships more than two weeks to beat out of the Mediterranean ('I cannot get a fair wind, or even a side-wind. Dead foul! – dead foul!'), and as he approached Gibraltar at last, a frigate brought a rumour that Villeneuve had continued westward. This uncertainty complicated the simple plan of falling back to join the Channel defenders, 'for I cannot very properly run to the West Indies, without something beyond mere surmise; and if I defer my departure, Jamaica may be lost.' He stopped the shortest possible time at the

Rock – so short that, when the wind came fair and the fleet weighed again, its washing was left on shore – and then in Lagos Bay, near Cape St Vincent, the surmise was positively confirmed. 'My lot is cast, and I am going to the West Indies ...' At ten minutes to seven on the evening of 11 May, *Victory* 'bore up and made sail; Cape St Vincent NW by N, distance 7 leagues.' The chase was on.

It was Nelson's third hunt for the French, and the longest, but it can quickly be summarized. Altogether, from Cape St Vincent, across the Atlantic, through the West Indies and back over the ocean to Gibraltar again, his ships pursued those of Villeneuve and the Spanish Admiral Gravina, who had escaped from Cadiz, for seventy days, covering something like seven thousand miles; and in all that time and distance, the opposing fleets never saw each other. Meanwhile – knowing that Ganteaume was still in Brest, and believing (as many in England feared) that Nelson was in Egypt – Napoleon revised his ideas for Villeneuve yet again, and sent him a series of new and different commands. They arrived in the wrong order, and in some respects they contradicted each other; but put together, their essence was that since the admiral was in the West Indies and free from interference, he should spend a month there capturing British possessions. He was then to return to Europe, rescue fifteen blockaded Spanish ships that were said to be ready in Ferrol, and sail to Brest, where he would defeat the British blockading squadron and free Ganteaume. Together they would lead the combined fleets to Boulogne. 'There,' Napoleon told Ganteaume on 20 July, 'all is prepared; and there, master of the seas for three days, you will enable us to end the destiny of England ... When you receive this letter, we shall be in person at Boulogne-sur-Mer.'

This was a madly ambitious scheme that only revealed the Emperor's ignorance of naval limitations. The original plan had had an element of surprise, but this had none. It expected a major battle off Brest, against an English fleet that would be forewarned of it. The battle would have to be fought before Ganteaume could join in: Villeneuve was expected to fight it with his own fleet, after crossing the Atlantic twice and fighting for a month in the Caribbean, and with the addition of a Spanish fleet whose ships and admiral he could not even name. Confused by the contradictions and desolated by the impossible task, Villeneuve began faithfully to try and perform it. He attacked and captured a very small British island; but then he had news that the

Emperor's premiss was wrong – far from being in Egypt, Nelson was close behind him.

In this considerable dilemma, Villeneuve deserved more sympathy than he has usually received. Was he to carry on for the allotted time with the Emperor's plan of capturing islands? If he did, he would certainly have to fight Nelson, and after that could not expect to be fit for the second and more important part of the operations; so he decided to sail for Europe as soon as he could.

Although people accused him of cowardice, he was right to avoid a battle in the Caribbean; and though he did not know it, he was lucky as well. Nelson had completed his westward crossing of the Atlantic ten days faster than Villeneuve, and if it had not been for a series of bad intelligence reports – apparently authentic, but completely wrong – would have caught up with him. When he realized what had happened, Nelson was bitter: 'But for that false information ... our battle would have been fought on the spot where the brave Rodney beat De Grasse.' And he added gloomily, 'I am rather inclined to believe that they are pushing for Europe, to get out of our way.'

On 10 June Villeneuve left the Caribbean; three days later, so did Nelson. 'What a race I have run after these fellows', he said, and Hardy agreed: 'I think we shall have had a pretty good round of it.' But it was not over yet, for the month's lead had been almost entirely whittled away. 'God is just,' remarked Nelson philosophically, 'and I may be repaid for all my anxieties.' Hardy's view was more robust: 'We still hope to ketch the Rascals, should they be bound for Cadiz, before they get there.'

On 20 August, that was exactly where Villeneuve ended up; but he had not intended to go there. Both his fleet and Nelson's left the Caribbean on northerly courses, aiming to pick up the trade winds to carry them across to the east. Eight days after leaving, Nelson saw three planks floating, which he guessed came from the French ships, and seemed to show he was on the right track. Yet if he caught up, he was not certain what he would do, for by then he knew their fleet must be about twice as strong as his. That might be used to advantage – 'Mine is compact, theirs must be unwieldy; and though a very pretty fiddle, I don't believe that either Gravina or Villeneuve knows how to play on it.' To his ten captains, he explained: 'We shall find them not less than eighteen, I rather think twenty Sail of the Line, and therefore do not be surprised if I should not fall on them immediately ... I think they will be glad to let me alone, if I will let them alone; which I will do, either till we approch the shores of Europe, or they give me an advantage too tempting to be resisted.' And he added reassuringly that, once they were sighted, whatever else happened, 'we won't part without a battle.'

However, about the latitude of Gibraltar, he turned his ships due east, aiming for the Straits; and about the same place, just a few days ahead of him, Villeneuve turned north-east, aiming for the Bay of Biscay. Each day after that, the distance between the fleets widened as their courses diverged. On 18 July, Cape Spartel – the cape close to Tangier – was sighted from Nelson's ships, and he knew the chase was lost. 'My dear Collingwood,' he wrote, 'I am, as you may suppose, very miserable at not having fallen in with the enemy's fleet ...'

Two days later, he landed at Gibraltar. 'Went on shore', he recorded, 'for the first time since June 16th, 1803, and from having my foot out of the *Victory*, two years wanting ten days.' Hardy found the Rock 'as hot and unpleasant as ever', but learned one piece of good news: 'I cannot say I am sorry to find that Sir John Orde has struck his flag, for in the first place he is senior to Lord Nelson, and in the next place he is a most unpleasant man to sail under.' Collingwood had taken over the blockade of Cadiz, with a very small squadron. Like Orde, he had worked out the French plan, and on 21 July explained it to Nelson, ending: 'Their flight to the West Indies was to take off the naval force, which was the greatest impediment to their undertaking.' Perhaps feeling that this implied some criticism – Nelson had taken the bait completely – he added, 'This summer is big with events: we may all perhaps have an active share in them; and I sincerely wish your Lordship strength of body to go through with it, and to all others your strength of mind.'

In fact Nelson was exhausted, physically, emotionally and mentally. Once again, though he wanted very much to go home, he prepared to conform to the defence system; after replenishing his ships and giving the Mediterranean command to Bickerton, he would take most of his fleet north to join the Channel defenders. What neither he nor Collingwood knew, though, was that the longed-for battle was about to be fought, on the very next day. In mid-Atlantic Nelson had detached a frigate to take news to Britain. On the way, it had sighted and shadowed Villeneuve's fleet, counted the sails and estimated their direction. As he approached the Bay of Biscay, the English knew he was coming. Sir Robert Calder took his own squadron off the blockade of Ferrol, and on 22 July, in a fog off Cape Finisterre, intercepted Villeneuve at last.

Nelson was thankful he had managed to drive the French from the West Indies with so little loss to Britain, but the success seemed small in comparison to what he might have done. When he reached Ushant, he was immediately allowed to proceed homeward. Very despondent, he wondered what unpleasant fate the Admiralty and public opinion had in store for him. But when he learned of Calder's action and heard what people thought of it, he was deeply embarrassed – because everyone said that he would have done a great deal better. The battle was inconclusive; indeed, it has never even been given a name. Calder captured two of the Spanish ships, then let the others, and the French ones, escape into Vigo. A few decades earlier it would have been considered a respectable result, for he lost none of his own vessels; but ever since the Nile, people in Britain expected the annihilation of the enemy.

The cry was out for Calder to be brought home and court-martialled. Yet his unnamed fight had a crucial consequence. 'In the fog,' Villeneuve wrote a little later, 'our captains, without experience of an action or of fleet tactics, had no better idea than to follow their second ahead, and here we are the laughing-stock of Europe.' The action almost completely demoralized the French admiral. His Spanish colleagues accused him of running, and leaving them to suffer; all the ships of both fleets were in bad repair, and thousands of their men were sick. From Vigo they went briefly to Ferrol, and put to sea again on 13 August. By then Villeneuve knew the most powerful fleet the English could assemble must be waiting for him in the Channel mouth, and he knew his own fleet was no match for it. The situation, he thought, had changed entirely since the Emperor's orders were written. In the dark one night, he saw the lights of another fleet and assumed it was English. He was wrong – it was French – but that, with contrary winds, decided him. He turned south to Cadiz, the option given to him in the Emperor's first order.

On 18 August 1805, after two years and three months away, Nelson stepped on shore at Portsmouth, and Hardy, making ready to go home to Dorset, wrote to his family: 'We fancy ourselves very unfortunate, after so many anxious moments, to have missed the combined squadrons.' Three days later, from Cadiz, Collingwood scribbled a hasty letter to his wife. 'I must tell you what a squeeze we had like to have got yesterday. While we were cruising off the town, down came the combined fleet of thirty-six sail of men-of-war: we were only three poor things, with a frigate and a bomb, and drew off towards the Straits – not very ambitious, as you may suppose, to try our strength against such odds.' The enemy briefly gave chase, then sailed in to the port. 'We, in our turn, followed them back, and today have been looking into Cadiz, where their fleet is now as thick as a wood. I hope I shall have somebody come to me soon ...' He did not have long to wait. Over the next six weeks, outside Cadiz, the English fleets assembled.

'I met Nelson in a mob in Piccadilly,' wrote Lord Minto, 'and got hold of his arm, so that I was mobbed too.' For months the admiral had wanted to come home; for weeks he had feared to, knowing how savage the anger of a frightened, frustrated people could be. But far from being torn limb from limb, 'it is really quite affecting', Minto continued, 'to see the wonder and admiration, and love and respect of the whole world; and the genuine expression of all these sentiments at once, from gentle and simple, the moment he is seen. It is beyond anything represented in a play or a poem of fame.'

It was, however, all that Nelson had fondly dreamed of, when far from England: the walls and ramparts of Portsmouth thronged with cheering crowds from the moment *Victory* was sighted; the home he cherished filled with ecstatic friends and family, with beloved Emma and enchanting little Horatia, giggling, learning to read, four and a half years old; the corridors of government open to him as ministers queued for his advice on the war at sea. Newspapers reported every detail, and 'timid widows and spinsters are terrified at his foot being on shore'. Though he had fought no battle and the enemy still remained, people understood and marvelled at what he had done: 'Either the distances between the distant quarters of the globe are diminished, or you have extended the powers of human action.' Five years earlier in Dresden, Hugh Elliot – Lord Minto's brother – had sniffed in disdain at the antics of the Hamiltons and Nelson. Now he spoke for England, with unreserved praise: 'After an unremitting cruise of two long years in the stormy Gulf of Lyons, to have proceeded, without going into port, to Alexandria, from Alexandria to the West Indies, from the West Indies back again to Gibraltar; to have kept your ships afloat, your rigging standing and your crews in health and spirits, is an effort such as never was realized in former times nor, I doubt, will ever be repeated by any other admiral. You have protected us for two long years, and you saved the West Indies by only a few days.'

'Should providence once more favour him, he will be considered our guardian angel' – Radstock had been right. Nelson could no longer doubt he was a national hero; yet in the midst of all the praise he felt a sudden, unfamiliar instinct of caution, recognizing that the nation was half-hysterical with invasion fever. 'I am now set up for a *Conjuror*,' he thought, 'and God knows they will very soon find out I am far from being one ... If I make one wrong guess the charm will be broken'.

Of all the periods he spent in England, this was the happiest and most glorious; it was also the busiest, the shortest and the last. He was on shore for twenty-five days, and fourteen of them involved meetings at the Admiralty or in Whitehall. From the beginning he expected he would have to go back to sea; by the ninth day he knew it for certain. No one in England was sure where the Combined Fleets had gone after their departure from Ferrol, following Calder's action. The Cabinet believed Villeneuve might return to the West Indies; Nelson was sure he would not, and convinced Pitt that the target must be Cadiz or Toulon. On Sunday 1 September, prime minister and admiral agreed how many ships should be sent to oppose them; then Pitt said, 'Now, who is to take command?' Loyal to his old friend, Nelson replied at once: 'You cannot have a better man than the present one – Collingwood.' 'No. That won't do', Pitt answered firmly. 'You must take the command.'

At five o'clock the next morning, a light, fast carriage arrived at Merton. Nelson was already dressed, and met his visitor, a young naval captain, without surprise: 'I am sure you bring me news of the French and Spanish fleets, and that I shall have to beat them yet.'

'Thank God!', wrote Lord Radstock to Nelson. 'Thank God a thousand times that these Jack o' Lanterns are once more safely housed without having done that mischief which was justly dreaded. The papers tell us you will shortly be after them.' The enemy were known to be in Cadiz, and every ship that could be spared was directed there. For Nelson, there remained two weeks on shore – 'a fortnight's dream', said Emma – crammed with naval, social and family activity; and it was then that he and she were married. Once, after Sir William's death, she wrote unhappily: 'My love is no common love. It may be a sin to love – I say it might have been a sin when I was another's, but I then had more merit in trying to suppress it. I am now free and must sin on and love him more than ever; it is a crime worth going to hell for.' Countess Spencer, now a widow, who had seen Fanny in the heights and the depths with Nelson, was present when he and Emma took communion together. 'After the Service was over,' she wrote, 'Nelson took Emma's hand and, facing the priest, said: "Emma, I have taken the Sacrament with you this day, to prove to the world that our friendship is most pure and innocent, and of this I call God to witness."' Of course it was not, in any legal way, a valid marriage; but they exchanged rings, and it must have made them both happy: Emma knew that Nelson would have really married her, if it had been possible; and perhaps he felt that she was now his wife – as he had often said before – 'in the eyes of Heaven.'

She told a story later that he had not wanted to return to sea, that 'it was I bid him go forth', and that he replied, 'Brave Emma! Good Emma! If there were more Emmas, there would be more Nelsons.' Of course he was reluctant to go away again so soon – anyone would have been – and if she had chosen, Emma could have made it very difficult and unhappy for him; but she was certainly exaggerating when she suggested that he would not have gone if she had not told him to. Even with her to love, duty still overrode, and never more than now. However, a private scene of wifely encouragement undoubtedly took place, which must have been very hard for her; and not only he but all England owed much to her for that.

Nevertheless, when the time came, he could hardly bear to leave. Horatia, still less than five years old, was in bed asleep. He knelt by the little girl's bedside, prayed she might be happy, kissed her and stole out quietly; but he returned three times more to see her again. Finally, 'at half past ten, drove from dear, dear Merton, where I left all which I hold dear in this world, to go and serve my king and country.' He noted the day, but not the date: Friday night, the 13th of September.

At 6 a.m. he was in Portsmouth. From a too-short time in Dorset, Hardy was ready to welcome him, dismissing his own bad rheumatism – 'I continue to mend as fast as can be expected, and am in hopes that the Salt Air will again agree with me.' Final meetings with the Treasurer of the Navy and other officials took place, before lunch at the George Hotel; and it was afterwards that one of the most famous scenes of Nelson's life in England took place. The road outside the hotel was packed with people hoping to get a glimpse of him, so he left by a back way. But someone saw him and raised a shout. The crowd came pouring after him, 'pressing forward', said a contemporary, 'to obtain sight of his face – many were in tears, and many knelt down before him, and blessed him as he passed. England has had many heroes; but never one who so entirely possessed the love of his fellow-countrymen as Nelson.' With Hardy seated beside him, his barge pushed away, and he waved his hat to the people on shore. Guards could not control them; they pushed them aside, chased away an officer who gave an order to fix bayonets, and clambered on walls and parapets to watch the boat drawing from the shore. And while their cheers echoed over the water, Nelson turned to Hardy and said, 'I have had their huzzas before. I have their hearts now.'

At eight o'clock the following morning, 16 September, *Victory* weighed and made sail to the south-south-east. As the great warship gathered way, one last letter from Emma arrived by boat. At once, Nelson scribbled a reply: 'My beloved Emma, I cannot even read your letter. We have fair wind, and God will, I hope, soon grant us a happy meeting. The wind is quite fair and fresh. We go too swift for the boat. May Heaven bless you, and Horatia, with all those who hold us dear to them. For a short time, farewell.'

Weeks passed, and Nelson's family kept Emma company: William and Sarah invited her down to Canterbury; from there she visited a friend in Ramsgate, and when she returned to Merton, Susannah, Nelson's eldest sister, came to stay. On the morning of 6 November, the two women were there together, Emma in bed and Susannah sitting beside her, when Emma raised herself on one elbow, saying she thought she heard distant gunfire. They guessed it might be from the Tower of London, ten miles away, and with nervous excitement Susannah wondered if it heralded news of her brother. Emma said not – 'Some victory in Germany' was her opinion – but privately she half-hoped, half-feared that Susannah might be right. A few minutes later a carriage rumbled to a halt outside. Now thoroughly alerted, Emma sent a servant to find out who had arrived.

'They brought me word, Mr Whitby, from the Admiralty. "Show him in directly", I said. He came in, and with a pale countenance and faint voice said, "We have gained a great victory." – "Never mind your victory," I said, "My letters – give me my letters."' But Whitby could not speak. His face was deathly white, and as Emma stared at him in horror, he began to cry.

26

'What a beautiful day!'

'FOR CHARITY'S SAKE, send us Lord Nelson, ye men of power!' Under Collingwood's command, the growing fleet outside Cadiz was not happy. His style of command was not Nelson's: he was conscientious, capable, shrewd and unquestionably brave; as a strategist he often seemed to know better than anyone else what the French intended to do. But he was also scholarly, pedantic, puritan and dour – at the age of fifty-five, a fatherly or even grandfatherly figure in a fleet whose average sailor was only twenty-two years old. He made a good admiral, but he might have made an even better bishop.

He had a reputation for being stern and strict, and yet of being just, and he seems to have been well respected on the lower deck. A boy named Robert Hays, who served under him in the Channel fleet in 1804, went so far as to say that a better seaman, or a better friend to seamen, never trod a quarterdeck. But he never unbent with his men, and not often with anyone else outside his immediate family. On board his ship his main companion was his dog: its name (the same as Hardy's dog) was Bounce, and it slept by his cot, largely reconciled to a life at sea – except that it hated gunfire.

He did not delegate much, and off Cadiz was absorbed in the details of administration and the importance of keeping watch on the French. So he had no time for what he considered social frivolity, and to the surprise of the captains who joined the fleet, none of them was invited to the flagship. Worse, he discouraged them from visiting each other. The weather was fine and calm, boats could easily be launched, and all of them wanted to call on their friends for some gossip, a drink and dinner – or, more seriously, to discuss their future tactics. Instead, with old friends sometimes in hailing distance, each was shut up in his own ship with his own subordinates, whose faces and conversation he already knew too well. They felt resentful. Brest and Toulon had been boring enough, but this was more frustrating. Fremantle confessed to Betsey that he had nothing to do and his temper was getting worse. His first lieutenant, he told her, had been in the ship much longer than he and could not bear the smallest contradiction, his steward was a drunkard, his servant was insolent, and the only goat on board had fallen down a hatch during a storm off Brest, so he had to drink tea without milk for his breakfast. It was a life of misery, he said.

Probably most of the captains would have agreed. 'We have got into the clutches of another stay-on-board Admiral' – so wrote *Orion's* captain, Edward Codrington, although he was a very different character to Fremantle. He was younger, only thirty-five, and he had a serious philosophical turn of mind; Fremantle often looked for the worst in people, but Codrington looked for the best. He had been married for two years to a girl called Jane, whom other people besides himself described as a beauty, and this was the first time he had left her, their year-old son and new-born baby. The pain of the parting had not worn off yet, and when he was alone he was very homesick. 'On the quarterdeck I am the captain,' he wrote to her. 'In my cabin I am the husband and the father.' And Collingwood's ruling left him too frequently in his cabin, alone and lonely. But on 28 September, *Victory* was sighted to the westward and the fleet recognized her flag; and in relief and wonder, Codrington wrote to Jane: 'Lord Nelson is arrived. A sort of general joy has been the consequence.'

The ships off Cadiz had never sailed before as a single fleet, and only six of their captains had been under Nelson's command. But that is not to say the captains were strangers to each other, or to him. There were not very many captains senior enough to command a ship of the line, and all of them had been officers all their lives: the chances are that they had all met before, somewhere, in years of voyaging. Codrington had not met Nelson, but he was young and new to command, and must have been an exception; and of course every captain, and every man in the fleet, knew Nelson by reputation at least. If there had been a man who had never heard of him, he would very soon have learned, because Nelson in those last three weeks of his life showed all the qualities his reputation had grown on – the bravery, clear thinking, understanding and tact, and the sudden unpremeditated kindness.

312

Codrington learned at once. Nelson called him on board *Victory*, greeted him in a friendly informal manner, and gave him a letter from his wife: being entrusted it by a lady, he said, he wished to deliver it personally. Fremantle was summoned too, for news of Betsey's latest production. 'Would you like a boy or a girl?' the commander-in-chief enquired. Fremantle said a girl. 'Then be content', Nelson said, and told him Betsey had had one and was well. And Captain Charles Tyler of *Tonnant*: he went to Nelson as soon as he arrived, with a private problem. His son, a young lieutenant, had jumped ship in Malta and run off to Naples with a ballet dancer, leaving a trail of debts. By now he was probably in prison – would Nelson use his influence to save him? Nelson not only wrote to Naples, but also, without telling Tyler, offered to pay the cost of having the boy set free.

Even Calder, who deserved it least of all, was treated with a generosity which was not just unnecessary, but reckless. One of Nelson's first and least pleasant duties on arrival was to tell him he must go home to face court martial for his indecisive battle. The question was, in which ship should he travel? The Admiralty intended a frigate, which was sensible but seemed a humiliating prejudgment of the issue. Calder, sixty years old, had been in the navy since childhood and at the Battle of Cape St Vincent had criticized Nelson's conduct. Now he was desperately anxious to keep *Prince of Wales*, his own splendid three-decker. Nelson hesitated, torn between common sense and support. From a strictly military point of view, it was indefensible to deprive the fleet of one of its most powerful ships simply to help one man's self-respect, and at first he must have refused, because Calder wrote to him: 'The contents of your Lordship's letter have cut me to the soul. If I am to be turned out of my ship, after all that has passed, I have only to request ... that I may be permitted to go without a moment's further loss of time. My heart is broken.' This was too much for Nelson. As soon as another three-decker, *Royal Sovereign*, arrived, he let Calder go in *Prince of Wales*, and wrote to the First Lord: 'I may be thought wrong, as an officer, to disobey the orders of the Admiralty ... but I trust I shall be considered to have done right as a man, and to a brother officer in affliction – my heart could not stand it, and so the thing must rest.'

When Calder got home, he was acquitted of cowardice, but severely reprimanded for not renewing the action. Collingwood had described it as 'rather a puzzled affair', but no naval officer liked the kind of civilian criticism which had appeared in newspapers before the trial.

Whatever the Admiralty thought of Nelson giving up a first-rate ship, officers off Cadiz thought he was right. The whole affair made a deep impression on them – the ingratitude, as they saw it, of people who could condemn a man at the end of a lifetime's service – and things were happier when Calder had gone and they could begin to forget it. But Nelson did not forget, and off Cape Trafalgar, when the first French shots began to fly, he said, 'What would poor Calder give to be with us now!'

When Nelson reached the fleet, without signal or salute ('it is as well not to proclaim to the enemy every ship which may join'), it was the eve of his forty-seventh birthday. A few weeks earlier, walking with Captain Richard Keats in the garden at Merton, he had started a conversation – almost a monologue – which Keats, who was not present at Trafalgar, treasured in his memory.

'No day can be long enough to arrange a couple of fleets and fight a decisive battle, according to the old system,' the admiral began. By 'the old system', as Keats realized straight away, Nelson meant the conventional parallel pair of lines ahead. 'When we meet them, for meet them we shall [and Keats was expected to be there], I'll tell you how I shall fight them. I shall form the fleet into three divisions in three lines. One division shall be composed of twelve or fourteen of the fastest two-decked ships, which I shall always keep to windward, or in a situation of advantage; and I shall put them under an officer who I am sure will employ them in the manner I wish, if possible. I consider it will always be in my power to throw them into battle in any part I may choose; but if circumstances prevent their being carried against the enemy where I desire, I shall feel certain he will employ them effectually, and perhaps in a more advantageous manner than if he could have followed my orders. With the remaining part of the fleet formed in two lines, I shall go at them at once, if I can, about one-third of their line from their leading ship.'

And then he stopped and asked, 'What do you think of it?' Surprised both by the idea and the sudden question, Keats hesitated, and Nelson instantly continued, 'I'll tell you what I think of it.' That was a typical phrase of his: five years earlier, travelling with the Hamiltons back from Palermo, he had stopped with Lord and Lady Minto in Vienna. When Lady Minto wished he commanded the Austrian army, he said to her, 'I'll tell you what: if I had, I would use only one word – advance.' In the garden at Merton, he swept on with the same immediate directness: 'I'll tell you what I think of it. I think it will surprise and confound the enemy. They won't know what I am about. It will bring forward a pell-mell battle, and that is what I want.'

Off Cadiz, knowing what he wanted and how to achieve it, he explained it – to those who would have to carry it out – in the best way he knew: personally, face to face. The day after *Victory* joined the fleet, he asked half the captains to dine with him, and the day after that, the other half. 'What our late chief will think of this I don't know,' Codrington wrote gleefully, 'but I well know what the fleet think of the difference.' The occasions were intended to be mainly what today would be called a briefing, but the first was his birthday, and in addition to the briefing, it developed into a birthday party. His guests made it plain how glad they were to see him; he said their reception of him was 'the sweetest sensation of my life. The officers who came on board to welcome my return, forgot my rank as commander-in-chief in the enthusiasm with which they greeted me.' And he vividly described the briefing to Emma: 'When I came to explain to them "the Nelson touch", it was like an electric shock. Some shed tears, all approved – "It was new – it was singular – it was simple!" and, from admirals downwards, it was repeated – "It must succeed, if ever they will allow us to get at them!"'

'The Nelson touch': it was a phrase he only used in his letters to Emma. Because its origin is unknown, and because he only used it privately, without explanation, its exact meaning has always remained a slight mystery. In later years, when those letters were made public, the phrase was commonly understood in two ways: in particular, to describe the tactical plan he made before Trafalgar, and in general as a cover-all description of his nearly indefinable touch of genius. Yet though these meanings are quite appropriate, people have continued to worry over the words, for they obviously meant something to Nelson, and no one knows exactly what. It may be, though, that 'the Nelson touch' was no more than a private standing joke, which he and Emma elaborated with time. As a pure guess, it might have started from the name of his old adversary at Boulogne and Toulon, Admiral de la Touche-Tréville, who had so angered Nelson by the public letter saying he had run away from Toulon. 'By God, if I take him, he shall *eat* it,' Nelson had said then, and he might well have added crossly, 'I'll give him La Touche – La Touche Nelson.' Perhaps, then, in her letters to him – all of which he burnt – or privately together, Emma used the phrase in a more intimate way, and the little joke grew. When he was sailing to join the fleet off Cadiz, Nelson wrote to Emma telling her how anxious he was to get there, 'for it would add to my grief if any other man was to give them the Nelson touch, which WE say is warranted never to fail.' And that too could have been another discreet elaboration, making fun of his own long-dead fears that she might be unfaithful to him. This might not be too fanciful an explanation for the phrase – for, leaving aside his romantic gratitude to any woman who showed him kindness in times of adversity, Nelson was always a man of two loves. One was his passionate love for Emma; the other was his compassionate love for the men under his command. And except when at last he felt absolutely secure with both loves, he was a jealous man. His touch worked with Emma; perhaps she teased him about how it must also guarantee success with the fleet, if only another man did not arrive first to take his place.

Certainly, on his forty-seventh birthday and the following night, neither he nor the captains who surrounded him felt the slightest doubt in each other or in his plan. Its essence, as he had told Captain Keats, was to approach the enemy's line with three divisions. The fastest would be kept in flexible reserve to windward, to be used as conditions demanded; the other two would break through one-third and two-thirds of the way down the opposing line, reducing it to manageable sections, and ensuring a local superiority over its rear and centre before the vanguard could turn to join in. Other admirals in other battles had done similar things – at the Saints, Rodney had broken the line in three places (though Nelson thought it was only one), and at St Vincent, Jervis had made one break. At the Nile, Nelson himself had used the wind to immobilize part of the enemy line while he concentrated his force on the rest. But Rodney and Jervis had taken unplanned opportunities, while at the Nile the enemy had been at anchor. To set out with the explicit intention of smashing a moving line was a revolution of naval tactics.

Although no one made a record of his verbal explanation, it was probably similar to the one he revealed to Keats; and a few days later he sent all his captains copies of a memorandum, putting it on paper. He had developed the idea during the chase to the West Indies, and then wrote a memorandum whose preamble now applied just as much: 'The business of an English Commander-in-Chief being first to bring an enemy's fleet to battle on the most advantageous terms to himself, (I mean that of laying his ships close on board the enemy, as expeditiously as possible;) and secondly, to continue them there, without separating, until the business is decided ...'

The Trafalgar memorandum made the same assumption: ships would be laid on board the enemy – that is, alongside and touching – and would stay there, and would win. In the clear unstudied language he always used, it provided for attacks to windward or to leeward, and some passages summed it up:

'The whole impression of the British Fleet must be to overpower from two or three ships ahead of their [the enemy's] Commander-in-Chief, supposed to be in the centre, to the rear of their fleet. I will suppose twenty sail of the enemy's line to be untouched; it must be some time before they could perform a manoeuvre to bring their force compact to attack any part of the British Fleet engaged, or to succour their own ships ... Something must be left to chance; nothing is sure in a Sea Fight, beyond all others. Shot will carry away the masts and yards of friends as well as foes; but I look with confidence to a victory before the van of the enemy could succour their rear, and then that the British Fleet would most of them be ready to receive their twenty sail of the line, or to pursue them, should they endeavour to make off ... Captains are to look to their particular Line as their rallying point. But, in case Signals can neither be seen or perfectly understood, no Captain can do very wrong if he places his ship alongside that of an enemy.'

It was adventurous, simple, thrilling in its flexibility, its opportunities for individual courage and brilliance, and in its trust: Nelson assumed without any question that every one of his captains was competent and brave. They fully returned his trust: 'You are, my Lord,' said one, 'surrounded by friends whom you inspire with confidence.'

Over the next three weeks, the confidence the captains felt in him spread right down through the ranks to the lower decks. This was partly due to their influence – a captain's mood always affects a ship – and partly to the legend Nelson brought with him. Very few of the seamen can have seen him, except *Victory*'s people, but they knew very well what he looked like: the empty sleeve from Tenerife, the blind eye from Calvi, the scar on his forehead from the Nile – such honourable souvenirs belonged more often to seamen than to admirals. And they knew the stories of the signal of recall he refused to see at Copenhagen, and of the two Spanish ships he had boarded at Cape St Vincent. They believed he was a man to lead them into danger, not send them.

There were also some small events which directly affected them.

317

Observing one day off Cadiz that his signal lieutenant, John Pasco, looked annoyed, Nelson asked what was the matter. A ship had just left with mail for England and was already some distance off, under full sail. 'Nothing that need trouble your Lordship', Pasco replied. But Nelson insisted, and Pasco told him: the bosun who had loaded *Victory*'s mailbags had forgotten to put in his own letter to his wife, and had found it in his pocket. 'Hoist a signal and bring her back,' the admiral said. 'Who knows that he may not fall in action tomorrow?' And the ship returned, and hove to while a boat was launched to carry the single letter. Stories like this went quickly around the fleet, and were gratefully remembered: old sailors, years afterwards, told them to their children and grandchildren. Of course it was not very hard to seem kind to men who seldom received much kindness. But to be kind and yet to maintain a standard of discipline is always a delicate balance. For a commander-in-chief to be kind to the lowest ranks of men without undermining his officers' authority is especially delicate, and most delicate of all when the discipline is harshest. Nelson succeeded because his kindness was inherent. 'Men adored him,' a sailor wrote simply, 'and in fighting under him, every man thought himself sure of success.'

On 19 October another friendly invitation was taken over to *Royal Sovereign*, Collingwood's new flagship. He had not wanted to shift into her – she had such a reputation for sailing slowly, she was nicknamed the West Country Waggon – but, after her recent return from England, he was finding how good her new clean copper bottom was: she was becoming the fastest ship in the fleet. 'What a beautiful day!' said the letter cheerfully. 'Will you be tempted out of your ship? If you will, hoist the Assent and *Victory*'s pendants.'

It was the last invitation Nelson sent out, and the last letter he ever wrote to 'my dear Coll'. On it, his second-in-command noted: 'Before the answer to this letter had got to the *Victory*, the signal was made that the enemy's fleet was coming out of Cadiz, and we chased immediately.'

In *Victory*, a young midshipman named R. F. Roberts from Burton Bradstock in Dorset was busy writing in his 'Remark Book', keeping what would now be called a narrative log – as a protégé of Hardy's, he may have been acting as Captain's Clerk. He noted that the fleet was sixteen leagues from Cadiz: Nelson had changed Collingwood's system of close observation to the one he had used himself off Toulon. Over the horizon, his fleet was invisible from the shore, but between the two a line of frigates was strung out, keeping watch and signalling to and fro. 'At 11.30,' Roberts wrote, 'another signal was repeated to us from the frigate that the enemy were out and had been three hours. Employed on board the *Victory* getting up a thousand shot on each deck, stowing away chests, etc. etc., clearing for action.' The wind, from the westward, was very light. Shortly after noon another message gave the enemy's course as south-south-east. Nelson concluded they were heading for the Straits of Gibraltar, presumably hoping to reach Toulon. 'In the evening a little breeze from the southward, going 3 or 4 knots; made sail all the night. Sunday morning [20 October] at daylight the fleet were upon the point of entering the Gut with a fine breeze, when we observed a frigate to leeward firing guns and making signals which was repeated to us by the *Royal Sovereign*, that the enemy's fleet were north. The Commander-in-Chief made the signal immediately to tack and shorten sail.'

The system of signals they used was new, and very simple. Devised by an admiral named Sir Home Popham and introduced in 1803, it involved large coloured flags or pennants for the numbers from 0 to 9, and for a few important words, such as points of the compass. The same flags were used for the letters of the alphabet, from 1 to 26, and each ship had a code book, in which common words and phrases were allotted numbers from 26 upwards. If possible, ships used the standard phrases or words. If any other word had to be used, it had to be spelt, the letters from A to I requiring one flag each, and the others two. The flags were hoisted to the upper yardarms or the mastheads, wherever they could be seen by the ships addressed. Sometimes a message needed a great many flags, giving the signalling ship a decorated appearance, and sometimes signalmen made mistakes; but to be able to speak so quickly at such distances still seemed almost miraculous. Henry Blackwood, who had fought *Guillaume Tell* almost to a standstill, was commanding the leading frigate *Euryalus* within four miles of the enemy and nearly sixty from *Victory*, yet still, as he told his wife, 'talking to Lord Nelson by means of Sir H. Popham's signals.'

Villeneuve's ships now appeared to be steering for Cadiz again; but at four o'clock in the afternoon, Blackwood signalled, 'The enemy seems determined to push to the westward, 30 north by east.' '30' was the number of their ships, 'north by east' their bearing, and Nelson replied from far away: 'I depend upon your keeping sight of the enemy during the night.'

'*Sunday evening*', Roberts continued. 'Our lookout ships showed their blue lights and sky rockets signifying that they were still in sight of the Enemy. English fleet to windward of the Enemy. At 8.40 wore and stood away from them. Wind W.N.W., drawing them off Cadiz as much as possible, they continuing on the same tack in our wake. Our lookouts continued showing their blue lights, rockets and firing guns, making signals of the Enemy's position in the night. *Monday morning* [21 October] – At daylight saw the Enemy's fleet in line of battle laying to the leeward. Dist. 10 or 11 miles, consisting of 33 sail of the line, 5 frigates, 2 brigs. A very fine morning, but little wind ... The signal was made by the Commander-in-Chief to bear up and set all sails, even studding sails. English fleet in two lines consisting of 27 sail of the line, and frigates, schooner and cutter. *Victory* Commander-in-Chief leading the weather line and *Royal Sovereign* second in command leading the lee line. Cleared away everything for action.'

To the British, it seemed the enemy were definitely offering battle – and doing it, Blackwood considered, in a handsome way. As senior frigate captain, he was the first of them to be summoned on board *Victory*, and was with Nelson before six o'clock. The admiral asked him what he would consider a victory. 'Considering their apparent determination for a fair trial of strength,' Blackwood replied judiciously, 'and the proximity of the land, I think if fourteen ships are captured, it will be a glorious result.' Nelson insisted on twenty, but he agreed it might be difficult to bring the prizes off the shore.

When he was still in command of the blockade, Collingwood had once written: 'We must beat them, or – never come home.' He was very tired, but not as despondent as that note made him sound: at the end of August, when a reinforcement gave him twenty-six of the line, he added, 'now a fig for their Combinations.' Just before Nelson came out, Collingwood wrote again: 'I watch them narrowly, and if they come out will fight them merrily; for on their discomfiture depends the safety of England, and it shall not fail in my hands if I can help it.'

No one can tell how well the fleet would have done in his hands, though certainly it would not have done badly. But now, with Nelson, there was never the slightest doubt of victory, only of how extensive the victory might be. Throughout the fleet the feeling was the same: mutual confidence had so pervaded it. But nobody from highest to lowest can go into battle free from doubt of his own survival; and that long morning, in which the tension slowly rose to a terrifying inevitable climax, gave ample time for private fear to grow. There was nothing for men to do, but wait and think.

In the hour after dawn, Nelson was not thinking of tactics; he had probably decided them in a moment. He was thinking of home again, and no doubt most of the men in both the fleets were doing the same. Eight days previously, Hardy had sent home a codicil to his will, saying that he trusted 'it will not be opened by my relations for many a year.' Now Nelson did the same. Hardy and Blackwood witnessed the document for him, and it was a strange and tragic one.

In his will, he had already provided for Fanny and the rest of his family, and had settled £4,000 in trust for Horatia; but unless he deprived his others relations, which he might well have thought unjust, he had nothing to leave Emma except Merton. By herself she could scarcely afford to stay there, and since she was not related to him she would not benefit from any pension, prize money or award if he were killed. So he wrote what has become known as 'the Last Codicil' (though the words do not occur in it), and bequeathed her and Horatia 'as a legacy to my King and Country, that they will give her an ample provision to maintain her rank in life.' He also requested that in future 'my adopted daughter, Horatia Nelson Thompson' would use 'the name of Nelson only. These are the only favours I ask of my King and Country at this moment when I am going to fight their battle.' For the debt the nation already owed him, it seemed little enough to ask.

He often thought of his own death: before battle it was one of his favourite topics. 'A peerage or Westminster Abbey!', he had said before the Battle of the Nile – just as his sailors, now before Trafalgar, were chalking 'Death or Glory' on their guns. He had often told Hardy what he wanted him to do with his body: to take it to England and bury it where he was born, at Burnham Thorpe in Norfolk, unless the country thought it proper to bury him at public expense. In that case he would prefer St Paul's Cathedral to Westminster Abbey, because he had been told when he was a boy that the Abbey was built on marshy ground and might in the distant future sink into it.

This kind of talk was not morbid; it was a healthy attitude of mind in a man who was sensitive and imaginative, and yet always ready to die in battle: it regarded death as no more than a part of life. But in the long morning before Trafalgar, he seemed to go further in his thoughts: he seemed to expect his own death as certainly as he expected victory – so certainly that people have wondered whether he wanted to die.

To believe that would be too simple. Not long before, he had written to Emma entreating her to 'cheer up; and we will look forward to many, many happy years, and be surrounded by our children's children.' He had also just written to his agent Alexander Davison, saying that if he survived the coming battle, he would need a long rest, and if he did not, it was the will of God. 'But do not think I am low-spirited on this account, or fancy that anything is to happen to me; quite the contrary. My mind is calm and I have only to think of destroying the inveterate foe.'

He was a man who, long before, had had to overcome all fear of death; and that day, one may suppose, he felt divided between his two loves, the love of Emma and the love of the men he worked with. Certainly, both loves were in his mind. He expected his victory would bring a peace to England, and if he lived he intended to go ashore for good, and settle down with Emma and Horatia, and grow old as a country gentleman. And yet, to achieve that ambition in peace of mind, the other love had first to be fulfilled. The fleet had demonstrated it, more clearly than ever before, since he came to Cadiz: they had set him on a pinnacle of trust. Their expectation could only be met by perfection in his conduct of the day; and in that light, all his actions can be seen to have been inevitable. His own ship must be first in the line; he must be the most conspicuous figure in her, as he always was; he must pace his quarterdeck, as he always did, to observe and direct the business – not inviting death, nor doing anything whatever to avoid it, but simply accepting it if it came. It was likely to come: he knew it, and everyone knew it. But in his life he had set such a standard of heroic conduct, to himself, and to the fleet, and to the nation, that death in victory had become its only true fulfilment.

To live in Emma's love or to die in the ultimate vindication of his friends' – if he was clearly aware of any choice, he believed the choice was not his. He went to his cabin again, a little later in the morning, and knelt at the table there, and wrote in a firm unhesitating hand his matchless prayer. 'May the Great God, whom I worship, grant to my country, and for the benefit of Europe in general, a great and glorious victory; and may no misconduct in any one tarnish it; and may humanity after victory be the predominant feature in the British Fleet. For myself, individually, I commit my life to Him who made me, and may His blessing light upon my endeavours for serving my country faithfully. To Him I resign myself and the just cause which is entrusted to me to defend. Amen. Amen. Amen.'

Nine o'clock: the enemy fleet at five miles' distance. Sombre thoughts were dispelled by an air of gaiety. The sun was well up, the sea was sparkling; the tension was relieved a little by music. Every captain who had a band ordered it up to the poop to do its best. Bands were a captain's conceit. Sometimes, they could be enrolled complete and ready to perform: Fremantle, before he left Plymouth, had been in negotiation for the band of a regiment of militia which was being reduced, and he had imagined himself giving splendid entertainments; but the deal had fallen through and he went into battle without one, taking comfort in the thought of how much it would have cost him to provide the instruments. But other bands were composed of volunteers from the crew, who learned their art on board and played on drums made of barrels, triangles bent out of ramrods, and whatever fifes, oboes and bassoons they had managed to find in captured ships. In the quiet air that morning, the bands could clearly be heard from ship to ship. They were all playing different tunes, some badly and some well, but the general effect was pleasant.

Every captain made his rounds as the morning wore on: so did Nelson and Collingwood, inspecting each deck, commending the junior officers on their readiness. Here could be seen the whole contrast between the ranks of the navy: the men stripped to the waist, barefooted, with kerchiefs ready to tie around their heads to protect their ears from the blast of the guns – and the officers dapper and elegant in frock-coats with epaulettes, immaculate silk breeches and stockings, and silver-buckled shoes. The contrast itself was reassuring. To the people, the captain was a superior being, whether they liked him or not, a man from a different world: he knew what was happening, he had talked to Nelson; and if he remained as elegant and unperturbed as usual and calmly spoke of a glorious victory, then a glorious victory it would be. The small processions moved along each gun deck; down to the cockpit at the after end of the orlop, where the surgeons had stropped their knives and their assistants, the loblolly boys, had dragged out the midshipmen's mess table, ready for the amputations, and spread out sails to lay the wounded on: down further still to the dim secluded world of the magazines, where gunners' mates stood waiting all alone in the light of a candle flickering through an air-tight window, cut off from everyone else by wet blankets hanging over the entrances, and by the stringent rules which kept unauthorized people away from the powder.

There was talk of glory, of course; but there was still more talk of going home, enriched with much prize money and many tales to tell.

Eleven o'clock: in two hours, the distance between the fleets had closed by two miles. Now *Victory* lay about three miles from the enemy line, and *Royal Sovereign* a little closer. Individual ships could be identified, and from both sides people could plainly see how the battle was going to open. As the moment approached, the tension grew almost unbearable; the waiting had been so long. Men suddenly remembered something quite mundane: they were hungry, and the battle was going to start exactly at dinner-time. Some captains had foreseen it and ordered the cooks to have the beef and biscuit ready an hour early; others less wise now ordered up cheese from the holds, and a half ration of rum. Officers, whose cabins had been dismantled, ate where they stood, or grouped around the rudder head, which they used as a table. Some captains called their junior lieutenants up from the gun-decks for a final word – mostly to tell them to hold their fire. Captain Hargood of *Belleisle* pointed out the black bulk of *Santa Ana*: 'Gentlemen, I have only to say that I shall pass close under the stern of that ship. Put in two round shot and then a grape, and give her *that*.'

Nelson also felt the tension, and the need for a final word. He said to Blackwood, who had been his most constant companion all morning, 'I will now amuse the fleet with a signal. Do you not think there is one yet wanting?' Blackwood said everyone seemed to know exactly what to do. Nelson thought for a moment, and then said, 'Suppose we telegraph, "Nelson confides that every man will do his duty".' The usage sounds odd to modern ears: he meant, in the parlance of the time, that he was confident all would do their duty. Someone suggested 'England' instead of 'Nelson', and he accepted the change with pleasure. With an air of boyish cheerfulness, he called to his flag lieutenant: 'Mr Pasco, I wish to say to the fleet "England confides that every man will do his duty." You must be quick, for I have one more to make, which is for close action.' Pasco asked to be allowed to use 'expects' instead of 'confides', because 'expects' was in Popham's signal book, but 'confides' would have to be spelt out. 'That will do, Pasco, make it directly', Nelson said. And at 11.35 the most famous battle signal ever made was hoisted to *Victory*'s yards and mastheads.

'England expects that every man will do his duty': the phrase has haunted and inspired generations of Englishmen, and it has been emulated even in other navies. Yet that day, the fleet did not receive it with unanimous pleasure. Ships cheered it, but in some of them the cheer itself had a dutiful ring. Collingwood, seeing the flags, said: 'I wish Nelson would stop signalling. We know well enough what to do' – but when the whole signal was read to him, he approved it cordially enough. In *Euryalus*, nobody bothered to repeat it to the crew; and in *Ajax*, the officer who was sent to read it out on the gun decks heard sailors muttering, 'Do my duty? I've always done my duty – haven't you, Jack?'

Nelson's first instinct had been right, as it always was in matters of that kind. 'England' was too impersonal; 'expects' was too mandatory. Nelson's confidence would have meant much more to the fleet than England's expectation. 'Nelson confides' – they would have cheered that all right; that was what they would have liked to hear. England was far away: England was not the navy, and this was a naval occasion. But Nelson was there, he was with them, one of them: he was their pride.

When the flags were hauled down, his last signal was hoisted: 'Engage the enemy more closely.' It flew at the masthead until it was shot away.

'Now I can do no more,' he said to Blackwood. 'We must trust to the great disposer of all events, and to the justice of our cause.' A few minutes later, he gave the frigate captains their final instructions and sent them back to their ships. 'God bless you, Blackwood,' he said. 'I shall not speak to you again.'

27

'Something which the world may talk of'

ADMIRAL VILLENEUVE had not wanted to leave Cadiz. He was not afraid – at least, not for his own skin – but he was a realist. Perhaps he knew in the back of his mind that a nation which had killed or driven out most of its experienced naval officers could hardly hope for victory at sea. Certainly he knew that ship for ship and man for man, the French were no match for the English, and that he was no match for Nelson. Thinking of the fleet waiting outside, he told Decrès frankly: 'I should be sorry to meet twenty of them. Our naval tactics are antiquated. We know nothing but how to place ourselves in line, and that is just what the enemy wants.' No doubt, in the months spent in harbour, he thought of the terrible sights he had seen in Aboukir Bay; and the few weeks spent at sea had only shown up his fleet's deficiencies.

However, the British were not Villeneuve's only enemies; he had others inside the harbour. If he had not been a Frenchman, Nelson might well have been his friend: he was first and foremost a professional officer, and could have felt at home in the other fleet. Indeed, when they captured him, they called him a very English kind of Frenchman, which was probably the highest compliment they could pay: Collingwood, who expected 'offensive vapouring and boasting', was pleased to find him 'a very well-bred man'. But in his own fleet, there was no band of brothers; Villeneuve lacked the personality or the conviction to create one. Some of his captains were efficient, some seemed to be loyal to him, and a few were eager for a fight. But some, too, were plotting against him; some were utterly discouraged by the endless demoralizing need to avoid battle; and the Spanish were unwilling allies. They had a longer and prouder tradition of seamanship than France, and were well aware of it, so they resented his command, saying openly that he had abandoned them in the fight with Sir Robert Calder. Stung to reply, Frenchmen made matters worse by saying the Spanish ships had been lost through their own incompetence, and through the same ill-feeling, Spanish officials in Cadiz made the supply of stores and services to French ships as difficult as possible.

His second-in-command was jealous of him; his third-in-command despised him; and his emperor was losing trust in him. Villeneuve half-expected dismissal, but on 28 September – the day that Nelson arrived off Cadiz – a message came from Paris which relieved and delighted him. It contained not even a mild rebuke, but instead a completely new set of orders, signed by Napoleon himself. He was not to attempt the Channel: at the first opportunity, he was to take the whole combined fleet into the Mediterranean, land his troops at Naples and return to Toulon. With the impossible plan thrown aside, it seemed he had another chance; and even with a clumsy, ill-trained fleet, the new task was within the bounds of possibility. To reach the Mediterranean was a very different matter from trying to reach the Channel. The inside of the Straits of Gibraltar was less than a hundred miles away; with a good north-easterly wind, there was a chance of creeping down unseen by the enemy, perhaps in a single night and day.

However, there was no explanation for the change, and Villeneuve could not have guessed what had happened – that Napoleon had cancelled the invasion of Britain, and did so even before he knew his fleet was in Cadiz. On 27 August, waiting in Boulogne with his soldiers, the emperor ordered the army to break camp and march towards the Rhine, where he launched the campaign in the east which led him to the triumph of Austerlitz; and no one knows precisely what made him change his mind. The fleet was late, winter was coming on; spies had reported Nelson was back from the Indies; events in the east, as Napoleon said himself, were growing in their menace. Analysing the move a century later, Colonel Edouard Desbrière acknowledged that 'although events were to justify the marvellous intuition the Emperor showed at this critical moment, no more serious decision can ever have been taken on less solid grounds.' Yet the fact for the imperial navy was that Napoleon abandoned the invasion at a time when, for all he knew, Villeneuve and Ganteaume were fighting their way up Channel. In so doing, he had mentally abandoned his navy as well.

It was not until the beginning of September that the emperor learned his fleet was in Cadiz. He may have realized it was better they should be intact in Spain rather than fighting a battle, now useless, in the Channel; but he was no longer interested, for by then he was engrossed in the new campaign – a straightforward land offensive which needed no help from the navy. He was tired of it, ashamed of its apparent inability to carry out the simplest order; and suddenly he felt the same about Villeneuve: 'Until you have thought of something convincing to say,' he told Decrès, 'kindly do not mention to me this humiliating affair, or remind me of that cowardly person.'

The new orders reduced Villeneuve's ships to the role of transport for the army, running the gauntlet of the British fleet to take a few thousand soldiers to Italy. Napoleon may have given the order in contempt, but Villeneuve looked on it as a reprieve, and told his officers: 'The fleet should view with satisfaction the opportunity it is offered of showing that character and daring which will ensure its success ... Our allies will fight with us, under the walls of Cadiz and under the eyes of their fellow citizens; the gaze of the Emperor is fixed upon us'. This greatly alarmed the Spaniards. Villeneuve's own optimism was brief: early in October he learned that among British reinforcements, Nelson was definitely present. Without anyone he could trust for advice, he called a council of war of the senior French and Spanish officers. 'Ought or ought not the Combined Squadron to put to sea,' he asked, 'seeing that it is not in such a superiority of force as to balance its inherent inferiority?' It was an honest and accurate assessment, but the words were those of a man already beaten by circumstances he could not control. The meeting was bitter and angry, with voices raised and swords half-drawn, as each side made sarcastic accusations of cowardice and incompetence, but the Council managed to produce a unanimous minute – a sad little record. 'All present recognized that the ships of the two allied nations are for the most part badly armed ... that many of them have not yet exercised their crews at all at sea ... that the enemy fleet in the offing is much more powerful than ours'. And they agreed to wait, as Napoleon said they could, until the first favourable moment, 'which may arise if the enemy fleet is driven off by bad weather or obliged to divide its forces.'

On 16 October, Nelson noted, the weather was good, with an east wind. 'The Combined Fleets cannot have finer weather to put to sea.' One of his favourite old ships, HMS *Agamemnon*, had recently joined the fleet, commanded by Sir Edward Berry, who always seemed to bring fights with him. 'Here comes that damned fool Berry,' the admiral remarked. '*Now* we shall have a battle!' To keep the fleet fresh, he had established a rota for squadrons to go and replenish in Gibraltar and Algiers. First to leave, much against their will, were William Hoste – now captain of the frigate *Amphion* – and a squadron of five ships under Rear Admiral Louis, veteran of the Nile. With him went another 'old Crocodile', Ben Hallowell. It has been suggested that Nelson despatched Hoste, his young protégé whom Emma called the 'second Nelson', to make sure he would survive. But when Louis said unhappily, 'You are sending us away, my Lord – the enemy will come out and we shall have no share in the battle', the admiral answered: 'The enemy will come out and we shall fight them; and I send you first to ensure your being here to help beat them.'

Villeneuve observed the weather, and the detachment of ships from Nelson's fleet; and on or about the same day, he heard a confusing rumour – a vice admiral named Rosily was on his way from Paris. At first it seemed good news, for Rosily was an experienced administrator who had not been to sea for many years; Villeneuve assumed he was coming to help him in his difficulties, and he looked forward to it. Quickly, though, the rumour became more specific: Rosily was to take command. Villeneuve would have been happy with that, and said so, 'if I am allowed to keep the second'; but then he guessed the truth. He did not yet know it, but Napoleon had ordered his recall, to 'account to me for his conduct.' On 18 October, suspecting just that, Villeneuve wrote to Decrès: 'It would be too frightful for me to lose all hope of a chance to prove I am worthy of better fortune ... Whatever the difficulties, if the wind allows me, I shall sail tomorrow.'

He was an astute man: his General Order on the morning of the 19th included a warning that if battle were joined, Nelson was likely to try an enveloping attack on the rear. Captains were told not to wait for signals, but to be guided by their courage, patriotism and love of glory; and with sad hopefulness, he added: 'There is nothing to alarm us in the sight of an English squadron ... In a month, we shall be as good as them. So everything joins to give us confidence in a glorious success, and a new era for the Imperial Navy.'

But it took the whole of the 19th to get just a dozen vessels out. The entire fleet included thirty-three ships of the line – eighteen French and fifteen Spanish – with five frigates and two brigs, altogether carrying more than 21,500 officers and men, including soldiers. Not until the afternoon of the 20th were they all free of the harbour, when Villeneuve signalled for a formation of three columns, with a squadron of observation out to windward. The ships had not emerged in any particular order, and to Villeneuve's dismay, and the chagrin of his more efficient captains, they could not carry out the command. They tried, but fell into a state of confusion from which they never fully recovered. The painfully clumsy manoeuvres were clearly seen by the enemy's frigates, and put an end to whatever hope there had been of avoiding battle.

No one alive today could manoeuvre a fleet of square-rigged ships, so nobody has the right to be critical of the French and Spaniards: one can only have sympathy for them, forced by the soldier emperor out to sea before they were ready. Even one of Nelson's ships, the 64-gun *Africa*, missed a signal and went astray during the night of the 20th, so that in the morning she was six miles away from his line. To take formation, or merely to keep it once attained, was much more subtle work than simply sailing a ship from port to port. It needed captains, masters and helmsmen who knew the feel of their own ships and the capabilities of the others, and it needed crews who at least could do what they were told, and do it quickly. It was not enough that some of them understood their business: they all had to. A few ships unable to reach their stations made it impossible for the rest; and within each ship, a few men who muddled their orders, cast off the wrong sheets or were slow in handling sails, could make havoc of what the captain was trying to do.

Still, they kept on trying. But throughout the night – some with angry frustration, some with hopeless bewilderment, and all in confusion – Villeneuve's captains saw vividly other marks of their fleet's inferiority. British frigates dodged into and out of gunshot, sending up rockets and blue lights to signal the enemy course, while French and Spanish frigates lurked in the safety of their own fleet. Not only were they sailing blind, but they had no means – apart from shouting – of communicating from ship to ship by night. With the uneasy feeling that they were being seen without being able to see, they could only sail on. And even when the sun rose over Cape Trafalgar on Monday 21 October, they were sighted first, because the light was behind them. At that moment, the British felt they had caught their enemy; the French and Spanish felt they had been caught.

Villeneuve's fleet was not unduly scattered: thirty ships at the standard interval of two hundred yards would cover about four miles of sea, and from van to rearguard his vessels were not much more than that.

But after the trials of the night, they were not in line. Some were in formless clusters, some in double lines masking each other's broadsides, and most were in nothing like the sequence he had ordered on leaving port. Half of Admiral Gravina's squadron of observation was still mixed up with the other three squadrons; Captain Jean Lucas, leading the fleet in *Redoutable*, was at least two miles and fifteen ships ahead of his proper station; even *Bucentaure*, Villeneuve's 80-gun flagship, had the wrong ships ahead and astern. In the early light, he and his staff could not see how confused the sequence had become, and he hoisted a signal which was almost impossible to execute: form line of battle in normal sequence. With the best of skill and the best of conditions, the manoeuvre would take hours; and conditions for the task were almost as bad as they could have been. The breeze was feeble, and a heavy swell on the beam rolled the wind out of the top-sails, so the ships were slow and uncertain on the helm. They tried. Lucas wore as soon as he read the signal, and sailed back to his station three ships ahead of *Bucentaure*, but it took him two hours to get there. Some others who were ahead of their stations did the same. But those astern of station could not catch up unless the rest of the fleet shortened sail to wait for them. The fleet was already moving very slowly – in the twelve hours of night it had made less than twenty miles – and forming line brought it almost to a standstill.

While British captains made the rounds of their ships, French and Spanish captains did the same. Lucas of *Redoutable* marched round his decks preceded by men with fifes and drums. He was an efficient, brave and fiery little man – the more fiery perhaps because he was under five feet tall – and he was extremely proud of his ship and crew. Since there had hardly been any opportunity to exercise the great guns, he had give his men regular practice with small arms – in throwing grappling irons and hand grenades, and in musketry from the tops. Within that limit they had become very proficient, and, imbued with their training, they shouted to remind him he had promised to let them board an enemy. But that kind of training was only second best: naval battles were not won by musketry. What they really needed, like all the other crews, was gunnery practice, which was impossible in harbour. At least, though, it gave them self-confidence; and it was to make its indelible mark in history.

In *Bucentaure*, the Imperial Eagle entrusted by the Emperor to the fleet was paraded round the decks, carried by two cadets and followed by the admiral and his staff – the captain of the ship, Magendie, and

General Contamine, who commanded the French troops who were embarked. Everywhere there were shouts of 'Vive l'Empereur! Vive l'amiral!' And the Eagle with its youthful guard was stationed at the foot of the mainmast for the battle.

By such means, a fighting spirit was aroused in the Frenchmen. Among the seamen it was sincere enough. No doubt they had often been told of their own shortcomings, but a time always comes, in any fleet or army, when criticism has to change to praise. Now, they were reminded of the Emperor's expectation and persuaded they were a match for anyone: gunnery teams felt satisfied at their own rate of fire, and did not know, or did not believe, that the British doing the same could do it twice as fast. Some of them, in what seemed the impregnable strength of their own ships, are said to have felt sorry for the British bearing down on them. But their senior officers knew what was likely to happen, and when they encouraged their men with talk of victory, it was hollow and insincere.

The Spaniards in general were closer to despair: it was not their battle. Centuries of war at sea had left a tradition among them that the British were murderous robbers, but in the last two months the French had seemed as hateful. They had no wish or reason to fight for Napoleon's glory; 'Vive l'Empereur!' meant less than nothing to them. There were brave men among them, ready to do their best; but their decks were cluttered with miserable landsmen and soldiers, two days at sea and still as sick as dogs. Their only comfort was in God: their navy was more pious in its observances than either the English or the French. While the French paraded their Eagle, the Spaniards hoisted crosses in their mizzen rigging, and in at least one ship, *San Juan Nepocumeno*, the captain assembled the whole of his crew for prayers and absolution. When his chaplain had administered the Sacrament to all hands, Captain Don Cosme Churruca made a speech to them which represented the last resort of naval command. 'In God's name,' he was quoted as saying, 'I promise eternal blessedness to all who do their duty.' Those who did not, he added, would instantly be shot, or, if they happened to escape his eyes and the eyes of his gallant officers, they would live the rest of their lives in wretchedness. A reward in heaven, summary execution, or misery on earth: this was all that was offered to the Spanish sailors.

The British fleet's advance was infinitely slow, and utterly relentless. There were twenty-seven sail of the line in it, and four frigates, a schooner and a cutter, crewed altogether by about 17,000 officers and men. Certainly there were some who were afraid, whose hearts sank at seeing themselves outnumbered, but the main feeling was excited anticipation – at last, the numbing boredom of blockade was going to end. 'I am sure', Nelson had written not long before, 'that all my brethren look to that day as the finish of our laborious cruise', and added: 'The event no man can say exactly; but I must think, or render great injustice to those under me, that, let the Battle be when it may, it will never have been surpassed.'

Because he had fewer than the forty ships he had originally expected, the fleet was divided into two rather than three columns, *Victory* leading the windward and Collingwood's *Royal Sovereign* the leeward. Since the last ships in each line would take longest to come within range of the enemy, they made, in effect, the flexible reserve, to be directed where most needed when the time came. To that extent the plan was followed, and the fact that practice differed from theory was irrelevant. Blackwood was ordered to remind each liner captain that 'if, by the mode of attack prescribed, they found it impracticable to get into action immediately, they might adopt whatever they thought best, provided it led them quickly and closely alongside an enemy.' But in one other respect, which theoretically could have been fatal, it seems the British approach was very different to the plan. No one can now be certain, because no one then drew a reliable plan of the battle, and in his memorandum Nelson made only one little diagram of his intended approach. This showed his own fleet in the three lines he had anticipated at first, with each parallel to the enemy's single line and preparing to cut through in comparative safety. But when the day came, Collingwood's squadron advanced at an oblique angle to the enemy; Nelson's came in nearly at right angles. Inevitably, the leading ships – their flagships – would be exposed to enemy broadsides long before they could bring their own guns to bear. Later generations often criticized the formation for its apparent naivety and evident danger – so often that more than a century after the battle, the Admiralty appointed a committee to investigate Nelson's tactics, and remind officers that they were not to be taken as an example.

Some people who write about history like to seem wiser than the people who made it, and ever since Trafalgar such people have implied that Nelson was foolish to take such an obvious risk. But there was one factor which made the unorthodox approach imperative, and another which made it less risky than it could have been. The first was that when Villeneuve's fleet began to wear into what eventually became its battle formation, it appeared to be turning back to Cadiz. After two years and more of uninterrupted blockading, the thought that the enemy might escape into port again was insupportable: to go for them directly was the only option. The second factor was the known poor quality of French and Spanish gunnery, which was bound to be made even worse as their ships rolled in the heavy swell. Of course there was still risk, but that was present in every battle, and the impulse to get it over with was shared throughout Nelson's fleet. From *Revenge* in the leeward line, Captain Robert Moorsom watched as 'Admiral Collingwood dashed directly down'; in *Victory* one of the able seamen noticed how everyone was 'anxious to be at it'; and following Nelson in the windward line, Edward Codrington wrote: 'We all scrambled into battle as best we could, each man to take his bird.'

'Dashing down' was an exaggeration: the wind was so light that even *Royal Sovereign*, with her new clean coppering, was barely going faster than a walking pace all morning. Yet that was faster than the others, and soon she pulled ahead, inevitably to be first to face a concerted enemy fire. Collingwood believed that a ship which could fire three well aimed broadsides in five minutes would be irresistible, and in his previous flagship, *Dreadnought*, he had brought that time down to three-and-a-half minutes, which was one reason he had not wished to move. At first he had not got on well with his new flag captain, Edward Rotheram, but now both were confident in each other and their ship's improved rate of fire; and that morning – indeed, with one marked exception, all day long – Collingwood displayed such superb calm that it has become part of the Trafalgar legend. At one point, in the height of the battle, he was observed carefully rolling a damaged sail into a tidy bundle: as he said, it would be needed again some other day. This was practical economy rather than bravado – at that time, fighting the ship was Rotheram's business. Until the battle was closer to its conclusion, the admiral had little to do, and rolling up a sail did not put him in any greater danger. Another instance: just after dawn, with the enemy in sight, he had dressed and shaved as calmly as on any other day. His composure astonished his servant, who wrote about it, and it is one of the little things people remember about that day; but there was no reason for Collingwood to do otherwise – an experienced sailor could tell that action must be hours away. His servant also related how the admiral advised his first lieutenant, John Clavell, to take off his boots and 'put on silk stockings, as I have done: for if one should get a shot in the leg, they would be so much more manageable for the surgeon.' That too was the common sense of experience, but it had a cool nerveless appeal for people who had never fought at sea. Clavell and the other officers followed Collingwood's suggestion; and when he had completed his rounds, visiting all the decks and making sure everything was in readiness, the admiral had one last thing to say to them – 'Now, gentlemen, let us do something today which the world may talk of hereafter.'

By a quarter to twelve, *Royal Sovereign* was almost within range. Everyone on the quarterdeck and upper deck could see they were about to come under fire at any moment; most people on the gundecks and below were aware of it; and there is no hint that any of them displayed any nervousness whatever. For the majority, this appearance of taut, confident readiness sprang from the sure knowledge of their duties, and if they were afraid, from the desire not to seem so in front of their shipmates. The same was true for Collingwood, but with something extra: he had the uncanny feeling that, more exactly than the likelihoods and possibilities which his experience made clear, he knew what was going to happen. This was 'a thing which made a considerable impression upon me', and afterwards he told his wife Sarah about it: 'A week before the war, at Morpeth, I dreamed distinctly many of the circumstances of our late battle ... I believe I told you of it at the time.'

At ten minutes to noon, the first guns fired as the French *Fougueux* sought *Royal Sovereign*'s range. A few seconds later, other French and Spanish ships near the rear of the line opened fire at her and at *Belleisle*, *Mars* and *Tonnant*. One of those first broadsides killed two of *Tonnant*'s bandsmen, still playing on the poop, and in *Royal Sovereign* Collingwood told his officers to 'see that all the men lay down on the decks, and were kept quiet'. Without aiming, an occasional gun was fired from the flagship, to cover her in smoke. Collingwood liked Spain, its people and particularly their language: he thought it the most elegant in Europe, and he hoped his daughters would learn it. This morning, though, his target was 'a Spanish perfection' which 'towered over the *Royal Sovereign* like a castle': Don Ignatio d'Alava's black-hulled flagship, *Santa Ana*. From every ship in the British fleet men watched *Royal Sovereign* in fascination as she stood on defenceless, with all her sails still set, into the fire of half a dozen enemies, without being able to bring her own guns to bear.

335

Three minutes astern of her, in *Belleisle*, Captain William Hargood also ordered his men to lie down, then climbed on to the carriage of a gun, the better to see the enemy ships ahead, which were already half covered by their own smoke. For a few minutes, people remembered, there was an awful silence. In *Belleisle* it was broken only by Hargood's orders, and the voice of the master repeating them: 'Steady – starboard a little – steady so.' But again the flashes from the enemy fleet, the smoke and thunder and echo of the guns, and the fire began to tell. *Belleisle*'s mizzen topmast was shot away and fell in a tangle of splinters; the ensign was shot away and hastily rehoisted; with a crash and a whirring sound a roundshot split the hull. Paul Nicholas, a sixteen-year-old officer of marines, saw and heard it all too clearly, standing on the forward edge of the poop, watching as a man was blown to bits. Almost everyone was lying down; he desperately wanted to do the same, but Hargood was standing, and so was the lieutenant of marines, pacing calmly up and down. Nicholas joined him and tried to look as composed. Inside ten minutes a dozen men lay dead on the decks and another twenty or more were being carried below to the surgeon, and the first lieutenant dared to ask: 'Shall we not show our broadside and fire?' 'No,' Hargood answered instantly, 'We are ordered to go through the line, and go through we shall, by God!'

So it was with Collingwood. 'See,' cried Nelson in *Victory*, 'See how that noble fellow Collingwood carries his ship into action! How I envy him!' And in *Royal Sovereign*, at about the same time, Collingwood was saying to Captain Rotheram: 'What would Nelson give to be here!' *Royal Sovereign* passed close under *Santa Ana*'s unprotected stern, and as she went she fired the fifty guns of her port broadside, double-shotted, and then within a minute fired half of them again – 125 roundshot delivered in the first moments of contact. Putting her helm hard to starboard (which turned the ship to port), she ranged up *Santa Ana*'s lee side, so close that the yards of the two ships locked together; and to the watchers in the fleet, both ships vanished in the shroud of their own gunsmoke.

'To tell you the truth of it,' wrote one of Collingwood's sailors, an Oxfordshire youth named Sam, 'when the game began, I wished myself at Warnborough with my plough again; but when they had given us one duster, and I found myself snug and tight, I bid fear kiss my bottom, and set to in good earnest, and thought no more about being killed than if I were at Murrell Green Fair, and I was presently as busy and as black as a collier.'

As the British fleet approached, Villeneuve observed their grim acceptance of his fire, and their determined refusal to return it too early. With despairing admiration, he said to his officers: 'Nothing but victory can attend such gallant conduct.'

The entire battle took place in an area only a mile and a half long and half a mile wide, yet it affected the whole world, and, for the men involved, was the whole world; and as Sam and his colleagues went into it, every particle of their attention was focused on it. But at that same moment, in the English university of Cambridge, the seventeen-year-old Lord Byron was settling in to his new rooms, which he had entered for the first time the previous day. In London, Sir Joseph Banks, President of the Royal Society, was entertaining in his library – open house from breakfast at 10 a.m. until four in the afternoon. That morning, in the British capital, three children died from smallpox, and Dr Moseley, who had served Nelson so well in Jamaica more than twenty years before, was writing a letter to the *Gentleman's Magazine*, condemning the 'filthy practice' of inoculation. And in Germany, at the abbey of Elchingen, five miles north-east of Ulm, the Emperor Napoleon was writing: 'I start at once for Strasbourg. I have made 33,000 men lay down their arms; I have from 60,000 to 70,000 prisoners; more than 90 flags; and 70 pieces of cannon. Never has there been such a catastrophe in military annals.'

28

'How dear is life'

As ENEMY GUNS began to find *Victory's* range, only one thought perturbed her officers. Leading the line and flying the commander-in-chief's flag, she was a doubly prime target; but much more than their own personal safety, they worried about Nelson's. He had already turned down proposals that he should shift his flag to a less noticeable vessel, or allow others to lead the way. A diffident suggestion that he should change his coat, or at least cover its four distinctive stars, was equally brushed aside – 'This is no time to be shifting coats', he said. A similar event took place in *Royal Sovereign*, where Captain Rotherham went into battle wearing a cocked hat of such size and sumptuousness that his friends felt it made him look silly, as well as unduly conspicuous. However, when they hinted that he might take it off, he replied with aplomb that he had always fought in a cocked hat and always would, and kept it firmly on his head. In both ships, the principle was perfectly understood: everything was to be as normal. But they still worried.

For his part, Nelson was thoroughly cheerful, and told his companions that the date had always been a happy one in his family. He did not say why; someone guessed that it was because that was the day of Burnham Thorpe's annual fair, and it was a long time before anyone remembered that thirty-eight years earlier, on 21 October 1757, his naval uncle Maurice Suckling had fought a successful battle against the French in the Seven Years' War. But then a shot tore a hole in *Victory's* main topgallant sail; the French saw it, raised a cheer and started to fire their broadsides; and almost at once, the admiral's secretary, John Scott, was cut nearly in half by a cannon-ball. Corpses were always thrown straight overboard, and when Nelson saw the body go, he said, 'as if doubtful', 'Was that Scott? Poor fellow!' Moments later, a double-headed shot killed eight marines, drawn up on the poop. On Nelson's order to their captain, the survivors were dispersed around the ship. The fire intensified, and *Victory* suffered from the sheer quantity of shot. Like *Belleisle*, her mizzen topmast fell, and all her studding sails were shot away. The ship began to slow, carried on mostly by the swell and her own momentum. A ball ploughed across the quarterdeck, cut the tiller ropes and broke the wheel: forty men were assembled below to man the tiller, and steering orders were sent or shouted down to them. Before she had reached the position where Nelson wished to open fire, twenty of *Victory*'s men were dead and thirty wounded. He and Hardy were walking on the quarterdeck in conversation when a shot struck the deck ahead of them, bounced and passed shrieking between them. They both stopped, and people saw them look at each other questioningly, each thinking the other had been wounded; but the only damage was to the silver buckle of Hardy's left shoe, dented by a flying splinter. Nelson smiled and said, 'This is too warm work, Hardy, to last long'; and as they resumed pacing to and fro, he added that in all his battles, he had never seen such cool courage as *Victory*'s men were displaying.

The attack developed in just the same way as *Royal Sovereign*'s. For about thirty or forty minutes, *Victory* stood on under fire, without replying, towards the enemy's crescent-shaped, concave, double line. All the French and Spanish in its centre could see she meant to cut through either ahead or astern of *Bucentaure*. Close ahead of *Bucentaure* was the massive four-decked *Santissima Trinidad* of 130 guns; astern, there was still a gap left by ships that had fallen to leeward. In *Redoutable*, Jean Lucas – a boastful person but an excellent seaman – made sail to close it, and succeeded in getting so near that he alarmed and annoyed the officers on Villeneuve's poop: they shouted to him that he was going to run them down, and by his own account, his bowsprit lightly touched *Bucentaure*'s stern rail.

Watching the manoeuvre, Hardy saw it left him no space to pass through, and he told Nelson it seemed impossible to break the line without going on board one of the enemy ships. 'I can't help it,' said Nelson. 'It does not signify which we run on board of – go on board which you please. Take your choice.' Hardy sent the master below to the tiller flat to order the helm to port, and slowly, she swung towards *Redoutable*. Having endured enemy fire without replying for more than half an hour, at last she was turning her own broadside to them. As she swung, *Bucentaure* fired a final scattered broadside at her; and about one minute to one p.m. – nearly a whole hour after *Royal Sovereign* first broke the line – *Victory* passed *Bucentaure's* ornate, beautiful, undefended stern. The two ships were so close that the French ensign hung practically over *Victory's* deck; and from that position she fired her port carronade – one of the fleet's largest guns, loaded with a 68-pound ball and a keg of five hundred musket-balls – straight into the windows of Villeneuve's cabin, followed by the whole fifty guns of the port broadside in a rapid ripple, each one firing as it passed by, all double-shotted and some treble-shotted. The impact was so violent that *Bucentaure* was seen to heel. Her stern was smashed to pieces; inside, hurtling the length of the decks, the scores of heavy shot immediately killed 365 men, wounded 219 more, and dismounted twenty of her eighty guns. The smoke of *Victory's* guns came billowing back across her; black dust and shattered woodwork blew over her; and with that one appalling blow, *Bucentaure* was virtually out of action.

Redoutable did not give way. *Victory* crashed into her port bow, pushing her head round to the eastward and bringing the sides of the two ships together. At once the crews of each responded to their training. *Victory's* starboard carronade, loaded like its partner on the port side, blasted out, clearing a bloody passage across part of *Redoutable's* upper deck; Lucas's men threw grappling hooks to bind the vessels together, and simultaneously – to the astonishment of men in *Victory* – slammed their gunports shut.

No British captain would ever have done that; it simply closed off the main armament. But it was part of the drill Lucas had taught his crew, and nothing could have persuaded him to do otherwise: though *Victory* carried a hundred guns and *Redoutable* only seventy-four, he positively welcomed the position he was in. The aim of his personal tactic was to board the enemy, armed with cutlass, bayonet and pistol and supported by a hail of musketry and grenades from the tops. That was the vision of glory he had put before his men, and to have fallen alongside the flagship of the enemy commander-in-chief offered a chance of glory higher than he had dreamed. A ship could be boarded from deck to deck, through the rigging or through the gunports. Although he could have continued to use his guns, despite their inefficiency, he shut their ports because he did not mean to risk being boarded through them: he intended to fight his battle on the upper deck and aloft, where he was strongest. There, in addition to grenadiers, he had a hundred musketeers, and as the two ships touched, they opened rapid fire – perhaps two hundred shots a minute – and several hundred short-fused iron grenades were hurled.

If Nelson's friends could have foreseen that chance would bring them alongside the ship of a man with such ideas, their anxiety for his safety would have become despair. After close action had been joined, his work was done, and so was Hardy's, until the outcome of the immediate conflict could be seen. And therefore they did what they always did at sea when they had no pressing business: they paced up and down the quarterdeck together, from the break of the poop to the hatch and back again. In spite of the swirling smoke, they could see the musketeers: some were only forty feet away. They could perfectly well see, too, their own people falling around them, hit by the murderous fire from above. But they probably never thought of taking cover, or of varying their routine in deference to the enemy. The code of conduct compelled them to ignore the danger, and indeed they may have been so absorbed in the progress of great events that they were hardly thinking of danger at all.

It is notoriously difficult to establish exact times of events in any naval battle of that period: navigational chronometers, the only precise timekeepers on board, were so valuable they were kept safely out of harm's way. Anyone detailed to keep a narrative log could only do so from his own pocket-watch, which was not usually synchronized with others in the fleet, or from an even less accurate hour-glass. In the frightening chaos around him, he might have to guess retrospectively for the time when some particular event occurred. That is difficult enough anyway, but during battle the passage of time can become completely subjective – in *Royal Sovereign*, it seemed to the crew that, after they had broken the line and before *Belleisle* joined them, hours passed. Even Collingwood thought it was twenty minutes; but in spite of their discrepancies, the various ships' logs show that it may have been as little as three minutes, and certainly was not more than nine.

Because of this, although it is known that the bullet which killed Nelson came from *Redoutable*'s mizzen top, it is impossible to say with certainty just when the little missile came flying down. It was absurdly small, only about an eighth of an inch in diameter. The anonymous man who fired it may have been aiming at Nelson, but probably he was not: the muskets were inaccurate, both ships were moving, and so, of course, was Nelson; and just before it happened – some time between a quarter and twenty-five past one, when the ships had been engaged for about fifteen minutes – he turned unexpectedly a pace or two earlier than usual, so that at first Hardy did not realize anything was wrong. But then he too turned and in abrupt shock saw Nelson kneeling, his back bowed, his head down, supporting himself on his single hand. Next moment it gave way, and Nelson fell to the deck, in the place where Scott had been killed: the secretary's blood was still sticky. 'They have done for me at last, Hardy', he gasped, and Hardy, in his consternation, could only reply, 'I hope not, my Lord.' Lying on his left side, 'Yes,' Nelson answered with certainty. 'My backbone is shot through.'

In the era of gunpowder, smoke was a factor which influenced every battle, and in the feeble breeze of the day of Trafalgar it shrouded everything. Sometimes an eddy cleared it for a moment, and sometimes, in lulls in the firing, it drifted away, suddenly revealing the whole of the panorama: including frigates, some fifty ships or more inside three-quarters of a square mile – many dismasted, several locked together in pairs, hull to hull, all with perforated sails and tangled, broken rigging trailing over the sides – and bobbing in the water, spars, barrels and dead bodies. A couple of miles to the north, the combined fleet's vanguard were beginning very slowly, and very belatedly, to turn; to the west, the last ships of the British lines were still advancing to the mêlée. But whenever the firing was heavy, the panorama vanished. Friends and enemies were hidden by banks of smoke, through which ships loomed unexpectedly, at the range of a pistol-shot: beyond them, only topmasts could be seen above the dense grey swirling vapours.

It is easy to imagine it as a fog, but fog suggests silence, and if anyone today was magically transported to the gundeck of a sailing ship in battle, it would seem like a picture of a medieval hell, a hell of noise and vision – cannon roaring, smashing back in recoil; shouts and yells, occasionally cheers, from hundreds of men as they loaded, rammed, hauled on the tackles or hove the carriages round with handspikes; awful rending crashes as enemy shot burst through the sides and splintered the timber; screams from the wounded. No one on a crowded gundeck could see far through the stinging smoke: gunports gave a dim square light; slow matches burning in their tubs made red glowing dots; the sudden jet of flames gushed upwards from the touchholes and scorched the beams above. And through the pandemonium, men shoved their dead and dying companions out of the ports and overboard; the powder-monkeys, small boys, ran to and fro carrying cartridges; the wounded staggered towards the hatches, clutching their injuries; the surgeon's assistants heaved up the wounded who could not walk; and in spite of the red paint which was meant to disguise it, blood flowed from side to side as the ship rolled, and made curious patterns on the deck.

All this was compounded when ships were locked together. The enemy's hull cut off the light from one row of ports, and made the scene even darker. Sometimes, at point-blank range, the red-hot blast of a gun came straight through a port and scorched everything and everyone inside it, or what the sailors called a slaughtering shot came directly in; and where the hulls were touching, the guns could not be run out, but had to be fired with their muzzles inside the ports, so that all their smoke came back on the deck, and the concussion deafened men for life. In the intensity of their excitement, men could be wounded without even noticing it – sailor Sam, the Oxfordshire youth in *Royal Sovereign*, lost three fingers from his left hand ('but that's not much, it might have been my head') and told his father: 'How my fingers got knocked overboard I don't know, but off they are, and I never missed them till I wanted them.' Many others showed the same lack of concern for themselves: an officer, noticing one sailor's toe cut half away by a splinter, told him to go and get it seen to. The sailor refused, saying he was not the fellow to go below for a scratch, and cut the toe off. Another, taking himself below to have his shattered arm amputated, sang 'Rule Britannia' while the surgeon operated on him; and the only thing people thought remarkable was that he knew all the words and sang the song right through.

'Sulphur and fire, agony, death and horror, are riding and revelling', wrote another; and though he never wondered what made men do such things, he suddenly realized the perverse and ghastly mental effect that battle could have – 'To see and hear this! What a maddening of the brain it causes! Yet it is a delirium of joy, a very fury of delight!'

Lucas was ecstatic. So fierce and successful was his musketeers' fire that a few minutes after Nelson was shot, *Victory*'s upper deck was almost empty of men. About fifty were wounded, and most of the rest had taken cover. The firing slackened, perhaps through lack of targets; and as *Redoutable*'s great guns had not fired once since the ships touched, Hardy thought she had surrendered, or was ready to surrender, and ordered *Victory*'s starboard guns to cease fire. But Lucas had not struck: on the contrary, he was sure he was winning, and when

Victory's guns fell silent it convinced him. He had a trumpet sounded, which was his signal to board, and afterwards proudly wrote that his boarding parties 'came up in such good order that one would have said it was only a practice.' He ordered his mainsail yard cut down, so that it would fall across the gap and make a bridge. While that was being done, a midshipman and four sailors clambered across *Victory*'s anchor and reached her deck. For a wonderful moment, Lucas believed he was capturing the flagship, and claimed ever after that he would have done so; but at that wonderful moment, the British *Temeraire* came out of the smoke and ran aboard him on the other side.

Lucas supposed that *Temeraire*, seeing *Victory*'s plight, had come purposely to rescue her. But in fact, Captain Harvey of *Temeraire* could not see anything at all. His ship had been in action with six enemies as she followed *Victory* through the line, and was badly damaged in the rigging; and then she had run into such a bank of smoke that he lost sight of *Victory*, though she must have been within a hundred yards. Fixed together, *Victory* and *Redoutable* drifted down on him, and he could not avoid them.

Lucas's position then was hopeless: his two-decked ship had a three-decker fast on each side, and both were firing at him, methodically beating his ship to pieces, above and below. On Hardy's order to recommence, *Victory*'s starboard gunners loaded their weapons with three round shot and a smaller than usual charge of powder, depressing the muzzles so that if their shot went through *Redoutable*, they would go through her bottom, without hitting *Temeraire*. No vessel could have withstood that treatment very long; and at the same time, *Temeraire*'s extra height brought her upper tier of guns level with Lucas's open upper deck, where the whole of his boarding-party was standing. With a single broadside, over two hundred of them were killed, or wounded so badly they could no longer fight. Lucas was wounded too, but did not leave the deck. By then, his ship was no more than a heap of debris; above her orlop, there was hardly a man unhurt. Her mainmast and foremast both fell over the starboard side, across *Temeraire*, and *Temeraire*'s topmast fell the other way, across *Redoutable*'s poop and quarterdeck, binding the ships together with hundreds of ropes and spars. And next, another crippled ship was seen in the smoke to leeward: the French *Fougueux*, victim of the British *Belleisle*. The three ships drifted helplessly down on her, and *Temeraire* fell aboard her. It was a sight old men said had never been seen before: four ships of the line close aboard each other, all more or less dismasted, and all heading the same way, as if they had been moored side by side at a pier. *Fougueux* surrendered with undisguised relief, Lucas and *Redoutable* with disgust; *Temeraire* ceased fire; and as the four ships began gently to drift away together, only *Victory* remained in action, still firing her port broadside at *Bucentaure* and *Santissima Trinidad.*

The thunder and concussion of the guns shook every part of the ship, and deep down in the cockpit, in the loneliness of his pain and impending death, Nelson groaned, 'Oh, *Victory, Victory,* how you distract my poor brain!'

He had been carried down, as gently as possible, through four decks, to the orlop; and there, attended by the purser, Walter Burke, and the chaplain, Reverend Alexander Scott, and surrounded by other wounded and dying officers and men, he lay for the last three hours of his life. It became one of the most famous scenes of death in British history, the most public of private agonies. Scott (who was no relation to the dead secretary John Scott) had met Nelson first at Copenhagen, when he thought the admiral a quixotic man, but since then, like so many others, he had come to love him very dearly. Appalled by the suffering below decks, he had been pushing his way up to the fresh air when Nelson was brought below. The sight so horrified him, he overcame his fear and followed the bearers back down. Afterwards, he never spoke about it publicly, except once, to say it was like a butcher's slaughterhouse. Privately, though, he and the others tried to remember everything that had happened, and everything Nelson had said; and the surgeon, Dr Beatty, wrote it down. It was he who had wanted Nelson to cover his four stars, and his description of those three hours gave the dying man a curiously formal turn of speech.

When Beatty examined the wound, he found the bullet had struck Nelson on the left shoulder, penetrated the left lung, and lodged in the backbone. Beatty asked Nelson his sensations, and he described them exactly: every minute he felt a gush of blood in his breast, he had no feeling in the lower part of his body, his breathing was difficult, and there was a severe pain in the part of his spine where he had felt the bullet strike. Beatty was immediately certain he was dying, but did not tell anyone except two of his assistants and Hardy, still on the quarterdeck, to whom he sent a message.

For the first hour, Nelson was in deep shock, preoccupied with pain and a feeling of suffocation; but it cleared, and he began to think again about the battle, and later, when he knew his death was very close, of Emma and Horatia. Beatty came and went, to the amputations on the gunroom table and to the other wounded men surrounding the little space that was cleared for Nelson; for the admiral was not alone, nor in any way secluded. John Pasco, his signal lieutenant, was one of those also wounded who lay close enough to speak to him; and someone rolled up the discarded bloodstained frock coat with the four stars, and put it under the head of a midshipman. Scott and Burke remained at his side, and tried at first to make him think he might recover. That only irritated him – 'Don't talk nonsense,' he said. 'I know it to be impossible.' But a little later, they heard him murmur: 'How dear is life to all men.' It sounded as though he was surprised.

Deep in the bowels of another ship, not very far away, sat another man, unwounded, who desperately did want to die. At about the time that Nelson was carried below, a chance breeze revealed the state of the battle to Admiral Villeneuve. What he saw was his rearguard in chaos, harried by Collingwood's squadron; his centre in no better condition; and his vanguard, under his second-in-command, Admiral Dumanoir, still sailing north, away from the battle. Four years later, Dumanoir was court-martialled for this extraordinary behaviour, and though he never gave a coherent explanation for his actions, he was exonerated. But at Trafalgar, as *Bucentaure* hastily signalled for the vanguard to return, all that Villeneuve knew for certain was that it would take them at least an hour and a half to reach the battle. And that was the last signal he ever made.

Bucentaure continued to fire as long as she could at ship after ship of Nelson's squadron, with her port broadside as they approached and with the starboard after they had passed. But as they passed her stern, she was raked in quick succession three times more by *Neptune*, *Leviathan* and *Conqueror*. Both *Leviathan* and *Conqueror* brought to on her leeward side and kept her under fire, while *Britannia* and *Ajax*, entering the fight, attacked her at longer range from the windward side.

Most of Villeneuve's immediate companions fell: the captain, first lieutenant, the master and a second captain acting as his chief of staff. More than half the crew were dead or wounded. All the guns on the upper deck were destroyed. The mainmast and mizzen mast were shot away. Falling off the wind, the ship's bowsprit collided with the stern of *Santissima Trinidad* and the foremast fell. All three fell to starboard, covering the ports and silencing the few remaining guns. The flag was hoisted on the stump of the mainmast: one of the two cadets entrusted with the Imperial Eagle was still there, with the staff of the emblem lashed around his waist. To save the lives of the men remaining on deck, Villeneuve sent most of them below; but he stayed there, pacing up and down as Nelson had done, and was heard to complain bitterly that he of all men should be left alive. Yet nothing touched him.

He was a man for whom fate always seemed to keep a final blow; and it happened again. Early on, he had ordered a boat to be towed astern, so that if *Bucentaure* were lost he could hoist his flag in another ship. Now she was indubitably lost, and so was the boat. Other boats on board had been obliterated by shot and falling masts. Without a boat he could not transfer to a ship with a mast remaining, and without a mast, unable to signal, he could not even attempt to control the battle. There was no French ship that could come to help him, and when he hailed *Santissima Trinidad*, nobody answered. His ship was wrecked; he was unhurt; he could not get away. Accepting his ultimate disgrace, he ordered his colours to be struck and the Eagle thrown overboard.

The marine officer who came on board from *Conqueror* did not feel sufficiently senior to accept Villeneuve's surrender, though he could perfectly well have done so. Leaving two of his men to take nominal charge of the ship, he took with him Villeneuve, Captain Magendie, General Contamine and two of the admiral's staff, and together they searched for *Conqueror*. But she, now fighting *Santissima Trinidad*, was invisible in the smoke, so they rowed on through the battle until they located *Mars*, drifting out of control from Collingwood's line. Her captain, George Duff, was dead, his head taken neatly off by a cannon-ball. His corpse still lay on deck, under a Union Jack, and thus *Mars*'s first lieutenant, William Hennah, became the one to accept the sword of the French commander-in-chief. And without any better place to put them, he sent the prisoners down to the orlop, where Villeneuve could only sit and listen to the muffled sound of the guns destroying his fleet.

Nelson asked to see Beatty again. He seemed to want somebody to admit he was dying, perhaps so that he could compose his mind by discarding any doubt; and when the surgeon arrived, he told him quite firmly 'what I forgot to tell you before, that all power of motion and feeling below my breast are gone. And *you* very well know I can live but a short time.' 'My Lord, you told me so before,' Beatty replied, and made to examine Nelson's feet and legs. The admiral persisted: 'Ah, Beatty, I am certain of it. Scott and Burke have tried it already. You *know* I am gone.' Even the doctor could scarcely bring himself to shape the words, but at last he said, 'My Lord, unhappily for our country, nothing can be done for you', and he turned abruptly away to hide his face. 'I know it', said Nelson, apparently completely calm. Turning to him again, Beatty asked if the pain was very great, and Nelson replied that it continued so very severe, he wished he could die quickly. Then, with labouring breath, he added in a lower voice: 'Yet one would like to live a little longer.' After a pause, he said in the same tone: 'What would become of my poor Lady Hamilton if she knew of my situation?' Scott and Burke fanned him with pieces of paper, gave him lemonade and diluted wine to sip, and rubbed his chest, which relieved the pain a little; and all around, in the dim claustrophobic stuffiness of fifty orlop decks, removed for ever from the brilliant Spanish sun, thousands of other men lay dying, each in his own unapproachable solitude.

Everything about *Santissima Trinidad* was bigger than any other ship – masts, sails, armament and hull. With 130 guns, she was a most formidable sight – and a most alluring prize. The 74-gun *Conqueror* beat at her from her lee quarter, and at the same time Captain Henry Digby's 64-gun *Africa* – the smallest ship in Nelson's fleet – arrived from the distant position she had strayed into during the night. On his way down, Digby, who had already made his fortune in prize money, exchanged fire with every French or Spanish ship he passed. Breathless but undamaged, he hove to on *Santissima Trinidad*'s weather bow, diagonally opposite *Conqueror*. Both the smaller ships had placed themselves where the giant could scarcely touch them, and under their fire all her masts collapsed. The whole majestic mass of sails, spars and rigging swayed, crumpled and plunged into the water: a man in *Conqueror* thought it was one of the most magnificent sights he had ever beheld. As her fire ceased, Digby did not wait to admire, but instantly sent a boarding party to take possession. Rowing over, they climbed up her side and presented themselves among the wreckage of her quarterdeck. There they were informed that her flag-officer, Rear Admiral Don Hidalgo Cisneros, had been wounded, as had his commodore and the ship's captain; but the officer who received them told them with the greatest courtesy that they were mistaken – the ship had not struck, and was still in action. It was true: *Santissima Trinidad* did not surrender until the battle was finished, when she struck to HMS *Prince*; but *Africa*'s boarding party were politely escorted back to her side, and allowed to return to their own ship.

North-west and south-east, the guns could be clearly heard at Cadiz and Tangier, each thirty miles away. At Gibraltar, forty-five miles distant, nothing was heard, but occasionally the echoes penetrated into the mountains of Granada as far as Ronda, sixty miles from the battle. Admiral Rosily, Villeneuve's intended successor, knew nothing of it: at three o'clock in the afternoon, delayed by a broken carriage-spring, he was still in Cordoba, 150 miles from Cadiz. At London Bridge, the tide was on the turn; at Eton School, near Windsor, the Remove class was beginning its afternoon session. One of the thirteen-year-old boys, Percy Bysshe Shelley, was that afternoon translating lines from the Greek poet Homer – '*Thus by the beaked ships the Achaeans drew up for battle ...*' Five hundred miles south-east of the English classroom, General Bonaparte and his Grand Army were advancing from Ulm towards Augsburg; three hundred miles further east, enraged at Napoleon's imperial title, Beethoven was conducting a rehearsal of his only opera, *Fidelio*, a celebration of freedom and faithfulness. And at about the same time, twenty minutes past three, Captain Hardy came down to *Victory*'s orlop deck for the second time, and the scene took place which ever since has confounded all those who like their heroes to be 'manly'.

During the first hour of his agony, Nelson was much agitated by the thought that Hardy was dead, and was only reassured by the arrival of a midshipman with a formal message – 'Circumstances respecting the fleet require Captain Hardy's presence on deck, but he will avail himself of the first favourable moment to visit his Lordship.' Unable to see clearly, Nelson asked who the messenger was. 'It is Mr Bulkeley, my Lord.' 'It is his voice,' Nelson said to himself, and added aloud: 'Remember me to your father' – they had fought together in Nicaragua, twenty-five years before.

Hardy, indeed, had more than enough to do: until Collingwood could be informed that Nelson was out of action, he was not only captain of the ship but acting commander-in-chief – the fleet would still look to *Victory* for signals. It was not until half past two that he was able to come down for the first time, and his stay was brief: shaking hands with Nelson, he told him that twelve or fourteen of the enemy had struck, that their vanguard was turning, and that *Victory* was protected by two or three of their own fresh ships. 'I hope none of our ships have struck?', Nelson asked. 'Oh no, my Lord,' Hardy answered in a positive tone. 'There is no fear of that.' Faintly, Nelson requested him to make sure that Lady Hamilton was given his hair, to which Hardy agreed. But he could not hide his concern altogether: 'Is your pain great?', he asked. 'Yes,' said Nelson, 'but I shall live half an hour longer yet', and, after shaking hands again, Hardy left.

Three-quarters of an hour passed before he could return, and when he did, it was clear that the admiral's death was imminent. Again they shook hands formally. This time, noticing that Nelson's hand was completely cold, Hardy did not let go. As Nelson's left lung filled with blood, it was becoming increasingly difficult for him to breathe, and his vision was still worse than before. He lay half-upright, supported by the chaplain and the purser. Standing beside him, stooped under the deckhead, Hardy offered his congratulations on a brilliant victory: at least fourteen or fifteen ships were taken, and perhaps more. Acknowledging the news with pleasure, Nelson said: 'But I bargained for twenty,' then added with urgency, '*Anchor*, Hardy, *anchor*.'

Very hesitantly, Hardy suggested that Collingwood should take charge. With a frightening jerk, Nelson sat up and exclaimed indignantly, 'Not while I live, I hope!' He fell back again. 'No, do *you* anchor, Hardy.'

'Shall we make the signal, sir?', Hardy asked him. 'Yes,' said Nelson, 'for if I live, I'll anchor.'

They paused in silence, and the dying man's thoughts reverted to himself and the love and friendship he was relinquishing. A sudden pitiful fear came to him: 'Don't throw me overboard, Hardy.' The captain could only reply, 'Oh no – certainly not.' 'Then you know what to do,' Nelson concluded. 'And take care of my dear Lady Hamilton, Hardy. Take care of poor Lady Hamilton. Kiss me, Hardy.'

The big bluff man knelt down and kissed his cheek. 'Now I am satisfied,' Nelson murmured. 'Thank God I have done my duty.'

Hardy stood again, and gazed at his friend for a minute or two. He knew he would never see him alive again, and at this last opportunity may have wanted to show, without being asked or ordered, the depth of his emotion, and to give a final touch of human affection before Nelson slipped beyond it for ever. Kneeling down once more, he gently kissed the admiral's forehead. Nelson could not see, and asked who it was. Without addressing him by title or rank, the captain told him, and Nelson blessed him for it.

Hardy left then, picking his way among the other wounded, and returned to the quarterdeck. Nelson spoke very little more, and when he did it was with great difficulty. He was turned on his right side, which relieved the pain, but made the right lung start to fill with blood. Scott continued to rub his chest; both he and Burke fanned him and gave him drinks to sip. 'I wish I had not left the deck,' he whispered, and then, to the chaplain, 'Doctor – I have not been a *great* sinner ... Remember, I leave Lady Hamilton and my daughter as a legacy to my country.' He had never referred publicly to Horatia as his daughter, and now said again, 'Never forget Horatia.' They heard that clearly, although they could not always make out his words; and with the ceaseless noise and movement around them, neither was quite certain whether his last words were 'God and my country', or, as the chaplain thought, 'Thank God I have done my duty', which he had said several times. But soon he said nothing more at all. The chaplain, worn out with stress and emotion, automatically carried on rubbing his chest; and until the surgeon came again, Scott did not realize that Nelson was dead.

29

'The greatest of misfortunes'

NELSON DID MANY extraordinary things in his life, and the victory he won under sail that afternoon established a supremacy at sea which lasted a hundred years; but the most extraordinary thing he ever did was to bind people to him, even those who did not know him, with such ties of affection that at sea or on shore, the elation of victory vanished in sorrow for his death.

The men of the fleet were already vulnerable, open to extreme reactions after extreme effort, and to them the news caused a unique and overwhelming shock. Writing from *Royal Sovereign* to his 'honoured Fathre', sailor Sam described what everyone felt: 'Our dear Admiral Nelson is killed! so we have paid pretty sharp for licking 'em. I never set eyes on him, for which I am both sorry and glad; for to be sure, I should like to have seen him – but then, all the men in our ship are such soft toads, they have done nothing but blast their eyes, and cry, ever since he was killed. God bless you! chaps that fought like the devil sit down and cry like a wench.'

Sam never dreamed how famous his letter would become: because of its simple honesty, it has been quoted by almost every one of Nelson's many biographers. And in every ship that has left any record, there was the same reaction. An officer from *Tonnant*, one of Collingwood's ships, went to report on board the flagship, and, seeing the expressions on people's faces, guessed at once what had happened: no other conceivable event could have caused such sadness. A boat from the cutter *Entreprenante* brought the news to *Belleisle*: all work on board came to a halt, and veteran seamen wept. Some ships were not told, and after nightfall saw *Victory* in darkness, and the commander-in-chief's night signal carried by Blackwood's frigate *Euryalus*, with *Royal Sovereign* in tow; and they could not bring themselves to believe what that implied. One of the officers said it seemed as if each individual had lost a friend, and Collingwood wrote to his brother-in-law: 'I cannot tell you how deeply I was affected. My friendship with him was unlike anything that I have left in the navy – a brotherhood of more than thirty years.' ('As bold as a lion, for all he can cry!' said Sam. 'I saw his tears with my own eyes, when the boat hailed and said my Lord was dead.') Even publicly, in his official despatch, he was hardly less restrained, saying 'My heart is rent with the most poignant grief.' A fellow admiral wrote, 'I too have lost a friend I loved and adored'; Ben Hallowell could barely support himself; Henry Blackwood admitted he had never been so upset in his life, adding that at such a cost, it was a victory he wished he never had seen. Hardy echoed him: 'It has cost the country a life that no money can replace, and one whose death I shall for ever mourn.' One of *Victory*'s seamen wished out loud that the shot had hit him instead of Nelson; another, a bosun's mate, was so overcome with tears that he could not pipe an order – 'I can't do it! To lose him now!... I can't think of parting with Nelson.' Others who were not at Trafalgar felt it just as deeply: 'Not to have been in it', said William Hoste, 'is enough to make one mad; but to have lost such a friend is really sufficient to overwhelm me ... I cannot get over the loss of our late noble commander-in-chief.' Both Sir Richard Keats and Thomas Louis wrote distraught letters to Emma, Louis asking for some personal memento: 'I never made such a request before and never shall again,' he explained, 'for no man can ever have the warmth of my heart and soul so strong and sincere.'

And Scott, who held and comforted Nelson as he died, spoke for all: 'When I think, setting aside his heroism, what an affectionate fascinating little fellow he was ... I become stupid with grief for what I have lost.'

In Shakespearian tragedy, the death of a hero or the subversion of the natural order is attended by weird events – owls hoot at midday, horses run backwards – and to those who heard of it in later years, the great gale which followed Trafalgar, rising to a hurricane, seemed a fittingly grand and theatrical climax: when Nelson died, even nature and the heavens heaved in despair. Admiral Collingwood, his officers and men, and their twenty thousand French and Spanish prisoners, saw no such romantic nonsense in the storm. Eighteen enemy ships had surrendered; another, uncontrollably on fire, had blown up. The total fleet under Collingwood's command was one of the hardest to manage that any admiral ever had, and no sailing fleet was ever in such a perilous position: nearly fifty ships on a lee shore, many of them dismasted, each with dozens and some with hundreds of wounded and dying men on board.

The hurricane blew for seven days, straight in to the hostile shore. At first the victors tried to tow the most damaged vessels away from the coast. Their logs had been sparse in recording the battle – usually the master or officer of the watch wrote them up, and they were not men experienced in describing fights. But when the storm began, they could precisely describe the problems of seamanship, and they did so with a simple eloquence which, even through its ancient technical terms, still evokes the nightmarish dangers.

Euryalus at midnight: 'Strong gales and rain with heavy squalls. The fore topmast staysail split and blown away by a heavy squall from the westward. At 2, sounded in 45 fathoms.'

Victory: 'Bent a main topsail, old one shot to pieces. Got a jib-boom up and rigged for a mizzen mast. Carpenters employed stopping the shot holes ... Got up a jury fore topmast, and a main top-gallant yard for a fore topsail yard ... At 4.15, heavy squalls. At 5.10, carried away the main yard. Split the main topsail and mainsail all to pieces. Cleared away the wreck. At daylight saw the *Royal Sovereign* with signal 314 flying [ship in distress and in want of immediate assistance].'

Royal Sovereign: 'At 5.30 our foremast went by the board, and with it the sails, standing and running rigging. Cleared the wreck. At 5.40 carried away the tow-rope. Rigged a jury foremast ... Sounded every half hour. Lost overboard one of the poop carronades by the violent rolling of the ship.'

Naiad, frigate: 'Took the *Belleisle* in tow, she being without a mast or bowsprit ... At 5 [p.m.], parted the stream cable in towing the *Belleisle*. At 7.40, strong breezes with continual rain. The *Belleisle* fell on board us, endeavouring to take her in tow. Damaged the jolly boat and carried away the greater part of the starboard quarter. Could not accomplish it by boats, the sea running so high ... At 5.40 [a.m.] saw the *Belleisle* very near the shore to the eastward of Cape Trafalgar.'

In *Euryalus*, Collingwood sailed round and round the scattering fleet, bombarding the ships with signals: sometimes Blackwood's signalmen hoisted ten in a single hour for him. No doubt he felt he had to take active command of a situation which grew steadily worse, and Blackwood, happy to be able to help him in any way, said he had done all an admiral could do. But added to the oppressing loss of Nelson and the extreme ordeal of the weather, other captains were angered by what seemed an unnecessary extra burden – 'The poor man does not know his own mind five minutes together', Fremantle wrote, and Codrington exclaimed, 'What he is doing, God knows!'

The options were starkly simple. The ships that were still intact could probably save themselves, either by weathering Cape St Vincent and giving themselves sea-room in the Atlantic, or possibly by beating down to Gibraltar; but none could do so, close-hauled to the gale, while they had others in tow. It was out of the question to abandon a disabled British ship, and no captain, except in a last extremity, would abandon the prizes that meant a life of wealth. Until the wind changed or moderated, they could only claw off the land, or anchor; and many of them, including *Victory*, did not have that choice, because their anchors had been lost, or their cables cut by shot.

Nelson's dying insistence that the fleet should anchor had been a difficult order for Hardy to receive, knowing both that it would be Nelson's last order and that Collingwood would soon be in command. Later, when it was publicly known, it was a source of criticism for Collingwood, for on the day of Trafalgar, neither Hardy nor he did make the signal to anchor; and because it was Nelson's last command, people found it difficult to admit that he could have been mistaken, and argued that if he had been obeyed, later events would have turned out more happily than they did. But this was to honour his memory too highly: he was out of touch, and Hardy and Collingwood, second to none in seamanship, knew what they were doing.

'I can only say', Collingwood wrote later, 'that in my life I have never seen such exertions as were made to save those ships; and would rather fight another battle, than pass such a week as followed it.' But on 24 October, with the hurricane still as furious as ever, 'I found it necessary to order the captures – all without masts, some without rudders, and many half full of water – to be destroyed, except such as were in better plight.' He did not like to do so, for it robbed everyone of prize money, but, he said, 'my object was their ruin, and not what might be made of them.' Of course some people resented it, after all they had been through, but by then it was the only thing that could be done, and was much more excusable than Hyde Parker's destruction of prizes after Copenhagen; and at least one of the sailors recognized that. Straightforward and philosophical, Sam condensed a week of storm and misfortune into one sentence: 'We have taken a rare parcel of ships, but the wind is so rough we cannot bring them home, else I should be rolling in money; so we are busy smashing 'em, and blowing 'em up wholesale.'

They were able to save only four of the prizes; but the great achievement was that after enduring battle and gale, none of the British ships was lost. One by one, in the following fortnight, they limped into Gibraltar, looking for repairs for the voyage home; their crews were dead weary, and already the battle seemed long ago.

'Hasten the very moment you receive this', wrote Scott, 'to dear Lady Hamilton, and prepare her for the greatest of misfortunes.' In the early hours of 6 November, news of Trafalgar reached the Admiralty. Messengers sped to inform the king at Windsor; with daylight the official announcement was made. People hurried to buy the *London Gazette Extraordinary*, and salutes were fired from the Tower of London: these were the guns which Emma and Susannah heard, ten miles away in Merton – their first intimation of what had taken place.

In the fleet, a kind of warmth had been extinguished at the time that Nelson died, and as they grieved, the sailors who wrote of it, of whatever rank or rating, expressed the same emotion: not only – not even mainly – respect and admiration, but love: 'a friend I loved', 'our beloved Admiral', 'our dear Admiral Nelson'. The word love can never have been used so much about any man by others; and on shore, in England, it was the same. *The Times* reported the universal feeling: 'We do not know whether we should mourn or rejoice. The country has gained the most splendid and decisive Victory that has ever graced the naval annals of England: but it has been dearly purchased. *The great and gallant NELSON is no more.*' Illuminations were set up to mark the victory, but most of them were draped in black and purple; in provincial towns the news was read out by the mayors, and 'instead of the air being rent with enthusiastic vociferations, and extravagant huzzas, a sullen gloom pervaded every countenance, and a dead silence ensued, which at length terminated ... when "POOR NELSON", with a faltering voice, and inarticulate sigh, was mournfully repeated by all who were present.'

The sigh was echoed even in distant Naples; Coleridge heard the news there, and when they saw him weeping in the street, sympathetic Italians guessed he was English, and came to embrace him. 'It seemed', he said, 'as if no man was a stranger to another: for all were made acquaintances in the rights of a common anguish.'

Astonishingly stoical under physical pain, the Georgian British were not ashamed to show emotional pain and confusion: 'It was a sensation at once of patriotism, of pride and of gratitude', said one newspaper. 'Not a man who would not have given up his life to achieve such a victory. Not a man who would not have surrendered every part of the victory (except the honour of Britain) to save the life of Lord Nelson.' 'The loss of Lord Nelson was more lamented than the victory was rejoiced at', wrote another; and a third said with certainty, 'If ever there were a hero who merited the honour of a public funeral, it is the pious, the noble and the gallant NELSON, the darling of the British navy, whose death has plunged a whole nation into the deepest grief.'

Perhaps it can never be exactly true that a whole nation is plunged into grief. But it is true that the same feeling of sorrowful loss spread out from Nelson's many friends, first through the fleet as a whole, and then – in diminishing degrees but to a unique extent – to people further and further removed from naval affairs. Eight years after Trafalgar, the poet Robert Southey remembered clearly that 'the death of Nelson was felt in England as something more than a national calamity. Men started at the intelligence, and turned pale, as if they had heard of the loss of a dear friend. An object of our admiration and affection, of our pride and of our hopes, was suddenly taken from us; and', he added with thoughtful accuracy, 'it seemed as if we had never, till then, known how deeply we loved and reverenced him.'

'They have behaved well to us', wrote one of *Victory*'s seamen, James Bayley, to his sister. The cause of his satisfaction was that, in Gibraltar, he and his colleagues had staged a small rebellion against an obvious injustice, and gained their point. Because of *Victory*'s battered condition, someone proposed that Nelson's body should return to England in another ship. Naturally the sailors who had fought closest to him were much offended. 'They wanted to take Ld. Nelson from us,' said Bayley indignantly, 'but we told Captn., as we brought him out, we would bring him home'; and they did. After repairs, *Victory* sailed for England on 2 November, accompanied by *Belleisle*. Through adverse winds and her own decrepit state, the voyage took nearly five weeks. After the battle, without sufficient lead on board to make an airtight coffin, and without either the knowledge or equipment for embalming, Dr Beatty had tackled the unfamiliar problem of preserving a corpse sensibly and well. Cutting off Nelson's hair to give to Emma, he made a brief autopsy, and the body was placed in a large barrel of brandy, lashed to the mainmast on the middle deck. In death as in life, the body was guarded day and night by a marine; one night, still struggling towards Gibraltar, the sentinel on duty had the shock of his life when the lid of the barrel began to rise up. To quieten the hair-raising rumour that Nelson was returning from the dead, Beatty explained it was only due to the natural release of internal gases from the corpse; but he was concerned about its condition, especially when he learned that it might lie in state physically exposed to public view.

In Gibraltar, the brandy was exchanged for spirits of wine, drawn off and renewed twice during the long voyage home. *Victory* reached Spithead on 5 December, anchored there for a week and then proceeded slowly to Sheerness, at the mouth of the Thames. During this terminal stage of a difficult journey, Beatty opened the cask and took the body out. He was much relieved to find that apart from the lips, which were slightly discoloured, it still looked very life-like, with the features peaceful. He made a complete autopsy then, removing the internal organs and noting their good condition for a man of forty-seven; and finally he extracted the musket ball. A fragment of blue cloth and the gold lace of Nelson's epaulette were still stuck to it.

For Beatty, there was a professional satisfaction in finding how well he had succeeded in preserving the body; but even if he had failed, he need not have worried about the possibility of its being placed in public view – that had only been a rumour, without any foundation. On the way to Sheerness, Nelson's own coffin – the one made by Ben Hallowell from the wood of *L'Orient*, blown up at the Nile – was brought from London and taken on board *Victory*. It had been waiting for him since that day when, finding his officers staring at it on *Vanguard*'s deck, he had told them with amusement, 'You may look it, gentlemen, as much as you please, but depend upon it, none of you shall have it.' And during the afternoon of 22 December, as Hardy and Scott watched, he was placed in it at last.

Trafalgar Night

In Portsmouth, on 21 October every year, the morning ceremony is brief. The order of Service states its purpose: 'to celebrate the victory off Cape Trafalgar, and to commemorate the death of Vice Admiral Horatio Viscount Nelson.' The two remain inseparable; and the third purpose is made clear by the chaplain's bidding: 'We are also met together to give thanks for the life of Horatio Viscount Nelson.' There are three prayers – Nelson's own incomparable one written just before the battle, the Lord's Prayer and the Naval Prayer. Before them comes Collingwood's General Order after the battle, which, thanking God for the victory, was a kind of prayer too; and after two hymns and a blessing, 'the Commander-in-Chief lays a wreath where Admiral Lord Nelson fell.' With the Last Post and Reveille, it is all over well before nine o'clock: for everyone involved, there is a normal busy day ahead.

It may be that the famous signal, spelled out in Popham's code, is not actually shown as it was on the day of battle: it requires twenty-eight flags, and going into battle with all sails set, even studding sails, it would have been very difficult -- perhaps impossible – to hoist them all at one go, using the masts in the regular order of precedence, and to be certain the whole was visible. Indeed, it may have taken as many as eleven separate hoists on the mizzen, and if so, it is no wonder that Collingwood said testily, 'I wish Nelson would stop signalling'; for quite apart from his own and the fleet's confidence, it would have appeared as a positive flurry of flags. Today, no one can be certain, but it does not matter dreadfully: as Collingwood said, 'We know well enough what to do.'

The funeral pageant, on 9 January 1806, was said to be the greatest which London had witnessed for centuries, and was certainly the most

359

splendid in living memory: royalty and nobility, ministers, admirals, generals, sailors and soldiers formed a procession so long that its head reached St Paul's Cathedral before its end had started from Whitehall, a mile and a half away. The day was bright and fine; the crowds along the streets were immense, silent except for a sighing sound like a wave advancing ahead of the funeral carriage, as, unbidden, thousands of hats were removed and heads respectfully bared. There were reckoned to be thirty-one admirals and a hundred captains present. Forty-eight men from *Victory* carried the ship's shot-torn ensign; at the cathedral steps, a dozen of them bore the coffin inside, while six admirals held a canopy above them, and in a place of foremost prominence, Hardy and Blackwood carried banners of emblems depicting Nelson's victories.

It was not actually very naval. There were ten thousand soldiers in the procession, which many people thought far too large a number: some observers said they would rather see *Victory*'s men than all the rest. The service too, apart from being very long, was so full of heraldic ceremonial that some felt it almost irrelevant. But it proceeded for four hours with orderly dignity, until the time came for the coffin to be lowered into the crypt. When that happened, the seamen were supposed to fold the ensign and place it on the coffin; but they did not. Just as in Gibraltar, they had decided privately what was right and proper; and when the moment of parting came, they suddenly ripped a huge piece off the ensign. Tearing their memento into fragments, each stuffed one into his uniform. Whatever the authorities said, they were going to bid their own farewell to their admiral.

The authorities apparently said nothing, though some may have been shocked by the spontaneous breach of protocol. But Captain Codrington's beautiful wife Jane was there, and her reaction was probably shared by all the naval people: 'That was *Nelson* – the rest was so much the Herald's Office.'

Among the nobility was William, Nelson's only surviving brother, who (though he had done nothing whatever to deserve it) was created Earl Nelson, in honour of the deceased. Emma and Horatia, who had done more than most to make Nelson happy, and who meant more to him that anyone else at all, were shamefully ignored. Neither was invited to the funeral; much worse, though, Nelson's bequest of them to his king and country was rejected. Perhaps it seems a naive thing for him to have imagined that a pension of public money might be provided for his mistress and illegitimate daughter; but when the

statesman Charles James Fox died in 1806, he left an illegitimate
daughter too, and she was provided for from the public purse.

It had not been much to ask in return for an unequalled life and
death in the service of his country, and had it been public knowledge
there can be no doubt that voluntary donations would have provided
all that was needed; but the country, in the form of governmental
obstinacy and inertia, turned him down. At first there seemed some
possibility that his last wish might be fulfilled, and with this small
token the nation's great debt to him redeemed, for William Pitt was
still prime minister, and sympathetic to the idea. But he was ill, and
died before the end of the month; and thereafter, in spite of repeated
pleas from Emma herself and from others on her behalf, the problem
was quietly shelved.

Emma's gentle husband Sir William had predicted that if she carried
on her spendthrift ways after his death, she would end her days in
penury, and he was right. She was already deeply in debt, and had to
sell Merton; but even that was not enough. While Nelson's sisters were
granted £15,000 each, while Fanny was given an annual pension of
£2,000, and while the new Earl Nelson enjoyed an annual pension of
£5,000 and a grant of £99,000 towards the purchase of a suitable
estate, Emma became destitute. 'Days have passed on,' she wrote
forlornly, 'and I know not how they end or begin – nor how I am to
bear my future existence.' In 1812, and again in 1813, she was
arrested for her debts. During her imprisonment she wrote to the
Prince Regent, begging his help, with some optimism. Nelson had once
feared that His Royal Highness would seduce Emma, and had written
about it in his letters, but the Prince – who had not attempted
seduction, and did not know Nelson's thoughts – had become a firm
supporter of his memory. Unfortunately, at that very time, a sensational revelation took place. A man named James Harrison, who
with his wife and family had been cared for by Emma in days when
he had been poor, had stolen Nelson's private letters to her. Now he
published them. Some people thought they were forgeries; others
thought Emma had published them for the money – Lord St Vincent,
transported with fury, wrote: 'What a diabolical bitch!' But everyone,
including the Prince Regent, could read what Nelson was supposed to
have written: 'Don't let him touch you, nor sit next to you; if he comes,
get up. God strike him blind if he looks at you – this is high treason
and you may get me hanged by revealing it. Oh God, that I were! ...
Does Sir William want you to be a whore to the rascal? ... We know

he [the Prince] is dotingly fond of such women as yourself, and is without one spark of honour in those respects.' True enough, but any hope of royal help instantly vanished.

Nevertheless, Emma was bailed out by a friend; and in the middle of 1814 she left England to live with Horatia in Calais. Food, drink and lodgings were cheaper there, and the summer was happy for them both. But she had less than fifty pounds when she arrived, and by the autumn impossible demands from English creditors were piling up. All her life she had drunk too much; now, after jaundice, she fell ill with pneumonia. She still tried to care for Horatia, pawning her last bits of jewellery to buy food for the girl; yet she herself merely drank and became, said Horatia, 'extremely irritable' – scarcely surprising, considering all the circumstances. As an old lady Horatia remembered that 'for some time before she died, she was not kind to me'. But she had done as much as she could. On 15 January 1815 she died, alone except for Horatia. Lloyd's agent in Calais paid for her funeral, which cost £28, and her wine and spirits bill, which was £77; and if he had not whisked Horatia back to England, she, though only thirteen years old, would have been held by the French authorities as hostage against Emma's other debts. Nelson, always a generous and grateful man, had never begun to imagine quite how churlish a government could be.

He would have been deeply hurt by Horatia too. As she grew up, she came to know that he was her father, but many years passed before she learned that Emma was her mother; and then she would not believe it. She dismissed his published letters as forgeries, and Emma, for whatever reason, never told her the truth. As far as Horatia was concerned, her origin remained a mystery. In time, by a rather touching coincidence, she married a Norfolk curate whom she met in Burnham Market, just a few miles away from the Parsonage House where Nelson was born. Then in 1849, when she was forty-eight and the mother of nine children, Nelson's letters to Emma were authenticated and republished. Horatia's full parentage was proved, and a matter of public fact; but to her dying day (and she lived until 1880) she refused to accept it. She adored her father's memory, and the publication pained her: she said the letters would 'sully his fame', and to their mid-Victorian audience, they may have done. Perhaps the cult of Nelson, the unsullied hero, was too great for her to react otherwise. It was certainly powerful by then, and she was one of its first devotees; yet presumably it did not occur to her that her refusal to absorb the truth of her father's one great love would have pained him more than anything else.

What of Fanny, Dowager Viscountess Nelson, the admiral's only wife in the eyes of Earth, and what of Josiah? 'Do, my dear husband, let us live together. I can never be happy till such an event takes place ...' Despite her supposedly frail constitution, much tried by those bleak long-distant winters in the Parsonage House, she lived to be seventy-three. She never lived again in a house of her own, but moved frequently between London, the West Country and the south coast. Occasionally she travelled abroad, once to Lyons and once, surprisingly, to Switzerland to go boating with Lord Byron on Lake Geneva. The impression is of a comfortable but despondent retirement, a sad little creature flitting from one shadowy retreat to another; and dreaming, perhaps, of a bright sunny day long ago in Nevis, when Prince William congratulated Nelson on carrying off the principal favourite of the island. Certainly she remained in touch with the prince, even when, following the Prince Regent's death, he ascended to the throne as King William IV; and early in May 1831, not long before her death, she was visited by an admiral who, as a midshipman, had been present on her wedding-day. He found her 'in great dejection of spirits ... the very picture of illness and despondency.' There was much reason for her gloom: she had outlived not only her husband but her son. Josiah – 'who', Nelson hoped at the beginning, 'I shall ever consider as one of my own', and who ended by wishing his stepfather might fall and break his neck – quit the navy in 1800, and was never asked to serve again, though it is doubtful if he would have wanted to. After joining because he admired and loved his stepfather, he had been unable ever to live up to the example, and Nelson's betrayal of his mother tainted the whole service for him. He kept his natural father's name all his life, and went into commerce, dealing in stocks and shares on the Bourse and the London Exchange. There he prospered, and at the age of forty he married. The lady of his choice was a god-child and relative of Fanny's, and, in a faintly unhealthy touch, shared her maiden name, Fanny Herbert; and after ten years of marriage, in which he bought a yacht and fathered a large family with the second Fanny Nisbet, Josiah died of pleurisy.

Admiral Villeneuve's fate was peculiar. 'To any other nation,' he said after Trafalgar, 'the loss of a Nelson would have been irreparable; but in the British fleet off Cadiz, every captain was a Nelson.' Taken to England by Blackwood in *Euryalus*, he was interned, then in April 1806 released on parole and allowed to return to France. Stopping at an hotel in Rennes, he wrote a tragic letter to his wife. 'How will you receive this blow? The fact is, I have reached a point where life is a disgrace and death a duty. Here, denounced by the Emperor, rejected by his minister who was my friend, charged with an immense responsibility in a disaster for which I am blamed and to which I was led by fate, I have to die. I ask your forgiveness for it, but it must be done ... How lucky I have no child to receive my awful heritage and be burdened with my name! Ah, I was not born for such a fate, I never sought it, I have been forced to it despite myself. Adieu, adieu.'

Discovered next to his body, the letter was seized and suppressed by Napoleon's chief of police. Villeneuve's wife was not told how he died, and still no one knows for sure. Napoleon said it was suicide, to avoid court martial, but officials noted that the body had six stab-wounds, which seems rather excessive for self-destruction. Some Frenchmen, then and ever since, have suspected he was assassinated. However, the death was convenient: all the blame could be put on him. Long afterwards, the emperor said a court martial would have shown Villeneuve had disobeyed his orders, which, he claimed, had been not to sail from Cadiz and not to engage the English. That was precisely the opposite of the last imperial orders Villeneuve had received. Had Napoleon forgotten? In his dislike of the navy he never understood, could even he have deceived himself so much? Truth could be twisted and any man disgraced to preserve the myth of Napoleonic infallibility; but a just court martial, if justice had been possible, could not have condemned Villeneuve; it could only have placed the weight of the blame for Trafalgar on the emperor himself.

Collingwood's letters after the battle make sad reading too. Mourning Nelson, he reflected that 'there never was such a combat since England had a fleet', but feared that 'there will be some in England who will ask, what have they done with their prizes? I can only say, if they are not satisfied, they are hard to please.' Some things happened which made him happy: he was promoted to Vice Admiral of the Red; he received 'the praise of every officer of the fleet'; and he was made a baron. When he heard the news, he wrote to Sarah, his wife: 'Blessed may you be, my dearest love, and may you long live the happy wife of your happy husband! I do not know how you bear your honours, but I have so much business on my hands, from dawn till midnight, that I have hardly time to think of mine, except it be in gratitude to my king ... I never dreamed I was to be a peer of the realm. How are my darlings?'

He yearned to return home – 'How I long to have a peep into my own house, and a walk in my own garden!' – but he was never allowed to. Ordered to take over Nelson's Mediterranean command, he remained on active duty at sea. During those last years of his life, his dog became a closer companion than ever, an outlet for private humour and affection; 'I am out of all patience with Bounce. The consequential airs he gives himself since he became a right honourable dog are insufferable. He considers it beneath his dignity to play with commoners' dogs, and truly thinks that he does them grace when he lifts his leg against them. This, I think, is carrying the insolence of rank to the extreme; but he is a dog that does it.' Even Bounce, though, suffered from the tedium of being eternally cooped up in a ship – 'very well and very fat,' Collingwood observed, 'yet he seems not to be content, and sighs so piteously these long evenings that I am obliged to sing him to sleep.' And from the admiral's cabin, on January evenings in 1807, the marine guard might hear a gentle crooning:

> Sigh no more, Bouncey, sigh no more,
> Dogs were deceivers never;
> Though ne'er you put one foot on shore,
> True to your master ever.
>
> Then sigh not so, but let us go
> Where dinner's daily ready,
> Converting all the sounds of woe
> To heigh phiddy diddy.

Bounce had a long life, doted on by his lonely master; but during the night of 12–13 August 1809, he fell overboard and drowned. 'He is a great loss to me,' Collingwood said sadly. 'I have few comforts, but he was one, for he loved me.' Less than seven months later, on 6 March 1810, Collingwood died too, of stomach cancer, and was taken home at last, to be buried near Nelson in St Paul's.

Hardy's life after Trafalgar was both longer and, on the whole, happier than Collingwood's. He was made a baronet just after Nelson's funeral, and stood for parliament, but did not get in. Thereupon he returned to sea, spending three years in Halifax, Nova Scotia, where he married

Anne Berkeley, his commander-in-chief's daughter. In 1809 he was on the Lisbon station, receiving the rank of honorary commodore in the Portuguese Navy; and in 1812, when the United States declared war on Britain, he crossed the Atlantic again to take part in the blockade of the East Coast ports. There, in July 1813, he and his crew in HMS *Ramillies* went through the unnerving experience of a submarine attack. The assailant probably did not know that his target was Nelson's flag-captain, but whether he did or not, fortunately the attack failed.

Five years later, in a steady professional progress, Hardy became commodore of the South America station. Flag rank followed in 1825, and in 1830, on King William's recommendation, he was appointed First Sea Lord, which surprised him very much. Rather to his embarrassment, he found he had to give orders to officers he was accustomed to think of as seniors: after the first occasion he said shyly, 'I really can't believe I am First Sea Lord – the tables are so entirely turned.'

Knight Grand Cross of the Bath was added to his baronetcy in 1831, the year Fanny died; he went to her funeral. In 1834 he became Governor of the Naval Hospital at Greenwich, which could have been a sinecure, but he worked hard to introduce many popular reforms; and there, having attained the rank of Vice Admiral of the Blue in 1837, he died in 1839. He had no son, so his baronetcy died with him, but one of his three daughters married another baronet; and the family's titles did not stop there. Lady Hardy, a woman much younger than her husband, had a romantic reputation – once, in 1816, Hardy had successfully sued a newspaper which said she was having an affair; he had also fought a duel with Lord Buckingham for the same reason. After Hardy's death, romance took practical form: on 22 March 1840, six months and two days from the day he died, Lady Hardy left off her widow's weeds; three days later, she informed her daughters that she was engaged to be married. And so she was, to Lord Seaford, an old family friend; and as Lady Seaford, she lived another thirty-seven years, while Hardy lay in the mausoleum at Greenwich, with a favourite miniature of Nelson beside him.

The signal remains hoisted throughout the day, and in the evening, in Royal Navy ships and shore establishments everywhere around the world, the Trafalgar Night dinners begin, culminating with a simple toast used exclusively for Nelson: 'The Immortal Memory'. The words descend from his own day, when it was fashionable to call heroes immortal – in his lifetime, after the Battle of the Nile, the word was applied to him constantly. For at least fifty years after he died, the memory was still sufficiently strong for mummers to include a portrayal of his death in their plays:

Nelson – 'Hardy, I be wownded.'

Hardy – 'Not mortually I hopes, my lord.'

Nelson – 'Mortually I be afeared. Kiss me Hardy, thank God I've done my duty.'

This, said Hardy's biographers, 'never failed to provoke the utmost enthusiasm'. In medical terms, Nelson died by drowning, which was appropriate for a sailor, and in his own blood, which might be thought appropriate for a warrior. Sailing and fighting were his business, and he was exceptionally good at both; but many other admirals were almost as good and are now all but forgotten. Death in battle, however heroic, is no guarantee of immortality.

Of course, no one and nothing can be remembered literally for ever; yet once one knows of him, Nelson is an unusually hard person to forget, or even to want to forget. The reasons for remembering him have changed often, with time, fashion and individuals – the idea of Nelson as martyr entered into it very quickly, and grew to Christ-like proportions; dying not only for his country, but for its salvation. Even in his lifetime he was regarded by many as a national guardian angel, as Lord Radstock said, and afterwards he became virtually a secular patron saint – although some people felt Emma's claim that during battle, he would cry out 'For Emma and England', was going a bit far. ('Nelson was always cried up as much for his devotion as his bravery,' Lord Holland remarked, 'but if this mode of invocation were commonly known, it would ruin his standing with the Saints.') In Japan, had he been Japanese, he would certainly have been rated as a *kami*, a guiding, guarding spirit of place, and people would have prayed to him quite naturally. But though Victorian Britain was generally more pious than today, and though people in time of trouble would ask themselves, 'What would Nelson have done?', actual prayers to deceased mortals have never figured highly in Anglican thought; and however plausible and emotionally satisfying the idea of a messianic sacrifice may have seemed a hundred years ago, today – except to a devout mind with a hint of paganism – it cannot be more than a remote if pleasing intellectual concept.

It may be that the cult of Nelson was deliberately fostered in its early days, to divert national attention from Napoleon's continuing achievements on land, against which it seemed, for many years more, that Britain could do nothing. But if that was all there was, he would have been long forgotten by now. To the very unsophisticated, he may still be imagined as a kind of comic-book superhero, defeating the arch-villains, the French. But (though St Vincent remarked, 'I do not say the enemy cannot come; I only say they cannot come by sea', and would probably spin in his grave at the thought of a Channel Tunnel) official relations with the French have improved since, and if Nelson were only the hammer of the Frogs, his fame would be very unfashionable now.

The theatrical element of his life was perceived as quickly as the pious, the sacrificial, the violent and the ardently nationalist elements: trying to console Emma, a friend and neighbour pointed out that 'his time was to die', and Nelson's old friend Lord Minto came to feel that his death, at the hour of victory, was 'the finest close and crown, as it were, of such a life'. One contemporary, Lady Bessborough, went so far as to say, 'It makes me feel almost as much envy as compassion – I think I should like to die so.' Aside from the pain, who would not? The moment is inevitable, and he would have liked to live; but dying, we must all relinquish our loves, and few can face that passage surrounded by devoted friends, and confident of an outstanding achievement. The theatrical side certainly has an enduring appeal, which is why people continue to read and write about Nelson, and to make and watch films on him: whichever way the succeeding generations interpret it, he left a perfectly formed story which still grips the imagination of each.

A great many people have tried to explain the unique response that Nelson could win from almost everyone. All such explanations must be more or less subjective: everyone can select attractive aspects from such a many-sided character, and everyone so inclined can find something to disapprove of. 'That man', said Dr Scott, 'possessed the wisdom of the serpent with the innocence of the dove.' Less poetically, Lord Minto observed: 'He is in many points a really great man, in others a baby.' Some people dislike what they read of his boyish vanity, or his apparent self-pity when he was feeling ill, or his love for Emma; some are still embarrassed by his dying request for a kiss from Hardy. They may choose to ignore all these, and to glorify the violence of his life and death, his nationalism or his reverence for the monarchy; but that must be a mistake. Others, preferring to take the opposite view, make the same mistake: for if you take out one part from the whole, the man is lost. Yet there is one part which, more than any, distinguished him from other heroes – even those of comparable stature.

One such was Arthur Wellesley, Duke of Wellington, Britain's other great hero of the Napoleonic Wars. There were numerous similarities, large and petty, between the two men – their victories, their devotion to duty, their fondness for children, their youthful infatuations with married women and, when married, their infidelity; and not least, the confidence their men felt in them. During the Peninsular campaign, in 1811, one young rifleman said of Wellington, 'We would rather see his long nose in a fight than a reinforcement of ten thousand men any day.' Yet the first thing that everyone remembers about Wellington now is his nickname, the Iron Duke. Lady Bessborough, who envied Nelson's way of death, never met him, but she did meet Wellington, in Paris in 1814. Writing to her own ex-lover, she deplored how in the absence of the Duchess of Wellington, the Duke carried on publicly with the opera singer Giuseppina Grassini, one of Napoleon's seven mistresses. In spite of her disapproval, she was honest enough to admit that the Duke was 'so civil to me, and I admire him so much as a hero, that it inclines me to be partial to him'; but contrast that with her reaction, nine years earlier, to Nelson's death – 'I hardly imagined it possible to feel so much grief for a man I did not know.' And consider too Captain Sir Pulteney Malcolm. As a naval officer, he might be suspected of bias; yet unlike Lady Bessborough, he knew both Wellington and Nelson intimately, and he was firm in his opinion: both were outstanding leaders, 'but Nelson was the man to *love*'.

Nelson and Wellesley met once, and once only. The chance encounter took place at the Colonial office in Downing Street, during Nelson's last twenty-five days in England, on or about 12 September 1805; and because the Colonial Secretary, Lord Castlereagh, kept Wellesley waiting, it lasted nearly an hour. Wellesley, than a young major-general in his middle thirties, recognized the one-armed admiral instantly, and they began to talk. The conversation, however, did not get off to a good start.

Though Wellesley's victories were already renowned, Nelson had not the faintest idea who his chance acquaintance was, and he did not bother to inquire. Instead, said Wellesley later, he talked 'all about himself, and, really, in a style so vain and silly as to surprise and almost disgust me'. Eventually, though, Wellesley managed to say something which 'made him guess I was *somebody*'; Nelson left the room, presumably to find out who his companion was; and when he returned, 'all that I had thought a charlatan style had vanished ... in fact, he talked like an officer and a statesman'. They spoke of the state of the country and of Continental affairs; Wellesley mentioned Calder's inconclusive battle with Villeneuve, comparing it unfavourably with the annihilation Nelson had 'taught the country to expect'; Nelson hoped that Wellesley would be given the chance to attack the French in Sardinia. Later, Wellesley had his own mental picture of an ideal naval captain, a man who saw fleets as part of a global strategy, and there cannot be much doubt that the ideal image grew out of that meeting. Certainly, Nelson's first presentation of himself was unfortunate, but as soon as he understood he was talking to an experienced military man, he abandoned the tone of patronizing boastfulness. And, like almost everyone, Wellesley succumbed to the Nelson touch – the natural, unforced charm, the feeling of mutual confidence and consultation between professionals, ignoring differences in rank and age. Remembering it decades afterwards, the Duke still said, 'He really was a most superior person ... I don't know that I ever had a conversation that interested me more.'

Perhaps, if Wellington had died victorious on the battlefield of Waterloo, the theatrical element would have entered his life as well; respectful, admiring and strong as it is, the folk-memory towards him might be warmer, less deferential. But probably not: Nelson's dramatic death in victory contributes to his legend, yet it is not that which makes him so fondly remembered. Wellington is only one example, useful because he was contemporary, of a man remembered with high regard; but not many leaders are remembered with both the regard and the informal good humour that Nelson attracts.

In purely martial terms, it is certainly better to have an unpopular commander who wins victories than to be led by a likeable loser. But Nelson was helped to his unprecedented victories partly for the very reason that he was so immensely likeable, and both the navy and the nation were sensible enough to realize how exceptionally lucky they were. It made him hard to follow, though. 'He is a terrible ancestor', said Joseph Conrad. In 1905, during celebrations of the hundredth anniversary of Trafalgar, Fred T. Jane – the originator of *Jane's Fighting Ships* – complained there was 'Too Much Nelson'. The 'cult of Nelson' was, in his view, 'pure and unadulterated moonshine', and he reckoned that no sailor would become more efficient just because 'England expects ...' was plastered on his ship. Jane was right; a hundred years of virtually uninterrupted peace at sea, with the oceans dominated by the Royal Navy, gave Britain and its fleets a feeling of casual superiority; England did not expect to be challenged, but if challenged, expected to win without much effort. Collingwood had almost prophesied that – off Cadiz, in the midst of the stress and strain of war, he wrote: 'A dull superiority creates languor; it is a state like this that rouses the spirits, and makes us feel as if the welfare of all England depended on us alone.' That true root of naval inspiration and dedication, which Nelson brought to flower, was something which Napoleon never grasped. After Trafalgar, as usual in naval matters, he got it wrong again, and ordered that each of his surviving vessels should bear a prominent inscription: *La France compte que chacun fera son devoir* – 'France expects . . .'

Today, nearly two hundred years after Nelson's death, with two world wars and other naval conflicts behind us, we may perhaps be a little nearer than most of the intervening generations to the moral values of his own Georgian England: we can value humane behaviour and kindness more highly than strict rectitude. During his lifetime, his portrait was often painted, and he said that hardly any of the pictures looked exactly like him – once, indeed, an artist refused a commission, and when asked why, explained: 'There is such a mixture of humility and ambition in Lord Nelson's countenance that I dare not risk the attempt.' Since then, perhaps rashly, many writers have risked the attempt, and no doubt none of their pen-portraits is exactly like him either. Yet we can certainly know him better than many did a century ago, be glad that he was not a saint, and like him better for it. He was a man like any other, but unlike almost any; and simple though it is, that, more than anything else, is probably why people today still feel both admiration and affection for him, and think it is worth while remembering him.

Index